10659893

When Movements Become Parties

Why do some parties formed by social movements develop top-down structures, while others stay more open and responsive to their social bases? The first rigorous comparative study of movement-based parties, this book shows not only how movements can form parties but also how movements contribute to parties' internal politics and shape organizational party models over the long term. Although the existing literature argues that movement-based parties will succumb to professionalization and specialization, Anria shows that this is not inevitable or preordained through an in-depth examination of the unusual and counterintuitive development of Bolivia's Movement Toward Socialism (MAS). Anria then compares the evolution of the MAS with that of other parties formed by social movements, including Brazil's Workers' Party (PT) and Uruguay's Broad Front (FA). In a region where successful new parties of any type have been rare in the past three decades, these three parties are remarkable for their success. Yet, despite their similar origins, they differ sharply in their organizational models and relationships with their social bases.

SANTIAGO ANRIA is Assistant Professor of Political Science and Latin American Studies at Dickinson College. His research focuses on social movements, political parties, and democracy in Latin America and has appeared in journals including *Comparative Politics*, *Comparative Political Studies*, the *Journal of Democracy*, and *Latin American Politics and Society*. He received his PhD in Political Science from the University of North Carolina at Chapel Hill.

Cambridge Studies in Comparative Politics

General Editors

Kathleen Thelen *Massachusetts Institute of Technology*
Erik Wibbels *Duke University*

Associate Editors

Catherine Boone *London School of Economics*
Thad Dunning *University of California, Berkeley*
Anna Grzymala-Busse *Stanford University*
Torben Iversen *Harvard University*
Stathis Kalyvas *Yale University*
Margaret Levi *Stanford University*
Helen Milner *Princeton University*
Frances Rosenbluth *Yale University*
Susan Stokes *Yale University*
Tariq Thachil *Vanderbilt University*

Series Founder

Peter Lange *Duke University*

Continued after the index

When Movements Become Parties

The Bolivian MAS in Comparative Perspective

SANTIAGO ANRIA

Dickinson College

CAMBRIDGE
UNIVERSITY PRESS

CAMBRIDGE
UNIVERSITY PRESS

University Printing House, Cambridge CB2 8BS, United Kingdom

One Liberty Plaza, 20th Floor, New York, NY 10006, USA

477 Williamstown Road, Port Melbourne, VIC 3207, Australia

314-321, 3rd Floor, Plot 3, Splendor Forum, Jasola District Centre, New Delhi - 110025, India

79 Anson Road, #06-04/06, Singapore 079906

Cambridge University Press is part of the University of Cambridge.

It furthers the University's mission by disseminating knowledge in the pursuit of
education, learning and research at the highest international levels of excellence.

www.cambridge.org
Information on this title: www.cambridge.org/9781108446327
DOI: 10.1017/9781108551755

© Santiago Anria 2019

This publication is in copyright. Subject to statutory exception
and to the provisions of relevant collective licensing agreements,
no reproduction of any part may take place without the written
permission of Cambridge University Press.

First published 2019
First paperback edition 2019

A catalogue record for this publication is available from the British Library

Library of Congress Cataloging in Publication data
NAMES: Anria, Santiago, 1982– author.
TITLE: When movements become parties : the Bolivian MAS in comparative perspective /
    Santiago Anria.
DESCRIPTION: Cambridge, United Kingdom ; New York, NY : Cambridge University Press, 2018. |
    Series: Cambridge studies in comparative politics | Includes bibliographical references and index.
IDENTIFIERS: LCCN 2018023529 | ISBN 9781108427579 (hardback)
SUBJECTS: LCSH: Movimiento al Socialismo (Bolivia) | Social movements–Political aspects–Bolivia.
    | Morales Ayma, Evo, 1959- | Bolivia–Politics and government–1982-2006. | Bolivia–Politics
    and government–2006- | BISAC: POLITICAL SCIENCE / Government / General.
CLASSIFICATION: LCC JL2298.M28 A67 2018 | DDC 324.284/074–dc23
    LC record available at https://lccn.loc.gov/2018023529

ISBN 978-1-108-42757-9 Hardback
ISBN 978-1-108-44632-7 Paperback

Cambridge University Press has no responsibility for the persistence or
accuracy of URLs for external or third-party internet websites referred to in
this publication, and does not guarantee that any content on such websites is,
or will remain, accurate or appropriate.

To Anne and Carmelo

Contents

Figures

Maps

Tables

Acknowledgments

I began working on this project in 2008. Since then, I've spent almost 13 months in Bolivia, divided into different trips in 2008, 2012, and 2013, conducting field research for this book. During all that time, I had the opportunity to speak with hundreds of people, including social movement leaders, politicians across the political spectrum, academics, journalists, and grass-roots activists. It would be nearly impossible to list them all here without the risk of forgetting some. And since I would rather not run that risk, I will thank them collectively. Every person who participated in this project, or with whom I discussed my research, profoundly influenced my understanding of the internal politics of the MAS. For that I'm forever grateful. Although I suspect that many of them will not read this book, this research would not have been possible without their input. Thank you.

This book grew out of my dissertation at the University of North Carolina, Chapel Hill. I'm above all thankful to Evelyne Huber, my dissertation chair and intellectual hero. Evelyne's generosity with her time, her dedication to and belief in my project, and her precise comments on virtually every single thing that I wrote for this book contributed immensely to my development as a scholar. To focus on her contributions to my intellectual development, however, would be nothing less than an understatement. Since we first met in 2009, Evelyne has been a continual source of support, encouragement, and calm. Although she set the bar remarkably, if not impossibly, high, I hope that one day I can be the type of mentor to others that Evelyne has been to me.

I also owe a debt of gratitude to the rest of my advisors at Carolina. Graeme Robertson provided extensive feedback, helped me see important gaps in my argument, and encouraged me to think more carefully about issues of path dependency. Milada Vachudova helped me to think about the broader comparative implications of my research and how a study of a small subset of Latin American movement-based parties might inform European debates on parties with similar origins. Lars Schoultz was extremely generous with his time and coached me patiently on how to write better for a non-specialist audience. John Stephens offered constructive criticism all along and always asked difficult questions. I learned a great deal – and possibly grew some gray hair – in trying to answer those questions. Although they were not on my dissertation committee, Cecilia Martínez-Gallardo and Jonathan Hartlyn pushed me to develop sharper arguments in specific chapters, and just talking with them about Latin American politics was a highly stimulating exercise.

I'm also thankful to several informal advisors. Eric Hershberg, at American University, deserves a special mention. Eric was my MA advisor, and I credit him as the person who challenged me to explore contentious politics beyond Buenos Aires, introducing me to the complex and fascinating world of the Andes. His advice, support, and friendship over the past decade have been invaluable, and his deep knowledge on Latin American politics has been inspiring. In addition, the time that I spent at the Center for Latin American & Latino Studies (CLALS), which Eric directs at American University, was especially productive, and I'm grateful to him and to the staff there for providing an ideal working environment in 2014. I'm also grateful to Judy Rein for her friendship and the feedback she has offered all along. Max Cameron, at the University of British Columbia, also offered continuous intellectual support and input on almost every chapter of this book. His passionate teaching, clear thinking, and patient mentoring had an immense impact on my professional and intellectual development, and I'll never forget our discussions of Guillermo O'Donnell's work over coffee. I cannot thank you all enough.

Countless colleagues in Chapel Hill read portions of this book and helped to improve it. In particular, I'd like to thank Russell Terry, Juan Bogliaccini, and Sara Niedzwiecki, who in the process became some of my closest friends. I'm also thankful to other graduate student colleagues who have provided challenging criticism, support, and detailed comments since this project started: Federico Fuchs, Claire Greenstein, Cole Harvey, Nick Howard, Hanna Kleider, John Lovett, Tamar Malloy, Elizabeth Menninga, Paula Mukherjee, Vicky Paniagua, Bilyana Petrova, Zoila Ponce de León, Casey Stegman, and Ali Stoyan. I'm especially grateful to Russell for the time he took to help me develop the maps featured throughout this book and to Bilyana, Claire, and Casey, who read, provided feedback, and edited major portions of this book.

This project also benefited greatly from the detailed feedback and constructive criticism I received from scholars in the broader academic community. I'd like to thank Tulane University's Center for Inter-American Policy & Research (CIPR), where I was fortunate to hold a book workshop that brought together a remarkable group of scholars: Evelyne Huber, Raúl Madrid, Ken Roberts, and Eduardo Silva. They offered thoughtful comments on every chapter and helped transform my dissertation into a book manuscript. Their generosity and the quality of their advice are beyond words. Ken Roberts remained engaged with this project even after the book workshop, although, in fairness, his advice had begun much earlier: had I not read his 1998 book, *Deepening Democracy?* I probably wouldn't have become an academic in the first place. His overall impact on my work is hard to measure. I'm also grateful to Mariano Bertucci, Riitta-Ilona Koivumaeki, Don Leonard, and Virginia Oliveros, who during the book workshop raised questions and afterwards provided helpful suggestions on different aspects of this project.

Many other people – colleagues and dear friends – contributed to the development of this book by providing feedback on significant portions of the manuscript or specific chapters and even by providing references to literature that I wasn't familiar with. I'm particularly thankful for the advice provided by Robert Albro, Rodrigo Barrenechea, Merike Blofield, Miguel Centellas, Christopher Chambers-Ju, Tim Gill, Agustina Giraudy, Tulia Falleti, Wendy Hunter, Herbert Kitschelt, Juan Pablo Luna, Lindsay Mayka, Al Montero, Jana Morgan, Brian Palmer-Rubin, Rafael Piñeiro, Jessica Price, Jessica Rich, Fernando Rosenblatt, David Samuels, María Paula Saffón, Jason Tockman, Rich Snyder, Alberto Vergara, and Kurt Weyland. I'm also deeply grateful to Candelaria Garay and Jenny Pribble, who went out of their way to give me multiple iterations of feedback on some of the longest chapters. Their efforts greatly helped to improve those chapters. Jennifer Cyr also deserves special credit; she read major parts of this book and gave me detailed feedback all along. Finally, my colleagues at Dickinson College in the Department of Political Science and the Latin American Studies program have been both welcoming and constant sources of support since I arrived at my new academic home.

In Bolivia, I was fortunate to receive a warm welcome from academics, politicians, and friends. I'd first like to thank Judith Hoffmann and Sebastián Michel for providing a home away from home. I will never forget the Saturday lunches and heated discussions at their house, as well as how much we enjoyed watching *The Strongest* soccer games. In La Paz, I especially appreciate the support of Moira Zuazo at the Friedrich Ebert Stiftung (FES) Foundation, Fernando García Yapur at the United Nations Development Program (UNDP), Ricardo Aguilar at *La Razón*, Erika Brockmann, and Fernando Molina, all of whom provided crucial guidance in the early stages of my fieldwork. Manuel Canelas, Nelson Carvajal, Walter Chávez, Adolfo Mendoza, Manuel Mercado, Rebeca Peralta, and Juan Carlos Pinto helped me ensure my fieldwork was a successful experience. I'm equally thankful for their friendship. In Cochabamba, I greatly appreciate the support of Fernando Mayorga at the Universidad Mayor de San Simón's Centro de Estudios Superiores Universitarios (CESU), Jorge Komadina, José de la Fuente, and María Teresa Zegada. I also thank René Recacochea and his family for their kindness and friendship, and for helping to ensure that my time in Cochabamba and the Chapare was a success. In Santa Cruz, I'm especially grateful to Gabriela Montaño, Hugo Siles, and Henry Zeballos, who assisted with my research in countless ways and provided crucial insight into Santa Cruz politics.

Financial support for this project came from several sources. The field research in Bolivia was possible thanks to the generous funding I received at UNC, including a Mellon Endowment Dissertation Fellowship through the Institute for the Study of the Americas (ISA) and a Graduate School Off-Campus Dissertation Research Fellowship. While these two sources allowed me to cover expenses and travel costs, a Dissertation Completion Fellowship from the Graduate School at UNC allowed me to focus exclusively on dissertation writing on my return from Bolivia. After graduation, Tulane's Center for Inter-American Policy & Research (CIPR) made the transformation of my dissertation into this book possible by providing a comfortable workplace, a vibrant intellectual community of Latin Americanists, and the necessary resources to organize a book workshop. CIPR and Dickinson College also provided support to present the research for this project in multiple conferences. I'm grateful for the support from these institutions.

Sara Doskow at Cambridge University Press has been an incredible editor to work with. Sara was strongly supportive of this project from the very beginning, and she made sure that my initial manuscript went through a rigorous peer-review process with excellent reviewers. And in fact, the comments I received from them were among the most thoughtful and helpful I've seen since I started working on this project. Sara not only made sure that I received the comments in a timely manner, but also her thoughtful summary of key points helped make the book appeal to a broader audience. Some material in this book has appeared in articles that I wrote earlier, and I'd like to thank the publishers for allowing me to use portions of those articles: "Democratizing Democracy? Civil Society and Party Organization in Bolivia," *Comparative Politics* 48, 4 (2016): 459–78; and "Social Movements, Party Organization, and Populism: Insights from the Bolivian MAS," *Latin American Politics and Society* 55, 3 (2013): 19–46. I would also like to thank Danielle Menz, Claire Sissen and the production crew at Cambridge University Press, Divya Arjunan of SPi Global, and Penny Lyons for her excellent copy-editing. And, finally, I humbly thank Kathleen Thelen and Erik Wibbels for their warm welcome into the series.

I'm forever grateful to my family and friends in my home country, Argentina, for their continuous understanding and tireless support. My parents, Luis Anria and Patricia Netri, always encouraged me to pursue my goals, and they have always been there in the good and in the difficult times. This project could not have been completed without them. My sister Clara also deserves special credit, as she provided research assistance by collecting data for several chapters. I'm also thankful to my friends Ignacio Jardón and Matías Puente in Buenos Aires, who, despite the distance and my long periods of poor communication, remained my closest allies as I pursued my path. My US family has been equally supportive, and both George and Susanna DeCecco have helped in countless ways – from dog sitting while I was in Bolivia to editing some of the roughest chapters. My other adopted family, my boxing team in New Orleans, was crucial as I began transforming my dissertation into a book; it provided a necessary grounding, and I learned a great deal from our conversations and the countless sparring sessions. Especially influential was my dear coach, the one and only Steven "Spyder" Hemphill, who became an informal mentor on this project and in life. Thanks to each one of you for the support you have given me and for making my life happier.

More than anybody else, Anne DeCecco, my wife, made the research and the writing of this book possible. Pursuing my academic goals meant living in several countries, adapting to new places, and sometimes living far apart. Her commitment to this project and her unwavering belief in me helped keep this project afloat more than even she knows. Anne was always there for me and, together with our steadfast chihuahua Pancho, accompanied me through my many ups and downs since the very inception of this project. In the process of writing this book we became the proud parents to our beautiful son, Carmelo, who has brought us endless joy and happiness. After a decade of continuous research, writing, and rewriting, I could not have finally taken this book across the finish line without the much-needed downtime and laughter provided by our tickle, peekaboo, and singing sessions. At the risk of sounding clichéd, a risk I'm not ashamed of taking, life with him changed immensely for the better, and he's my most precious treasure. I'd like to thank Carmelo and Anne for helping me to understand the real meaning of home and for making home a fun place to be. With much love and gratitude, I dedicate this book to both of you.

Acronyms and Abbreviations

AD	Democratic Action (Acción Democrática – Venezuela)
ADN	Nationalist Democratic Action (Acción Democrática Nacionalista)
ALAS	Legal Advisory Branch of the Workers' Union in Santa Cruz
ANC	African National Congress – South Africa
AP	Popular Action (Acción Popular – Bolivia)
ASIP	Popular and Solidarity Alliance (Alianza Popular Solidaria)
ASP	Assembly for the Sovereignty of the People (Asamblea por la Soberanía de los Pueblos)
AU	Uruguay Assembly (Asamblea Uruguay)
BCB	Bolivian Central Bank (Banco Central Boliviano)
CEDIB	Bolivia's Center for Documentation and Information (Centro de Documentación e Información Bolivia)
CEJIS	Center for Juridical, Institutional, and Social Studies (Centro de Estudios Jurídicos e Investigación Social)
CIDOB	Confederation of Bolivian Indigenous Peoples (Confederación de Pueblos Indígenas de Bolivia)
CIPCA	Center for Research and Promotion of the Peasantry (Centro de Investigación y Promoción del Campesinado)
CNMCIOB-BS	"Bartolina Sisa" National Confederation of Campesino, Indigenous, and Native Women of Bolivia (Confederación Nacional de Mujeres Campesinas Indígenas Originarias de Bolivia "Bartolina Sisa")
COB	Bolivian Workers' Central (Central Obrera Boliviana)
COMIBOL	Mining Corporation of Bolivia (Corporación Minera de Bolivia)

CON	Regular National Congress (Congreso Nacional Ordinario)
CONALCAM	National Coordinator for Change (Coordinadora Nacional para el Cambio)
CONAMAQ	National Council of Ayllus and Marcas of Qullasuyu (Consejo Nacional de Ayllus y Markas del Qullasuyu)
CONDEPA	Conscience of the Fatherland (Conciencia de Patria)
COR	Regional Labor Federation (Central Obrera Regional)
CPO	Causal Process Observation
CSCIB	Syndicalist Confederation of Intercultural Communities of Bolivia (Confederación Sindical de Comunidades Interculturales de Bolivia)
CSO	Civil Society Organization
CSUTCB	Unique Confederation of Rural Laborers of Bolivia (Confederación Sindical Única de Trabajadores Campesinos de Bolivia)
CUT	Unified Workers' Central (Central Única dos Trabalhadores)
DALP	Democratic Accountability and Linkages Project
EP	Progressive Encounter (Encuentro Progresista – Uruguay)
FA	Broad Front (Frente Amplio – Uruguay)
FEJUVE	Federation of Neighborhood Boards (Federación de Juntas Vecinales)
FENCOMIN	National Federation of Mining Cooperatives (Federación Nacional de Cooperativas Mineras de Bolivia)
FESUCARUSO	Unique Federation of Peasant Communities in the Urban and Semi-Urban Radius of El Alto (Federación Única de Comunidades Campesinas del Radio Urbano y Sub Urbano de El Alto)
FETCT	Special Federation of Peasant Workers of the Tropics of Cochabamba (Federación Especial de Trabajadores Campesinos del Trópico de Cochabamba)
FEYCH	Special Federation of the Yungas of the Chapare (Federación Especial Yungas del Chapare)
FMLN	Salvadorian Farabundo Martí National Liberation Front (Frente Farabundo Martí para la Liberación Nacional)
FSNL	Nicaraguan Sandinista National Liberation Front (Frente Sandinista de Liberación Nacional)
FSTMB	Union Federation of Bolivian Mineworkers (Federación Sindical de Trabajadores Mineros de Bolivia)
INE	National Institute of Statistics of Bolivia
IPSP	Political Instrument of the Sovereignty of the Peoples (Instrumento Político por la Soberanía de los Pueblos)
ISI	Import Substitution Industrialization

IU	United Left (Izquierda Unida)
LAPOP	Latin American Public Opinion Project
LCR	Radical Cause (La Causa R – Venezuela)
LJ	Liberty and Justice (Libertad y Justicia)
LPP	Law of Popular Participation (Ley de Participación Popular)
M-19	19th of April Movement (Movimiento 19 de Abril – Colombia)
MAS	Movement Toward Socialism (Movimiento al Socialismo)
MDB	Brazilian Democratic Movement
MIP	Pachakuti Indigenous Movement (Movimiento Indígena Pachakuti)
MIR	Revolutionary Left Movement (Movimiento de Izquierda Revolucionaria)
MMP	Mixed-Member Proportional Electoral Systems
MNR	Revolutionary Nationalist Movement (Movimiento Nacionalista Revolucionario)
MPP	Popular Participation Movement (Movimiento por la Participación Popular)
MPS	Movement for Sovereignty (Movimiento por la Soberanía)
MRTKL	Revolutionary Liberation Movement Tupaq Katari (Movimiento de Liberación Revolucionaria Tupaq Katari)
MSM	Movement without Fear (Movimiento sin Miedo)
MST	Landless Movement (Movimento Sem Terra – Brazil)
MVR	Fifth Republic Movement (Movimiento Quinta República – Venezuela)
NC	National Council (Plenario Nacional – Uruguay)
NFR	New Republican Force (Nueva Fuerza Republicana)
NGO	Non-governmental Organization
NM	New Majority (Nueva Mayoría – Uruguay)
OTB	Territorial Grass-roots Organizations (Organización Territorial de Base)
PACHAKUTIK	Ecuadorian Pachakutik Plurinational Unity Movement – New Country (Movimiento de Unidad Plurinacional Pachakutik – Nuevo País)
PBC	Bolivian Communist Party (Partido Comunista Boliviano)
PC	Communist Party (Partido Comunista – Uruguay)
PED	Processo de Eleicoes Diretas (Direct Election Process)
PJ	Justicialist Party (Partido Justicialista – Argentina)
PL	Liberal Party – Brazil
PMDB	Brazilian Democratic Movement Party
PODEMOS	Social and Democratic Power (Poder Democrático Social)
PPB-CN	Plan Progress for Bolivia – National Convergence (Plan Progreso para Bolivia – Convergencia Nacional)

PRD	Party of the Democratic Revolution (Partido de la Revolución Democrática – Mexico)
PRI	Institutional Revolutionary Party (Partido Revolucionario Institucional – Mexico)
PS	Socialist Party (Partido Socialista – Chile)
PSDB	Brazilian Social Democracy Party (Partido da Social Democracia)
PSUV	United Socialist Party of Venezuela (Partido Socialista Unido de Venezuela)
PT	Workers' Party (Partido dos Trabalhadores – Brazil)
SMD	Single-member District
TIPNIS	Isiboro Sécure National Park and Indigenous Territory (Territorio Indígena y Parque Nacional Isiboro-Sécure)
UCS	Civic Solidarity Union (Unión Cívica Solidaridad)
UDI	Chilean Independent Democratic Union Party
UJC	Cruceñista Youth Union (Unión Juvenil Cruceñista)
UN	National Unity (Unidad Nacional)
UNDP	United Nations Development Program
UNIR	UNIR Foundation (Fundación UNIR)
UNITAS	Union of Institutions of Social Work and Action (Unión Nacional de Instituciones para el Trabajo de Acción Social)
V-DEM	Varieties of Democracy Project

Introduction

Political parties have undergone deep changes in recent years. As mass party membership has arguably become a relic of the past for many of them (Levitsky and Cameron 2003; Mainwaring and Zoco 2007; Van Biezen, Mair, and Poguntke 2012), political parties founded as ad hoc electoral vehicles to sustain the support of a single charismatic leader have become increasingly common phenomena in "young" and "old" democracies alike – prominent examples include the Movimiento Quinta República (MVR) under Hugo Chávez and Alianza País under Rafael Correa (Ellner 2013), as well as the Italian Forza Italia and the Popolo Della Libertá under Silvio Berlusconi (McDonnell 2013), among others. In these parties, the locus of organizational power is squarely at the top. By contrast, other newer parties, such as the Green left-libertarian or the anti-austerity "movement parties" in Western Europe, reject personalism in the interest of boosting internal participation and resisting oligarchic tendencies and top-down control.[1] However, success in achieving and maintaining internal grass-roots participation and bottom-up influence, particularly after assuming national power, has generally proven to be elusive for political parties (Jachnow 2013).

This book develops a thick "anatomy" of the Bolivian MAS (Movimiento al Socialismo, or Movement Toward Socialism) – an example of a party formed by social movements organized around the political inclusion of the poor and underrepresented, and one that 20 years after its genesis, and more than a decade in power, still deviates from the conventional wisdom on parties. I argue that the MAS has found ways to at least partially counteract trends toward

---

[1] The term "movement party" comes from Kitschelt (2006: 280). For a review of these parties – particularly left-libertarian ecology parties – and their experience in government, see Müller-Rommel (1989) and Müller-Rommel and Poguntke (2002). Della Porta et al. (2017) studies anti-austerity movement parties in Europe.

top-down control, a widely held expectation in the literature, due in large part to elements traceable to the party's social movement origins and to the ongoing strength of autonomous civil society mobilization. To test the generalizability of my arguments, I then compare the MAS with two additional parties that share common origins in social movements but vary in terms of the extent to which their structures disperse political power and allow bottom-up participation in decision-making. A central goal of this book, then, is to explain *why* some movement-based parties develop more top-down structures designed to enhance the power and autonomy of the party leadership while others remain more open to bottom-up participation and responsive to the interests, demands, and preferences of their social bases. Through an in-depth examination of the origins, organization, and internal politics of three parties formed by and with strong ties to grass-roots social movements in Latin America, this book develops an original theoretical framework for explaining variation in their internal power distributions, organizational models, and leadership patterns.

New parties have been especially important in Latin America (Levitsky et al. 2016). One of the most salient developments in the region is the recent emergence and ascendance to power of left parties that represent the interests of the politically and socially marginalized (Cleary 2006; Castañeda 2006; Cameron and Hershberg 2010; Weyland, Madrid, and Hunter 2010; Levitsky and Roberts 2011).[2] Some of those parties began life as social movements. Usually described loosely as "movement-based" parties (Van Cott 2005: 39; Hochstetler 2013: 242), they draw organizational strength from connections to grass-roots social movements. Key examples include the Brazilian PT (Workers' Party), the Uruguayan FA (Broad Front), the Colombian 19th of April Movement (M-19), the Nicaraguan FSNL (Sandinista National Liberation Front), the Salvadorian FMLN (Farabundo Martí National Liberation Front), the Venezuelan LCR (La Causa R), and the core case studied in this book: the Bolivian MAS.

Movement-based parties are not just a Latin American phenomenon; they have also emerged in Africa (LeBas 2011), the Middle East (Roy 2013), Western Europe (Mair 2013; della Porta et al. 2017), Eastern Europe (Glenn 2003), and North America (Schwartz 2006). Despite their importance and rise in popularity (de Leon 2013: 5, 158–9), we know little about how these parties work internally. Research has tended to overwhelmingly focus on the origins of movement-based parties and their rise to prominence (e.g., Kitschelt 1989a; Keck 1992; Bartolini and Mair 1995; Bruhn 1997; Goldstone 2003; Chandra 2004; Van Cott 2005; Madrid 2012), meaning that the internal politics of these

---

[2] Left parties are parties committed to the values of equality and solidarity (Huber and Stephens 2012: 28). Strategically, they seek to use state power to "protect individuals from market failures, reduce socio-economic inequality, and strengthen underprivileged sectors" (Levitsky and Roberts 2011: 5).

parties remain both underexamined and undertheorized. The work by della Porta et al. (2017) is a partial exception.

In Latin America, the rise in popularity and ascension of movement-based parties to national-level power generated some optimism about the prospects for building internally democratic organizations that encourage grass-roots social movements to participate both widely and substantively in making collective decisions (Van Cott 2008; Handlin and Collier 2011; Goldfrank 2011a; Madrid 2012; De la Torre 2013). Extending direct grass-roots participation, which has been associated with the post-Cold War notion of "deepening" democracy, is a historic goal of the political left in Latin America (Roberts 1998: 3; Goldfrank 2011b). Scholars such as Levitsky and Roberts (2011: 13) and Pribble (2013: 178) have shown that new left parties and political movements in power in Latin America vary in the extent to which their internal structures disperse power and political authority, but more fundamental questions still remain unanswered: How do these parties work internally? How democratic are they in their organization and internal operations? What are their relationships to grass-roots allies in civil society? And what causes these parties to exhibit such a wide variation in the manner in which they concentrate and disperse political power in their internal organization? To put it simply: why do some succumb to the trend toward top-down control, as the conventional wisdom would expect it, while others resist that trend more strongly?

These questions have a long lineage in political and sociological thought. They had great relevance to Moisei Ostrogorski's (1964 [1902]) classic theoretical work on democracy and the dangers of oligarchic tendencies within political parties in *Democracy and the Organization of Political Parties*, Max Weber's (1946) writings on parties in *Politics as a Vocation*, and Robert Michels's research on parties and oligarchy theory in his seminal book, *Political Parties* (Michels, 1962 [1911]). The short version of Michels's "iron law" of oligarchy is arguably one of the most generalizable and prominent statements in political science.[3] Now over a hundred years old, Michels's argument on the organizational development of parties predicts the inevitable rise of top-down, elite-dominated hierarchical structures that concentrate power and de-emphasize bottom-up participation. Michels's oligarchy theory is of special interest here because influential analyses of party organization either explicitly

---

[3] I distinguish between a "short" and a "long" version of Michels's oligarchy theory. While the former is about the *centralization of authority* and the progressive decrease of opportunities for participation in decision-making by the grass-roots, the latter is about the growing *difference between the preferences* of the office-seeking leadership and those of the rank and file, and about a prevalence of decisions made in favor of the self-regarding political interests of the leaders. For a discussion on the multiple understandings of, and ambiguities in, Michels's work, see Linz (2006: 37–45); also Kitschelt (1989b).

confront or arrive at this same conclusion.[4] Framed as an authoritative, "fundamental sociological law of political parties," it denies the very possibility of democratic modes of governance within parties regardless of party type or differences in their founding organizational characteristics. The assumption is that, even if parties have different genetic endowments (Panebianco 1988), they will all end up the same – particularly as they contest elections, institutionalize their structures, and access high electoral office.[5]

Michels's work has deeply shaped scholarly thinking about political parties. And indeed, there is a clear teleological expectation in the scholarly literature of comparative political parties that *even* where parties begin as social movements (or as distinctively bottom-up organizations), they all evolve until they are dominated by a specialized, professionalized caste of political elites who are highly detached from and unaccountable to their social bases. In response to electoral imperatives and other pressures discussed in Chapter 1, the movement transforms into a political machine or, even worse, a closed and powerful political cartel with distinct interests from the movements (Katz and Mair 1995). Under conditions of cartelization, there is a widening gap between party leaders and social bases, and the latter wield little power in internal party affairs.

This book challenges this highly influential body of literature by showing that such a teleological course of organizational development is *not* inevitable or preordained. I argue that Bolivia's MAS, a party formed directly by social movements, has found ways to at least partially counteract Michelsian oligarchic trends. This outcome is largely attributable to the party's social movement genesis and the strength and ongoing capacity of autonomous social mobilization by its social base. I demonstrate that, against theoretical expectations, the party's grass-roots social base wields significant influence over the selection of candidates for elective office and in the policy-making sphere. Although oligarchic temptations are readily present by the party's top leadership, historical causes traceable to the party's early development as well as constant causes linked to its power base provide countervailing, "bottom-up" correctives to hierarchy and concentrated authority.

Although the question of *who* wields power in political parties and the related idea of internal party democracy are the subject of an age-old debate, they recently regained attention in comparative party analyses (Hazan and Rahat 2010; Cross and Katz 2013; Cross and Pilet 2013; de Leon 2013; Mudge and Chen 2014), partly in response to the widespread crisis of representation and the decline of mass party membership. Thus, the broader theoretical question that I address in this book – the conditions and mechanisms under

---

[4] The classic works of Duverger (1954), McKenzie (1955), Michels (1962 [1911]), Kirchheimer (1966), Katz and Mair (1995), and Panebianco (1988) are examples of this trend.

[5] This is captured in the statement: "it is organization which gives birth to the dominion of the elected over the electors, of the mandatories over the mandators, of the delegates over the delegators. Who says organization says oligarchy" (Michels 1962 [1911]: 365).

which political parties can counteract a seemingly inevitable course of oligarchic organizational development – is both a classic question of political sociology and a pressing issue of practical relevance in contemporary societies.

WHY THIS BOOK

Parties are crucial, if not indispensable, for democratic politics.[6] They do much more than make democracy "workable" for voters and politicians.[7] Parties are key for political interest aggregation and for the translation of programs into policies. Their organizational properties, moreover, have implications not only for the dynamics of interparty competition (Panebianco 1988; Kitschelt 2000; Roberts 2015a), but also for shaping normatively important public policy outcomes. For example, the politics of redistribution can be better understood by looking at the organizational attributes of parties – and, specifically, their balance of power among internal stakeholders – since more power-dispersing parties generally push social policy in a bolder, more redistributive, and universalistic direction.[8] Thus, there is a potentially high payoff for research on the sources of variation in the internal distribution of power within and between parties.[9] This could then be linked to rich and nuanced explanations of macro-level processes, such as social policy reform.

The question of whether, to what extent, and how parties can defy the tendencies toward top-down control and remain open to societal input is not just an academic exercise; it has important practical and political consequences at both the party and the regime levels. As multiple studies have made abundantly clear, when democratic participation within governing parties is deficient, those parties can more easily become vehicles for the unrestrained will of political elites and even dominant single leaders. In such contexts, the voices of regular citizens or even of the party's own social bases may not be heard, thereby hindering the average citizen's participation in political life while enhancing the discretion of the party leadership – a condition conducive to personalistic politics. At the party level, using Hirschman's (1970) terminology, where groups and individuals that constitute a party's social base have limited opportunities to exert "voice" in party decisions, it is generally much harder to establish and maintain high levels of organizational "loyalty," partisan engagement, and mobilization capacity (Anria and Cyr 2017; Pérez, Piñeiro, and Rosenblatt 2018; Rosenblatt 2018). At the broader regime level, where instances

---

[6] As Schattschneider (1942: 1) writes, "modern democracy is *unthinkable* save in terms of political parties" (emphasis added).

[7] "Democracy," writes Aldrich (1995: 3), "is *unworkable* save in terms of parties" (emphasis added).

[8] For excellent analyses pointing in this direction, see Huber and Stephens (2012), Pribble (2013), Schipani (2016), and Garay (2017).

[9] See Mudge and Chen's (2014: 320) call for research on this question.

for bottom-up input are significantly reduced while in power, "bait-and-switch" policy-making becomes more likely (Roberts 2015a). This, in turn, can affect negatively the consistency of the party "brand" and impact the stability of the overall party system (Lupu 2016).

When governing parties are more open to bottom-up input, by contrast, there are greater opportunities to establish checks on the decisions of their leaders and constrain their strategic behavior and hierarchical control. In such contexts, it is less likely that the party will become a vehicle to advance the goals of a personalistic leader – even if oligarchic temptations are readily available. The presence of channels to exert "voice" provides incentives for the social bases to shape important decisions, as these bases become de facto veto actors within the organization. Developing greater opportunities for bottom-up input, moreover, makes it comparatively easier for these parties to maintain strong grass-roots linkages as well as to breed organizational loyalty, partisan engagement, and mobilization capacity (Rosenblatt 2018). At the broader regime level, when a governing party establishes and upholds well-developed opportunities for bottom-up grass-roots participation, instances of bait-and-switch policy-making are less likely – a condition conducive to policy stability. This, in turn, makes the consistency of the party brand more likely to stick and the party system more stable (Lupu 2016).

In addition, when governing parties (especially those formed by popular organizations pushing for inclusion) are more open, they may generate opportunities and incentives for the political empowerment of traditionally marginalized groups by boosting their input in the political power game.[10] Seen from this angle, arguments about internal power dispersion can be seen as arguments about "democratizing" or "deepening" democracy.[11] My goal here, then, is neither to refute Michels's "iron law" of oligarchy nor to prove that it does not apply everywhere. Rather, the goal is to use original, systematic evidence to explain the conditions, mechanisms, and processes under which broader and substantive bottom-up participation can be promoted and sustained within contemporary governing parties that have social movements, peasant associations, labor unions, and other popular organizations as their

---

[10] Thus, in parallel to *workplace* democracy (Pateman 1970; Huber 1980), party democracy can promote the involvement of groups and individuals in the making of collective decisions that affect their social life. It can achieve so not only by promoting their participation, but also by extending substantive decision-making authority and influence.

[11] While the term "democratizing democracy" is taken from Santos (2005), the idea of "deepening democracy" is taken from Roberts (1998). Both terms are similar; they presuppose a move from a "shallow" formal democracy to a more "participatory" mode of democracy – one that expands the opportunities for popular sectors to exert meaningful influence on the political process (see also Huber, Rueschemeyer, and Stephens 1997). In this view, democracy is not just about its formal institutions, but it also has to do with increased empowerment of its citizens, especially subordinate groups in society.

core social base.[12] The scholarly literature gives scant theoretical guidance to assist with the empirical exploration of this puzzle.

Beyond its substantive and practical relevance, this book helps address significant gaps in the scholarly literature of comparative politics. Understanding the organization and internal operations of movement-based parties adds to one of the most strikingly underdeveloped and fragmented bodies of literature in comparative politics: the debate about what happens inside the "black box" of parties and party decision-making (Levitsky 2001). As scholars have noted, political parties "are not what they once were" in older and younger democracies alike (Schmitter 2001, cited in Roberts 2015a: 37). Yet, although parties remain weakly organized in much of the developing world (Cyr 2012), the era of party-building is far from over (Tavits 2013; Van Dyck 2014), and movement-based parties seem to be well-equipped to build strong and durable organizations (Levitsky et al. 2016: 21). In Latin America, a region notorious for its populist tradition and personalistic politics (Weyland 2001; De la Torre and Arnson 2013; Roberts 2017), vibrant social movements have spawned electorally successful parties that even gained national-level power. This is by itself a remarkable development. Even more remarkable, some of these parties have become better than others at generating spaces for bottom-up influence and counteracting the trends toward top-down control associated with party bureaucratization and concentrated executive authority – a pattern that is promising because it can contribute to breaking with the historic mold of party organizations subordinated to the political authority and interests of dominant leaders. And yet the literature has few insights to help explain this variation.

This book provides a timely addition to the study of the internal politics of movement-based parties, and in so doing it tries to build bridges across the scholarly literatures on political parties and social movements. The book not only shows how movements can form parties, as they sometimes do, but also how they shape and constrain internal party organizational and leadership patterns. Indeed, as discussed in the pages that follow, movement attributes become a critical source of variation in parties' internal power distributions and organizational models, both within and across cases.

MOVEMENTS, PARTIES, AND MOVEMENT-BASED PARTIES

The scholarly works of literature on social movements and political parties have often traveled parallel roads with little conversation between them (della Porta et al. 2017: 3). However, scholars have recently been paying more attention to the multiple overlaps between parties and movements linked to

---

[12] My approach is thus akin to the one followed by Lipset, Coleman, and Trow (1977 [1956]: 13) in their seminal study of the conditions affecting *union* democracy, whose goal was to explain the mechanisms that might enable or hinder the maintenance of democracy in organizations.

them (Goldstone 2003; Heaney and Rojas 2015; Tarrow 2015). Social movements, usually defined as networks of groups that seek to change some aspect of the social and political structure through extra-institutional means (Tilly 1978), influence the internal politics of parties in various ways; they often infiltrate parties, introduce new issues on their programs, provide mobilizational power, and help parties expand their bases of support by establishing linkages with voters, among other things (Bartolini and Mair 1995; Thachil 2014; Brooke 2017). In extreme cases, as McAdam and Tarrow (2010: 533) note, "movements turn into political parties themselves." In this book, I call these movement-based parties. They are one of "the main political consequences of movements at the structural level" (Amenta et al. 2010: 289).

Movement-based parties share two key defining attributes. First, they are parties directly formed by social movement activists and leaders. This means they have a different logic of party formation than what the dominant, Downsian models of party formation stipulate (Downs 1957). In those highly influential models, parties are seen as the creation of strategic legislators; they are depicted simply as electoral vehicles for political elites and as structures largely detached from their social bases (Aldrich 1995: 29–50). By contrast, movement-based parties are the direct creation of militant movement activists and grass-roots leaders forged in the heat of social mobilization, who decide to enter into the electoral arena and compete for office while sustaining collective action in the streets; they are generally formed as opposition parties or as regime challengers, and they follow a distinctively "bottom-up" logic of party genesis. In short, if in Aldrich's (1995) dominant model the logic of party formation consists of rootless political entrepreneurs in search of social bases, movement-based parties stand out because they follow the reverse logic. They begin life as movements (Tarrow 2015: 95).

Second, movement-based parties are parties with a core constituency of grass-roots social movements.[13] This definition parallels Levitsky's (2003: 4) definition of labor-based parties, with grass-roots social movements rather than organized labor as the sponsoring organizations and core constituency. In my conceptualization, movement-based parties are also different from Kitschelt's (2006) analytical characterization of "movement parties," which are almost always the electoral vehicles of a social movement mobilized around a single issue (Kitschelt 2006: 283). By contrast, movement-*based* parties are broader alliances of various movements and other popular organizations and, as such, they are better prepared to incorporate a broader set of issues, actors, and demands. My conceptualization is also different from della Porta et al.'s (2017: 4, 7) definition

---

[13] The term "core constituency" comes from Gibson (1992, 1996). It refers to specific sectors that provide financial resources, policy-making support, and guidance to a political party. In the case of movement-based parties, movements also provide mobilizational power. In the remainder of this book, I shall use the terms "social movements," "grass-roots movements," and "popular organizations" interchangeably.

of "movement parties," which stresses the strength of the organizational linkages between parties and movements. In that definition, movement parties are those that have particularly strong organizational and external links with social movements. My definition of movement-based parties also considers those connections but emphasizes that these parties are the creation of social movements. They are, in short, founded *directly* by movements.

In contemporary Latin America, examples of these parties include, but are not limited to, the Bolivian MAS, the Brazilian Workers' Party (PT), the Ecuadorian Pachakutik Plurinational Unity Movement – New Country (Pachakutik), the Farabundo Martí National Liberation Front (FMLN), the Uruguayan Broad Front (FA), and the Venezuelan Radical Cause (LCR). Outside Latin America, additional examples of movement-based parties include, but are not limited to, the African National Congress (ANC) in South Africa, the Congress Socialist Party (CSP) in the Indian state of Kerala, and even the Muslim Brotherhood in Egypt, as well as "historic" cases such as Solidarity in Poland and even the Republican Party in the United States, which emerged from the abolitionist movement in the context of the American Civil War (McAdam and Tarrow 2010: 533).[14] Table I.1 has additional examples and details about their sponsoring movements and core constituency.

Clearly, many of these parties have lost their bottom-up characteristics and become hierarchical party organizations. What I am going to explain in this book is why some of them have been able to preserve a vibrant and participatory internal life.

Movement-based parties follow what Roberts (1998: 75) calls the "organic" model of party development, in that they are organizationally hybrid: they engage in extra-institutional social mobilization, such as street protests and mass demonstrations, and they also compete for office in the electoral arena.[15] As della Porta et al. (2017: 7) note, "to different degrees, they have overlapping membership." And, in fact, members and leaders who run for electoral office tend to be "drawn directly from social movements rather than from the ranks of a separate, professional political caste" (Roberts 1998: 75). While these parties may vary in terms of ideology and programmatic orientation, they almost always share a rejection of top-down hierarchical control by an autonomous and all-too powerful party leadership, as well as an explicit commitment to maximizing opportunities for democratic participation at the grass-roots level (Carty 2013).

Movement-based parties are often seen as "transitional phenomena" (Kitschelt 2006: 288; della Porta et al. 2017: 24), but the "transitioning into what" question is not settled. One salient argument suggests that the highly participatory and "bottom-up" decision-making patterns that are generally

---

[14] The mid-nineteenth-century French Republican Party is another key historical movement-based party that has received some attention in the social-movement literature. See Aminzade (1995).
[15] De Leon (2013: 158) calls them "omnibus" parties, acknowledging that it is "difficult to discern where the party begins and where it ends."

TABLE I.I *Examples of movement-based parties.*

Party	Country	Sponsoring organizations and core constituency	Sources
Movement Toward Socialism (MAS)*	Bolivia	Coca growers; peasant movements	Van Cott (2005); Madrid (2012)
Workers' Party (PT)*	Brazil	Labor unions; ecclesiastical communities	Meneguello (1989); Keck (1992)
Broad Front (FA)*	Uruguay	Labor unions; student movement	Luna (2007); Lanzaro (2011)
Pachakutik Plurinational Unity Movement	Ecuador	Indigenous movement	Van Cott (2005); Yashar (2005)
Farabundo Martí Natl. Liberation Front (FMLN)*	El Salvador	Guerrilla groups; labor unions	McClintock (1998)
African National Congress (ANC)*	South Africa	Anti-apartheid movement; labor movement	Marais (2011)
Muslim Brotherhood	Egypt	Pan-Islamic, religious movement	Wickham (2015)
Solidarity	Poland	Labor unions	Garton Ash (2002)
Congress Socialist Party (CSP)	India (Kerala)	Anti-colonial, anti-caste movements	Desai (2003)
British Labor Party[a]	Great Britain	Labor unions	Bartolini (2000)
Christian Democratic Party[b]	Germany	Catholic lay organizations; confessional organizations	Kalyvas (1996)
Green Party[c]	Germany	Environmental movement	Kitschelt (1989a)

Notes: The list is not exhaustive. Asterisks indicate movement-based parties that won national-level elections, and not as a member of a coalition. The list also excludes cases such as Podemos in Spain, Syriza (Coalition of the Radical Left) in Greece, and M5S in Italy. These have a core constituency of and strong connections with anti-austerity protest movements in each country (della Porta et al. 2017: 24–55), but they are not *sponsored* directly by movements.

[a] Labor unions, in alliance with other civic associations, also sponsored social democratic or labor parties in many other countries, including Belgium, Sweden, and Australia, among others (see Bartolini 2000: 246).

[b] Religious communities and associations also formed confessional political parties in countries like Belgium, the Netherlands, and Austria, among others (see Kalyvas 1996).

[c] Environmental movements, in alliance with other social movements, also spawned Green parties in several other Western European countries, including Belgium, Finland, France, and Italy.

present at early stages in the life of a movement-based party are viable for only a short time, as the logics of electoral competition and territorial representation will inevitably push parties to subordinate their mobilizational strategies to the imperatives of organization and the exercise of power. However, movement-based parties may not evolve in a unilinear or uniform way. It is also theoretically plausible that such parties follow contingent structural and strategic incentives that make it possible for them to return to the organizational patterns common in their early phases.[16] In other words, there are no a priori reasons to assume that parties formed by social movements will inevitably, or by necessity, transition to a form of party that is hierarchical, exclusive, and centralized, following an "iron law" of organization.

Because movement-based parties are fundamentally moving targets whose organizational boundaries are "fuzzy and permeable" (Goldstone 2003: 2), they offer unique opportunities to examine potential forms of political organization that challenge conventional notions of how parties work internally and how they shape broader political transformations.[17] Their bottom-up genesis in autonomous grass-roots mobilization and their hybrid features may create favorable conditions for opposition among allied groups to check elites' power from within and to generate pressures from below in ways that constrain the decision-making power and autonomy of the party's top leadership. This dynamic has the effect of encouraging democratic control from below. However, not every movement-based party develops such structures of accountability, where movements continue to influence, constrain, and hold the leadership accountable over time. As I argue in this book, the realization of this potential depends heavily on the organizational strength, density, and autonomous capacity for social mobilization by popular constituencies.

THE MAS AS A MOVEMENT-BASED PARTY

The core case that I analyze in this book is the Bolivian MAS. I treat the case as an example of a movement-based party in national power and argue that it is theoretically relevant because it deviates from the existing wisdom about this type of party: defying theoretical expectations, it has followed a remarkably different organizational trajectory that has facilitated grass-roots impact and constrained elite control, even after assuming power at the national level.[18]

---

[16] For a parallel argument, see Kitschelt (2006: 286).

[17] The challenge is to identify patterns that are sustainable both in the short and in the long run.

[18] This is the story of the MAS so far; I am not claiming that it will remain open to grass-roots input in the future. It is likely that it will become increasingly centralized if it becomes a hegemonic power holder, like South Africa's ANC, but it is also theoretically plausible that if it loses power it will seek to revitalize linkages with the grass-roots. The broader point is that, theoretically, there are no good reasons to assume a priori that movement-based parties like the MAS will develop in a uniform manner, as the bulk of the existing literature predicts.

This case is particularly important for study because conventional accounts of movement-based parties focus on cases that develop a strong organizational infrastructure of collective action before assuming national power, such as the Brazilian PT (Samuels 2004; Ribeiro 2008, 2014; Hunter 2010). Consequently, previous studies' conclusions tend to stress the "normalization" of these parties, their tendency to become more centralized, and the difficulties of sustaining bottom-up participation when they govern at the national level (Hunter 2007).

As a deviant comparative case, or as an organizational "anomaly" in comparative politics, the MAS serves to develop and refine existing arguments of party organizational development. It does so by demonstrating that such a teleological course of organizational development, where parties begin as movements but evolve into a cartel of incumbents, is not preordained or inevitable. The central contributions of this type of deviant case study are therefore to identify the boundaries of existing theory – the conditions under which existing theoretical propositions that predict a unilinear course of oligarchic development do not hold true – and to explain the mechanisms and processes that help to counteract expectations widely held in the literature.[19]

THE MAS IN HISTORIC AND STRUCTURAL CONTEXT

Given the centrality of the MAS for this book, some contextualization is in order. A good place to start is by recognizing that the MAS is – chronologically speaking – Bolivia's second "mass-mobilizing" party, the first one being the Nationalist Revolutionary Movement (MNR). The MNR emerged as a product of the anti-oligarchic mobilization that started in Bolivia in the late 1920s and which intensified in the aftermath of the Chaco War (1932–6). It was formed in 1941 by a small group of middle-class nationalist intellectuals, who, in order to successfully attain state power, allied with the organized working class and peasant organizations. By the early 1950s, the MNR was committed, first, to overthrowing the dominant tin-based oligarchy, dubbed *La Rosca*, and, second, to an agenda of tin nationalization, universal suffrage, and mass educational reform. Through these measures, the party intended to weaken the power base of traditional elites and promote the incorporation of marginalized groups into national political life.

---

[19] On the importance of "deviant" cases in comparative politics, see Lijphart (1971: 692) and Emigh (1997). These cases, in short, can contribute to theory building by challenging and extending established propositions. The term "anomaly" is taken from Keck's (1992) study of the origins of the Brazilian PT, and it intended to capture the party's novelty and exception in Brazilian politics. Similarly, today the MAS stands for its novelty in Bolivian politics and in the broader Latin American region – a novelty due to its process of formation and its patterns of internal organization.

After seizing power through a successful revolt in 1952, the MNR nationalized tin mines, established universal suffrage, expanded mass education, and implemented an ambitious land reform. These policies helped to incorporate into politics large segments of the, by then, predominantly rural population. Land reform, which was instituted in response to pressures from the peasantry, was especially important; it not only allocated land to the landless, particularly by expropriating valley estates (*haciendas*) in the highland indigenous areas, but also freed them from a condition of personal servitude.

These reforms had lasting legacies. Although the underlying structure of the country's economy changed little after 1952, with mining industries remaining the dominant source of foreign exchange, important advances toward the incorporation of popular groups were set in motion. Just days after the revolution, labor organized a separate, national-level organization called the Bolivian Workers' Central (COB), which was headed by militant tin miners. As the MNR expanded its territorial reach and consolidated its predominant place in Bolivian politics, the COB consolidated its organizational presence throughout the country while maintaining some degree of autonomy from the MNR. The MNR offered the COB direct representation in government agencies, as in classic corporatist arrangements, and did not seek to integrate labor into the party (Mitchell 1977: 44). A similar approach prevailed vis-à-vis peasants. Regardless of how we label that approach, the MNR provided new channels for representation of peasants and workers in organized politics, facilitating their incorporation into the political system (Crabtree 2013). This cemented the MNR as the country's first mass-mobilizing party directly representing the interests of the marginalized (Anria and Cyr 2017: 1261).

Although the MNR was overthrown in a military coup in 1964, the policies put in place by the party triggered major social change; they transformed Bolivia from being a strikingly poor, illiterate, rural, and mostly indigenous society into a wealthier, literate, increasingly urban, and *mestizo* society (Grindle and Domingo 2003; Klein 2011). The country urbanized rapidly, but peasant groups remained crucial allies for both the MNR (1952–64) and successive military-authoritarian governments (1964–78). During this time, rural syndical organizations became crucial for the mobilization and participation of the peasantry in both the highlands and in the amazon lowlands. While authoritarian regimes sought to control them by what came to be known as the "military-peasant pact," some groups with no commitments to parties or the military maintained autonomy and strengthened their organization. The most powerful organization to emerge was the Unique Confederation of Rural Laborers of Bolivia (CSUTCB). Formed in 1979 by the *katarista* Aymara indigenous movement in the highlands and in close connection with the COB and other labor organizations (Yashar 2005: 178), the CSUTCB focused on promoting peasant unity and demanding both improved social conditions in rural areas and a greater role for indigenous people in mainstream society (García Linera, León, and Monje 2004: 113–5). It would then play a leading role in the restoration of democracy in 1982 after almost two decades of military dictatorships.[20]

By the 1980s, urban migration had radically transformed Bolivian politics by giving rise to a new urban-popular class highly organized into neighborhood and syndical organizations, which, in a context of persisting poverty and lack of sufficient labor absorption, would demand better social and economic conditions. This urban class grew in number with the sudden dismantling of the state mining sector (COMIBOL) in the mid-1980s, when large groups of relocated miners migrated to cities like La Paz, El Alto, and Santa Cruz and strengthened local community organizations. The attacks on COMIBOL, which were central to Bolivia's "shock-therapy" shift to neoliberalism since 1985, weakened the country's labor unions and deepened unemployment in the traditional mining centers of Oruro and Potosí, a pattern that led to continued migrations to both rural and urban areas. Neighborhood organizations flourished exponentially between 1989 and 2006 and blended together class-based demands of ex-miners and claims for improved basic services, such as a water, electricity, and sanitation (Lazar 2008).

Despite increasing urbanization, decentralization reforms in the 1990s, a part of the neoliberal reform package, encouraged the mobilization of peasant and indigenous movements (Yashar 2005: 220–1) and unleashed a "ruralization" of Bolivian politics (Zuazo 2008: 23). New opportunities for participation at the municipal level, in particular through the 1994 Law of Popular Participation, led to "the increased presence of *campesino* and indigenous peoples in formal politics" (Klein 2011: 59). By recognizing a multiplicity of forms of local and community organization as legal vehicles for civil society representation – including indigenous groups, peasant unions, and neighborhood organizations – the LPP contributed to the strengthening of civil society (Kohl 2003: 162). It also encouraged the formation of new political parties through which organized groups gained increased representation at the local and the national levels, such as the Aymara-based Pachakuti Indigenous Movement (MIP) and the MAS, redressing historical exclusions. Although a central idea behind the LPP was to facilitate popular participation in organized politics, the strengthening of newly legally recognized organizations also turned them into more effective channels for contentious political mobilization. In 2000, mass popular protests staged by social movements and directed against neoliberal policies in Cochabamba, a series of events dubbed the Water War, opened up a period of high-intensity mobilizations that united both rural and urban-popular movements in a broad-based coalition for the defense of improved living conditions, greater state control over the economy, and a fuller incorporation of popular groups into social and political life (Silva 2009: 123–42). This period of mass mobilizations

---

[20] For the slower-paced development of indigenous organizations in the lowlands, see the rich accounts provided by Healy (2001), Yashar (2005), and Lucero (2008).

also set in motion political dynamics that made the rise to power of the MAS in 2005 increasingly likely, as explained in Chapter 2.

Unlike the MNR, the MAS, Bolivia's second mass-mobilizing party, stands out for its genesis in a highly organized and disciplined social movement of *cocaleros* (coca producers) mobilized for decades against coca eradication programs and neoliberal reforms. Founded in Bolivia's coca-growing Chapare region in the mid-1990s, it became the country's largest party in less than a decade. Its leader, Evo Morales, won three presidential elections (2005, 2009, and 2014) with absolute majorities, an unprecedented feature in Bolivian politics. The MAS is a different case from other movement-based parties in the region (and, indeed, elsewhere) because it represents indigenous constituencies – in fact, even more unusually, it grew directly out of the mobilization of these constituencies. To be clear, to state that the MAS represents indigenous constituencies is not to say that it is an "indigenous" party. Instead, we can conceive of the MAS as a party that presents itself using an ethnic discourse but that also tries to appeal to a wider constituency by blending class and ethnic elements in a manner that tolerates ethnic diversity.[21]

As an organization, the MAS emerged from the belief of *cocaleros* and other peasant groups that they should take advantage of the new opportunities opened by the LPP and have a "political instrument" to contest elections on their own, rather than in alliance with the existing political parties.[22] The resulting instrument, a loosely organized party, engaged in electoral politics at the local level, making rapid gains, specifically in the Chapare region. Early electoral successes in the Chapare helped to consolidate coca growers as the leading group within the party's central leadership. It also helped boost the representation of coca growers at the national level. The party's rapid ascension to power, in turn, occurred through the construction of an unusually strong rural–urban coalition crafted via different types of linkages between the MAS and organized popular constituencies. This development took place in the midst of a severe social crisis and period of mobilizations that, as was noted above, shook the country between 2000 and 2005 (Silva 2009; Anria 2013: 26–8). Ever since assuming power, the MAS has been characterized by its high degrees of pragmatism – in its rhetoric, its policies, and its alliance-building approach (Harten 2011; Gray Molina 2013; Farthing and Kohl 2014; Anria and Cyr

---

[21] Madrid (2008) uses the term "ethnopopulism" to describe the MAS. Ethnopopulist parties are "inclusive ethnically based parties that adopt classical populist electoral strategies" (Madrid 2008: 475). These parties present themselves with an ethnic discourse but try to appeal to a wider constituency. The difference between these and exclusionary indigenous-based parties is that the latter cannot make broad appeals beyond a specific and territorially defined ethnic group. Examples of these are the Pachakuti Indigenous Movement (MIP) and the Revolutionary Liberation Movement Tupac Katari (MRTKL).

[22] The "political instrument" – as the MAS is still referred to by its founders and allied movements – was created around the idea of achieving the "self-representation" of popular groups.

2017). This pragmatism has made the MAS elusive to simple classifications, and consequently many scholars have avoided such efforts.

Despite this pragmatism, the MAS maintains a grass-roots social movement core, particularly in rural areas. The organizations that founded the MAS, and particularly the *cocaleros*, still constitute its "core constituency" (Gibson 1996: 7), shaping the party's identity to a large extent. The weight of such groups in internal party affairs is unrivaled in the case of the MAS, as they have played a central role in setting priorities, agenda items, and political action. In sum, then, the party's genesis as a political organization was undoubtedly from the bottom up. This foundational characteristic, together with the fact that the MAS has retained a core constituency of grass-roots social movements even after gaining state power, makes the MAS a clear example of a movement-based party. While the party as a bureaucratic organization remains relatively weak 20 years after its emergence, its main source of organizational power derives from its close ties to a wide array of rural and urban-popular movements and associations, which provide a formidable mass base and coalition of support. Today, 12 years after it gained power for the first time, the MAS remains the only truly national party in Bolivia and is that country's undisputed governing party.

OVERVIEW OF THE ARGUMENT

The framework I develop in this book stresses the impact that both historical and constant causes have on power distributions within movement-based parties. This distinction between "historical" and "constant" causes is taken from Stinchcombe (1968). On the one hand, historical causes are dynamics that occur once in the early stages of an institution and have long-lasting effects. On the other hand, constant causes are ongoing and have to be reproduced. In other words, they are dynamics that operate more or less continually and help to reproduce a given outcome.

In my framework, historical causes comprise party organizational attributes traceable to a party's origins and early institutional development, the experience accumulated before gaining national power, and the conditions surrounding a party's access to power. Constant causes, in turn, correspond with the organizational strength and density of civil society – or its overall "configuration" (Rueschemeyer, Stephens, and Stephens 1992). A strong, autonomous, and well-developed civil society (one rich in voluntary associations for collective organization independent of the state or economic elites) can serve as a power base for movement-based parties. It can play not only an important party-building role by facilitating territorial expansion but can also shape internal power distributions and leadership patterns by generating pressures from below and constraints on the power and strategic behavior of the party leadership. Two caveats must be discussed here, however. First, high organizational density in society can also bring about enhanced power concentration.[23] The *autonomy* of civil society from the state and its independence from economic elites is key; if civil society is created from above, or is rendered dependent on resources and financing from the state or economic elites, it can be more easily controlled from the top or do little to enhance internal party democracy. In short, for bottom-up correctives to concentrated authority to be operative, what is truly crucial in my framework is the ongoing capacity for autonomous social mobilization that is not controlled from the top down.

The historical explanation focuses on internal organizational structures and practices adopted during the party's foundational phase and early development. It pays special attention to the organizational linkages with mass civic associations and social movements, the degree of emphasis on building bureaucratic structures, and the level of centralization in decision-making processes. In concrete, I argue that the close links with social movements and civic organizations developed by the MAS in its formative years, combined with a high emphasis on grass-roots input and low levels of bureaucratization and centralization, left indelible marks on the organization and internal power distributions of the party. They created an inclination for the party to develop a bottom-up pattern of organization that has proved to be resistant to change – a phenomenon that historical institutionalists refer to as a "weak" form of path dependence.

The party developed a bottom-up pattern of organization since its genesis. Spawned by a rural social movement and embedded in a rich tradition of participatory politics found in base organizations, it promoted internal grass-roots participation as a founding organizational characteristic. Adopting a loose bureaucratic structure facilitated the emergence of opposition among allied groups that check power from within and keep open channels for agenda setting from below. The fast trajectory of the MAS from its founding to gaining national power, as it unfolded, helped to reproduce and consolidate early organizational patterns – it served, in short, as a mechanism of reproduction underpinning path dependence. This process, moreover, entailed two partly divergent developments of its relationship to its constituency. On the one hand, the expansion to urban areas and access to power brought about greater leadership autonomy from the party's core constituencies. On the other hand, the contribution of allied social movements to the overthrow of two prior unpopular governments, which propelled the party to national office, meant that allied social movements in Bolivia remained relevant political actors once their partisan allies captured the presidency. Early success through mobilization made both party leadership and rank and file movement leaders more likely to

---

[23] That was in fact the essence of corporatism, like the cases of Peronism in Argentina or the Institutional Revolutionary Party (PRI) in Mexico, where strong and densely organized social actors were linked to – but heavily controlled by – centralized, top-down parties (Collier and Collier 1979).

continue using those tactics, and movement leaders used them even against the party leadership. These movements would then gain policy influence and place real constraints on the authority and decision-making power of the party's central leadership via their autonomous mobilization capacity. The story, then, is that the MAS does not operate under a purely bottom-up logic, but rather as a hybrid model that combines both top-down leadership and the bottom-up power of autonomous social mobilization by popular constituencies.

The ability of the rank and file in major popular movements to hold the movement leadership accountable and sustain autonomous mobilization capacity is what, in turn, helps to keep the MAS accountable to its social bases. This issue – that the movements themselves are internally vibrant and that the party leadership could not easily co-opt movement leaders – is not only key for resisting the trend toward top-down control but, in my framework, is also another critical mechanism of organizational self-reproduction that undergirds path dependency. In other words, the constant cause of strong, autonomous civil society mobilization is crucial to reproduce the founding organizational characteristics over time.

It is here where the case of the MAS differs from other cases examined in this book (Chapter 5), such as the Brazilian PT, where social mobilization withered, and with cases like Venezuela under Hugo Chávez (1999–2013) and Nicolás Maduro (2013–present), where mobilization is strong but largely controlled from above. It is also the constant cause of *autonomous* civil society mobilization that distinguishes the MAS from earlier experiences with corporatism in Latin America, where strong and densely organized social actors were linked to – but generally controlled by – centralized, top-down parties like Peronism in Argentina or the Institutional Revolutionary Party (PRI) in Mexico (Collier and Collier 1979).

The argument that strong and autonomous civil society organizations matter for shaping internal power distributions, leadership patterns, and party organizational models is developed on the basis of evidence from candidate selection for both national and local office within the MAS. My analysis demonstrates that in contexts where civil society organizations are strongly organized, autonomous, and united in support of the party, civil society organizations can play an important role in resisting the trend toward internal power concentration; where civil society organizations are weak, top-down elite choices are more likely to prevail. Strong civil society organizations can also be aligned with an opposition party, however, or they can be aligned with multiple parties. In both of these cases, elite choices are likely to triumph.

Strong civil society organizations also act autonomously and shape the degree of power concentration in the national policy-making process. First, civil society organizations may have the ability to set agenda items, priorities, and party action and to use pressure to ensure the responsiveness of an allied party. However, the capacity of allied groups to wield power in policy-making varies by policy area and is contingent on the relative power and autonomous mobilization capacity of groups pushing for reform. My analysis demonstrates that the greater the organizational strength and autonomous mobilization capacity of allied groups, the greater the degree to which their participation in decision-making will translate into influence on desired policy outcomes.

Second, allied groups and movements may have constraining power or an ability to block or modify legislative proposals pushed forcefully by the party's central leadership. It is in this area that top-down decision-making is most constrained in the case of the Bolivian MAS. Allied groups can place limits on the authority of the party's top leadership and keep the party internally responsive to particular societal demands, thereby wielding control over party decision-making. Success in blocking or modifying proposals is contingent on the breadth of the veto coalition that mobilized groups manage to configure, and on their autonomous capacity to mobilize. In general, if a mobilized allied actor opposed to a policy decision builds a broad-based coalition with multiple sectors of society, and if the rest of the party's core constituency is not fully aligned with the leadership in power, then the veto coalition is more likely to succeed in forcing policy change.

A comparison of the origins, organizational development, and power structures of the MAS with that of the Brazilian PT and the Uruguayan FA provides further support for the argument about the impact of historical and constant factors. All three parties emerged out of social movements and made it to power at the national level. Like the MAS, the PT and the FA were also reelected to several consecutive presidential terms, although Dilma Rousseff (2011–16) was impeached and forced out of power in Brazil in 2016.

Although all three parties are based on movements, they do not share the same "starting point" in their founding organizational characteristics. In the conventional wisdom, however, it does not matter whether they start out different; the key assumption is that they will all end up the same. Yet, despite this expectation, the MAS, the PT, and the FA also followed dissimilar paths of development. While the PT experienced a clear Michelsian shift in its character, with a trend toward organizational centralization, greater leadership autonomy, and a widening political gap between the leadership and the social bases, the MAS and the FA remained comparatively more open and internally responsive to their bases, although in different ways. Comparative evidence allows for tracing the roots of this variation. In reflecting on the similarities and differences between the three cases, the key explanatory factors helping to prevent or consolidate the trend toward top-down are to be found in historical and constant conditions, processes, and mechanisms. Historical causes – organizational elements and practices traceable to parties' genesis, and in particular the type of initial institutional structures – create an inclination to develop a more or less bottom-up pattern of organization from early on. However, it is the constant cause of strong and autonomous civil society mobilization that plays a crucial role undergirding path dependency. Its presence or absence helps to reproduce early organizational patterns over time.

THEORETICAL AND EMPIRICAL CONTRIBUTIONS

Civil Society and Party-Building

A key theoretical contribution of this book is to demonstrate that civil society, when it is strongly organized and retains autonomous mobilization capacity, has important effects on the internal politics and leadership patterns of movement-based parties – a point that bridges the scholarly literatures on political parties and social movements. The analysis stresses, first, that these parties are not the creation of strategic legislators devoid of social bases (à la Aldrich 1995), but are rather the direct creation of densely organized social constituencies. Second, it stresses that movement-based parties are neither unitary nor homogenous actors under the tutelage of a unified leadership.[24] The analysis stresses, third, that they are not uniformly bureaucratic organizations. The internal operation and organizational form are dictated neither by the political institutional contexts in which they operate nor simply by their ideological orientation.[25]

Rather, movement-based parties are best described as highly flexible organizations; the boundaries between such parties and civil society allies tend to be fluid to the point that they may in fact be virtually inseparable.[26] Some of them, such as the Bolivian MAS, lack an elaborate bureaucratic structure, and they look and operate differently in different environments based on the structural composition of civil society and on the kinds of connections they establish with social movements and other organized social actors. They also invest differently in formal party structures across social constituencies, and as a result they experience strikingly diverse development trajectories in differing contexts. By focusing on the impact of civil society on internal power distributions in the party, and how civil society interacts with other variables (electoral systems, party alignments, etc.), this book contributes robust evidence and offers an explanation for this diversity. Social movements not only spawn parties, but, in this book, they are a critical source of variation in parties' organizational models.

Understanding this variation is of great theoretical importance. Other scholars have made similar arguments, recognizing that parties (movement-based and otherwise) are decentralized systems of actors and organizations that

---

[24] Inspired by the work of Downs (1957), much of interparty competition theory makes this simplifying assumption (Robertson 1976). The major tenets of this approach to parties are epitomized by Aldrich's (1995) argument that election-minded legislators create parties to solve collective action and social choice problems.

[25] Internal party structures are often viewed as reflections of formal institutional rules governing a polity (Harmel and Janda 1982; Carty 2004) or as reflections of party ideology (Bolleyer 2012).

[26] The boundaries between them are even more diffuse when movement-based parties are in power. It becomes increasingly harder do discern where the movement, the party, and the state start and where they end.

relate differently to different constituencies in multiple settings.[27] However, existing studies focus disproportionally on the linkages between parties and individuals or voters (Kitschelt 2000; Kitschelt et al. 2010; Luna 2010a, 2014), whereas the present book, by contrast, looks at how parties develop different linkages to their movement base and other organized social constituencies. Specifically, it identifies conditions of societal and political structures where hypotheses formulated about power centralization (as developed by a rich tradition in the literature initiated by Michels) do not fully apply, allowing for greater participation of organized civil society in party decision-making. Internal processes, like the selection of candidates for elective office, provide good examples of how parties operate differently depending on how the political space is structured across a country's territory. As this book demonstrates, examining how organizational dynamics vary according to structural conditions provides the most analytical leverage on complex decision-making mechanisms that reflect varying degrees of grass-roots participation and patterns of internal power distribution. It is only when we examine these differences with some degree of systematization that the full organizational complexity of movement-based parties becomes visible.

Other authors have made the argument that parties are not uniformly bureaucratic. Levitsky (2003), for instance, focused on organizational characteristics, such as informal and weakly institutionalized party structures, to explain coalitional and programmatic adaptation of labor-based parties in Latin America. In the case of Peronism, Levitsky's core case, informal party organization allowed the party leadership to act autonomously, with few bureaucratic constraints. As this book demonstrates, the obverse is true in the case of the MAS, where similar organizational attributes generally provide incentives and opportunities for the social bases to act autonomously, with little to none bureaucratic constraints.

Weak bureaucratization also helps to explain *within*-case variation in the degrees of grass-roots participation. The lack of an elaborate bureaucratic structure facilitates adaptation to varying political spaces and thus encourages truly eclectic party-building dynamics. For example, movement-based parties with weak bureaucratization are more likely to look and operate "like movements" in high-density organizational settings. In such contexts, they are less likely to invest resources in building a formal organizational party structure (that is, one with a paid staff of professionals and a physical infrastructure of communications) to mobilize the already organized, and they are less likely to

---

[27] Examining the dynamics of the Justicialist Party (PJ) in Argentina and the PRI in Mexico, Gibson (1997) notes that populist parties in Latin America tend to have different rural and urban social constituencies and adopt different organizational logics in each environment. In Chile and Uruguay, Luna (2014) notes that the same parties relate differently to their constituencies in some municipalities, and that campaigns at the national level are in some cases more programmatic whereas at the local level they can be more clientelistic.

invest in the development of formal channels to solve collective action problems; instead, they are more likely to embed their structures on preexisting networks and emphasize some form of grass-roots democratic, participatory coordination among allied groups. By contrast, in areas of low organizational density, they are more likely to invest in developing a formal party structure and to operate in a more centralized manner – a pattern that generally grants more power and autonomy to the leadership and allows less influence from below. Weak bureaucratization, in short, can work in two different ways for movement-based parties: it can promote the development of accountability structures and thus contribute to pushing internal structures in the direction of power dispersion, but it can also push the other way. As Chapter 3 shows, these diverging patterns are likely to vary according to how the political space is structured.

Studying the operations of movement-based parties in differing structural contexts is therefore a crucial lens for gaining insight into broader patterns of organizational development. While the "density" of civil society has been used in recent scholarship to explain variation in the emergence and organizational expansion of movement-based parties in Latin America (Levitsky et al. 2016), this book places greater emphasis on how it shapes internal party organizational and leadership patterns. On the basis of an examination of the MAS, and drawing also on cross-case comparative evidence from the PT and the FA, I highlight how variation in civil society characteristics and the nature of their political alignments affects the overall distribution of power inside parties.

Civil Society and Its Relation to Democracy

The findings that robust civil societies can contribute to keeping an allied movement-based party open and internally responsive are important for theoretical reasons, but they require further elaboration here. Conventional wisdom says a dense civil society is good for democracy because it generates social capital and trust, both of which are seen as necessary to make democracy work (Putnam, Leonardi, and Nonetti 1993). More critical views see well-organized civil societies as either threats to democratic stability, or as potential foundations for authoritarian mass-based movements (Huntington 1968; Berman 1997; Riley 2010). Instead of taking sides with one of these "either or" positions in the existing literature, the central argument of this book is more in agreement with the "configuration of civil society" argument advanced by Stepan (1985), Collier and Collier (1991), and Rueschemeyer, Stephens, and Stephens (1992). A well-developed, autonomous civil society, especially one filled with associations organized around social and political inclusion of the poor and the underrepresented, can facilitate the development of more open structures of an allied movement-based party because it creates favorable conditions for those social groups to coordinate interests, thereby increasing their chances to counterweigh the power of the party leadership. In this book, I explain not only the impact of divergent configurations of civil society on internal power distributions within the case of the MAS, but also across different cases of movement-based parties. I also provide an explanation of the conditions under which strong, well-developed civil societies can facilitate the inclusion of the socially and politically excluded through organizational mechanisms and expand their influence on agenda setting and policy-making more broadly, thereby generating conditions conducive for a shift from a "formal" to a more "participatory" or "deeper" democracy (Huber, Rueschemeyer, and Stephens 1997; Roberts 1998).

A contrast between Bolivia under Morales and Venezuela under Chávez (from 1998 until 2013) and Maduro (from 2013 until the present) is illustrative. As this book and the work of others show, Morales has gradually marginalized some existing movements and has attempted to co-opt and gain control over "umbrella" and base organizations either as part of a strategy for electoral growth, as a governing tactic, or even as an attempt to build hegemony (Zuazo 2010; Anria 2013; Weyland 2013). Yet, despite these attempts, strong civil society groups that predated the emergence of the MAS have maintained significant degrees of autonomy from the state after the MAS captured national power, exerting influence on national policy-making and serving at times as a counterweight to state power. This has not meant refusing support and political alignment with the MAS, but rather engaging with the state in collaborative terms in some matters of common purpose (such as assisting in the passing of contested policies and reforms) while at the same time mobilizing against it in other instances.

In Venezuela, by contrast, the state engaged actively in a more clearly top-down approach to organization building that is not apparent in the Bolivian case (Smilde and Hellinger 2011; De la Torre 2013; Silva 2017). While some of this state-led popular organizing was evident since Chávez's rise to power, it intensified after the attempted coup d'état in 2002. Multiple forms of popular organization sponsored by the Chávez government, some of which were designed to defend the socialist transformation of Venezuela, including the Bolivarian Circles and the Communal Councils, among others, added density and plurality to Venezuela's civil society (Hawkins and Hansen 2006). On the one hand, these popular organizations and other more recent efforts to strengthen the role of communes in order to build a "communal project" have enhanced the mobilizational capacity of the poorest and most marginalized segments of society and, in a context of gross inequalities, boosted their inclusion and participation in politics (Ellner 2011; McCarthy 2012). On the other hand, they became heavily dependent on funding and political control from the executive branch, a condition favorable to turning popular organizations into instruments of state power and subjects of intense clientelism – all of which can overwhelm their democratic potential.[28] It bears stressing that while in the Bolivian case co-optation attempts (as well as threats, intimidation, and repression to divide social movements and NGOs) have become common over time, similar levels of state-led organizing and top-down control over popular organizations, as in Venezuela, are not immediately apparent.[29]

The second caveat is that evidence of bottom-up influence by disadvantaged groups in collective decision-making is not, by itself, indicative of greater regime democracy; such input is a necessary but not sufficient condition to have "full" democracy in Dahlian terms, an ideal model in which there is no gap between collective decisions and the preferences of all citizens (Dahl 1971). Changes in the overall distribution of power are also crucial to approximate that model. Due to the central role played by the MAS in the Bolivian political system, and due to its strong ties to organized social forces, the analysis of the MAS offers important insights into the connection between civil society and regime type. Some scholars have argued that once Morales was reelected for a second term in 2009 – when the MAS also gained absolute majorities in both houses of Congress – Bolivia became a "competitive authoritarian" regime (Levitsky and Loxton 2013; Weyland 2013; Sánchez-Sibony 2013). That line of inquiry highlights significant illiberal features and democratic deficiencies that are present in Morales' Bolivia (which in fairness, it should be noted, were also present between Bolivia's transition to democracy in the 1980s and the rise to power of the MAS): Power is too concentrated in an executive administration that too often treats opponents and the press with raw hostility. Institutions are inefficient, liberal rights are poorly safeguarded, and courts are feeble and politicized. The growing personalization of power is real, particularly since 2014, when the MAS declared Morales indispensable and decided to avoid cultivating a new leader for the party. A large group of academics, journalists, opposition politicians, and citizens more generally share similar concerns (multiple interviews; also see LAPOP 2012).

Such concerns are legitimate, but classifying Bolivia as "competitive authoritarian" offers only a partial lens for interpreting contemporary politics in the country, particularly when placed in the long arc of Bolivian history. While I do not minimize the weakening of institutional checks and balances on presidential authority in Bolivia and Morales' authoritarian temptations, I offer a different regime characterization – one that is informed by both the relative class power model of democratization (Rueschemeyer, Stephens, and Stephens 1992),

---

[28] State funding should not be automatically seen as conducive to reduced autonomy; it should be seen as a condition that makes depreciated autonomy more likely. For a survey of independent organizations – such as opposition unions and independent communal councils, among others – and a critical discussion on their complex relationships with the state in "Bolivarian" Venezuela, see Ciccariello-Maher (2013).

[29] A similar assessment can be found in Silva (2017).

which highlights the organizational power of subordinate classes for the promotion of democracy, and Dahl's (1971) classic two-dimensional conceptualization of polyarchy, consisting of participation (inclusion) and institutionalized contestation (horizontal checks and balances). I argue that the experience of the MAS in power has resulted in important shifts in domestic power relations at the state and social levels that have empowered large rural and urban segments of the population that were historically in the margins of social and political life. Those shifts have led to the development of more inclusive modes of political and economic decision-making and greater regime responsiveness to the interests of groups that were previously marginalized.

The greater inclusiveness of Bolivian politics is real, as this book demonstrates, even if checks and balances on presidential authority have weakened. Inclusion created a "new normal" in the Bolivian political arena. Larger numbers of Bolivians do enjoy rights of citizenship and greater input into political decision-making and into determining who gets what, when, and how. Indigenous people and other subordinate groups do enjoy increased access to the state. They are better able to shape decision-making around issues, claims, and objectives of their concern either via "inside" channels (by infiltrating representative institutions and state bureaucracies) or via "outside" channels (by autonomous forms of social mobilization).

People from groups that were long subordinated are included, therefore, not only as voters but also as makers of policy in between election cycles. In this sense, by stressing the continuous impact of social movements on the internal politics of the MAS, and those shifts in domestic power relations, I provide a contribution to a scholarly debate that is too often partial or superficial. I demonstrate, in short, that while the institutional checks and balances have indeed deteriorated sharply, Bolivia has also moved aggressively in a more democratic direction on the participation axis – with social mobilization, inclusion, and accountability remaining robust.

Structure of Left Parties and Broader Processes

Studying the MAS in comparative perspective can also contribute to refining the scholarly understanding of the Latin American Left and the impact of party organizational attributes on bigger-picture outcomes. The rise to power of leftist parties and leaders led to several analyses of their origins, their performance in office, and the sources of their policy orientations once in office. Thus, there is a copious literature on the topic of the Latin American Left. Building on different political and normative concerns, the existing literature tends to group together Bolivia, Venezuela, and Ecuador in the "radical" or "contestatory" strand of the left (Castañeda 2006; Weyland et al. 2010). In a classification of left parties that takes into consideration organizational factors, Levitsky and Roberts (2011: 13) classify the MAS as an example of the "movement left," for it is a new political organization (rather than an established or "institutionalized" party) whose internal structures disperse power among many grass-roots actors and is therefore more likely to be held accountable by those grass-roots actors. Despite this welcome correction and the abundance of works in this general area of inquiry, the literature on the Latin American left remains insufficiently attentive to the critical sources of variation in parties' organizational models, as evidenced by the scarcity of careful examinations of individual and comparative cases.[30]

In a way, this book brings "society back in" to the center of the analysis.[31] By studying the MAS as a case of a movement-based party that has found ways to at least partially counteract Michelsian oligarchic tendencies, an outcome largely attributable to the party's social movement origins and the ongoing strength of autonomous social mobilization, this book generates new ideas about the conditions under which these parties can become effective organizational actors for the empowerment of popular groups and how they can deal with the "tension between governing and maintaining grass-roots linkages" (Levitsky and Roberts 2011: 421). Several new left parties in the region have become personalistic tools for the self-regarding goals of a charismatic leader, as with the MVR in Venezuela and Correa's Alianza País in Ecuador. Although it might be argued that Morales shares similar impulses to Chávez (and Maduro) and Correa, this book shows that he operates under a remarkably different organizational foundation that continues to influence and constrain his power from below in ways that are not evident in Ecuador and Venezuela. Neither Ecuador nor Venezuela had the kind of sustained, autonomous social mobilization from below that the MAS has had in Bolivia, and that differentiates Bolivia from the leftist experiences in those other cases.

When organizational factors and the nature of party–society linkages are examined, this book argues, the MAS is not only radically different from the two other cases with which it is usually grouped together (Venezuela and Ecuador) but also quite similar to other cases with which the party is rarely compared. For example, in my account, the Uruguayan FA, which is often classified as belonging to the "moderate" camp of the Latin American Left, is a good case to compare with the MAS. The FA's origins in bottom-up social mobilization are similar to those of the MAS, and it too developed from early on as an organization whose internal structures diffuse power and encourage grass-roots input and mobilized participation in ways that greatly constrain the party leadership in power. In turn, the Brazilian PT, which is also a clear case of a movement-based party, can be seen as a contrasting example – one that evolved increasingly in the direction of greater centralization and leadership autonomy with relation to the party's social base. This book develops a framework to explain the roots of these diverging trajectories and shed light

---

[30] For a notable exception, see Pribble (2013). For a reflection on the limits of existing typological efforts in the literature on the Latin American left, see Bruhn (2015).

[31] I am grateful to Ken Roberts for this point.

on the factors that make the MAS both similar and different from other leftist parties. It highlights that social movements are a critical source of variation in parties' power distributions and organizational models.

In addition to explaining that variation, my framework gives us some theoretical purchase in explaining broader macro-level processes. In the Bolivian case, for example, building and maintaining vibrant grass-roots linkages has been crucial for the successful incorporation into politics of traditionally excluded and marginalized social actors, particularly indigenous and peasant groups linked to the formal and informal labor sectors, which in turn "boosted [their] political participation and satisfaction with democracy" (Weyland, Madrid, and Hunter 2010: 142). By contrast, leftist parties classified as "moderate" or "institutionalized" have had greater difficulties in sustaining those linkages. Some of them, such as those in Brazil and Chile, experienced declining citizen participation in politics and an increasing disconnect between political elites and civil society, resulting in a legitimacy crisis in the former and a crisis of representation in the latter (Luna 2016; Hagopian 2016).

As this book demonstrates, looking closely at the factors shaping party–society linkages can therefore help us gain a better understanding of diverging patterns of representation and political incorporation in contemporary democracies, which involve new social actors and occur through more fluid structures than in the earlier periods of incorporation that Collier and Collier (1991) described for Latin America in the late 1930s and 1940s.[32] Differences in the strength of party–society linkages also have effects on the extent to which governments can move toward more universalistic coverage in social policy, as others scholars have firmly established (Pribble and Huber 2011; Huber and Stephens 2012; Pribble 2013), which is fundamental for advancing an agenda of social incorporation. Therefore, analyzing the nature of those linkages and the resulting power distributions within governing parties, as this book does in great detail, helps to highlight similarities between left parties commonly classified in different typological boxes, which in turn can be linked to more nuanced accounts of outcomes.

A Comprehensive Account of the MAS

Finally, this book develops the first English-language, comprehensive and theoretically informed, explanation of the Bolivian MAS at the national level

---

[32] For the burgeoning literature on the politics of "new incorporation" in contemporary Latin America see, among others, Levitsky and Roberts (2011), Roberts (2015a), Rossi (2015), and Silva (2017). These works tend to conceive of Latin America's "second incorporation crisis" (a parallel to the first one that enfranchised subordinate groups during the import-substitution industrialization model) as reflecting the reactive politics of popular sectors to neoliberal restructuring. Other scholarship has linked the politics of incorporation to participatory innovations and the "deepening" of democracy (Goldfrank 2011b; Cameron, Hershberg, and Sharpe 2012).

with insights into its operation in several rural and urban segments.[33] It first traces its origins as a grass-roots social movement and its electoral growth to then examine the challenges of transitioning from regime challenger into an organization that gained control of the state. My analysis does not discount the influential role of the party's charismatic (and still undisputed) leader, Evo Morales, but it rather places greater emphasis on the internal organizational level of the MAS as a movement-based party: it explains the complex and often contentious power relations between constitutive social actors with different, yet overlapping, logics of political mobilization (i.e., social movements, the MAS as a party), as well as explaining the structural constraints on the political choices of the leadership in office.

The MAS has been the subject of significant attention in the political science literature over the past decade. Most of this literature concentrates on documenting its bottom-up genesis in Bolivia's rural syndicalism and the *cocalero* movement (Stefanoni 2003; Yashar 2005), its transformation into an electoral vehicle (Van Cott 2005; Komadina and Geffroy 2007; Zuazo 2008), and its rise to power (Albro 2005a; Stefanoni and Do Alto 2006; Silva 2009; Harten 2011; Madrid 2012). The literature also features studies evaluating the experience of the MAS and Evo Morales in power (Postero 2010; Zuazo 2010; Pearce 2011; Webber 2011; Zegada et al. 2011; Crabtree 2013; Dunkerley 2013; Wolff 2013; Farthing and Kohl 2014), and detailed biographies of Evo Morales documenting his humble origins, his trajectory as a social movement leader, and his road to becoming Bolivia's – and also Latin America's – first "indigenous" president (Subercaseaux and Sierra 2007; Sivak 2010). With a few exceptions,[34] not much attention has been given to how the MAS is structured internally and how it functions as a governing party by providing theoretically informed analyses of its internal organization and detailed accounts of how it operates in key decision-making areas. Also missing from the existing literature is an explicit comparison between the MAS and other cases, and in fact there is a tendency to study the case in relative isolation – a point also raised by Centellas (2015: 240). This book redresses these shortcomings in the existing scholarly literature and in so doing provides crucial qualitative data on the state–society relations that exist in Bolivia's current democratic period, while also placing the empirical findings in a broader comparative perspective.

---

[33] Unlike the Brazilian PT, which has been the subject of excellent comprehensive analyses of its formation, organization, and evolution as a national party (Meneguello 1989; Keck 1992; Ribeiro 2008; Amaral 2010; Hunter 2010), to date, and to my knowledge, there are no parallel "foundational" or landmark works on the MAS.

[34] My earlier works (Anria 2009, 2010, 2013), as well as empirical research by Do Alto and Stefanoni (2010), Zuazo (2008, 2010), and Crabtree (2013), are partial exceptions that have incorporated party organization and development as variables that explain party behavior. Harten (2011) examines internal organizational issues but does not follow the transformations of the MAS in the face of the challenges of transitioning from regime challenger to governing entity. His focus is rather on the period leading to the ascent to power.

It is important to emphasize here that researchers investigating other mass-mobilizing parties in Latin America, like the PT, have an easier time accessing empirical data on internal organization and processes than researchers investigating new parties such as the MAS.[35] Like the landmark texts on the PT (Meneguello 1989; Keck 1992; Hunter 2010), or on other parties like the Mexican Party of the Democratic Revolution (PRD) (Bruhn 1997) and the Argentine Justicialist Party (PJ) (Levitsky 2003), this text is an important step to generate robust evidence that can be used to advance cumulative knowledge on a poorly understood case that stands for its novelty in both Bolivian politics and the broader Latin American region. Future works on the MAS will benefit from the materials presented in this book and from improvements in the collection and analysis of new empirical data.

[35] On this point, see Amaral and Power (2015: 164).

I

Theoretical Framework and Methods

The question of whether, to what extent, and under which conditions tenden-cies toward power concentration can be mitigated has been key in political sociology analyses of parties. Building on Michels's "iron law" of oligarchy, a large body of literature holds that the logics of organization, competition, and the exercise of power will inevitably lead to hierarchy, elite entrenchment, and to the decreasing power of the grass-roots activists in internal party affairs. These studies, of which Duverger (1954), Kirchheimer (1966), and Panebianco (1988) are among the best-known early proponents, conceive of parties as dynamic, evolving units. This type of literature assumes that while parties might emerge from the bottom-up as political expressions of grass-roots movements and develop strong linkages with civic associations, age, maturation, and the pressures of the electoral marketplace will cause parties to become gradually detached from their social bases. This is why in general many movement activists are wary of political parties and why they often are opposed to creating a party or participating in electoral contestation.

Several factors are said to detach parties from their bases and push internal structures in the direction of power concentration. Some authors emphasize changing preferences and assume that the preference structures of the party leadership change over time, as elites' enthusiasm for listening to the bases tends to gradually go away (Michels 1962 [1911]; Panebianco 1988). In those accounts, the leadership will sooner or later abandon the interests of the party's social movement bases in favor of privileging the logics of electoral competition and political power, meaning that the leadership will sideline the grass-roots from internal decision-making processes. Other authors link detachment to the imperatives of electoral contestation. In other words, when parties become increasingly preoccupied with participating in mainstream electoral competi-tion and adopt "catch all" strategies of recruitment, they need to distance themselves from their original constituencies, and this gap between party elites and rank and file members pushes their structures in the direction of power concentration (Kirchheimer 1966: 193). Yet other authors emphasize a changing societal environment and organizational imperatives. According to Panebianco (1988: 264–7), for instance, parties might start their lives as mass organizations, but in response to electoral imperatives in an era of capital-intensive campaigns they will sooner or later move toward becoming "electoral-professional" organizations led by a specialized, professionalized caste of political elites who are highly detached from and unaccountable to their social bases.

More recent research on parties in advanced industrialized countries has generated important explanations for the ways in which power within parties tends to become increasingly concentrated when parties win elections and hold public office (Katz and Mair 1995: 13). These studies advance a Michelsian-Weberian argument claiming that as parties become closer to the state, they tend to become separated from citizens and social groups. Western European parties, Katz and Mair argue (2009: 753), "increasingly function like cartels, employing the resources of the state to limit political competition and ensure their own electoral success." For these authors, the key factors leading to this outcome are a series of social and political transformations. The growing importance of the mass media, for instance (and the rising costs of political campaigns), push party leaders to rely less on their rank and file members and more on public financial subsidies (Katz and Mair 2009: 754). By depending on state-based funding rather than on membership contributions, advocates of the cartel party thesis argue that such developments have brought about party professionalization, bureaucratization, and hierarchy. As Cedric de Leon (2013: 161) argues, this line of argumentation represents "yet another kind of Michelsian party oligarchy for the twenty-first century." An observable implication of the cartel party thesis is a trend toward top-down control, which is, in turn, closely linked to a growing political gap between party elites and the party's social bases. While using different parlance, scholars of social movements have reached similar conclusions. Schwartz (2006) argues that parties based on movements tend to lose their movement features as minorities within their structures gain control over party affairs and become too preoccupied with the logics of political power and electoral competition.

The cartel party thesis has been sharply criticized,[1] particularly because the experience of Green parties in government has shown that some of these parties have avoided extensive hierarchical development and have maintained vibrant connections with their grass-roots bases.[2] Additionally, some have argued that the concept of cartelization does not translate well into non-European contexts, where party organizations are generally weaker and less

---

[1] For critiques on the cartel party thesis, see Koole (1996) and Kitschelt (2000).
[2] See Frankland, Lucardie, and Rihoux (2008) for an assessment with mixed conclusions.

institutionalized. Whether the cartel party thesis, as formulated by Katz and Mair (1995, 2009), is empirically accurate or not is indeed a stimulating question, but with or without cartel parties, the trend toward internal power concentration and leadership entrenchment in political parties is pervasive in the real world of politics.

Although, as seen above, there is disagreement about the causal mechanisms that induce movement-based parties to become increasingly top-down over time, a general consensus exists in scholarship about the overarching evolutionary trajectory of movement-based parties. Latin American parties are no exception to this trend. For some authors, this Michelsian challenge is so central that it provides a core explanation of a general pattern of fragile and volatile political representation that characterizes the region (Roberts 2012; Luna 2016). It affects parties of all kinds, and it is pervasive. Indeed, many scholars have shown that Latin American parties, including movement-based parties, have followed the general trend toward internal power concentration and become increasingly separated from citizens and social groups. In general, this literature takes the form of in-depth case studies of major parties, and it is focused on explaining their internal dynamics in response to changing environmental conditions. Existing studies tend to focus on specific dimensions of internal party organization, such as adaptive capacity (Roberts 1998; Levitsky 2003), institutionalization (McGuire 1997), issues related to emergence and consolidation (Bruhn 1997), and factionalism (Coppedge 1994). While these studies do not focus on explaining patterns of internal power distributions and why they vary within and across cases, they provide powerful evidence in support of a trend toward top-down control within parties and a widening political gap between party elites and their social bases.[3]

Hunter (2010) is an excellent example of one such study; her work focuses on how the Brazilian PT, another classic instance of a movement-based party that reached national power (examined in detail in Chapter 5), lost a great deal of its initial bottom-up participatory thrust. As Hunter convincingly demonstrates, participation in electoral arenas caused the party to adopt a partisan logic that crowded out or tended to suppress the movement logic of autonomous social mobilization that shaped its founding characteristics; the imperatives of electoral contestation helped to consolidate an organizational oligarchy. This behavior, as other studies demonstrate, enabled a widening gap between the PT and its organized social bases.[4]

This course of organizational development is widely recognized. And indeed, there is an overwhelming teleological expectation in the literature that even where parties begin as distinctively bottom-up organizations formed by

---

[3] More recent comparative works point in a similar direction. See, for instance, Nogueira-Budny's (2013) study of left party adaptation in Latin America.

[4] Hochstetler (2008) reaches a similar conclusion in her study of the relationships between Lula's first government (2003–6) and organized civil society in Brazil.

movements, they will evolve until they are dominated by a caste of political elites who are highly detached from and unaccountable to their social bases. The assumption is that this course of organizational development is preordained or inevitable, even in cases where we would least expect it. Such a trend begins before parties come to power and intensifies when they switch from opposition to government.

Though the above works make important contributions to the study of parties based upon movements, and although in many ways they serve as models for analyzing internal party politics, they do not engage systematically and comparatively with the questions of internal power distributions.[5] This is an important gap that the present book seeks to redress. Given that social movements are quintessential bottom-up organizations, why do some parties spawned by movements become top-down organizations, structured to enhance the power of the leadership and increasingly distanced from their social bases, whereas others stay more open to bottom-up input influence and internally responsive? What are the contexts or conditions under which this trend does not hold, and what mechanisms help impede it? As the present book demonstrates, not only do movement-based parties vary considerably in terms of how they are internally organized and how authority and power are allocated within them, but also they do not evolve uniformly by following a distinctive path toward top-down control. There are mechanisms to counteract this course of organizational development. Movement-based parties are not developmentally unidirectional but their internal power distributions are path dependent and are conditioned by attributes defined in early stages of development and by conditions of societal structure. In the pages that follow, I explain the factors that account for this variation and the mechanisms that undergird path dependency.

STUDYING POWER DISTRIBUTIONS

A central question driving this book is the degree to which – and the conditions under which – grass-roots social movements can wield control over national party affairs and hold party elites accountable to their interests within movement-based parties. To measure degrees of internal power concentration and grass-roots control, I therefore study the balance of intraparty power in processes of candidate selection and in processes of national policy-making. These two dimensions attract perhaps the highest level of agreement as valid indicators of intraparty power distribution in the party literature, and they are arguably the two measures with the broadest scope for comparative analysis. Candidate selection is commonly regarded as *the* best measure for internal

---

[5] A partial exception is Gómez Bruera (2013: chapter 3). His focus, however, is on how the exercise of power has transformed the PT's agenda, not its internal structures.

power distribution (Gallagher and Marsh 1988; Bille 2001; Field and Siavelis 2008: 620; Hazan and Rahat 2010: 6–12).[6] It shapes who rises to leadership positions and who actually gets into public office. When a party elite gains control over the process (and outcome) of candidate selection, it is more likely to become a caste of political elites that is self-selecting and self-reproducing. In this book, then, power concentration in this realm is high when the party's central leadership, or even a single individual, controls the selection process and its outcome; and it is lower when grass-roots groups maintain some capacity to control candidate selection.[7] Their capacity to wield control is essential to internal party democracy and vertical accountability.

However, in contexts of high poverty and inequality, where issues like patronage and clientelism are generally widespread, candidate selection may not be, by itself, a robust enough proxy to measure internal grass-roots control. In such contexts, the party's social bases may wield control over candidate selection (and thus determine *who* gets into office), but they may be irrelevant in other party decisions, such as in the policy-making realm.[8] It is therefore crucial to integrate both dimensions and examine whether greater bottom-up control over the selection of candidates also translates into greater substantive input into, and control over, party policy (Katz and Mair 1995: 10–11; Loxbo 2013). Taken together these two dimensions in the life of a party can tell us a great deal about how power is allocated internally and the extent to which organized actors at the grass-roots are genuinely empowered in relation to party elites and power holders. In short, as the pages below demonstrate, this book integrates theoretically two questions that are at the core of politics and democratic rule: do the party's social bases determine who rises in leadership positions and gets into office? And if they do, do they influence "who gets what, when, and how" once in office? Do they constrain and hold the leadership accountable? Figure 1.1 codes the three movement-based parties examined in this book in terms of their degree of internal power concentration along these two dimensions (see Chapter 5 for the different placement of the PT in the two cells).

Why Candidate Selection Matters

The selection of party candidates is arguably the single most important activity that distinguishes political parties from other organizations (Schattschneider

---

[6] In an earlier contribution, Schattschneider (1942: 64) goes so far as to claim that "the nature of the nominating process determines the nature of the party; he who can make the nominations is the owner of the party. This is therefore one of the best points at which to observe the distribution of power within the party."

[7] Low degrees of power concentration imply the empowerment of the bases in relation to party elites.

[8] In other words, grass-roots control of selection processes can be seen as an empirical manifestation of civil society co-optation.

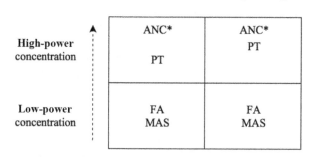

FIGURE I.I Power distributions within movement-based parties. *The African National Congress (ANC), which is not examined in this book at length, is an example of a movement-based party in power in South Africa and is also a distinctively negative case – one that moved clearly in the direction of power concentration and top-down control.

1942: 64; Field and Siavelis 2008: 620; Hazan and Rahat 2010: 6–12). It can be defined as the "process by which a political party decides which of the persons legally eligible to hold an elective public office will be designated on the ballot and in election communications as its recommended and supported candidate or list of candidates" (Field and Siavelis 2008: 621).[9]

The selection of candidates is of central interest because it sheds light on the dynamics of party power struggles among leaders themselves – and between them and aspiring leaders.[10] Understanding how individuals become candidates is central to the analysis of representation and internal power distributions (Gallagher and Marsh 1988; Katz 2001; Siavelis and Morgenstern 2008a; Hazan and Rahat 2010).

Although the significance of candidate selection has been underscored for decades, research on the topic has remained rather underdeveloped until recently, particularly when compared to the extensive literature on party and electoral systems. Recent research into this topic has noted that candidate selection methods have political consequences on various democratic dimensions, including representation, participation, competition, and responsiveness

---

[9] Long ago, French political scientist Maurice Duverger (1954) described candidate selection as "a private act which takes place within the party. Often it is even secret, as parties do not like the odours of the electoral kitchen to spread to the outside world" (Duverger 1954: 354). Selecting candidates is therefore a rather mysterious intraparty affair, and due to its hidden secrecies it is still often seen as a "secret garden" of politics (Gallagher and Marsh 1988).

[10] The importance of candidate selection has been acknowledged for over a hundred years. Authors such as Schattschneider (1942), Weber (1946), Duverger (1954), Michels (1962), Ostrogorski (1964), and Panebianco (1988) have noted that the processes of candidate selection are of especial interest in the study of parties because they considerably determine the distribution of power within parties.

(Hazan and Rahat 2010: 3, 89–164). Other studies have noted that candidate selection processes generally create loyalties to particular groups or individuals, which in turn impact the behavior of legislators once they are in office (Siavelis and Morgenstern 2008b: 32–4). Moreover, the importance of candidate selection rests on the idea that selection processes can shape patterns of sociopolitical incorporation by including historically excluded sectors into the political process (I return to this point in the Conclusions).

Party oligarchy has been generally associated with exclusive procedures for candidate selection and centralized decision-making, a model of organization whereby a unified party elite or single leaders have complete control over candidate selection. Conversely, internal party democracy has been loosely associated with more inclusive selection procedures that spread responsibilities and power among many political actors and that ensure leadership accountability (Bille 2001; Hazan and Rahat 2010). From this perspective, the contemporary literature has linked internal party democracy to the idea of power diffusion. If the idea is to limit power concentration in and top-down control by centralized authorities, demonstrating that candidate selection procedures effectively diffuse power among several political actors can serve to advance theory by showing ways of organization that can generate genuine empowerment of the grass-roots in relation to party elites.

The literature focusing on candidate selection within Latin American parties is rapidly growing (Siavelis and Morgenstern 2008a, 2008b). The existing case studies lend overwhelming support to a Michelsian notion of party politics, and Michels' theoretical argument about power concentration seems to apply to almost every case, independent of the specific party type. Examples include, but are not limited to, the Venezuelan Democratic Action (AD) Party in the 1990s (Coppedge 1994), the Argentine Justicialista (PJ) and Radical parties (McGuire 1997; Jones 2008), the Chilean Independent Democratic Union (UDI) Party (Navia 2008), the Mexican Institutional Revolutionary Party before 2000 (Langston 2008; Wuhs 2008), and the Mexican Party of the Democratic Revolution (PRD) (Bruhn 1997). In all of these cases, candidate selection is an activity dominated by a small party elite that wields overwhelming power. Even the Brazilian PT – the other classic example of a movement-based party in contemporary Latin America – appears to be following this pattern (Ribeiro 2014).

Why Policy-Making Matters

At the most basic level, the way in which parties set agenda items, priorities, and policy choices is of central interest because it provides useful insights into a central question of politics: *who* actually wields power? If we look at governing parties, moreover, understanding how decisions are made sheds light on where effective – or "real" – authority falls within the party and the larger system in which it is embedded. Policy-making is key to the study of participation and internal power distributions; it reveals crucial information about how power is organized and exercised.

The core Michelsian argument expects that parties formed by social movements will succumb to party bureaucratization and top-down control and will suppress the bottom-up logic of mobilization that generally characterizes social movements (Panebianco 1988: 164–8). Michels argues that even in the case of leftist parties formed by labor movements, which use the language of grass-roots participation, top-down decision-making will inevitably emerge as parties become detached from the movement and a caste of political elites dominates their internal operations. The resulting image of internal party politics is one of party leaders pursuing their own selfish interests, as opposed to their party's collective goals, and striving to limit the influence of the party's social bases on party strategy and policy choice.

This is due, in large part, to the imperatives of electoral competition and office or vote seeking, where the objectives of the party or its top leaders may diverge from those of the social movements at the grass-roots. Social movement activists are generally political minorities that tend to be more ideologically oriented than regular citizens. In the conventional models of party development – stretching from Michels (1962 [1911]) to Kirchheimer (1966), Przeworski and Sprague (1986), and Katz and Mair (1995), among others – party elites tend, over time, to pull away from their movement bases so that they can have greater strategic flexibility to appeal to the less ideological "median voter." In this account, then, the evolution of movement-based parties is associated with a process of ideological dilution or programmatic moderation – a dynamic that reinforces the detachment between leadership and bases. In this view also, the parties' social bases are seen as oddly passive actors with few claims of participation in party decisions, and thereby leaving decision-making to the party's leadership. In short, leadership entrenchment and grass-roots passivity reinforce each other and hinder bottom-up influence. If social allies find ways to influence, constrain, and hold the leadership accountable, however, then there should be observable policy consequences. Studying this is therefore crucial.

The implicit or explicit acceptance of the Michelsian argument is even more common in studies of governing parties. These predict the almost inevitable emergence of hierarchical elitist structures in which the interests of the party's social bases would be increasingly marginalized. While the emergence of hierarchy will start before a party ever achieves governmental power, as described above, hierarchy and power concentration will intensify when the party does come to power. This is in part due to decision-making efficiency; complex task structures associated with governing a country push governing parties to both be efficient in the administration of the state *and* to respond to political and economic pressures that come from sectors well beyond the party's social base (Deschouwer 2008: 10). Reaching decisions is complicated and inefficient in complex organizations (Burchell 2001; Bolleyer 2011). Therefore, hierarchy, specialization, and a caste of professionalized politicians who are detached from the social bases become necessary to generate decisions.[11]

Governing parties – whether they have a social movement base or not – tend to delegate authority to their leaders in the executive branch (Coppedge 1994: 64). The general expectation is that governing parties will generate support for any initiative designed by the executive. Yet, despite the tendency toward executive autonomy, there is still significant variation. In Argentina during the 1990s, President Carlos Menem could expect support for most of his initiatives, including reforms that were detrimental to his party's historic core constituencies (Levitsky and Way 1998). In Uruguay, however, the market reform process of the 1990s was slower than in Argentina, in part because the executive branch never enjoyed comparable levels of autonomy in relation to the governing parties (Pribble 2008, 2013; Bogliaccini 2012).

Movement-based parties are well equipped to resist pressures toward top-down control associated with concentrated executive authority. Such parties exist as electoral vehicles for other organizations, from which they receive external loyalty. As Panebianco notes, these parties tend to never fully institutionalize, and this is because the sponsoring and allied organizations almost always do not feel compelled to grant full autonomy to the electoral vehicle (Panebianco 1988: 62). At the same time, they are generally composed of diverse grass-roots movements and organized social actors, whose heterogeneity tends to increase as these parties expand their electoral base. The hybrid nature of movement-based parties may encourage democratic control from below by providing opportunities for sponsoring and allied movements to check political power from within and keep open channels for agenda setting from below. It is more likely that they will do so if those movements are strong and can act autonomously.

When it comes to the policy sphere, all movement-based parties encounter similar challenges when they assume national-level power: tensions emerge between the executive branch, the party's representatives in Congress, the party's top leadership, and the leaders and grass-roots members of sponsoring and allied organizations. These tensions often interact in unpredictable ways, and they have not been fully investigated by social scientists.[12] Most notably, however, governing movement-based parties share a problem of organizational

---

[11] At the same time, this logic almost always leads to a popular disenchantment with the ability of parties to reform state–society relations and generate more inclusive procedures of democratic decision-making. However, this is still an empirical matter. Governing parties can also transform existing structures through the adoption of new institutions of participation and decision-making and state–society linkages.

[12] When dealing with movement-based parties in power, sociologists tend to look at social movement activity, failing to link it to party activity (Fung and Wright 2003). Political scientists tend to look at their contributions to local government institutional innovation, failing to link these innovations to the issues that arise when these organizations gain national-level power (Van Cott 2008: 99).

legitimacy. As Kitschelt (1989a: 130) notes, "an organization enjoys legitimacy when its members accept its decisions as authoritative and final even if they personally disagree with them." Although his focus is on *individual* compliance and legitimacy (that is, at the level of individual members or activists), it is plausible to make a similar argument centered on the *organizational* level (that is, at the level of collective actors). Movement-based parties enjoy organizational legitimacy when their social bases, usually a diverse set of social movements and popular sector organizations, accept the supremacy of the party over the individual constituent part. Drawing on Hirschman (1970), this presupposes a sense of "loyalty" to the party, the acceptance of its decisions as authoritative and final even if they go against particular interests.

When in power, movement-based parties are particularly susceptible to suffering challenges to their legitimacy. This occurs because governing a country involves reconciling the interests of different groups affected by government policy. It also requires harmonizing (or trying to reconcile) the often-diverse interests of the party's social bases. These groups can under certain circumstances successfully challenge government decisions if they disagree with them or if their interests are seen as not properly taken into account. As a result, governments headed by movement-based parties are likely to find themselves at odds with their organized social bases, which can become an obstacle to the parties' programmatic agenda. This refers to what I term the "constraining capacities" of the party's social allies, or their veto and counter-mobilization power.

The existing literature would expect the suppression of such constraining capacities via the co-optation of sponsoring and allied movements or via other mechanisms of demobilization (Piven and Cloward 1979). Participation in elections may cause movements to demobilize; one of the first steps in demobilization is when social activists redirect the bulk of their activities to the partisan and electoral spheres (Przeworski and Sprague 1986; Hipsher 1996). Another crucial step in that direction is when their partisan allies reach power, which may make social allies less likely to protest (Heaney and Rojas 2015). Yet, social movements may also, under certain circumstances, mobilize and challenge their own partisan allies if some issues, claims, or objectives that they care about are threatened or not adequately taken into account by those in power. This mobilization is something that takes place at least partially outside the electoral arena and in a permanent or at least semi-permanent manner, in between elections. Social allies may challenge party decisions with various degrees of success, however, depending to a large extent on their power resources and their capacity to sustain autonomous collective action.[13] As an empirical matter then, we would expect that the stronger the organizational

---

[13] For example, movements rooted in production or economic activity are generally stronger than other movements, and therefore can keep movement-based parties more open and can constrain governments based on these parties more effectively.

power of the sponsoring and allied groups, and the greater the capacities of these groups to act autonomously and mobilize people into the streets, the more likely they can constrain the leadership and keep it responsive to the social bases.

Studying policy-making would be incomplete until we consider what I term the "creative capacities" or positive policy formulation power of the party's social bases. With this I refer to their ability to generate decisions by determining which issues and claims enter the public domain and by proposing solutions to them. When movement-based parties assume office, they almost always confront the issue of the role of sponsoring and allied movements and organizations in the policy process. Yet, because the bottom-up, social movement genesis of these parties generally precludes the construction of firm institutions and clear participatory channels (Panebianco 1988: 53), the influence of their social allies risks being limited and isolated. The new opportunity structures associated with the exercise of state power can expand influence of constituent organizations, but they can also hinder it.[14]

In summary, the classic Michelsian bureaucratic argument would lead one to expect an increasing marginalization of the party's social bases in the policy process. Moreover, this tendency is expected to intensify if movement-based parties, as governing entities, consolidate a dominant position in the political system, for it means that they may have fewer incentives to be responsive to their social bases (Magaloni 2006; Carbone 2008; Heller 2009). As an empirical matter, then, we would expect that the longer these parties stay in national power, the less likely it becomes for their social allies to project themselves into the state and exert continued influence on the policy-making process. In addition, however, we should expect movement influence to vary widely across policy spheres. Their influence should be greater in ministries whose policies affect large groups of well-organized constituencies linked to these movements than in ministries whose policies affect broader cross-sections of society.

HISTORICAL AND CONSTANT EXPLANATIONS

My explanation of the conditions under which movement-based parties can remain open, internally responsive, and accountable to their social bases in the two dimensions outlined above is based on a combination of "historical" and

---

[14] On the one hand, access to power can come at the expense of moderation (Meyer and Tarrow 1998: 21) and it can also lead to suppression of contentious action via the co-optation of sponsoring and allied groups (Foweraker and Landman 2000). On the other hand, though, moderation can also be "the price to pay for the emergence of agile political actors that can negotiate with incumbent regimes" (Foweraker 1995: 103). At the other extreme, when sponsoring and allied groups reject to moderate and to abandon militant forms of contentious action, they can be excluded from positions of influence in the government, and their ability to shape the agenda can be reduced (Meyer and Tarrow 1998: 21).

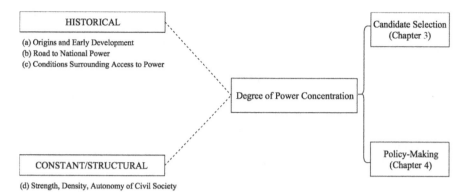

FIGURE 1.2 Summary of main argument.

"constant," or ongoing, causes.[15] On the one hand, historical causes refer to dynamics that occur in early stages of an institution, or in its genesis, and produce lasting legacies down the road (Stinchcombe 1968: 103). In my explanatory framework, they include: (a) organizational attributes embedded in the parties' origins and early development, (b) their experience before gaining national power, and (c) conditions surrounding their access to power. In Figure 1.2, (a) is a historical cause that creates a "weak" version of path dependency subject to positive feedback and self-reproducing mechanisms that are present in (b) and (c) (Mahoney 2000; Pierson 2000).[16] Initial institutional structures, and the ensuing power distributions they produce, are path dependent (Pierson 2015: 133); though not impossible, it is difficult to deviate from them over time.

On the other hand, constant causes refer to dynamics that operate more or less continually and help to reproduce a given outcome over time; they may change slightly in the short-run, but most often they stay fairly stable (Stinchcombe 1968: 101). In my explanatory framework, conditions of societal structure linked to the parties' power base (or the strength and density of civil society) constitute a constant cause (Collier and Collier 1991; Rueschemeyer, Stephens, and Stephens 1992). Those conditions interact closely with more cyclical attributes of civil society (the process of autonomous mobilization) to reproduce early organizational patterns over time. As discussed in the

---

[15] The distinction between historical and constant causes is taken from Stinchcombe (1968: 101–3). Historical causes, as conceptualized by Stinchcombe, undergird most conceptualizations of path-dependency (Mahoney 2000: 512; Pierson 2000: 263).

[16] "Weak" forms of path dependence are historical patterns in which each step in a particular path makes it more difficult to reverse course (Pierson 2000). In other words, each step down a path increases the *probability* of a given outcome to continually reoccur. "Hard" forms of path dependence see path dependence as sequences marked by contingency followed by a more *deterministic* pattern (Goldstone 1998).

Introduction, strong and densely organized societies can serve as a potential power base for political parties. In my framework, however, while the organizational strength and density of civil society may be important for keeping an allied party open and internally responsive, what is truly decisive is the ongoing capacity for *autonomous* social mobilization. This is because strong, well-organized civil societies can be thoroughly controlled from the top down, contributing little to enhancing internal democracy. Autonomy, in short, is crucial for my argument. When strong and densely organized social actors can sustain autonomous collective action, they can shape internal party governance by generating pressures from below in ways that constrain the power of the top leadership.

This combination of historical and constant causes sets movement-based parties into distinct trajectories and shapes their internal power distributions – the degree of power concentration or dispersion – and organizational models. Figure 1.2 provides a summary and illustration of the main arguments explaining the factors shaping the degree of internal power concentration.

Historical Explanations

Origins and Early Development
The core historical explanation is traceable to the party's origins and early development.[17] It relates to what Panebianco (1988: 50–3) calls the "genetic model" of a party, which refers to the Weberian-inspired intuition that the founding moments of institutions create enduring legacies. In developing my argument, I borrow the idea that parties' founding organizational characteristics matter greatly. However, instead of using Panebianco's term genetic model (or genetic "endowments"), I use the terms "origins" and "early organizational development," and use them specifically in regard to the set of internal institutional structures and patterns of behavior adopted at a party's early development.[18] These traits can be theorized as "starting points" in the parties' founding organizational characteristics. They create a "weak" form of path dependency – an inclination to develop a greater or lesser top-down pattern of organization down the road.

Specifically, I argue that the bureaucratic development of the party and the level of organizational centralization of power in the early development of a party matter greatly in the long run. These two features embedded in the

---

[17] The literature emphasizing the lasting consequences of a party's origins has a long lineage that can be traced back to the classic works of Duverger (1954), Lipset and Rokkan (1967), Weber (1968 [1922]), and Panebianco (1988).

[18] In Panebianco's work, a party's "genetic model" – its organizational "DNA" – is defined by three factors traceable to a party's founding moment: its initial territorial strategy, the presence (or absence) of an external sponsoring group, and the role of charisma in the formative phase.

parties' early years require further elaboration because they trigger particular patterns of organizational evolution down the road.

I conceptualize the bureaucratic development of the party as the degree of emphasis on constructing rules about membership and delegation of authority. According to Weber (1968 [1922]), the logic of bureaucratization breeds hierarchy, professionalization, and specialization. It works to ensure that the internal lives of parties end up run by the party leadership and a professionalized staff, with the party's social bases playing a marginal role in internal processes such as candidate nomination (Weber 1968 [1922]: 1129) and the drafting of party programs (Weber 1968 [1922]: 1396) – the two key dimensions under analysis here. Rules about membership and delegation of authority can generate power concentration, but it is also theoretically possible that, under certain conditions, such rules can contribute to prevent hierarchical control.[19]

In turn, I conceptualize the level of organizational centralization as the degree to which internal structures initially generate incentives for consultation with organized social bases, and the effects of internal voting rules on intraparty affairs (with majoritarian internal rules generally resulting in more power concentration than proportional rules). At one extreme, high levels of centralization are associated with limited input from the social bases in decision-making. At the other extreme, low levels of centralization involve more opportunities for grass-roots input.

Movement-based parties may share overarching similarities in their origins, including the sponsorship by social movements, but they may not necessarily have the same "starting point" in their founding organizational characteristics – their bureaucratic development and their level of centralization. Different starting points may leave enduring organizational legacies on parties, but, in my framework, those differences do not have deterministic properties.[20] And, in fact, it is worth emphasizing here that, as described above, in the conventional wisdom it does not matter whether starting points in their founding organizational characteristics vary; the central assumption in the conventional wisdom is that movement-based parties will develop in the same direction, given the pressures of the electoral marketplace.

However, that is not always the case. In explaining the sources of variation in internal power distributions and parties' organizational models, initial institutional structures have some explanatory power. They create a weak form of path dependency with self-reproducing dynamics. As actors within the party get used to working in those structures, the structures become more effective and

---

[19] Much of this is related to the type of electoral rules within parties, as will be seen in Chapter 5.

[20] Using Panebianco's (1988) biological language, these elements – the organizational sponsors and their commitments – can be thought of as elements that leave "birth marks" on a party rather than immutable "genetic" features.

they create vested interests – a set of "winners" and "losers" (Pierson 2015: 133).

This can be briefly illustrated with examples. In the case of the PT, for instance, its early development as a bureaucratic, centrally organized party with hierarchical leadership structures and majoritarian decision-making mechanisms allowed one faction to gain substantial advantages and consolidate power within the party. Control over those structures guaranteed control over the organization and few limits on the strategic decisions of the party's top leadership. This difference in "starting points" is important for understanding why the MAS and the FA differed so sharply from the PT from early on. Unlike the PT, the structures of both the MAS and the FA created more opportunities for contestation, consensus building, and negotiation, as well as more dispersed sets of winners and actors with decision-making – and "constraining" – powers. Once these early organizational patterns were set up, it became increasingly difficult to switch course.

As explained in the following pages, early organizational patterns can be reinforced, first, in response to electoral imperatives and by conditions surrounding the parties' access to power. They can be reproduced over time, second, by the "constant cause" associated with the strength and density of civil society, and its autonomous mobilization capacity.

Road to National Power

While institutional structures set up in the early stages of a party's organizational development may create a greater or lesser top-down impetus, the parties' road to power, as it unfolds, can help reinforce such trends. To put it in other words, electoral pressures and the circumstances that shape the path to power can serve as "self-reinforcement processes" of particular trends (Pierson 2015: 133). In general, due to the imperatives of electoral contestation and office/vote seeking, party elites tend to, over time, pull away from their movement bases so they can gain strategic flexibility in order to appeal to the "median voter," who is generally less ideologically motivated than social movement activists.[21] The movement thus can get progressively transformed into a machine, or worse yet, into a cartel of incumbents.

The time it takes for movement-based parties to transition from opposition into governing parties has some explanatory power. In general, the longer it takes for movement-based parties to take national office, the stronger the pressures toward moderation and top-down control. As movement-based parties win elections, institutionalize their structures, and exercise power at subnational levels, it becomes increasingly difficult to consult the movement bases and to sustain bottom-up participation. However, the pressures of

---

[21] To put it in other words, processes of change in party organization, ideology, and social constituencies are closely intertwined.

electoral contestation do not have uniform effects on internal power distributions, and nothing in that course of organizational development is preordained or inevitable. Organizational structures, as described in the section above, and characteristics linked to the parties' social bases, also play a role.

This can be best illustrated with examples. In response to electoral imperatives, all three parties examined in this book underwent a process of ideological dilution or programmatic moderation, from an advocacy of socialism to a more pragmatic position of reforming capitalism to protect the interests of the underprivileged. This move toward the center was a reflection of office-seeking strategies and a result of their experience in subnational governments. As the bulk of the literature would have expected (e.g., Kirchheimer 1966; Przeworski and Sprague 1986), in the process, all three parties increased their pragmatism and expanded the scope and nature of their alliances – a dynamic that contributed to pulling away party elites from the social bases and created strong incentives for top-down control.

While they all experienced this general trend, the trend varied sharply in intensity across the cases. Slow electoral progress in the case of the PT created strong incentives for the party leadership to make strategic adjustments, moderate its ideological platform, form broad alliances, and strengthen its internal hierarchical control. Although this was facilitated by the party's already centralized organizational structures, as described above, the party's slow electoral progress helped to reinforce those structures over time. The FA also experienced slow electoral progress, but institutional rules defined early on and the strength of its social pillars allowed the party to retain strong bottom-up characteristics even after several decades in opposition. Similar electoral pressures and time in opposition, in short, may produce common incentives to centralize but they may not invariably produce a Michelsian shift in the parties' character. Finally, the MAS's vertiginous growth, its comparatively shorter experience in subnational governments, and its rapid ascent to power meant that the leadership encountered weaker incentives to centralize authority, creating stronger incentives for autonomous bottom-up mobilization. This would, in turn, continue to reproduce founding organizational characteristics over time.

Conditions Surrounding Access to National Power

The mode of access to power, and especially the institutional position and availability of political resources once in office, can also help to reinforce existing organizational trends and internal power distributions. On the one hand, gaining power in a context of intense social mobilization, where democratic institutions are in deep crisis, as opposed to via routine turnover or in a context where democratic institutions are not in crisis, can create stronger incentives for mobilized participation and power dispersion within the party. This may not always be the case, however. The availability of institutional resources (the degree of control over representative and other core state institutions) is also important; it creates different incentives and political challenges for movement-based parties when they reach power. While having stronger control of core state institutions creates incentives in the direction of power dispersion and fosters stronger ties with the party's social bases, having a weaker institutional position pushes in the other direction – the latter pushes a party to generate legislative majorities by allying with forces that are often seen as "distasteful" by the social bases, widening the gap between the two. However, the effects of such institutional constraints are rarely uniform; they are highly contingent on previously adopted organizational patterns that condition parties' responses to such constraints.

Two contrasting examples may help to illustrate the point. The MAS captured office when social mobilization was in ascent and in a context of a profound economic and social crisis – and a deep crisis in democratic institutions. In this case, that context generated long-lasting legacies that shaped its organizational characteristics as a governing party. For example, social movements in Bolivia remained vibrant once their allies captured the presidency because these same founding and allied social movements had just contributed to the overthrow of two prior unpopular governments and played a crucial role in propelling the party to national office. From the perspective of the governing party, this civic engagement meant that the party could rely on continued mobilizational strategies both as a policy-making tool and in electoral campaigns. This enabled the party to overcome resistance from the guardians of the *ancien régime* – which dominated Congress – and pass key legislation that would fundamentally re-shape Bolivian politics. It also meant that even after assuming office, the party retained many of the founding organizational characteristics. Although once in power the party leadership attempted to co-opt the leadership of allied movements, grass-roots leaders could not always guarantee the compliance of the rank and file with the government's policies. As discussed in greater detail in the pages below, this ability of the rank and file to mount and sustain *autonomous* mobilization capacity contributed to keeping the party open and responsive to movements once in office and created pressures for power dispersion – in spite of the adverse institutional context and the oligarchic temptations of the party leadership.

By contrast, the PT came to power via routine turnover. Like the MAS, however, it also came to power with a weak position in Congress and weak control of core state institutions. This meant that a central political challenge was to generate a legislative majority to pass laws and support its policies. Instead of relying on mobilization, the PT responded to divided government by engaging in broad alliance making – a pattern it had found useful in its experiences of local administration, and one that could only be pursued once the more radical factions committed to bottom-up politics had declined in influence within the party. Ultimately, this need to establish and maintain coalitional deals pushed its internal structures toward more top-down control and eroded linkages with the social bases. Having a weak position in Congress served as a mechanism of organizational self-reproduction; it kept pulling the PT leadership in a direction that further reinforced the detachment from the party's social movement bases.

Constant Explanations

Constant explanations or causes are stable conditions that contribute to reproducing an outcome and to explaining its continual reoccurrence. The "configuration" of civil society – particularly its strength or density – is a constant cause. It interacts closely with more cyclical attributes of civil society – the process of autonomous mobilization – to shape outcomes like power distributions within parties. By "civil society," I mean the totality of politically oriented associations that contribute to the self-organization of society, which can be the basis for collective action and political mobilization.[22] These associations include, but are not limited to, grass-roots social movements, labor and peasant unions, neighborhood associations, self-help organizations to obtain services, mining cooperatives, and organizations representing the urban and rural poor, including the unemployed, artisans, pensioners, advocacy groups, and street vendors, among others.[23] The focus of this book is on voluntary associations that facilitate the political mobilization of the socioeconomic segment of society generally designated as "popular sectors" (Oxhorn 1998; Silva 2009, 2017; Rossi 2015). These associations, as has been firmly established in the empirical literature, provide different kinds of resources to political parties, which "enable them to be the primary connectors of state and society" (Vergara 2011: 74). Parties pursue connections to civic associations to expand territorially, recruit leaders, distribute the party's program, collect local information, mobilize voters, and so on. Whether on the left or on the right, parties have traditionally benefited electorally from their linkages to unions and other, less formal grass-roots movements.

Early theoretical works,[24] as well as more recent empirical research on party-building, have established that strong and densely organized civil societies – *high* organizational density in society – can serve as mobilizing structures for new movement-based parties.[25] The general expectation in that literature is

---

[22] This definition of civil society is a modification of Huber and Stephens' (2012: 26) definition.

[23] This is clearly a restrictive definition of civil society. It focuses on associations that can provide resources to parties. It excludes groups, such as sports leagues, choral societies, card-playing groups, etc., that can also contribute to strengthening civil society but may not necessarily play an important role in shaping the internal politics of parties.

[24] See, particularly, the works of Duverger (1954), Lipset and Rokkan (1967), and Huntington (1968).

[25] On the importance of linkages between civic associations and parties for party building in Latin America, see Collier and Collier (1991), Van Cott (2005), Vergara (2011), and Levitsky et al. (2016); on African parties, see LeBas (2011); on European parties, see Panebianco (1988), Kitschelt (1989a), Bartolini and Mair (1995), Kalyvas (1996), Bartolini (2000), and Glenn (2003).

that the organizational infrastructures of politically oriented associations or other collective actors[26] may contribute to building strong parties by reducing costs and coordination problems associated with those efforts (LeBas 2011). This "organizational inheritance" – as Levitsky et al. (2016: 21–3) argue in a recent contribution – can provide invaluable resources to new political parties and contribute to their long-term empowerment. For these authors, new parties are more likely to take root, and also to persist over time, where politicians build upon the infrastructure of preexisting organizations. Movement-based parties, even if initially loosely organized and held together, are well positioned to become strong parties in the long run because they draw on the resources of a multiplicity of social movements and civic associations that provide crucial assets for party-building.

Existing studies highlight the theoretical importance of the organizational context in helping to explain the emergence and the strength of movement-based parties, as well as how that context contributes to electoral competition. In the present book, I take the idea that the existence of a dense organizational context matters, but I move beyond the party formation stage and beyond the competition aspect. I add the insight that variation in both the organizational strength and in the *autonomous* mobilizational capacity of civil society actors can also affect the internal governance structures of parties and their tendencies toward power concentration. Concretely, I argue that the presence of civil societies that are strongly organized and that retain an ongoing capacity for autonomous social mobilization can generate politically consequential pressures from below that can serve as limits on the autonomy and decision-making power of the party's top leadership. These pressures may also defy trends toward internal power concentration by helping to keep channels open for agenda setting from the bottom to the top, and thus they can contribute to keeping parties responsive and accountable to their social bases. In short, the strength, density, and autonomy of civil society mobilization can help to explain the continual reproduction of early patterns of party organizational development.

The above terms require some further elaboration. "Strongly organized" civil societies are those with high organizational density, measured as the percentage of the population that are members of grass-roots organizations. "Autonomy" refers to the capacity of social movements and other civil society organizations to engage in a bottom-up dynamic of sociopolitical mobilization, as opposed to a type of state-sponsored mobilization or one induced from the top down. "Highly mobilized" societies, finally, are those where the majority of the population is capable of self-organizing and articulating demands in the

---

[26] These might include labor and agrarian unions, community associations, religious associations, indigenous movements, and other "new" grass-roots movements.

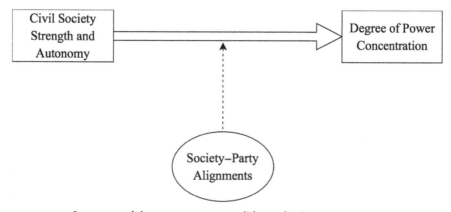

FIGURE 1.3 Summary of the argument on candidate selection.

political arena via contentious bargaining.[27] As stated previously, these different attributes shaping the nature and strength of civil society are power resources that can help resist a Michelsian shift in the character of an allied movement-based party.[28] All these attributes are not always clearly distinguishable, however. Theoretically and empirically, the effects of these attributes are intertwined.

The strength and autonomous mobilization capacity of civil society organizations first contribute to resisting pressures toward internal concentration in the realm of candidate selection, as the example of the MAS demonstrates. Top-down decision-making by the party leadership is less likely to take place where civil society is strong, well organized, and autonomous. In such contexts, the grass-roots organizations are more likely to wield power over who rises to leadership positions, thereby constraining the power of the party leadership. Strong and autonomous civil society organizations, however, are more likely to have an influence on candidate selection if they have close ties to the party. Figure 1.3 provides a summary and illustration of the argument, which I unpack further in Chapter 3.

In the absence of strong bureaucratic constraints within the party, civil society strength and its capacity to mobilize autonomously also affect the degree of internal power concentration in the policy-making sphere. Figure 1.4 provides a summary and visual illustration on the dimensions of analysis and the main components of the argument in the policy realm, all of which is explained further in Chapter 4. On the one hand, the explanation focuses on

[27] In a democracy, a highly mobilized civil society is itself a double-edged sword. It enables subordinate groups to make their weight felt between elections and to check state power, but it can also make democracy ungovernable and even undermine it.

[28] They are power resources because groups in civil society, especially popular sectors, can use them to expand their substantive influence (Rueschemeyer, Stephens, and Stephens 1992).

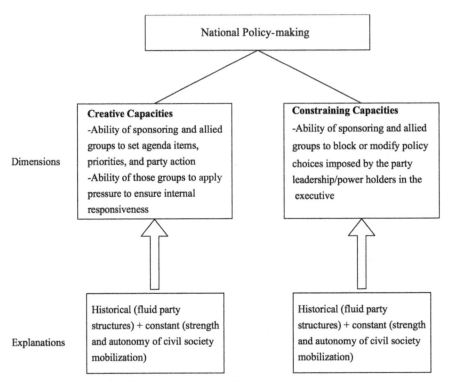

FIGURE 1.4 Summary of the argument on policy-making.

what I term the "creative capacities" of the party's social movement bases. This term refers to the ability of sponsoring and allied groups to put issues on the agenda and to use pressure to ensure governing parties respond by passing certain policies. Strong and autonomous civil society organizations are more likely to have creative capacities where the policies affect them in their productive roles.

On the other hand, the explanation centers on what I term the "constraining capacities" of sponsoring and allied groups. This concept refers to the veto and counter-mobilization power of the party's social movement base. These are usually strong collective actors that can mobilize autonomously and impose effective constraints on the authority of power holders and decision-making power of party leaders by either blocking or modifying legislative proposals that are on the agenda.

Not every group has the same capacity to pressure the governing party from below and block or modify policy proposals, however. A group's success is contingent on the breadth of the veto coalition that mobilized popular actors manage to configure and on the group's autonomous mobilizational capacity. In general, if a mobilized grass-roots actor builds a broad-based veto coalition with multiple sectors of society, then the veto coalition is more likely to succeed in forcing policy change. At the other extreme, if a mobilized grass-roots actor acts alone and cannot build a strong veto coalition, it is more likely that the party in office will defeat attempts from below to push policy change. Whether a policy initiative has the support of the party's political core is also important, but the effects of this variable are conditioned by the strength of the veto coalition. In short, in the realm of policy-making, meaningful advances toward the mitigation of top-down control within governing movement-based parties require mobilized pressures from below: the broader and better coordinated the pressures, the greater the chances of enhancing the governing party's responsiveness to its social movement bases. These arguments are developed further in Chapter 4.

Alternative Explanations

There are at least three reasonable critiques of my explanation based on a combination of historical and constant causal factors. A prominent explanation focuses on time, or the distance between the founding of the party, its ascent to power, and the moment in which it is examined. This argument, inspired by Michels and grounded on a unilinear understanding of party organizational development, would claim that the passage of time will inevitably lead to top-down control and to a widening political gap between party elites and the party's social bases. Sooner or later, the argument goes, parties with similar origins will develop similar – bureaucratic, centralized, "top-down" – organizational structures. In the end, the "iron law of oligarchy" was formulated on the basis of the experience of the German Social Democratic Party, a party that had been around for decades when Michels formulated his organizational theory.

Critics might then argue that, given the young age of the MAS, it might be "too early to tell" whether the trend toward top-down control has had time to fully develop. In this view, the observations advanced in this book – that the party has maintained important spaces for bottom-up input in candidate selection and policy-making – may simply be a reflection that the party is still relatively close to its own origins, close to the moment of social mobilization that predated its rise to power, and more strongly connected with a vibrant social movement tradition in the country at the time of my study. But all this could change. While this might be a reasonable expectation, it need not be the case. The experience of the Uruguayan FA, developed in detail in Chapter 5, helps to discount the argument that time has uniform effects on organizational development. The party has been around for over 45 years and (at the time of this writing, in March 2018) over 14 of these years in national government, and yet it has maintained well-developed spaces and opportunities for grass-roots participation and bottom-up governance that at least partially help to counteract the trend toward top-down control associated with party bureaucratization and executive authority (Pérez, Piñeiro, and Rosenblatt 2018).

Two additional critiques might be, firstly, that my explanation fails to capture some of the nuanced ways in which domestic and international economic pressures may contribute to facilitating or hindering internal grass-roots participation, and, secondly, that it ignores leadership qualities that favor top-down control within parties. My argument does not discount economic or leadership factors, but it holds that historical and constant elements discussed above better explain the extent to which governing parties can help to counter-act the pro-oligarchy pressures that economic and leadership factors might exert. Comparative evidence of other parties with similar origins in social movements but otherwise different organizational development supports the explanatory power of the historical and constant dimensions developed above (Chapter 5). Domestic and external economic pressures do not explain why, when confronted with similar pressures, some movement-based parties remain open to input from below and more internally responsive than others. If we were examining ideological or policy issues, these three statements would hold true: (1) a severe crisis context provided strong incentives for the MAS to enact more "radical" reforms and rely on mobilization as a policy tool, thereby keeping the party more open to movement influence; (2) the absence of a crisis – but threat of a potential crisis – in Brazil contributed to a process of ideological moderation; and (3) severe economic pressures in the aftermath of the Argentine collapse of 2001 set priorities and the broader policy agenda for the FA in Uruguay that remained strongly change-oriented. However, policy choices or ideological positions do not dictate organizational patterns, or how power and authority are allocated within movement-based parties. In all these instances, organizational legacies outweighed exogenous pressures. Such pressures, in short, do not have uniform effects on internal power distributions.

Charismatic political leaders – those that command overwhelming legitimacy and internal authority – are widely seen as inimical to internal power dispersion and bottom-up governance. Charismatic authority is usually seen as conducive to concentrated power and top-down control. When parties do not manage to outgrow leaders over time – that is, when they do not "routinize" charisma – there is a sense that the leaders "own" the parties and that they can single-handedly make decisions.[29] Empirically, as Huber and Stephens (2012: 266) note, dominant personalities "do not have a good track record when it comes to building strong political parties that would become organizational actors independent of their leaders." At the core of this is the idea that charismatic political leaders generally eschew building parties that can limit their power and autonomy. Latin American history does indeed offer several examples of political parties that, regardless of their origins, turned into personalistic vehicles for charismatic leaders who control much of the party's

---

[29] On this point, see Weber (1968 [1922]: 1121).

internal life from the top and according to their own taste. Even the Brazilian PT, which is typically portrayed as an example of bottom-up, rank and file governance has experienced this. As Amaral and Power (2015: 169) note:

After eight successful years in the presidency (2003–10), Lula's position in the party was so strong that he could single-handedly emplace the relatively unknown Dilma Rousseff as his party's candidate for president in 2010. This personal decision by the incumbent president (an outcome that would have been unthinkable only a few years earlier) was met by uncritical silence within a party long accustomed to vibrant internal democracy.

In Bolivia, Evo Morales qualifies as a charismatic leader. This book underscores that Morales does indeed command significant legitimacy and undisputed internal authority within the MAS. Rooted in the struggles for the party's foundation, the centrality of his leadership (as well as its growing "personalism") cannot be overlooked (Madrid 2012).[30] He is the dominant figure who helps binds together a wide array of loosely connected popular movements and organizations, and he inspires devotion among supporters, especially in rural areas. Yet, although Morales more often than not tends to dominate party affairs, his word within the MAS is not always the "last word." Decision-making involves a great deal of negotiation and compromise (Silva 2017). The party combines top-down charismatic leadership with bottom-up opportunities for "voice," and highly mobilized groups recurrently challenge Morales' authority from below in ways that are not evident in the case of the PT. In short, while one may associate charismatic leadership with greater levels of top-down control, the effects of charismatic leadership on internal power distributions are not straightforward. They should be studied rather than assumed.

As I argue in this book, the fluid nature of the MAS's internal organization generates incentives against top-down control, as do the dynamics of autonomous social mobilization by popular constituencies that take place in the streets. It is an empirical question as to whether the growing personalism of Morales's leadership, and the fact that there are no obvious successors being cultivated from the bottom, might lead to a growing power concentration in the party in an eventual next term in office. The answer to this question will require time and will depend heavily on the continuing strength and autonomous mobilization capacity of allied groups in civil society.

METHODOLOGICAL APPROACH

I address the puzzle of what options movement-based parties have to mitigate the trend toward top-down control by using a within-case research design for theory-building purposes. Figure 1.5 summarizes the research design. First,

---

[30] This trend intensified dramatically in the context of the 2016 referendum to allow Morales to run again for the presidency in 2019. Highlighting the indispensability of Morales' leadership, Vice-President García Linera went as far as to say that "If Evo is not allowed to run, the sun will hide away and everything will be sadness."

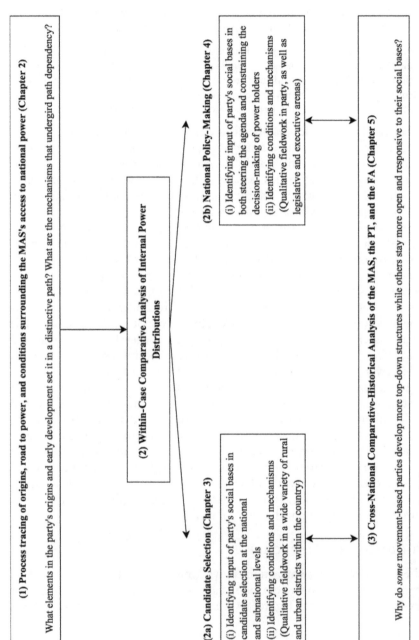

(1) Process tracing of origins, road to power, and conditions surrounding the MAS's access to national power (Chapter 2)

What elements in the party's origins and early development set it in a distinctive path? What are the mechanisms that undergird path dependency?

(2) Within-Case Comparative Analysis of Internal Power Distributions

(2a) Candidate Selection (Chapter 3)

(i) Identifying input of party's social bases in candidate selection at the national and subnational levels
(ii) Identifying conditions and mechanisms (Qualitative fieldwork in a wide variety of rural and urban districts within the country)

(2b) National Policy-Making (Chapter 4)

(i) Identifying input of party's social bases in both steering the agenda and constraining the decision-making of power holders
(ii) Identifying conditions and mechanisms (Qualitative fieldwork in party, as well as legislative and executive arenas)

(3) Cross-National Comparative-Historical Analysis of the MAS, the PT, and the FA (Chapter 5)

Why do *some* movement-based parties develop more top-down structures while others stay more open and responsive to their social bases?

FIGURE 1.5 Summary of research design.

I develop a "historical" explanation of how organizational attributes adopted during the MAS's early development created a "weak" form of path dependency that is resistant to change. I rely on process tracing to tease out the initial organizational attributes that set the party in a distinctive path and explain the mechanisms that undergird path dependency (Chapter 2).

I then unpack the party's internal operations and place more emphasis on the "constant" explanations. Using the empirical case of the MAS, I explore variation in patterns of candidate selection for national and local-level office, according to the strength of civil society, the nature of the political alignments between the MAS and civil society, and the electoral strength of the MAS in different areas of the country (Chapter 3). I then explore variation in patterns of policy-making in different policy spheres, according to the autonomy and mobilizational power of civil society and the alignments between the MAS different social actors (Chapter 4). While other scholars have already offered qualitative descriptions of the diversity of the MAS's decision-making processes and mechanisms (Komadina and Geffroy 2007; Do Alto 2007; Zuazo 2008, 2010; Do Alto and Stefanoni 2010; Harten 2011; Madrid 2012; Crabtree 2013), this book generates more robust descriptive evidence and a more systematic explanation for this heterogeneity by focusing on explaining internal power distributions and the role of the party's social bases in shaping candidate selection and national policy-making.

To test the generalizability of the arguments presented in this book, I then compare the MAS with the PT and the FA (Chapter 5). This comparison helps to create more variation in my dependent variable (i.e., power concentration) with the case of the PT as a movement-based party that became highly top-down, as conventional wisdom would have expected, and the FA representing an intermediate case. The comparison also helps to create more variation in independent variables (i.e., longevity) with the case of the FA as a party that even after many years since its foundation remains participatory and anchored in its movement roots. The comparison thus strengthens the explanatory power of my theory and sheds light on the factors that make the MAS both similar to and different from other movement-based parties.

The MAS is in some ways an organizational anomaly, which, as has been noted, makes the case theoretically interesting and can help us understand non-anomaly cases as well. It has a dominant and highly personalistic leader, Evo Morales, who concentrates a great deal of power in his own hands, but yet its internal mechanisms have given meaningful voice and influence to groups that were previously on the margins of political life. By maintaining a fair amount of its initial bottom-up participatory *élan* and strong connections with its movement roots, the MAS has defied pressures toward top-down control and has proven to be an organization not easily controlled from the top even after assuming national-level power.[31] Thus there is much to be gained from an in-depth examination of the conditions and mechanisms under which top-down control can be attenuated, if not avoided, in a scenario where high degrees of power concentration would be clearly expected.

To accomplish such an examination, an in-depth case study approach remains fundamental.[32] Although the case study approach has its drawbacks, as all research methods do, such an approach is particularly strong at yielding internal validity and discovering causal mechanisms through process tracing.[33] And while case studies have recently been the target of harsh criticism, often on the faulty assumption that one case equates to one observation (King, Keohane, and Verba 1994), the case study approach remains a crucial tool for understanding power relations among collective actors (in this book grass-roots social movements and political parties) and the conditions of societal and political structures that may restrain elite behavior. Qualitative data, or causal process observations, are absolutely critical to capturing the internal dynamics, organization, and behavior of movement-based parties.[34]

To collect causal process observations, I carried out two rounds of field research in Bolivia, the first one between July and September 2008 and the second between August 2012 and May 2013.[35] During this time, I conducted more than 170 in-depth interviews with party elites at the national, state, and municipal levels, as well as with a wide variety of civil society actors, including union leaders, activists, journalists, and academics. These interviews provide the basis for my analysis of legislative candidate selection for national office, which focuses on the electoral process leading to the 2009 general election. This was a key moment for analyzing internal power distributions because the MAS was in its most expansive phase, and as a result, the lead up to that election can be conceived of as a likely scenario for high degrees of power concentration. My analysis draws on systematic interviews with more than 50 incumbent representatives from the departments of La Paz, Cochabamba, Oruro, and Santa Cruz.[36] These are the country's most populated departments, they form

---

[31] An observation also noted elsewhere (see Anria 2013) and by other scholars (Crabtree 2013).

[32] Gerring defines the case study approach as "the intensive study of a single case where the purpose of that study is – at least in part – to shed light on a larger class of cases" (Gerring 2007: 20). In other words, from case studies we can learn something about political phenomena that is well beyond the mere description of a particular case.

[33] On the issue of internal validity, see Adcock and Collier (2001).

[34] A causal process observation, CPO, is "an insight or piece of data that provides information about context, process, or mechanism, and that contributes distinctive leverage in causal inference" (Brady and Collier 2004: 2). These observations imply and require process tracing and within-case analysis. For an extensive discussion on CPOs' distinctive leverage in causal inference, see Mahoney (2010).

[35] Preliminary results of the first round of fieldwork have been published elsewhere (see Anria 2009, 2010, 2013).

[36] Departments in Bolivia (a unitary country) are the equivalent of states or provinces in federalist countries.

the "central axis" of the country, and they are the places where I carried out fieldwork.[37] One's take on top-down or bottom-up candidate selection processes heavily depends on whom you speak to. On the basis of the large number of interviews I conducted I am confident that the account I provide is as accurate as possible. Out of 93 seats in the 4 departments of interest, the MAS obtained 66 in 2009. Of those 66, I interviewed 57 (or 86 percent of those elected).

While those four departments in the country's "central axis" obviously do not constitute the entire country, the patterns observed there were also common elsewhere, as confirmed through interviews with actors who have privileged access to the internal politics of the MAS, as well as secondary sources and newspaper archives. All these "thick" data helped me to compare and contrast observations gathered in Bolivia's major departments and to see how generalizable my findings are to other districts.

It is difficult, however, to paint a single picture of a complex governing organization when local contexts shape internal characteristics and behavior. This is particularly difficult to do in countries with large rural–urban divides, high levels of inequality, or other major sources of diversity. To create a more accurate account of the MAS, I also include an analysis of candidate selection for local office, which focuses on the lead up to the 2010 municipal elections. The analysis draws on in-depth interviews with over 30 elected officials at the local level, as well as unsuccessful aspirants and a variety of local party elites, regional brokers and notables, grass-roots leaders, and activists. This research was conducted in five municipalities, three urban (La Paz, El Alto, and Santa Cruz) and two rural (Achacachi and Villa Tunari). I selected rural and urban municipalities with the following electoral configurations: (1) the MAS as electorally dominant at all levels of competition, both national and municipal, as in Villa Tunari and El Alto; (2) opposition parties dominant at all levels, as in Santa Cruz; and (3) mixed or split, where neither the MAS nor opposition parties are clearly dominant, as in Achacachi and La Paz.[38] Although the five municipalities are not representative of the country as a whole, they are included in this book to capture the diverse organizational patterns and practices that prevail within the MAS in both rural and urban settings. Subnational comparisons have important advantages. As Snyder (2001) points out, by "scaling down" the unit of analysis, subnational comparisons greatly expand the number of observations and help to uncover processes that are harder to observe at the country level.

Regarding my interviews, I employed a semi-structured format but also included a number of structured questions in order to be able to identify and

[37] However, the majority of my interviews with incumbent representatives were conducted in the country's administrative capital, La Paz.

[38] This allowed for an exploration of the organization of the MAS in its strongest area of support (Villa Tunari) and also in strongholds of the opposition (Santa Cruz).

compare patterns across regions.[39] Most of the interviews with incumbent representatives and local level elected officials were recorded, and these were then transcribed and processed in NVivo to find patterns emerging from individual accounts. All interviews were conducted in Spanish.

My analysis of the policy-making process also draws on a wealth of original interviews with a wide range of politicians (MAS leaders, representatives, bureaucrats, advisors) and civil society actors. The focus of the analysis is centered, on the one hand, on the degree of input of grass-roots actors in the positive formulation of policies through internal party structures or through their representatives in Congress. Interviews with top-level party officials, incumbent representatives, and grass-roots leaders, as well as participatory observations in party congresses, were central to developing this analysis. To evaluate degrees of grass-roots impact on decision-making via their access to the executive branch, on the other hand, I relied on interviews with top- and mid-level officials in the ministries of Rural Development, Mining, and Economy, as well as in the Office of the Vice Presidency. These four offices exhibit significant variation in terms of their degree of "permeability" to bottom-up input. Interviews in this arena helped to compare and contrast different degrees of grass-roots influence across government bureaucracies. This in-depth information collected through original interviews was supplemented with data from secondary sources and from newspaper archives. These additional printed data helped to establish general timelines for the policies under study and to cross check the accuracy of retrospective accounts from interviews.

Finally, to examine the conditions under which the party's social movement bases can constrain the decision-making power of power holders and force policy change, I selected a wide array of major initiatives by the executive branch. These included instances where the national government proposed a policy and was forced to reverse decisions as a result of bottom-up pressure, as well as other instances in which the leadership did not change the policy course in spite of the, often intense, sociopolitical pressures from the party's social bases. Interviews with politicians and with a large number of civil society actors allowed me to reconstruct the positioning, perceptions, and calculations of key players during conflicts of high intensity. I supplemented this information with data from newspaper archives.[40]

---

[39] Although I was always prepared with a series of questions and probes, interviews were often more open-ended than I anticipated – or even *wanted*. However, allowing participants to "tell their stories" allowed them to feel more comfortable about telling their side of the story, which yielded richer information.

[40] To assist with this, I relied on reports compiled by Bolivia's Center for Documentation and Information (CEDIB) in Cochabamba. CEDIB has one of the largest newspaper archives in the country, and it allows researchers to compile reports based on searches by keyword. For each of the policies under consideration I prepared a compilation of their coverage in Bolivia's major newspapers. This allowed me to have access to every article mentioning the policies under consideration, to create timelines of events, and to identify key actors. I also relied on social conflict data generously provided by the *Fundación UNIR*.

A final component of my research strategy was to gather official documentation by the MAS. These documents provided useful information on the party's internal debates and helped identify relevant political actors within the organization. I also consulted a vast literature of published and unpublished works on the MAS, most of which is not available in English. I looked at local publications, as well as theses produced by students at leading universities in the country. Because Bolivia is sharply polarized between those who passionately support the MAS and those who are equally passionate in their opposition, it was crucial to obtain a wide variety of perspectives. I interviewed journalists and academics who are sympathetic to the MAS government, as well as those who are avid opponents, who shaped my understanding of the trajectory and organization of the MAS. Finally, my fieldwork also included participatory observation in party congresses, which helped me to understand how some of the party's decisions are made and communicated internally.

While the heavy lifting for causal inference derives from a within-case comparative examination of the Bolivian MAS, I also develop a cross-national comparison of the origins, organizational evolution, and power structures of two major movement-based parties in Latin America: the Brazilian PT and the Uruguayan FA. These comparisons help to further support the theoretical claims about the importance of historical and constant factors for shaping the degree of internal power concentration in these kinds of parties. Like the MAS, both the PT and the FA share a common origin in grass-roots social movements, and all three came to national-level power for the first time during Latin America's left turn (in 2006, 2002, and 2005, respectively). Despite their common origins as electoral vehicles for social movement entrepreneurs, they differ sharply in terms of the extent to which their structures concentrate or disperse power and the kinds of linkages they have with their social bases: while the PT became highly top-down, the FA represents an intermediate case, and the MAS represents an example of a movement-based party that remains highly participatory and anchored in its social movement roots.

To explain *why* they have followed different trajectories, a "contextualized comparison" using comparative historical analysis is fundamental (Mahoney and Rueschemeyer 2003). This method allows me to trace the origins and causes of political outcomes that are harder to observe in a single case. In order to collect causal process observations about these comparative cases, this analysis draws mainly on secondary sources and on the analysis of LAPOP survey data.[41] In each of the comparative cases, I begin the narrative by tracing the foundational moment and early development of the party, the experiences in local level government before gaining national-level power, and the mode of

---

[41] Hosted at Vanderbilt University, LAPOP (Latin American Public Opinion Project) conducts surveys of public opinion in Latin America every two years. I used their data to examine the relationship between partisan engagement and participation in associational life, which in turn served as an indirect measure of the potential for support for mobilization that the three parties under consideration have, as well as of the kinds of pressures from below they might confront.

access to state power. The comparative analysis helps to detect factors preventing or facilitating the development of top-down structures that would not be made immediately apparent by studying a single case over a short period of time. In so doing, the comparative analysis helps improve the overall evidentiary base of this book and strengthens it theoretically.

A final word on the value of my methodological approach is in order. The choice of a case study approach combined with comparative historical analysis was driven by the logic of the research question animating this book, not the other way around. The collection of causal process observations via qualitative techniques is crucial for unpacking the "black box" of movement-based parties and for uncovering processes that parties often prefer to keep behind the scenes. The internal life of parties and the political logic behind internal decisions can be fully grasped only with an in-depth knowledge of the cases and "a healthy dose of political sociology" (Smith et al. 2014; see Roberts' contribution, p. 18). An understanding of the conditions that can facilitate or help counteract the trend toward top-down control within movement-based parties cannot be fully attained by relying on already existing party datasets.[42] Thus, my approach accepts the plea made by Murillo, Shrank, and Luna (see Smith et al. 2014) for the generation of more empirically grounded and context-sensitive theoretical work, and it also builds on a rich tradition of comparative historical and political sociology approaches to parties (Duverger 1954; Lipset and Rokkan 1967; Panebianco 1988; Levitsky 2003; Luna 2014; Roberts 2015a). The result of this fieldwork-intensive study is a series of testable hypotheses that, built on the experiences and organizational development of Latin American movement-based parties, can be tested empirically elsewhere.

---

[42] This is particularly true for Latin American parties, where the quality of the existing datasets is strikingly low.

2

Origins and Ascendance to Power

In this chapter, I develop parts of the historical explanation through a discussion of the origins, evolution, and ascendance to power of the MAS. I explain how attributes adopted during the party's early development created a "weak" form of path dependency – an inclination to develop a distinctive bottom-up pattern of organization – that is resistant to change. The MAS grew organically from the autonomous mobilization of social movements. It promoted active participation since its foundation and created channels of consultation through which sponsoring and allied movements could have "voice" and influence over decision-making in areas such as candidate selection, programmatic development, and party electoral strategy. This would allow them to at least partially determine the party's agenda, select party candidates for public office, and exercise veto powers over the authority of the party leadership. The existence of such channels facilitated the early emergence of social accountability structures headed by groups and movements that, years after the party's founding, still check power from within and keep open channels for agenda setting from below.

This chapter describes how both party and rank and file movement leaders became used to working in these structures, how structures became effective (but informally institutionalized), and how deviating from them became less promising over time even while the party experienced important transformations. The chapter also traces the relationships between the MAS and its social bases during the party's dramatic territorial, organizational, and sociological expansion preceding its rise to power. It discusses the extent to which this expansion, as it unfolded, posed challenges to the party's "genetic model" and how, despite those challenges, early organizational patterns consolidated and reproduced over time through the ongoing capacity for autonomous mobilization that is not controlled from the top down, by the party or by Morales.

THE MAS AS A HYBRID PARTY

Parties are deeply affected by their origins and early development, as the literatures on historical institutionalism and on comparative political parties have established.[1] Organizational structures adopted during the formative phase of a party leave indelible marks on its life, as they condense early power struggles and shape the development of the organization in a path-dependent process. Panebianco (1988) describes this in his classic "genetic model" of party development, saying:

[A party's] organizational characteristics depend more upon its history, i.e. on how the organization originated and how it consolidated, than upon any other factor. The characteristics of a party's origins are in fact capable of exerting a weight on its organizational structure even decades later. Every organization bears the mark of its formation, of the crucial political-administrative decisions made by its founders, the decisions that "molded" the organization (Panebianco 1988: 50).

This model is too deterministic, however. It posits that almost every aspect of a contemporary party organization can be traced to "the crucial political choices made by its founding fathers, the first struggles for organizational control, and the way in which the party was formed" (Panebianco 1988: xiii). Yet, despite Panebianco's determinism, his analysis is useful here because it brings to the fore the dimension of "organizational power," which consists of "explaining the functioning and activities of organizations above all in terms of alliances and struggles for power among the different actors that comprise them" (Panebianco 1988: xii). His insight, in short, serves as a starting point for the analysis that follows.

Originating in Bolivia's Chapare region in the mid-1990s as a small, localized party, the MAS experienced vertiginous growth over a short period of time. It expanded to Bolivia's largest cities and became the country's largest party in less than a decade, as its leader, Evo Morales, was elected to the presidency in 2005 and then reelected in 2009 and 2014. The coca growers who formed the MAS still conceive of it as *their* "political instrument."[2] As such, the party's genesis as an organization was distinctively from the bottom up, making the MAS a clear example of a movement-based party, a hybrid fusion of movement and party networks.

---

[1] See Panebianco (1988), Collier and Collier (1991) and Mahoney and Thelen (2015).

[2] The "political instrument" was founded on the idea of "self-representation" of the masses (see García Linera, León, and Monje 2004). Political leaders of the MAS's organizational core reject the "party" designation because they associate parties with institutions that divide rather than unite popular forces. Leaders stress that they are spokespeople, or messengers, for their constituencies, as opposed to their representatives. That they do not intend to build a conventional party has much to do with this. Based on the idea of "self-representation" of the masses underpinning the MAS, its political core has privileged the sustaining of social mobilization in relation to the institutionalization of the movement as a party.

The MAS has followed this model: a sponsoring group, namely a rural social movement of *cocaleros*, generated its own political leadership, formed a political vehicle to compete in elections, and maintained some degree of autonomy and leadership accountability (Van Cott 2005: 67–71). That the MAS grew directly out of the autonomous social mobilization of an indigenous constituency makes it a different case from other movement-based parties in the region and beyond (Yashar 2005). However, to state that the MAS represents indigenous constituencies is not to say that it is an "indigenous" party. Instead, it is a party that presents itself using an ethnic discourse but tries to appeal to a wider constituency by blending class and ethnic elements in a manner that tolerates ethnic diversity.

The genesis of the MAS in Bolivia's *cocalero* movement has been the subject of attention in both the scholarly and non-scholarly literature (Van Cott 2005; Stefanoni and Do Alto 2006; Komadina and Geffroy 2007; Escóbar 2008; Madrid 2011, 2012). Existing studies of the MAS's rise to power have focused on the "populist" leadership of Evo Morales and how he was able to woo indigenous and non-indigenous voters, who were disenchanted with the traditional political parties and the neoliberal policies these parties had implemented. Madrid (2012) has described Morales and the MAS's tactics as an example of "ethnopopulism," meaning that the movement relied on generic "indigenous issues" devoid of particular cultural referents to provide the basis for the construction of a multi-class coalition around a charismatic leader (see also Albro 2005a; Harten 2011).

Yet, despite all the attention paid to Morales's leadership and his "populist" electoral strategies, less attention has been paid to how the party developed organizationally. More specifically, the literature has overlooked how the MAS's growing electoral success has been contingent on the construction of an unusually strong rural–urban coalition that was built on the basis of different linkages between the MAS and organized constituencies in urban and rural areas. Maps 2.1 through 2.4 highlight this point; they show that the MAS grew electorally from a very geographically concentrated constituency in rural areas of Cochabamba to the national level with support in rural and urban areas throughout the country, and that it did so in a very fast manner.[3] This chapter addresses this angle of the MAS's evolution and rise to power.

---

[3] These maps were built using ArcGIS 10.2 Mapping Software. They use municipal level data for both presidential elections and municipal elections between 1995 and 2010. The data were broken down by urban and rural municipalities. Thirteen municipalities were coded as urban. These include the capitals of Bolivia's 9 departments, in addition to El Alto and every other city with a population over 100,000. The remaining municipalities were coded as rural. For additional maps on municipal elections, see Appendix 2.

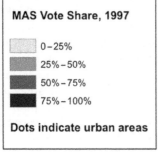

MAP 2.1 1997 presidential election United Left (IU) vote (rural and urban).
Note: The Assembly for the Sovereignty of the People (ASP), a movement organization that preceded the MAS, took over the United Left (IU), a defunct left party, and ran its own candidates.

Gibson's (1996) approach to party electoral coalition building will help to articulate the claims advanced in this chapter.[4] Gibson (1996: 7) argues that, in

---

[4] Although his study focuses on parties on the right, the conceptual distinction between core and non-core constituencies is amenable to the study of parties on the left. For empirical examples that support this claim, see Luna (2014).

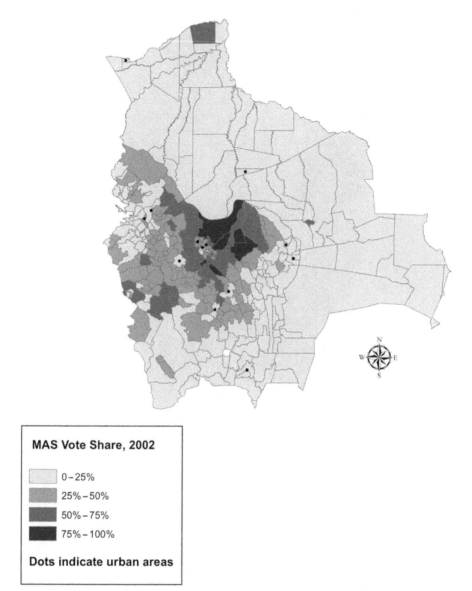

MAP 2.2 2002 presidential election MAS vote (rural and urban).

order to persist over time, conservative parties in Latin America tend to rely on two constituencies: a "core" constituency and a "non-core" constituency. Although the core constituency provides financial resources, policy-making support, guidance, and mobilizational power, it is generally incapable of making the party a viable electoral force, let alone an electoral winner. In order to expand their electoral base, parties make inroads into non-core or

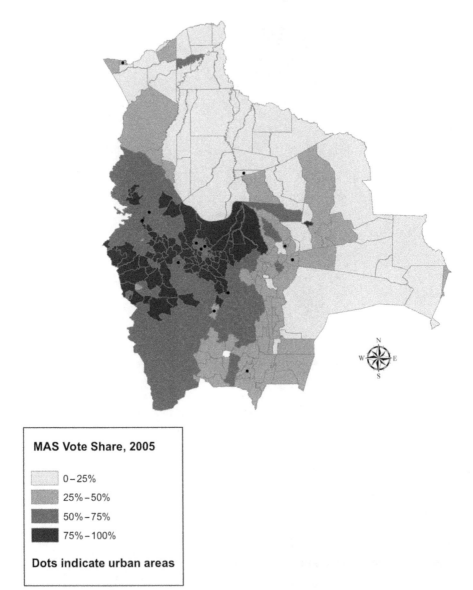

MAP 2.3 2005 presidential election MAS vote (rural and urban).

"peripheral" constituencies. The strategy for reaching these constituencies generally de-emphasizes ideology and is less programmatically oriented than the one directed at core groups. As a result, the non-core constituency consists of a less ideologically committed coalition designed to provide enough votes to guarantee the party's viability.

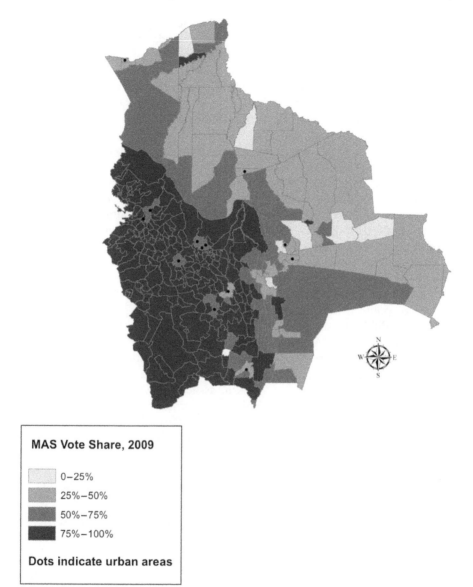

MAP 2.4 2009 presidential election MAS vote (rural and urban).

One central claim of this chapter is that MAS can be described as having two distinctive social coalitions. The central coalition is highly targeted. It is based on Bolivia's rural sector and consists of the *cocaleros* in the Chapare, as well as three national-level peasant organizations, which conceive of the MAS as their "political instrument" (interviews with Modesto Condori, Felipa Huanca,

Román Loayza, Dionicio Núñez, Rodolfo Machaca, Segundina Orellana, Concepción Ortiz, Juan de la Cruz Villca, and Leonida Zurita).[5] These social movement organizations distrust political parties and think of them as obsolete types of organizations that can slow down social and political change. In this segment of its central coalition, the MAS is organized distinctively from the bottom up and relies on the collective, assembly-like (*asambleísta*) style of decision-making utilized in Bolivia's rural social movements.

The peripheral coalition, in turn, relies on a broader set of urban-popular organizations in Bolivia's largest cities, where neighborhood associations, trade unions, and other forms of local collective organization play a key articulatory role. This expansion of the party to urban areas was based, on the one hand, on the ability of the MAS to aggregate interests and bundle issues together by finding common programmatic ground, articulating the claims for a remarkably diverse array of rural and urban movements that were mobilized in opposition to neoliberalism and extractive policies – a process by which the MAS became an "instrument" for a broader set of subordinate actors. On the other hand, the electoral strategy used to attract these peripheral constituencies combined attempts to co-opt the leadership of popular organizations with the pursuit of political alliances with established center-left parties in hopes of reaching middle-class segments.

In this regard, the MAS provides a clear example of a party that relies on a segmented linkage strategy to mobilize different constituencies (Luna 2014: 315–19). The different electoral strategies pursued by the MAS to reach core and non-core constituencies are, in turn, associated with different *organizational* strategies. On the one hand, the MAS's rural roots reflect patterns of bottom-up organization and organic movement–party linkages, a pattern that has facilitated a grass-roots control over the leadership and is associated with the party's "movement" origins.[6]

On the other hand, the MAS's vertiginous growth and extension into urban areas – and the evolution of the party "apparatus" in power, which facilitated

---

[5] These organizations are the so-called *trillizas* (the triplets), which include the Unique Confederation of Rural Laborers of Bolivia (*Confederación Sindical Única de Trabajadores Campesinos de Bolivia*, CSUTCB); the Syndicalist Confederation of Intercultural Communities of Bolivia (*Confederación Sindical de Comunidades Interculturales de Bolivia*, CSCIB); and the Bartolina Sisa National Confederation of Campesino, Indigenous, and Native Women of Bolivia (*Confederación Nacional de Mujeres Campesinas Indígenas Originarias de Bolivia "Bartolina Sisa,"* CNMCIOB-BS).

[6] Unlike other parties that emerged from social movements (such as the Brazilian PT), which consolidated a relatively autonomous and institutionalized bureaucratic structure, the MAS emerged as an extension of an indigenous social movement. During its initial stages, there was no clear distinction between the movement and the party "apparatus." As one of the MAS's founding members, Dionicio Núñez, commented in an interview, in this segment "the political structure is married to the social structure as a result of those early decisions," and because of that it may be "hard to visualize a divorce between the social movement and the political instrument" (interview with Dionicio Núñez).

access to state and patronage resources – fostered the emergence of top-down mobilization strategies and co-optative practices reminiscent of earlier experiences with populism and neopopulism, a process that at times has threatened to compromise the autonomy of allied groups. While this dramatic territorial and organizational expansion posed important challenges to the party's foundational characteristics, social movements found ways to reproduce its genetic imprint (as expansion occurred) through their ongoing activism and capacity for autonomous collective action.

In the pages below, I stress the hybrid attributes of the MAS and argue that it operates through a model that functions on the basis of a combination of autonomous collective action with top-down attempts of co-optation by a charismatic, and highly personalistic, leader. This hybrid fusion reflects the party's social movement origins as well as the pressures of electoral imperatives that allowed the MAS to reach core and non-core constituencies and craft a broad social base in opposition to neoliberal extractivist policies. Interest aggregation has not been an easy task, however, especially in the period since the MAS took national power and proceeded with a form of state-led extractivist policies (Mazzuca 2013; Weyland 2013). This is where the "bundling" began to break down and interest aggregation became more complicated, leading to conflicts between the MAS and its social movement bases over aspects of policy. Despite co-optation attempts, groups linked to the MAS maintained a strong capacity for autonomous social mobilization. Their ongoing capacity to mobilize autonomously helped to reproduce the party's initial "genetic imprint" over time. In so doing, social movements and other grassroots groups found ways to at least partially counteract the Michelsian trend toward top-down control.

ORIGINS AND ASCENDANCE TO POWER

The origins of the MAS as an electoral arm for a movement of coca producers and its fast rise to power were shaped by at least four elements. One was the implementation of neoliberal reforms, which created economic losers who would then resist neoliberal policies, and the crisis of neoliberalism, which opened up space on the left. The second factor was the resistance to coca eradication programs and the state repression associated with such programs, which acted as a unifying force and strengthened peasant and indigenous movements around the defense of their interests. A third factor was a changing institutional context associated with decentralization reforms, which provided opportunities for indigenous social movements and new parties to compete and thrive in local elections. Fourth was a crisis of Bolivia's political party system and state institutions that became acute in the context of anti-neoliberal protests in the early 2000s.

Bolivia implemented draconian neoliberal reforms during the period 1985–2005, and the consequences of these reforms profoundly shaped the rise of the MAS.[7] Central to these policies was the closure of state-owned and state-operated tin mines, which were no longer profitable by the mid-1980s. This meant that thousands of miners were forced to "relocate" to other sectors of the economy (Gill 2000: 73). Some of these workers, who were the vanguard and most combative sectors of the Bolivian proletariat, left the mining camps and moved to cities like El Alto (Lazar 2008), which could not absorb this labor force. Hence, this situation accelerated the growth of the informal, predominantly artisan economy. Others moved to the coca-producing regions of the Chapare, where they began to produce coca and organize with the *cocaleros*. Relocated workers brought with them a Trotsky-ist union-organizing background and a history of militant struggle and soli-darity, which would influence the discourse of the coca growers by introducing elements of Marxism and nationalism (Stefanoni 2003; Stefanoni and Do Alto 2006; Guillermoprieto 2006; Escóbar 2008). Still, it is worth noting that while relocated miners played an important role in organizing the coca growers around the idea of forming their own party, the coca grower movement preceded these mid-1980s developments.

A second important contributing factor involved the position of coca produ-cers in relation to coca eradication policies. As Postero (2010: 22) notes, *cocaleros* "came of age in a low-intensity war on drugs led by the U.S Drug Enforcement Agency." Indeed, it was due to Bolivian Law 1008, which framed the United States-sponsored drug war, that such groups were able to gain strength and self-confidence (interviews with Modesto Condori, Filemón Escó-bar, and Dionicio Núñez). The promulgation of this law was followed by state repression and conflicts in which many *cocalero*s died. But state repression worked as a catalyst for the *cocalero* unions, prompting their participation in the formal political system by constituting a relatively united political front with other peasant and indigenous organizations (Albro 2005b). In this con-text, the leaders of the *cocalero* movement hatched the idea of building a "political instrument" through which *cocaleros* could challenge US imperialism and neoliberal economic policies, both in the halls of Congress and on the streets (interviews with Condori, Escóbar, Loayza, and Villca; see also Van Cott 2005: 103; Escóbar 2008; and Hylton and Thomson 2007: 171). Through much of the 1990s, though, *cocaleros* were to a large extent focused on resist-ance to coca eradication. During this time, the broader anti-neoliberal move-ment was relatively weak, and the MAS did not play a large role in it.

The fact that the MAS gained force and that it became a national organiza-tion so rapidly had much to do with the circumstances of *cocaleros* in relation to the national political scene. A permissive institutional environment opened new channels of participation for social actors in local elections and municipal governance (Van Cott 2003; also 2005: 50). The Bolivian institutional context

---

[7] For a review of the neoliberal period in Bolivia, see Kohl and Farthing (2006) and Silva (2009).

changed deeply in the mid-1990s thanks to the 1994 Popular Participation Law (LPP) and the 1995 Law of Administrative Decentralization, both of which were passed under the first government of Gonzalo Sánchez de Lozada (1993–7). These laws involved the creation of hundreds of municipalities throughout the country and instituted direct elections for mayoral and council member positions. The LPP, in particular, created institutional opportunities for social actors to participate in decision-making processes at the local level, for instance by engaging in the elaboration and oversight of municipal development plans (Kohl 2003: 153). It also established that civil society representation should be based on territory rather than on corporate or functional lines. As a result, the government recognized nearly 15,000 preexisting territorial-based organizations, whose functions would be to provide checks and balances to municipal governments (Boulding 2014: 56). The LPP was a major change that created opportunities for the inclusion of traditionally underrepresented groups into organized politics. It was, in short, a reform that bolstered rural civil society and would later help the MAS.[8]

In addition, Bolivia's constitutional reform under Sánchez de Lozada's first presidency introduced single-member districts to one tier of the lower chamber in Congress, creating the so-called "uninominal" representatives (Chapter 3). As the Bolivian political scientist Moira Zuazo (Zuazo 2008; interview with Moira Zuazo) notes, all of these institutional changes unleashed a process of "ruralizing" politics, meaning that the reforms recognized rural and indigenous communities as actors in municipal-level decisions and expanded citizenship rights to indigenous peoples; one example of this is that the government began recognizing collective titling for indigenous territories (Postero 2007: 5–6). Indigenous movements formed their own electoral vehicles and, taking advantage of the new opportunity structures, engaged in electoral politics at the local level, which resulted in rapid gains in access to local offices (Van Cott 2005, 2008; Collins 2006; Albó 2008). Undoubtedly, the most successful of these newly created parties was the MAS, though its success was not immediate.[9]

Because the *cocaleros* were not able to gain registration for their "political instrument," they initially borrowed the registration of other left parties. At first, what is known today as "the MAS" took form as the Assembly for the Sovereignty of the People (ASP) – a movement organization of peasants and coca growers led by Quechua peasant leader Alejo Véliz (Burgoa and Condori

---

[8] Although the LPP helped redress the historical exclusion of indigenous peoples at the municipal level and particularly in rural districts, it did little to improve the *quality* of representation at the national level. Parties and the legislative branch were weakened by the late 1990s, illustrating some of the recurrent democratic deficits in Bolivia.

[9] Other indigenous parties include the Pachakuti Indigenous Movement (MIP), headed by Felipe Quispe, and the Revolutionary Liberation Movement Tupaq Katari (MRTKL), headed by Genaro Flores. These did not become as electorally successful as the MAS (Madrid 2012: 35–73).

2011: 20). ASP never ran for office; it took over the United Left (IU), which was by the mid-1990s a moribund left party, and ran their own candidates in the municipal elections of 1995 and the national elections of 1997. *Cocaleros* in Cochabamba provided an important flow of votes, helping the IU (with coca growers/peasant candidates) gain ten municipal governments in 1995 and four congressional seats to represent the Chapare region in 1997.[10] However, Alejo Véliz, who was both presidential and congressional candidate for the ASP formula, did not get elected to Congress. Following his defeat, he accused Morales of sponsoring the "crossed vote" in the Chapare, and thus the alliance between the two, as well as the ASP, dissolved.[11]

When Véliz and Morales split, Morales, who was by then a popular political figure and a congressman, rose to the fore of the *cocalero* movement in the heat of the cycles of contention around coca eradication (Sivak 2010). Morales had started as the Secretary of Sports for his local union in 1982 – the San Francisco Syndicate – but then worked his way up the union ladder and was elected as the Executive Secretary of the Federation of the Tropics in 1988 (Sivak 2010: 42). His leadership was distinctively bottom-up. *Cocalero* unionism, as Sivak (2010: 43) notes, was Morales' political school. It marked his "political origin, and for many years he understood politics as the sum of assemblies, negotiations with politicians and officials, and fights in the streets and roads."

Together with peasant leader Román Loayza, Morales formed yet another movement organization: Political Instrument for the Sovereignty of the Peoples (IPSP), which, just like the ASP, was based on the idea of "self-representation" of popular social actors. Unlike the ASP, however, IPSP became the actual electoral vehicle of the coca growers'/peasant movement (García Linera, León, and Monje 2004; Burgoa and Condori 2011: 40) and fielded candidates in municipal elections. For legal reasons, IPSP borrowed the legal registration of a dying party, the MAS-U, which was a left splinter of the Bolivian Socialist Falange party and a member of the IU (interviews with Alejandro Almaraz, Modesto Condori, Filemón Escóbar, Sergio Loayza, Isabel Ortega, and Juan de la Cruz Villca).[12] This would also allow IPSP to participate in national elections using the MAS's legal registration.

[10] Evo Morales, Román Loayza, Néstor Guzmán, and Félix Sánchez became uninominal deputies for the Chapare. Evo Morales received 70 percent of the vote in his district. As Madrid (2012: 48) notes, however, "outside of Cochabamba, the party fared poorly, winning only 1.2 percent of the total vote."

[11] The "crossed vote" consisted of voting Jaime Paz Zamora (the Revolutionary Left Movement [MIR] candidate) for the presidency, and voting Evo Morales (the ASP candidate) for a uninominal deputyship. According to several testimonies collected during my fieldwork, Morales sponsored the "crossed vote" to neutralize the leadership aspirations of Alejo Véliz within the peasant movement.

[12] David Añez Pedraza, who was the former president of the MAS, gave the registration to Evo Morales and the coca growers. This explains why in the party statute Mr. Pedraza is formally recognized as life and honorific president of the MAS (interviews with Juan de la Cruz Villca,

From the beginning, the MAS engaged in electoral politics, and its leaders conceived of it more as a "political instrument" of the social movements than as a traditional political party (Van Cott 2005: 103). Its first electoral experience as "the MAS" was in the municipal elections of 1999, in which it obtained 3.3 percent of the national vote, and it was in Cochabamba, specifically in the coca-growing Chapare, where it obtained the most votes (Rojas Ortuste 2000; Ballivián 2003). These early electoral results helped to consolidate the *cocaleros* in the Chapare as the leading faction of Bolivia's peasant movement, and they also consolidated the leadership of Morales in relation to other peasant leaders such as Felipe Quispe (Zuazo 2008: 29–30). Having established an anchor in the Chapare – and having decided to pursue an electoral path to be elected to the government at the national level – the challenge for the MAS was to nationalize its appeal by winning as many votes as possible.

The crisis of neoliberalism and the related decomposition of the party system played a key role in accelerating the electoral ascendance of the MAS and its organizational growth (Cyr 2017: 173). Market-oriented reforms were imposed in Bolivia by parties that had campaigned *against* neoliberal orthodoxy, giving rise to a sense of "bait-and-switch" that de-aligned the party system and eroded institutional channels for dissent (Roberts 2015a: 274). This opened up space on the left, which was initially filled by a neo-populist left party, Conscience of the Fatherland (CONDEPA) (Madrid 2010: 509–10). The traditional parties (Nationalist Revolutionary Movement [MNR], Revolutionary Left Movement [MIR], and Nationalist Democratic Action [ADN]), all of which supported neoliberal reforms, rotated in office until 2003; they traded offices among themselves while promoting orthodox neoliberal policies. Slater and Simmons (2013) rightly call this "promiscuous powersharing."

By the early 2000s, this system and its economic policies were in crisis as mass protests gained momentum thanks to a massive economic crisis (Silva 2009). As CONDEPA faltered, the MAS capitalized on the explosion of these protests by creating a "master frame" of opposition to neoliberalism and the traditional parties that took turns managing it. In the process, it developed into a national political party by articulating the claims for a remarkably diverse set of urban and rural movements.

Protests against water privatization (the "water wars") were the beginning (Simmons 2016); they helped extend the reach of the MAS to urban areas and expand its social base by denouncing the traditional parties and their policies and combining them with ethnic appeals (Madrid 2010: 600). The MAS used this crisis context to its advantage and adopted a "supraclass strategy" of

---

Modesto Condori, and Carlos Burgoa). The letter "U" (an homage to Óscar Únzaga de la Vega, a historic anti-communist leader of the MAS) was eliminated at a party congress in 2001, once Morales and the coca growers were in control of the party (Burgoa and Condori 2011: 70). That party congress also formalized the name of the party as MAS-IPSP. It will be referred to here simply as "the MAS," however.

electoral recruitment (à la Przeworski and Sprague 1986: 70).[13] Albro (2005a) described this period in terms of a "plural popular" strategy of coalition building – one in which indigenous issues became the framing plank for successful political articulation among groups as diverse as *cocaleros*, indigenous movements, peasant associations, urban labor unions, and neighborhood associations. Morales played a key role – mostly via charismatic appeals – uniting a remarkably diverse set of subordinate actors into a powerful coalition that converged around the MAS (Madrid 2012: 62). Clearly, these relationships were less organic than what the MAS had with *cocaleros*, yet in the process the party was able to become their "instrument" as well.

Expanding the base of electoral support, however, was anything but a straight line. Initially, the MAS sought to include left-leaning and nationalist intellectuals, as well as the urban indigenous and non-indigenous middle classes, for example, by naming first José A. Quiroga and then Antonio Peredo as vice presidential candidates in 2002 (interviews with Filemón Escóbar, Antonio Peredo, and José Antonio Quiroga; see Escóbar 2008).[14] But forging what Anria and Cyr (2017: 1256) call "extensive" linkages – that is, loose political ties based on an exchange of more particularistic goods – with individual figures was not the only component of its repertoire.

The MAS also expanded organizationally. While from the beginning it grew embedded within a rich tradition of participatory politics and grass-roots consultation that characterizes Bolivia's rural social movements (Crabtree 2013: 284), during its road to power it opened up even further. It did so, for example, by opening up party lists to local leaders who ran for electoral office under the MAS ticket at three levels of government (national, departmental, and local; see Harten 2011: 135). This allowed the MAS to "benefit from specific local dynamics" in the realm of candidate selection (Harten 2011: 131), helping to ensure massive turnout for the party's candidates. Such a strategy, in turn, led to the large-scale arrival of candidates nominated by popular sector organizations (Zegada and Komadina 2014: 57), and provided them with a mechanism of representation and bottom-up participation (or "voice") in internal decision-making. These newly incorporated groups included peasant unions, cooperative miners, transportation unions, and urban workers in Bolivia's large "informal" sector, among others.

---

[13] This vote-maximizing strategy entails turning to groups other than the core constituencies of a party in order to gain the support necessary for electoral majorities. Party leaders are generally willing to pursue this kind of strategy once they know they enjoy sufficient support among their core constituencies.

[14] Quiroga was invited to run as Morales's vice-presidential candidate but declined the offer, asserting personal reasons (interview with José Antonio Quiroga). Morales then selected Antonio Peredo, a renowned journalist and teacher associated with the Bolivian Communist Party (PCB), and Peredo accepted the candidacy (interview with Antonio Peredo).

This organizational strategy promoted the political support of these local organizations and created incentives to develop close ties between local elites and the party, as the latter became the common entity to articulate their interests at the subnational and national levels of political representation (Crabtree 2013: 285; Zuazo 2008: 36–41). It also helped to expand the size of the party's core constituency, increasing the number of potential veto actors, encouraging the emergence of opposition among allies, and making the possibility of internal power dispersion more likely. Although the MAS did not win the presidency in 2002, it finished second and accrued significant institutional positions in Congress that served as a power base for future elections.[15]

Mobilizations continued between 2003 and 2005. They shook the old order and led to the overthrow of Sánchez de Lozada first and then of Carlos Mesa (Silva 2009: 132–41). While the MAS did not initiate these protests, it used this continued upheaval to perform a classic representative and programmatic function of parties: it bundled issues together by finding common programmatic ground with a remarkably diverse set of rural and urban movements, which allowed the party to expand its following. As Webber (2010) argues, by adopting the discourse of the most mobilized groups during these popular struggles and incorporating their claims and demands, Morales and the MAS ultimately managed to shift the prevailing balance of social forces to their advantage, winning the 2005 presidential election. On this occasion, the electoral formula of Evo Morales and Álvaro García Linera was elected to the executive in a landslide victory (53.7 percent of those who voted).

To summarize, the MAS emerged organically from the bottom up, out of the autonomous mobilization of grass-roots social movements, and grew embedded within a rich tradition of participation and accountability that is common among Bolivia's rural movements. Although the MAS was born as a small, localized party that was seen as an "instrument" of a specific social group, it then experienced a vertiginous growth in a short period of time to become an instrument for a much broader set of subordinate actors. The MAS's ascent to power was fast – it took less than 10 years – and in the process the party expanded both territorially and organizationally and integrated new social actors as organizational pillars. It built strong ties with a wide array of grass-roots groups, for example, by opening up party lists for elective office at all levels

---

[15] Three days before the 2002 election, US ambassador Manuel Rocha warned Bolivians about the risks of voting for a candidate associated with coca-growing activities. Together with Morales's expulsion from Congress months earlier, Rocha's statement appears to have contributed to the increase of support for Morales. Inspired by Juan Peron's electoral campaign in 1945, who campaigned with the slogan "Braden or Perón" (Spruille Braden was then the US ambassador to Buenos Aires), campaign advisors of the MAS used Rocha's words to inflame feelings of nationalism and anti-Americanism, and this boosted the support for the MAS. Voters rejected the US intervention in domestic politics and in the campaign, and many who were likely to vote for Reyes Villa or Jaime Paz Zamora decided to vote for the MAS as a sign of protest to the US Embassy (interview with Marcelo Quezada).

of electoral competition. This created important channels for social movements and movement organizations to select their own candidates through the internal mechanisms of the party, and thus exert "voice" and influence over *who* would represent their interests in high electoral office. It enhanced their leverage in decision-making while boosting the party's grass-roots support base.

As the pages below demonstrate, however, the MAS did not always rely on the same kinds of bottom-up, participatory politics that led to its formation – and that, to some extent, characterize its organizational expansion.

THE MAS IN URBAN AREAS: LA PAZ AND EL ALTO

This section traces the extension of the MAS into a major urban setting: the metropolitan area of La Paz and El Alto. It shows that in urban segments, in response to electoral imperatives, the party built on top of older political parties' structures and preexisting civic networks and, in so doing, adapted many of these other parties' practices and modes of operation. This process, as it unfolded, changed the "face" of the MAS: it made the party reminiscent of a populist machine in urban areas.

The metropolitan area of La Paz and El Alto consists of more than 1.5 million people. La Paz is Bolivia's principal city and administrative capital, and, together with El Alto, it comprises the biggest urban area of Bolivia, making both cities decisive players in national politics (Arbona and Kohl 2004; Albó 2006).

These cities, which were crucial to the organization and success of the 2000–5 protests, are often seen as critical to winning national elections and to ensuring governability. Indeed, they achieved international prominence when their residents took to the streets and confronted the military forces that occupied those spaces. Urban residents were central to the various mobilizations that had rendered the country ungovernable for several years, and they became key actors in the resignations of Sánchez de Lozada in 2003 and Mesa in 2005. Yet, although the MAS achieved territorial penetration in these cities, it did not consolidate a party structure that incorporated the interests and leaderships of these urban populations.

The MAS's experience in these cities is relatively recent, and it has been influenced by the protest activities that took place in September and October 2000 in the Department of La Paz. In September 2000, the conflicts that began in Cochabamba with the Water War spread to the highlands of La Paz, as Felipe Quispe ("the Mallku"), Aymara peasant leader and later head of the Unique Confederation of Rural Laborers of Bolivia (CSUTCB), led a series of mobilizations against the government of General Hugo Banzer. Protesters demanded that the government fulfill a series of agreements it had concluded with peasant workers (Esposito and Arteaga 2006). Although Quispe later formed his own party, the MIP, and rejected association with the MAS (Van Cott 2005: 77), his mobilizations acted as a blow to the "traditional" political parties and facilitated the expansion of the MAS in the city. Disenchanted with the status quo, *paceños* and *alteños* welcomed the MAS as a viable alternative.

TABLE 2.1 *Population of La Paz and El Alto.*

	La Paz		El Alto	
	1992	2001	1992	2001
Population	715,900	793,292	405,492	649,958
Poverty	297,507 (41.55)	263,783 (33.25)	261,845 (64.57)	424,504 (65.31)
Extreme poverty	78,200 (10.92)	74,420 (9.38)	95,529 (23.55)	111,697 (17.18)
Self-identification with indigenous peoples				
Aymara		275,253 (49.81)		291,977 (74.25)
Quechua		55,384 (10.02)		25,025 (6.36)
Other		3,175 (0.57)		1,399 (0.36)
None		214,296 (38.78)		73,556 (18.71)

Figures in parentheses denote percentages.
Note: The 1992 census did not include a question asking whether people self-identified as indigenous. That is why those values are not included in this table.
Source: Instituto Nacional de Estadísticas (INE) (2001).

But La Paz and El Alto differ in important ways, and these differences have shaped the ways the MAS as a rural organization adapted to these urban settings. Specifically, they differ in terms of their ethnic and class composition. Besides being Bolivia's fastest-growing city (Arbona and Kohl 2004: 258), El Alto is an urban community made up overwhelmingly of recent Aymara immigrants (see Table 2.1). In contrast, the *cocaleros* of the Chapare tend to be Quechua and – to the extent that they are *colonos*, as many are – they tend to come from the mining communities of Oruro and Potosí.

Table 2.1 also reveals El Alto's strikingly high levels of poverty. By contrast, La Paz is more of a "middle-class" city, with a significantly larger proportion of the population that does not claim an "indigenous" identity. Still, according to the 2001 census, close to 50 percent of the population over 15 years of age self-identifies as Aymara, and 10 percent as Quechua. Such ethnic and class differences between the MAS's "core constituency" and its constituency in La Paz and El Alto have made it difficult for the MAS to adapt to these settings, but this is particularly true of El Alto, which is a highly politicized social space with a strong Aymara identity (Albó 2006).

Table 2.2 shows voting trends in both cities in the general elections since 1989, when the data for municipalities became more reliable. Specifically, it shows that a neo-populist party (Conscience of the Fatherland, or CONDEPA) dominated the electoral preferences of El Alto during the 1990s, capturing over 45 percent of the vote in the general elections of 1989, 1993, and 1997. While CONDEPA was also an important force in La Paz, this city remained more committed to "traditional" parties (ADN, MIR, and MNR) up until the 2002 election. Table 2.3 provides additional evidence that El Alto was heavily penetrated by CONDEPA during the 1990s, while residents of La Paz remained

TABLE 2.2 *Voting in La Paz and El Alto, general elections, 1989–2009 (percent).*

	La Paz						El Alto					
	1989	1993	1997	2002	2005	2009	1989	1993	1997	2002	2005	2009
CONDEPA	30.1	27.6	31.5				47.1	47.9	55.1			
ADN	27.5		25.8				15.8		14.8			
MNR	22.9		15.5	23.4			14.1		6.8	8.7		
MIR	12.5		10.5	10.8			16.3		11.2	12.7		
MNR-MRTKL		35.7						24.5				
AP		16.4						8.3				
UCS		9.2	10.8					9.8				
MBL		5.4							8.1			
NFR				28.5						21.3		
MIP				6.8						17.9		
LJ				6.3						6.9		
MAS				16.2	55.7	63.1				27.9	77.1	87.5
PODEMOS					28.5						13.9	
UN					10.1	14.7						
PPB-CN						18.6						6.1

Notes: Empty cells denote parties that either did not participate in the electoral contest or received less than 5 percent of the vote. Parties that placed candidates but received less than 5 percent of the vote in the respective electoral contest are not included in the table.
Source: Fundemos (1998)

TABLE 2.3 *Voting in La Paz and El Alto, municipal elections, 1989–2010 (percent).*

	La Paz							El Alto						
	1989	1991	1993	1995	1999	2004	2010	1989	1991	1993	1995	1999	2004	2010
MIR-ADN	37.2							11.2						
AP		23.9							20.8					
UCS	5.4	18.8	3.4	4.8	2.8			10.8	27.1	5.8	10.8	2.8		
MIR			4.2	3.3	16.2	6.4				4.6	21.0	45.6	3.7	
ADN			5.3	20.2	17.8					2.9	3.1	4.1		
MNR	13.3	23.2	40.0	15.2	16.7		1.5	8.5	9.3	12.8	7.1	6.6		
MBL		4.5	5.1	8.3	0.8		1.7		3.9	3.4	2.2	3.6		
CONDEPA	40.4	27.4	38.1	38.2	5.7			64.8	35.6	61.8	49.2	19.6		
IU	2.2			0.9				2.8	3.4					
MAS					0.9	19.9	34.9					2.1	17.1	38.8
MSM					22.5	45.9	48.5					4.0	2.7	24.4
ASP							2.4							2.6
UN						12.3	9.7						1.2	30.4
PP													52.6	

Notes: Empty cells denote parties that did not present candidates in the respective election. Parties that presented candidates but received less than 5 percent of the vote are not included in the table, as they are not relevant to the arguments in this chapter.

Source: Organo Plurinacional Electoral; Fundemos (1998).

more committed to "traditional" parties (though with a gradual shift toward the center-left Movement without Fear, MSM, starting in 1999). Against this backdrop, the MAS pursued two divergent strategies to expand organizationally in these cities: whereas in El Alto it sought to co-opt the leadership of major popular organizations by distributing patronage and resources, in La Paz it sought to boost its support among middle-class voters by pursuing an alliance with the already established MSM. This was key to moderating the image of the MAS among urban, middle-class voters (Madrid 2012: 59).

At first, residents of La Paz and El Alto resisted the MAS. Due to its origins in coca-growing regions, they associated the MAS with illicit activities, such as drug dealing, and they associated MAS operators with drug traffickers (interviews with Bertha Blanco, Elvira Parra, Martha Poma, and Roberto Rojas).[16] On the one hand, this aversion meant that the expansion of the MAS was possible only once CONDEPA started to lose influence in cities, which allowed the MAS to directly capitalize on the neo-populist inroads and symbolic and cultural strategies used by CONDEPA. On the other hand, this process was complicated by the presence of the MSM, which, particularly in La Paz, had been a dominant force since the late 1990s.[17] This pushed MAS leaders to negotiate a strategic alliance with this party. According to Román Loayza, this was detrimental to the MAS because it forced the MAS to allow MSM members to run as MAS candidates and to include some MSM figures in important positions within the public administration (interviews with Román Loayza; also with Manuel Mercado, Sebastián Michel, and Marcela Revollo).[18]

Founded in 1988, CONDEPA emerged at the end of the 1980s to represent sectors that were "affected by adjustment policies and unrepresented by the established parties" (Mayorga 2006: 154). This party was built around the charismatic leadership of Carlos Palenque, and its political and symbolic practices combined the extensive use of clientelism, paternalism, plebiscitary appeals to the masses, unmediated relationships with constituents, and a strong anti-establishment discourse (Alenda 2003; Revilla Herrero 2006; Madrid 2012: 47). Partly because CONDEPA failed to consolidate a party structure or forge organic linkages with its constituency, the party practically died along with its founder in 1997. This party's loss of political power created opportunities for the MAS, which would build on top of the networks inherited from older parties and replicate many of its practices in the cities.

In the municipal elections of 2004, which were affected by the contentious events of the Gas War, the MAS emerged as the most electorally successful

---

[16] Bertha Blanco was one of the people who brought the MAS to El Alto. A former member of the National Federation of Campesina Women of Bolivia-Bartolina Sisa, she was, at the time of the interview, estranged from the MAS.

[17] One of its founders, Juan del Granado, served as mayor of La Paz between 2000 and 2010.

[18] Loayza was one of the founding members of the MAS and is now a dissident, since he was accused of betrayal and expelled from the MAS in April 2009.

party, especially in the western part of the country.[19] As noted, while the MAS was neither a chief instigator nor a key protagonist of the protests (Lazar 2006), it used the context to develop into a national party, articulating the claims for a diverse set of subordinate actors. After Mesa's resignation (or fall) in June 2005, some urban forces attempted to configure a "broad front" as a mechanism to incorporate a coalition of progressive forces into the MAS, both in order to develop a comprehensive long-term program of government and as a collective effort to democratize the MAS. The attempts to configure a broad strategic front failed, as the MAS insisted on the "zero alliances" formula (interviews with Iván Iporre and José Antonio Quiroga). That MAS leaders refused to form alliances with political parties had much to do with the idea of avoiding any kind of association with, first of all, the "traditional" parties, which were seen as inefficient and corrupt, and, secondly, with the unpopular neoliberal policies these traditional parties had implemented.[20] The anti-alliance position was also seen as an attempt to protect the MAS's anti-establishment stance and guarantee the party's survival.[21] But some of these forces, particularly the center-left MSM, decided to accommodate the MAS and negotiated an alliance with heavy personalistic components. In particular, the MAS–MSM alliance was designed to guarantee important spaces of power for MSM candidates (interviews with Manuel Mercado, Sebastián Michel, and Marcela Revollo). Before the presentation of lists to the National Electoral Court, then, the MSM placed some of its candidates on MAS's lists. As some of the MSM candidates performed fairly well in the elections, this situation generated discontent in the *masista* rank and file, which saw that their possibilities of getting a job in the new government were reduced (on this point, see Do Alto 2006). It also caused tensions within the party's core constituency, particularly with respect to nominations for government positions and ministerial posts.[22]

The MAS, therefore, was not an organic product of these cities. Rather, it inserted itself into La Paz and El Alto as something foreign. As such, it faced

---

[19] It is worth noting, however, that even though the MAS won almost every municipal government in the country, it did not win the municipalities of La Paz and El Alto.

[20] Neopopulist parties such as Conscience of the Fatherland (CONDEPA) and Civic Solidarity Union (UCS) joined governments led by "traditional" parties in the 1990s and 2000s. Not only did this undermine these neopopulist parties' anti-establishment credentials, but it also contributed to their collapse.

[21] Individuals such as José Antonio Quiroga, René Joaquino, and Juán del Granado, among others, had attempted to articulate a similar front in 2002, without success. This previous proposal was rejected by peasant leaders on the grounds of wanting to avoid any kind of association with the "traditional" political parties (interview with José Antonio Quiroga).

[22] In interviews conducted in 2008, a common complaint by peasant leaders was that the grassroots organizations that had formed the MAS and that had made its rise to power possible had lost influence in the nomination of candidates for key positions within the government, particularly in relation to new members that joined during the campaign (interview with Román Loayza and Orlando "Tito" Guzmán).

obstacles as it sought to organize a party structure of its own on top of political configurations and existing social networks of older parties, even though parties like CONDEPA had already broken significant popular ground for the entrance of the MAS. Along with this organizing, the MAS incorporated militants and party operators from other parties, such as CONDEPA. These incorporations were accompanied by a transfer of top-down schemes of participation, as well as a set of co-optative practices that are now characteristic of the MAS in urban segments – practices that differ sharply from the more organic, participatory politics that led to the formation and early development of the party.

POPULAR MOVEMENTS, *DIRIGENTES*, AND THE PARTY

We have seen social movements – especially *cocaleros* – played a constitutive role in the formation of the MAS; they generated a political leadership, Evo Morales, and carried him to power. In the process, and in response to electoral imperatives, the party did not fully abandon the patterns of participatory politics that led to its formation, but it adopted hybrid features, particularly in urban segments. This section adds a layer of empirical density to that claim. To do so, it examines the relationships between the party "apparatus" in power, the leadership of the popular movements and organizations that support the MAS, and the rank and file. Specifically, I focus on one rural district (Villa Tunari) and two urban areas (La Paz/El Alto and Santa Cruz), which represent very distinctive patterns of interaction between those three components and help to capture the extent of the hybridity that characterizes the party today. The resulting image that emerges from the MAS is one in which social actors (and bottom-up politics) are very influential in rural segments, but party bureaucrats (and top-down politics) are more influential in the cities. Although the expansion of the MAS pushed the party into a top-down direction and posed challenges to the party's founding organizational characteristics, the "constant cause" of strong, autonomous civil society mobilization helped to largely reproduce the party's founding organizational characteristics even as expansion occurred.

Villa Tunari

As has been shown, the MAS emerged from a very specific, localized social constituency, the *cocaleros* in the Chapare region of the Department of Cochabamba. Together with the country's main peasant organizations, they still conceive of the MAS as *their* "political instrument" under their control, and they view the MAS government as *their* government. That the MAS was formed in the Chapare meant that it was infused with collective decision-making traditions found in the unions, which provide a framework for decision-making embedded in a "culture of delegation and accountability" (Crabtree 2013: 284). In that region of the country, moreover, the MAS as a party does not appear to have an independent role vis-à-vis the coca-growing unions, and indeed, the two can be seen as fused.[23] As some have argued – years after its founding – *cocaleros* still view the MAS more as an extension of the union than as a classic party (Grisaffi 2013: 49). The boundaries between the two are notoriously blurred.

The dynamics between the coca-growing unions, the MAS, and the municipal government can help to illustrate this point. In Villa Tunari, which is the largest municipality in the Chapare, candidates for local office running with the MAS ticket are almost always drawn from the coca-growing unions (on this, see Chapter 3), and the relationships between elected officials and union leaders (*dirigentes*) are close and constant. As the mayor of Villa Tunari, Feliciano Mamani, commented in an interview:

There is a kind of overlap between social organizations and municipal authorities. We are constantly talking, either in person or by phone, and when we have acts of inauguration, sports events, and meetings, for example, they [the *dirigentes*] are there first (Interview with Feliciano Mamani).[24]

The candidates are generally males and females with considerable leadership experience within the union structure (interviews with Emiliana Albarracín, Erasmo Espinoza, Ricardo Henríquez, Segundina Orellana, Julio Salazar Edgar Torres; also with Fernando Salazar, Eduardo Córdova Eguivar, and Jean-Paul Benavides). Once in office, elected officials are expected to execute decisions made by the unions (interviews with Omar Claros and Segundina Orellana), to "work together in the development of the municipal development plan" (interview with Asterio Romero), and to "participate actively in the 'organic life' (*la parte orgánica*) of the union" (interview with Feliciano Mamani). In Villa Tunari, the headquarters of the largest and most militant of the coca growers' unions, the Special Federation of Peasant Workers of the Tropics of Cochabamba (*Federación Especial de Trabajadores Campesinos del Trópico de Cochabamba,* FETCT), serves as a meeting place for *dirigentes,* affiliates, and elected officials. Union affiliates thus maintain close links with both their *dirigentes* and their elected officials,[25] and they have the power to hold these delegates accountable to the rank and file. This community-led control scheme, known locally as "social control," happens on a regular and face-to-face basis,

---

[23] Indicative of this, in Villa Tunari, the site of my fieldwork, there were no party offices for the MAS. As Grisaffi (2013: 56) notes, "there is a total overlap between membership of the union and membership of the MAS party." The hegemony of *cocaleros* in Villa Tunari creates exclusions, however. It marginalizes people who are not affiliated with the unions from the political process and limits their access to resources.

[24] I attended several meetings where municipal authorities and *dirigentes* shared the credit for the delivery of public works. Usually, the *dirigentes* have the last word in these events.

[25] The mayor of Villa Tunari was present in all of the meetings I attended at the FETCT, for example.

occasionally forcing *dirigentes* and elected officials to resign before the end of their term. The argument is that "if the unions nominate authorities and put them in positions of authority, the unions can also remove those authorities from power" (interview with Jean-Paul Benavides).[26]

As Grisaffi (2013: 57) notes, because the MAS emerged infused with these community-based forms of decision-making, it came as no surprise that "when Morales won the 2005 election, the coca growers imagined that the national government would function in a similar way to local government, in other words, the *cocaleros* thought of the government officials as nothing more than spokespeople for decisions forged at their [the *cocaleros's*] union meetings." But governing a country involves responding to wider domestic and international pressures, so it is unsurprising to find some mismatch between inauguration and actual practices.

Of all the grass-roots actors that brought Morales to power, he has maintained strongest links to the *cocaleros* in the Chapare. Indeed, he has continued to be the president of the Six Federations of the Tropics of Cochabamba, which is the overarching union of coca growers. He travels there frequently to participate in their *ampliados* and other types of meetings, which serve to reaffirm his leadership and to collect valuable information from the rank and file. In my observations during these meetings, he usually begins by telling *dirigentes* and the rank and file that he is there "to listen to them," to "inform them about things we are doing in the government," and "to ask you [affiliates] and your leaders to come up with proposals." However, when *dirigentes* talk in these forums, it is rather common to hear complaints about problems of coordination between the grass-roots and the party in government. A union leader of Chimoré told me in an interview: "never ever did we have the opportunity to tell authorities to their faces what our problems and demands are. I thank the president for that, for always coming here to talk to the rank and file. But the representatives and the ministers usually do not come."

These kinds of complaints capture some of the tensions that exist between the bottom-up politics and collective decision-making that characterize union politics, on the one hand, and the top-down logics associated with governing a country, on the other. Sometimes decisions coming from the top can create tensions among the rank and file, in particular when these average

---

[26] These relationships can be highly contentious. While mayors may not enjoy full autonomy vis-à-vis the social movement bases (Van Cott 2008: 184), over time they tend to develop their own interests, and they are also constrained by legal structures, which may not allow them to follow through on the demands set by the rank and file. The highest-level female authority within the union structure, Segundina Orellana, commented: "there are norms in the municipality that mayors have to follow, [and therefore] we cannot impose [these norms] 100 percent of the time" (interview with Segundina Orellana). Conflicts between *dirigentes* and the rank and file arise if the former are seen as "protecting" the mayor and not respecting the decisions forged in the unions. This usually leads to divisions within the unions.

citizens do not feel that their *dirigentes* are putting sufficient pressure on higher-level authorities or are not carrying out the decisions made in the unions. However, Morales still commands overwhelming authority among the rank and file in the Chapare, and both he and the MAS enjoy strikingly high levels of support in that region of the country. *Dirigentes* play a key role in shielding Morales from grass-roots criticism, which helps to strengthen his leadership. When unpopular policies that affect the rank and file come from the top, for example, *dirigentes* usually blame ministers and representatives for what are seen as mistakes made by the government but induced by Morales's alleged disloyal aides.[27] Examples of these policies include the *gasolinazo* of 2010 (on this point, see Chapter 4) and, paradoxically, Morales's coca policy, which is seen by the base as a step in the right direction, but also as an imposition from the top (Grisaffi 2013: 60).[28] In both cases, the *dirigentes* could not generate full compliance with the policies and encountered popular resistance.

Despite these tensions, the MAS maintains strong organic links to its core constituency. While the *dirigentes* generally align with Morales and "protect" his government and his leadership, they do not command full control over the rank and file, and thus cannot always generate compliance of their base with governmental policies. As such, there is neither government co-optation of its core constituency nor full grass-roots autonomy, but rather permanent interactions and degrees of cooperation between the two. There are also strong pressures from below to keep the leadership accountable to the rank and file, a pattern that is closely associated with the movement origins of the MAS and with the legacies of social mobilization that forged the organization at its inception. These links and interactions are different in other areas of the country, however, which the MAS penetrated in later stages of its organizational development by using different strategies. The examples below illustrate two distinctive alternative patterns.

[27] When asked about the increment of fuel prices in 2010 (an event known as the *gasolinazo*; Chapter 4), Segundina Orellana commented: "the ministers made a mistake, they fooled the president" (interview with Segundina Orellana). Usually, the assumption is that ministers, especially those who do not come from the ranks of a trusted social organization, are not fully committed to the MAS's project and are instead driven by personal motivations.

[28] The policy eliminates forced eradication of coca crops but sets a restriction (1 *cato*, or 1,600 sq. meters) on the amount of coca that farmers can legally grow. It also replaces the old regime of police and military repression for a community-led form of "social control" (Farthing and Kohl 2010: 205). Although the policy was designed with the participation and input of the unions, many coca farmers believe that the ceiling of permitted coca growth was arrived at arbitrarily, and they complain that it is too low and does not allow them to guarantee their survival. In the meetings I observed, where the issue of coca production is a major topic of discussion, Morales also recurrently complained that, "there are several of you [union affiliates] that do not want to comply with the 1-*cato* ceiling."

La Paz and El Alto

As was noted in the previous section, penetrating the cities of La Paz and El Alto was crucial to the MAS's ability to win electoral majorities and become a national-level actor. There, the MAS came in as an outsider party and expanded in two ways: first, by building a territorial party infrastructure on top of preexisting networks from older parties, and second, by configuring a network of alliances with urban-popular organizations (see Anria 2009; also Anria 2013: 33–5). Although the MAS had been inching along with the latter path to expansion since 2002, alliances did not materialize until the 2005 general election campaign. Organizations representing groups as diverse as artisans, microenterprises, pensioners, transportation, street vendors, miners working for cooperatives, and other forms of community organization, such as neighborhood associations, perceived the alliance with the MAS as an opportunity to achieve parliamentary representation, occupy important positions in the government, and gain access to government jobs for their affiliates. For the MAS's part, by forging links to groups with great mobilizational capacity, the party dramatically expanded its support base and thereby its influence. Given that some of these organizations had been key protagonists in the protests that forced the resignation of two consecutive presidents, forging alliances with them was also seen as a way to ensure some degree of governability.

As anthropologist Sian Lazar (2008: 52–5) notes, El Alto is a highly mobilized and self-organized political space. The main civic organizations at the city level are the Federation of Neighborhood Boards (FEJUVE-El Alto) and the Regional Labor Federation (COR-El Alto).[29] These organizations are critical for ensuring governability in the city and gaining electoral majorities at the national level (García Linera, León, and Monje 2004; also Alenda 2003). As a result, party operators have historically attempted to infiltrate these organizations and control their leadership, and the MAS is no exception. Indeed, operators believe that infiltrating the leadership levels of these militant organizations allows the MAS to extend its influence and control throughout the territory and to recruit leaders who mobilize large numbers of voters.

While, in accordance with their statutes, these organizations do not have formal ties to political parties, the MAS has configured an umbrella of informal alliances with key *dirigentes* through which it has sought to insert itself into the cities to build a political base and acquire political influence. Trying to win over these organizations, *masista* operators have frequently used top-down co-optive

---

[29] The FEJUVE is a coordinator of residents, as well as neighborhood councils and associations, in El Alto. The COR is an umbrella organization of workers, which includes factory workers, teachers, journalists, and artisans but is dominated by street traders. A third organization, the Federation of Street Traders ("the Federation"), coordinates associations of street traders. Taken together, the three organizations possess an impressive mobilizational strength in the city.

practices (interview with Abel Mamani). These have consisted, for example, of offering positions in the government in exchange for organizational loyalty (or what in Bolivian parlance is known as *pegas*), providing services or infrastructure to particular organizations, and infiltrating the ranks of organizations to directly control their leadership. From the beginning, this approach was not aimed at building organic ties with these organizations. Bertha Blanco, one of the leaders who brought the MAS into El Alto, noted, "When we were constructing the MAS, we needed to find candidates [to run for office]. We didn't have candidates in the city, and nobody wanted to be associated with the MAS. And what did we do? We went to find persons within the organizations, for example in the COR. And there we talked directly with the *dirigentes* " (interview with Bertha Blanco).

What began as a search for candidates quickly turned into a penetration strategy aimed at eroding the autonomy of social organizations from the top, a pattern that became particularly clear after the MAS gained governmental power. As a *masista* representative for a "uninominal" district in El Alto commented in an interview: "We can't deny we do that. We aim for our people to become leaders in these organizations. It is an effort to control the social organizations from the top" (interview with Miguel Machaca). A *masista* delegate to the constituent assembly concurred:

The project we have had as MAS is to be able to take control over the social organizations. In order to do that, you need to start from working at the district level and from there you can start climbing. For FEJUVE's next congress, for example, we have the wish that we're going to take on FEJUVE's leadership [. . .] At least, that's what I can tell you that we'd like to happen (Interview with Elvira Parra).

These testimonies provide evidence for a deliberate plan to win over previously existing popular organizations at the regional level by penetrating their social networks and seeking to control them. But it should be noted that this is not something new in Bolivia. Rather, it reflects a general pattern of how different collective political interests have long contended for control of "umbrella" organizations in Bolivia, as the history of the Bolivian Workers' Central (COB) and the CSUTCB demonstrate (García Linera, León, and Monje 2004). In short, the MAS has not innovated much in terms of its practices for controlling base and umbrella organizations.

This strategy, however, creates a situation in which *dirigentes* of popular organizations perceive these entities simply as "a trampoline for launching oneself into a public administration position" (interview with Gerardo Morales). Becoming a *dirigente* is therefore a rather attractive role, for it is a path to getting a government job. The case of FEJUVE in El Alto provides a good example. Abel Mamani, the highest authority of this organization since 2004, was appointed as the water minister for the Morales government in 2006. His appointment translated into the direct presence of a FEJUVE representative in a high-level government position and into government jobs for some of its affiliates. On the one hand, this entailed growing capacities for the organization to negotiate corporativist demands from within the state. On the other hand, its presence in the government eroded its autonomy and created strong divisions within the organization (interview with Abel Mamani). As a high-level *dirigente* of FEJUVE commented in an interview:

We have lost considerable capacity for mobilization. Why? Because *dirigentes* have occupied ministries and other public offices [. . .] they have received quotas of power. But the people can see what their real interests are and thus it is difficult to strengthen the organization (Interview with Luis Huanca).

Much of this had to do with the mode of nomination used by Morales to form his cabinet. Mamani, for example, was appointed directly by Morales, and he accepted the nomination without having the chance to consult the rank and file, which alienated the lower-level members from the leadership (interviews with Abel Mamani, Néstor Guillén, and Fanny Nina).

In the case of the COR-El Alto, the linkage with the MAS is subtler and less direct. This organization has supported the government and the process of social transformation sponsored by the MAS. Unlike FEJUVE, the COR has never been represented directly in the government apparatus; in other words, the COR has not physically occupied spaces of power under the Morales government. But party operators and government officials have sought to infiltrate this organization, and they have established negotiations directly with the leadership, creating tensions between *dirigentes* and the rank and file. As Edgar Patana, the former COR executive in El Alto and El Alto's current mayor, commented in an interview:

Former executives of COR have always had rapprochements with political parties. Since 2002 they have been courting the MAS so that they could negotiate spaces of power, such as a candidacy for deputyship or something else. But we have never been 'organic' members of the MAS (Interview with Edgar Patana).

To summarize, the MAS became a national-level force only to the extent that it played an articulatory role among the experiences, demands, and internal structures of various base and "umbrella" organizations in urban settings. As noted above, part of this expansion was based on the ability of the MAS to aggregate interests and articulate the claims for a remarkably diverse set of urban and rural movements – performing the classic representative and programmatic functions of political parties. At the same time, the strategies for linking those urban movements and organizations and the MAS were also based on the negotiation of spaces of power and influence within the government. The MAS came to these cities as an outsider party and tried to win over existing community organizations. By co-opting their leadership into government positions, a strategy facilitated by having access to state resources and patronage, the MAS attempted to control these organizations from above and in so doing threatened their autonomy and independence. Whereas the rural dynamic that shaped the emergence of the MAS was one of bottom-up mobilization and active participation – a pattern that, as seen with the example of Villa Tunari, still characterizes the relationships between the MAS and its core constituency – the strategy for linking to its peripheral constituencies in urban areas is more top-down. Nevertheless, many of these organizations are the bearers of the legacies of social mobilization that brought down two successive governments, and they have not lost their capacity for autonomous collective action; even if *dirigentes* support the government or are co-opted by it, they cannot always secure that their base will be compliant with the government's policies.

Santa Cruz

Yet another pattern worthy of some elaboration here is found in Santa Cruz, which used to be a bastion of right-wing opposition to the MAS, particularly during Morales's first term in office (2006–9). In that department, the MAS has grown electorally from rural districts – particularly from areas recipient of collective peasant migration – to urban areas. In rural areas, the MAS has grown by forging links with peasant organizations and the lowlands' indigenous movement, which is organized around the *Bloque Oriente* (Eastern Block). The MAS has also built bonds on the basis of programmatic representation, particularly around the issue of land redistribution (interviews with Justa Cabrera, Lidia Choque, Hugo Salvatierra, and Lázaro Tacóo).[30] NGOs such as Legal Advisory Branch of the Workers' Union in Santa Cruz (ALAS), Center for Juridical, Institutional, and Social Studies (CEJIS), and Center for Research and Promotion of the Peasantry (CIPCA) played a central role in bringing together peasant and indigenous organizations, providing spaces for articulation, and providing legal advice and basic infrastructure (i.e., personnel, offices, suggestions for candidates, etc.) for the party "in times when nobody wanted to be associated in the MAS in Santa Cruz" (interview with Alejandro Almaraz; also with Lidia Choque and Hugo Salvatierra).[31] The MAS has faced the strongest resistance in districts where peasant or indigenous organizations are not well organized and where the political right is established and in control of well-functioning clientelistic networks (interview with Lidia Choque).

In the city of Santa Cruz, the MAS has grown in two directions: by pursuing alliances with powerful social actors with great mobilizational capacity, such as

---

[30] *Bloque Oriente* was an alliance of peasant and indigenous organizations with a presence in the departments of Santa Cruz, Tarija, Beni, and Pando. Many of my interviewees described it to me as a regional version of the Unity Pact. *Bloque Oriente* developed proposals for the Constituent Assembly, particularly focusing on common demands and proposals related to land.

[31] ALAS is an NGO directed by former minister of rural development, Hugo Salvatierra. CIPCA is the Center for Research and Promotion of the Peasantry, and it is an NGO supported by the Catholic Church. CEJIS is the Center for Juridical, Institutional, and Social Studies.

cooperatives, health care workers, transportation, street vendors, neighborhood associations, and school boards; and by configuring a strong territorial
party infrastructure around districts, which overlaps with the administrative
division of the city (interviews with Tito Sanjinez and Rodolfo Zeballos).
Although the first strategy has relied on practices reminiscent of those found
in El Alto, the novelty in Santa Cruz lies in the organizational strength of the
territorial infrastructure, which was built on top of existing networks of older
parties, such as the Nationalist Revolutionary Movement (MNR) and Civic
Solidarity Union (UCS).[32]

Santa Cruz is the only city that has an urban directorate.[33] This structure is
stable, in the sense that it operates not only during electoral cycles but also
between elections, and it operates with autonomy from both the peasant
organizations that control the departmental directorate (interviews with Lidia
Choque, José Quiroz, Tito Sanjinez, and Hugo Salvatierra) and the party
"apparatus" in power (interviews with Gabriela Montaño and Álvaro García
Linera). Although this territorial party structure yields considerable influence in
the nomination of candidates for local and national elective office, the party's
top leadership often bypasses it, thereby causing friction among the rank and
file and creating internal divisions. In the municipal election of 2010, for
example, Evo Morales formed an alliance with a right-wing party in Santa
Cruz, the Popular and Solidarity Alliance (ASIP), which guaranteed the nomination of one of ASIP's leaders as the mayoral candidate (interviews with
Gabriela Montaño, Hugo Salvatierra, Freddy Soruco, and Hugo Siles). This is
indicative of the limits on the territorial party structure's ability to generate
decisions autonomously and counteract the tendencies toward top-down control. As Tito Sanjinez, the Vice President of the urban directorate in Santa Cruz,
commented in an interview: "this agreement created discontent among the rank
and file, as it was seen as coming from the top" (interview with Tito Sanjinez).
While the MAS's top leadership praises the urban structure for its remarkable
mobilizational capacity (interview with Álvaro García Linera), it does not grant
full autonomy to this structure. At the same time, the leadership of the urban
structure recognizes the leadership of the peasant organizations, but maintains
tense and competitive relationships with it.

THE MAS IN POWER

I have so far examined the origins and evolution of the MAS, and shown that
between its founding and ascent to power the party experienced important

---

[32] Civic Solidarity Union (*Unión Cívica Solidaridad*, UCS) was a neopopulist political party
    founded by Max Fernández in the 1990s. It made significant electoral inroads and mobilized
    the urban poor in the peripheral areas of Bolivia's largest cities, including La Paz, El Alto, and
    Santa Cruz.
[33] Urban directorates are not recognized in the party's statute.

internal transformations. While the process leading to its formation responded to a distinctively bottom-up logic of mobilization, the party developed hybrid characteristics in response to electoral imperatives, especially as it penetrated urban areas. This section shows that although the party's expansion and exercise of power pushed the MAS in the direction of power concentration and led to a loss of its participatory *élan* (or challenges to its "genetic imprint," to put it in Panebianco's [1988] term), organizational patterns defined early on and autonomous social mobilization largely continued to influence party-movement relations and governing patterns after the MAS took power in January 2006.

Some observers have argued that the MAS has become increasingly detached from popular organizations as a governing party, and that it has, in fact, undergone a process of strong "personalization of power" since the 2000s (Madrid 2011: 241–2), a process that intensified since 2014, when the MAS declared Morales indispensable and decided to avoid cultivating a new leader for the party (Molina 2018). Other scholars have looked at the social composition and evolution of Morales's cabinet of ministers. While it is true that his first cabinet included a mix of leaders of rural and urban grass-roots organizations, some of whom came from popular or "plebeian" origins and had little or no previous experience in government,[34] the presence of these people in key positions of the cabinet has tended to decrease over time.[35] The participation of representatives drawn from popular organizations in top-level positions within the executive branch has been limited and isolated. With some exceptions, key positions have been occupied by a technocratic elite that is "invited" into the ranks of the party, that does not come from the ranks of grass-roots organizations, and that consequently has few checks from below. An example of this is Bolivia's minister of economy, Luis Arce Catacora, who was in office between 2006 and 2017. Of course, the appointment of these individuals is related to the need for expertise in certain technical ministries, and the lack of cadres from within the ranks of allied popular organizations with that expertise.[36]

Yet other scholars have examined the social composition of the Congress, revealing that despite the gradual concentration of power in the executive, the greater inclusiveness of Bolivian politics is real (Anria 2016; Silva 2017; Wolff 2018). A large number of representatives drawn from popular organizations can be found in this law-making body (Zuazo 2008: 36–41; Vergara 2011: 84;

---

[34] This observation led Bolivia's Vice-President to characterize the Morales government as a "government of the social movements" (García Linera 2009: 90) and to argue that, through the MAS, social movements are in control of the state (García Linera 2006). Empirical assessments of those claims can be found in Stefanoni and Do Alto (2006); Crabtree (2013); Soruco, Franco, and Durán Azurduy (2014); and Espinoza Molina (2015).

[35] See, for instance, Zegada, Torrez, and Camara (2008); Laruta (2008); Do Alto (2011); and Espinoza Molina (2015).

[36] This point is also developed in Wolff (2016).

TABLE 2.4 *Representatives' occupations (%) prior to being elected to Congress.*

	1993–7	1997–2002	2002–6	2006–10	2010–14
Public administration	14.2	16.3	21.9	16.5	18.6
Middle-class professions	48.7	37.8	28.1	25.0	17.7
Politician	4.3	4.1	7.6	7.3	11.1
Workers, artisans, and primary sector	3.9	11.2	11.2	18.6	26.3
Transportation	–	2.0	1.2	4.2	5.2
Business and private sector	24.0	26.5	27.3	27.4	19.0
Retirees, students, other	7.7	2.0	2.8	1.0	2.1
Sample size	74	98	80	96	97

Source: Zegada and Komadina (2014: 57).

Crabtree 2013: 285; Zegada and Komadina 2014). Table 2.4 illustrates this change. While the percentage of middle-class professionals has decreased from 48.7 percent in the 1993–7 legislative period to 17.7 percent in 2010–14, the percentage of peasants, artisans, and workers – groups linked with the MAS – has grown from 3.9 percent to 26.3 percent in the same period.

As I demonstrate in Chapter 3, part of this can be explained by the methods that the MAS uses to select candidates. Even after the party assumed power, the party's grass-roots social bases have retained significant influence over the selection of party candidates for elective office – a pattern that empowered groups that were traditionally subordinate and underrepresented. This is an area in which, as Dunkerley (2007: 166) notes, the "character of the leadership-mass relation is distinctly bottom-up."[37] This, in turn, led to the political incorporation of large segments of the population that were previously on the margins of social and political life. As a result, the social and demographic profile of elective representatives has changed dramatically, and now features more peasants, as well as indigenous people and members of urban-popular groups, with expanded influence of those groups on policy-making (Chapter 4). Seen from the long arc of Bolivian history, this was an exceptional change in a society characterized by deep ethnic divisions and exclusion.

Since Morales assumed office, he has tried to maintain participatory linkages between his leadership, the MAS, and the organized support base in the crafting of public policies (Roberts 2007a). To differentiate his government from those of Bolivia's "traditional" parties (and also to stay true to the party's social movement origins) Morales endorsed the principle of "ruling

[37] That elected representatives overwhelmingly come from organized popular groups does not mean automatically that these organizations have a strong influence on setting the legislative agenda (I elaborate on this in Chapter 4). Some scholars have pointed out that under the Morales government, representatives have had a "subordinate standing" in relation to the executive (Crabtree 2013: 287; also Fornillo 2008: 3).

by obeying." For Schiwy (2008: 9), this "means that if the organizations and movements that brought Morales to power find him failing to pursue their decisions, they are likely to force the president to step down." It also refers to being responsible for positive actions and maybe responsive to the will of its social bases while planning those actions. When Morales assumed office, for example, he addressed the demands set forth by the anti-neoliberal mass mobilizations of the early 2000s, which had, de facto, set the government's policy agenda.[38] Therefore, upon taking office, he increased royalties on extractive industries, proclaimed a New Agrarian Reform Law, and called for a constituent assembly through which popularly elected delegates would rewrite the country's constitution. These initial actions can be seen as examples of Morales's positive accountability to the popular movements and organizations that propelled him to power; that is, as attempts to fulfill his campaign promises. At the same time, they can be seen as efforts to consolidate Morales's leadership and to ensure governability during difficult political times, particularly when confronting elite-based opposition at the subnational level (Eaton 2007).[39]

Even since before the MAS took national power, there have been several attempts to establish mechanisms to channel the bottom-up power of social movements and remain true to the party's origins. In 2004, for example, the peasant organizations that constitute the MAS's core formed an alliance with large indigenous movements in the eastern lowlands, like the Confederation of Bolivian Indigenous Peoples (CIDOB), and in the Andean highlands, like the National Council of Ayllus and Marcas of Qullasuyu (CONAMAQ), and called it the Unity Pact. The Unity Pact operated independently from the MAS, although it had *dirigentes* involved with the MAS, and it served as a channel of regularized consultation with the social movement bases. The Unity Pact also organized mass mobilizations demanding the convocation of the constituent assembly after the MAS took power. And after years of deliberations full of tensions, it even produced a complete draft of a constitutional text and presented it to the constituent assembly (Garcés 2010, 2011: 57). Above all, it provided advisory consultation; its proposal for a "plurinational" state was debated and eventually shaped many of the features of the draft of Bolivia's new constitution. Since the new constitution was approved in 2009, however, the Unity Pact has not been visible or actively participatory in

---

[38] This was known as the "October Agenda." It was not a clear party program designed by the MAS, but more of a list of aspirations that emerged from the insurrection of El Alto in October 2003, which the MAS used for its campaign. The agenda included a wide array of popular demands to re-found Bolivia in the name of the poor and the indigenous majority. Among the key demands included in the agenda were the nationalization of hydrocarbons, an agrarian reform, and the call for a constituent assembly.

[39] During Morales's first term (2006–9), the political opposition controlled the Senate and was not willing to compromise. This period was highly contentious, and it reflected the regional dispute between the west and the east.

decision-making processes, as splinters of CIDOB and CONAMAQ have taken a critical stance against the government and peasant organizations have consolidated their hegemony within the alliance (interviews with Xavier Albó, Fernando Garcés, Walter Limache, Juan Carlos Pinto, and Raúl Prada). The MAS government promoted other channels of consultation beyond the constituent assembly process, such as the National Coordinator for Change (CONALCAM). However, there has been strong resistance to institutionalization by the party's movement base, in part because movement leaders think that institutionalization would be viewed as co-optative, with the MAS operating more like a conventional political party – one with formal and hierarchical structures.

To the extent that these structures do not take hold, the interactions between the party in power and allied groups in civil society remain fluid – even 12 years after taking power. The absence of strong party structures or effective state bureaucracies as "transmission belts" has indeed contributed to the concentration of power in the hands of the president, who plays the role of an arbiter, often at the expense of Congress, as well as the courts and non-partisan oversight agencies (Anria et al. 2010: 254–60; Madrid 2012: 163; Crabtree 2013: 287; also Anria 2016). This tendency was further aggravated by the 2009 Constitution, which, as I elaborate further below, strengthened executive power – and the trend intensified in 2014, when the MAS declared Morales "indispensable" and decided to avoid cultivating a new leader for the party. In addition, as we have already seen, having continued access to state resources encouraged the use of co-optative strategies vis-à-vis civil society groups, which at times compromised the autonomy of the party's grass-roots social bases.

However, this is neither to say that Morales's power is absolute, nor that he or his government can fully control social mobilization. There are strong limits to his authority and top-down command, in part because strong and well-organized groups in civil society have retained an ongoing capacity for autonomous collective action that allowed them to pursue their agendas with very few bureaucratic constraints and shape party action despite the government's attempts to control them (I elaborate on this in Chapter 4). In the absence of strong institutional controls and opposition parties, autonomous social mobilization by popular constituencies has been the strongest check on executive power. It erupted in 2010, forcing Morales to reverse his decree ending gasoline subsidies, and again in 2011 when the government had to drop its plan to build a highway through an autonomous indigenous territory – the Isiboro Sécure National Park and Indigenous Territory (TIPNIS).[40] In these two instances, and

---

[40] This is where the "bundling" that was crucial for the MAS expansion nationally began to break down, and interest aggregation became more complicated once the MAS took power. The MAS proceeded with a form of state-led developmentalism that alienated some of the indigenous groups that had come together behind the MAS when the party was in opposition.

in several others, an aroused society contributed to holding the government accountable to its social bases and countervailed against Morales's tendencies to dominate the political process.

It bears noting that such checks on executive power are imposed by grassroots social movements and popular organizations in Morales's own political camp. It also bears noting that, aside from those "social vetoes," Morales has had to yield to pressures from opponents from the right, particularly during his first term, and more specifically in the period of high regional polarization between west and east that took place between the convention of the constituent assembly and the approval of the new constitution (Stoyan 2014). The outcome of the constituent assembly was a text approved by pro-government delegates only (Lehoucq 2008: 110–11). The text needed to be submitted to the verdict of the citizens, which required that the Congress sanction a law specifying the schedule and other details for the constitutional referendum. As the MAS controlled the Chamber of Deputies but not the Senate, this bill was blocked in Congress until the events that followed the recall referendum of August 2008 shook the political arena. While Morales emerged victorious in that referendum, opposition governors (then known as "prefects") were ratified with large majorities in the Media Luna. These intensified their demands for autonomy. In September 2008, after a series of armed confrontations among autonomists and MAS supporters in Pando and Santa Cruz left several dead, the government and opposition politicians engaged in deliberations in Congress, where the text of the constitutional draft was negotiated and modified heavily with input from the opposition and with compromises on both sides (Romero, Bohrt Irahola, and Peñaranda 2009). The constitution was then ratified via popular referendum in January 2009, and in elections held in December 2009, Morales was reelected by 64 percent of the vote. The MAS also won over two-thirds of the seats in the Plurinational Legislative Assembly (as Congress was renamed in the new constitution) and maintained two-thirds majorities since then.

The 2009 Constitution condenses the tensions that mark Bolivian politics under the MAS: The document reinforces executive power and, at the same time, prioritizes the construction of a more inclusive state. It leaves vast discretionary authority in the hands of the president – and in this sense it has not altered the "engine room" of the constitution (Gargarella 2013) – but it also extends the effective rights of citizenship to those with no status and power, for instance by embracing their representation and boosting public input in political decision-making. As a step in this direction, the new constitution renames Bolivia the "Plurinational State of Bolivia," in recognition of its diverse character. It also admits different forms of democracy (representative, direct and participatory, and communitarian) that should, in principle, complement one another and supplement the electoral regime (Exeni Rodriguez 2012). For example, it establishes new processes to institutionalize participation and self-government, such as the institutions of prior consultation and indigenous autonomies.[41] Some of these mechanisms, including the recall vote, were used by Morales in 2008 to reaffirm the legitimacy of his administration – and to eventually reduce the number of opposition governors. Others, however, have been used successfully by grass-roots social movements, or even by indigenous communities, to gain greater control over their land and their resources.

Although institutional checks and balances remain weak, then, the greater inclusiveness of Bolivian politics is real. Inclusion created a "new normal" in the Bolivian political arena, where larger numbers of Bolivians enjoy effective rights of citizenship and greater input into political and economic decision-making – a point also made by Silva (2017) and Wolff (2018). Previously subordinate groups enjoy increased access to the state and are included not just as voters but also as makers of policy, as I discuss in Chapter 4 and in the Conclusions.

CONCLUSIONS

This chapter traced the origins and development of the MAS. It highlighted how truly organic the party and the leadership was in its founding. The chapter also showed that the MAS was born as a small, localized party that was an "instrument" of a very specific social group, the *cocaleros* in the Chapare, but yet it experienced a vertiginous growth in a very short period of time to become the electoral vehicle for a broad set of urban and rural social movements – and then a governing party. This process turned the party into a hybrid fusion of movement and party networks, and, as a result, the MAS today looks and operates differently in different rural and urban segments. Whereas the MAS's origins reflect a clear pattern of bottom-up mobilization and organic linkages to its core constituency, its dramatic territorial and organizational expansion fostered the emergence of top-down mobilization tactics and co-optative practices vis-à-vis the leadership of organizations in its peripheral constituency, particularly in the urban areas.

While this period of growth posed important challenges to the party's founding, bottom-up organizational characteristics, the party's grass-roots social bases found ways to replicate those initial characteristics as expansion occurred. Social movements and other grass-roots organizations in Bolivia retained significant degrees of autonomy from Morales and the MAS and continued to influence, constrain, and hold the leadership accountable as expansion unfolded – and even after the party took power. This is what makes the case such an anomaly, as discussed in the Introduction and Chapter 1. As this chapter demonstrated, the "constant cause" of strong, autonomous civil

---

[41] Both were introduced in response to demands that predated the Constituent Assembly, as attempts to deepen the participation of indigenous peoples in collective decision-making. Their implementation has yielded mixed results (Tockman and Cameron 2014; Falleti and Riofrancos 2018).

society mobilization helped to reproduce the party's founding characteristics over time (its "genetic imprint," to use Panebianco's parlance), rather than allowing the party to evolve toward professionalization.

The MAS developed from early on channels of consultation through which sponsoring and allied groups could influence internal decision-making in important areas such as candidate selection, programmatic development, and party electoral strategy. The MAS's weak bureaucratic development provided opportunities for the party's grass-roots social bases to act autonomously, with few bureaucratic constraints, facilitating the emergence of social accountability structures that would check power from within and keep open channels for agenda setting from below. These structures, in turn, created a "weak" form of path dependency resistant to change; they were consolidated and reproduced during the party's road to power through strong, autonomous civil society mobilization, and they influenced governing patterns after the MAS took office.

For example, early success through social mobilization in opposing neoliberal reforms made party and movement leaders more likely to continue using mobilization tactics as the party sought power – and movement leaders would later on use these tactics even against the party leadership in power. That some of the sponsoring and allied movements contributed to the overthrow of unpopular governments and propelled the MAS to power also meant that social movements and popular organizations remained vibrant and were able to maintain a remarkable capacity for autonomous collective action. Even if movement leaders supported the government, or were co-opted by it with government jobs or easier access to the state, they could not always guarantee the compliance of their bases with the government's policies. Mobilized pressure from below, as seen in the examples of the *gasolinazo* and the TIPNIS, forced the party leadership to negotiate and reach compromises with sponsoring and allied movements, contributing to keeping the party responsive to (at least parts of) its grass-roots bases and to attenuate the Michelsian tendencies toward top-down control.

As this chapter discussed, finally, Bolivia under the MAS experienced a critical shift in domestic power relations that empowered traditionally excluded groups. Groups linked to the MAS, especially rural indigenous and peasant movements that were on the margins of social and political life, have gained a greater say over who represents them in high electoral office (as will be discussed in Chapter 3) as well as expanded influence over economic and political decision-making (as will be discussed in Chapter 4). As a result, groups that were previously subordinate now have a greater say on determining who gets what, when, and how.

3

Candidate Selection Patterns

While the previous chapter examined the origins and development of the MAS and showed how movements found ways to largely reproduce early organizational attributes as the party's expansion occurred, this chapter looks closely at the internal politics of the MAS. Specifically, the chapter examines the degree of power concentration in the MAS in the realm of candidate selection. It looks at the extent to which sponsoring and allied movements have been able to retain control over the selection of party candidates for elective office, even though, as studies in the Michelsian tradition would have predicted, party leaders have sought to concentrate power in their own hands. Using original data collected through fieldwork in different regions of Bolivia, I identify the key conditions of societal and political structures where greater grass-roots control is most likely and the conditions where the trend toward top-down control does not hold.

As the chapter shows, national-level factors, such as formal electoral rules, do not explain well subnational variation in the degree of top-down control. At best, those rules create different opportunities and incentives for the party's grass-roots social bases to shape the process. Key to understanding variation in terms of degrees of grass-roots control over candidate selection is the strength and autonomy of civil society. But the effects of these civil society characteristics are mediated by the nature of party–society alignments (Figure 3.1).[1]

Regardless of the electoral rules and district size, top-down decision-making by the party leadership is less likely to take place in districts where civil society is strong, autonomous, and politically aligned with the party. In such contexts, the grass-roots organizations can effectively impose their choices for

---

[1] The term "political alignments" – or to be "politically aligned" – refers to a shared understanding that both civil society organizations and the party belong to the same political camp (in other words, it is not about *formal* organizational ties).

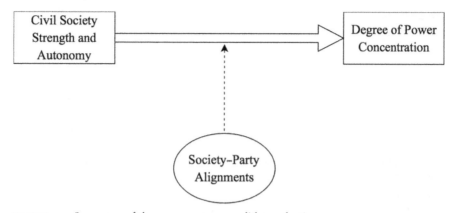

FIGURE 3.1 Summary of the argument on candidate selection.

candidates, constraining the power of the party leadership. By contrast, in contexts where civil society is strong but aligned with an opposition party, top-down decision-making in the hands of a small party elite – and even in the hands of one single prominent leader – is much more likely to occur. The same is true in contexts where civil society is strong but aligned with multiple parties. Where strong organizations manage to coordinate and agree on a candidate – where they unite – they can wield power within the party and nominate their desired candidate. However, where there are strong organizations but no consensus among them, a situation I designate as "coordination failures," the party leadership is likely to concentrate power and nominate desired candidates. Finally, contexts of weak civil society create organizational opportunities for power concentration in the hands of a few party elites, meaning that top-down elite choices tend to prevail.

The chapter is organized as follows. First, it develops a theoretical explanation of within-party variation in candidate selection in which civil society characteristics and party–society alignments interact with institutional elements. Second, the chapter provides an in-depth analysis of the MAS by looking at how the party selected legislative candidates in the 2009 general elections.[2] Third, to increase the number of observations and thus strengthen the evidentiary base for causal inference, the chapter develops subnational comparisons of how the MAS selected its municipal authorities in five municipalities for the

---

[2] The selection of *legislative* candidates is the best point from which to study power distributions within parties because they generally involve a broader set of actors and processes than executive elections. While the study of candidate selection for the executive branch could also be beneficial, it requires separate treatment since presidential races are more personalistic enterprises; they tend to strengthen the importance of strong personalities and thus contribute to undermine the role of candidate selection procedures in relation to individual groups or influential personalities that wield overwhelming power.

2010 elections.[3] Finally, the chapter draws conclusions from the findings and discusses their implications.

EXPLAINING VARIATION IN CANDIDATE SELECTION

Institutional and constant factors interact to shape candidate selection within movement-based parties. Institutional elements comprise aspects of a country's electoral system that create the space for the grass-roots to shape the selection process and elements related to the strength of the local party apparatus. Constant factors correspond with the organizational strength and density of civil society. Strongly organized societies can serve as a potential power base for movement-based parties. However, one can have very strong, well-organized civil societies that are largely controlled from the top-down in a corporatist fashion, doing little to enhance internal democracy. Autonomy is therefore key for my argument.

Institutional Elements

My analysis focuses on two institutional elements: electoral rules and the nature of the local party organization. Electoral systems affect party outcomes like discipline in Congress (Samuels 1999); they also affect candidate selection by creating space for civil society actors to shape the process (Siavelis and Morgenstern 2008b). Mixed-member proportional electoral systems (MMPs), like the one used in Bolivia, force parties to produce individual district candidates alongside a party list. As the literature shows, party leadership tends to become more central to selection and candidate list placement as district magnitude increases (Carey and Shugart 1995). Thus, it is likely that popular organizations will be able to exert more influence on selection for single-member district candidates than for proportional representation party candidates.

---

[3] Observing selection dynamics during those elections allows us to see the MAS in its most expansive phase. Since 2009, it has adopted a strategy of electoral recruitment conceived of as a deliberate plan to (1) control two-thirds in the legislative assembly that would allow the party to implement the newly approved constitution and (2) establish a strong presence in every municipality in the country and neutralize the opposition in the eastern departments (interviews with campaign advisor Jorge Silva and campaign communications strategist Manuel Mercado). That situation can be seen as a most likely case for top-down decision-making, given that the MAS expanded itself to the east and to areas where there were no strong grass-roots organizations that could serve as its base. Yet, the patterns observed in this chapter are consistent with those found by other researchers who undertook studies at earlier stages in the life of the party (Komadina and Geffroy 2007; Escóbar 2008; Zuazo 2008; Zegada, Torrez, and Camara 2008). Thus, there are reasons to believe that the deviant pattern is sustainable in the long run and that the trend toward top-down control can be held off if conditions are conducive. The expansion to the east, which is the strategic shift adopted by the MAS since 2009, only accentuated some top-down decision-making dynamics that already existed at earlier phases. It did not significantly alter the deviant pattern.

MMPs create distinct incentives for the party's top leadership, predisposing it toward the selection of different types of candidates. In single-member districts, the key for electoral success is the candidate's personal reputation and support within the district, which leads to three possible scenarios. First, a candidate that emerges with strong backing from grass-roots organizations can be accepted by the leadership to increase the probability of getting out the vote. Second, if there are strong organizations but contested nominations, the leadership can provide arbitration to maximize the chance of electoral success. In these cases, the option that maximizes the likelihood of success is for the leadership to choose a candidate that is most acceptable to a majority of local organizations. Third, where there are few social organizations linked to the party or where these are weakly organized, the central leadership can use nominations to build alliances to existing organizations or to attract the support of specific social sectors. However, for proportional representation candidates the key to electoral success is the overall strength of the party ticket. Parties often use these candidacies to diversify their lists and attract maximum electoral support. Candidates can emerge with strong organizational backing, but they are likely to be acceptable to multiple organizations or attractive to particular social groups.

Recent studies also highlight the relevance of the organizational strength of local party subunits for shaping party outcomes (Levitsky 2003; LeBas 2011; Tavits 2013; Van Dyck 2014). Tavits argues that local organizational strength helps parties survive.[4] In addition to mobilizing supporters and delivering votes, the literature shows that a strong local party organization can play a role in the aggregation of political interests, such as in the selection of candidates. It can either nominate candidates directly or serve as an arena for resolving conflicts among competing groups. However, variance in the organizational strength of party subunits does not fully explain variation in candidate selection patterns, nor how internal conflicts are resolved. In this chapter I show that a party's top leadership can serve as an arbiter-in-chief in conflicts where the local party organization is either weak or strong. However, the leadership more likely performs this role in contexts with a strong and heterogeneous civil society that is not fully aligned with the party. In other words, it is the failure of coordination among grass-roots actors that, in general, creates an organizational opportunity for the party leadership to centralize power. This finding suggests the importance of examining broader structural elements associated with civil society characteristics, and more broadly, with the organizational contexts where parties are embedded.

---

[4] Tavits (2013: 39–40) uses four indicators to measure party organizational strength: number of party membership, number of party branches, presence of a professional staff (as a percent of the electorate), and participation in local elections.

Constant Elements and Political Alignments

Factors associated with the strength, density, and autonomy of civil society are central to my explanation. Classic works in political sociology, as well as more recent empirical research on party-building, have established that densely organized civil societies can serve as a potential power base for parties.[5] The expectation is that the organizational infrastructures of politically oriented networks and associations may contribute to building strong parties by reducing costs and coordination problems. This "organizational inheritance" – as Levitsky et al. (2016: 21–3) argue – can provide resources to new political parties and contribute to their long-term empowerment. New parties are more likely to take root, and also to persist over time, where politicians build upon the infrastructure of preexisting organizations. Movement-based parties, even if initially loosely organized, are well positioned to build strong parties.

Following these insights, a significant factor affecting the internal governance of parties and their tendencies toward top-down control in the area of candidate selection is the variation in the organizational strength of their civil society allies. Specifically, I argue that the presence of civil societies that are strongly organized, autonomous, and *united* can generate politically consequential pressures from below that are crucial for shaping candidate selection processes. These pressures can serve as strong limits on the decision-making power and self-regarding political objectives of the top party leadership.[6]

Strongly organized civil societies are those with high organizational density (percentage of the district's population that are members of grass-roots organizations). Yet, one can have very strong, well-organized civil societies that are thoroughly controlled from the top but do little to disperse internal power. Autonomy is therefore crucial for my argument. It refers to the capacity of social movements and other civil society organizations to engage in a bottom-up dynamic of social mobilization. Finally, the term "united" means affinity of purpose – or the ability to privilege common purpose over narrow organizational interests in order to agree on decisions affecting common interests. Unity among organizations not only strengthens civil society, but it can also represent a counterweight to the centralizing tendencies of an allied party.

Strongly organized, autonomous, and united civil societies can play a central role in resisting pressures toward internal power concentration in the realm of candidate selection by wielding significant influence over the selection of party candidates. This is largely a function of how the political space is structured in a given electoral district and of the political alignments between civil society and the party.

---

[5] See Chapter 1 for a more thorough discussion.

[6] As I show in Chapter 4, this pressure may also defy the trend toward top-down control by helping to keep channels open for agenda setting from below, and can thus contribute to keeping parties responsive to societal demands.

As seen at the bottom of Figure 3.2, at least four "constellations" of party–civil society are theoretically possible: (1) strong civil society aligned with the party, (2) strong civil society aligned with opposition parties, (3) strong civil society with different political alignments, and (4) weak civil society (in which case political alignments are less relevant). I should add here a note of caution: although autonomy is crucial for my argument, I do not use the term in the remaining text of this chapter to avoid using the term excessively. But when I discuss strong civil societies, I am referring to those with autonomy of social mobilization, unless noted otherwise.

Based on the four "constellations" of party–civil society, Figure 3.3 presents my general theoretical expectations. Low-power concentration is more likely to

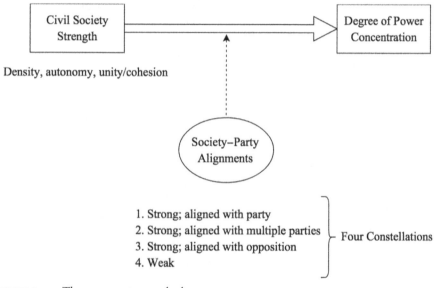

FIGURE 3.2 The argument unpacked.

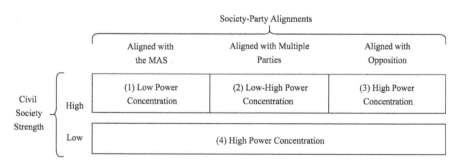

FIGURE 3.3 Theoretical expectations.

be observed in scenario (1), where civil society is strong and aligned with the party. High degrees of power concentration are more likely to be observed in scenarios (3) and (4), where civil society is strong and aligned with opposition parties, or where civil society is weak. Variable degrees of concentration are more likely to be observed in scenario (2), where civil society is strong but aligned with multiple parties.

Systematic evidence from candidate selection within the MAS, as discussed below, provides strong support to those theoretical expectations. It demonstrates that top-down decision-making by the party's top leadership is less likely to take place in districts where autonomous grass-roots groups aligned with the party are strongly organized, have mechanisms to arrive at decisions, and can agree on selection – a pattern most commonly seen in Bolivia's rural areas in the west of the country, where districts are generally more homogeneous and have strong organizations monopolizing the political space. In turn, in contexts where civil society is strong but has multiple alignments and cannot agree on a candidate, top-down decision-making is more prevalent – a pattern commonly observed in more heterogeneous environments, such as Bolivia's largest cities in the western part of the country. Similarly, where civil society is strong but aligned with opposition parties, the MAS leadership concentrates power in the hands of a small party elite, selecting candidates that will help to build alliances to existing organizations or to attract support from particular groups that may increase electoral returns. Selection in these cases is mostly an elite top-down affair, as it is in contexts of weak civil societies.

In short, the evidence highlights the importance of both the relative strength of civil society and political alignments of civil society in candidate selection. Thus, the evidence and findings are consistent with recent developments in the social movement literature inspired by the organizational ecology tradition (Soule 2012).

Though not yet connected to the literature on political parties, organizational ecologists emphasize the broader organizational field in which collective actors, including parties, operate (Robertson 2010). Similarly, the findings from the case of the MAS suggest that a potentially rewarding area for further research on the internal dynamics of political parties is the relevant contextual conditions, such as the impact of diverging patterns of party–civil society relations. Just as parties deploy different linkage strategies to attract and mobilize distinct electoral constituencies in unequal societies, and are therefore "segmented" in their appeals (Luna 2014), their local operations also vary widely according to how the political space is structured (I elaborate on this in the Conclusions).

WHY THE MAS IS RELEVANT

As discussed in the Introduction, the MAS is a particularly relevant case for studying power distributions inside movement-based parties because it deviates from the conventional wisdom. Although there are observable tendencies toward power concentration – as is evident in the growing personalization of power within the party – the party's grass-roots social bases have retained a strong capacity to control the selection of party candidates or who rises to leadership positions. Although oligarchic temptations are readily available, important spaces for bottom-up influence in the process of candidate selection have been preserved in districts where civil societies are strongly organized and autonomous, have mechanisms to arrive at collective decisions, and can agree on a candidate. The result has been striking variation in candidate selection outcomes across different geographical constituencies.

No clear rules guide selection processes. According to its statute, the MAS is "the political and ideological branch of the social organizations that represent Bolivia's cultural diversity in rural and urban areas" (Article 5). The statute further stipulates that: "members and activists participate in the different levels of the political structure [of the MAS] through their natural social organizations, which guide the work of these leaders and extend their own loyalty, work, and honesty to the structure of the MAS" (Article 9).

According to the party statute, moreover, the organizational structure of the MAS is decentralized along territorial and functional lines. The statute recognizes directorates at no fewer than eight levels: national, departmental, regional, provincial, municipal, indigenous territories, districts, and sectors (Article 12). For example, it recognizes the organizational structures of the social organizations and unions at the rural level, the districts and social sectors in urban areas, as well as the autonomous territories of indigenous peoples.

The highest decision-making authority within the MAS is the Regular National Congress (Congreso Nacional Ordinario, CON). Here the leadership of the peasant organizations is recognized by the rule that the CON should "respect the historical trajectory of the three core umbrella organizations that head the National Directorate of the MAS: CSUTCB, CSCIB, and CNMCIOB-BS" (Article 18, b).[7] This rule imposes a candidacy requirement for the National Directorate: having a background as a leader of one of the national-level peasant unions. The CON has the prerogative to select these leaders by "respecting internal democratic practices in free elections and through direct and secret vote. Their selection requires an absolute majority of the delegates attending the congress, or by consensus in accordance to the modality decided by the congress" (Article 18, a).

---

[7] These are the Unique Confederation of Rural Laborers of Bolivia (Confederación Sindical Única de Trabajadores Campesinos de Bolivia, CSUTCB); the Syndicalist Confederation of Intercultural Communities of Bolivia (Confederación Sindical de Comunidades Interculturales de Bolivia, CSCIB); and the Bartolina Sisa National Confederation of Campesino, Indigenous, and Native Women of Bolivia (Confederación Nacional de Mujeres Campesinas Indígenas Originarias de Bolivia "Bartolina Sisa," CNMCIOB-BS).

Although the party statute is clear on the definition of the internal mechanisms for selecting leaders for internal leadership bodies such as the National Directorate, it is much less clear on the procedures that regulate the selection of candidates for elective public office. Article 37 says that it is a responsibility of the National Directorate of the MAS to "coordinate and respect the modes of selection, as well as the norms and procedures used by social organizations for the creation of the candidate lists – for national assemblies, departmental assemblies, regional or provincial assemblies, municipal governments, districts and sectors – that the MAS will present in electoral contests." In other words, there is not a single and clearly stipulated candidate selection method: sponsoring and allied grass-roots organizations should select candidates through whichever means they con- sider appropriate. Given that the party's statute does not tell us much about the internal dynamics of candidate selection within the MAS, the case is attractive for studying the causes and impact of different selection mechan- isms across different districts in the country.

Examining this variation in a highly diverse country that uses a mixed- member proportional electoral system (MMP), such as Bolivia, is also useful because it allows for a systematic comparison of candidate selection strat- egies.[8] It allows us to see how the same party selects party candidates for different electoral lists, while keeping constant all other relevant contextual factors.

There have been some attempts to understand how the MAS selects its legislative candidates. Zuazo (2008) notes an important rural/urban cleavage in the realm of candidate selection, and her study has shed light on organiza- tional aspects of the MAS. Based on interviews with 85 MAS representatives in the 2005–9 Congress, she claims that there are horizontal decision-making mechanisms for the selection of candidates to run for Congress, particularly in rural areas. These mechanisms, which tend to guarantee high levels of participation "from below," vary greatly for each organization and each region, and they are rooted in unwritten indigenous customs and traditions. The candidates emerging from these mechanisms of direct participation are generally known as "organic," whereas other legislative candidates who are invited "from above" directly by the leadership are known as "invited." And they are predominantly urban. Zuazo's study does not explore this variation systematically, however, nor does it delve deeply into the internal dynamics of candidate selection procedures. The study also focuses on the selection of legislative candidates leading to the 2005 general election, and thus it fails to capture the internal transformations that the MAS has undergone since it

---

[8] No study of which I am aware addresses candidate selection within movement-based parties from this angle, nor do any of the existing studies on the case of MAS take full advantage of this institutional framework.

gained power, and particularly after 2009, when it adopted an expansive strategy of electoral growth by expanding to the east.

Do Alto and Stefanoni (2010) address candidate selection processes in a more systematic way. Their ethnographic study provides a "thick" socio-logical examination of the selection of legislative candidates for the 2009 general election, focusing on the internal dynamics of specific uni-nominal districts in the departments of La Paz, Santa Cruz, and Pando. Like Zuazo (2008, 2010), the authors observe the presence of mechanisms of direct democracy that guarantee high participation levels "from below," particularly in rural areas, and they provide detailed accounts of how these actually work. Do Alto and Stefanoni argue that while those mechanisms tend to be respected by the leadership of the MAS, in the absence of clearly established rules and procedures, the tendency is for those mechanisms to "favor the articulation of clientelist networks around leaders of social organizations" (Do Alto and Stefanoni 2010: 354). In short, by examining the micro dynamics of concrete cases, they point to a tension between the idea of "self-representation" – what they refer to as the "founding myth" of the MAS – and the actual relationships that exist between the social organ-izations and the MAS, and also among the social organizations themselves (Do Alto and Stefanoni 2010: 354–5). They argue that these power rela-tions not only shape candidate selection process but also largely determine the outcome.

While these studies offer some important insights on the selection of legisla-tive candidates and provide a wealth of qualitative information, they also leave some crucial questions unanswered. In general, they fail to address questions regarding the role of the MAS as an independent agent in candidate selection. For example, if the candidates are "nominated by a social organization" that decides to join the MAS, as many of them are, who or what party body approves the nominations, and at what level? If there is a rural/urban cleavage, does the MAS as a party play a more important role in one context than the other? Assuming that candidate selection processes are contested, does the MAS serve as an arbiter if conflicts emerge between different organizations that compete for the same space? If so, how are these conflicts resolved? In short, although existing studies acknowledge variation within MAS and pro-vide a wealth of qualitative information, they fail to explain what the main sources of that variation actually are.

My empirical analysis addresses this issue. It examines subnational variation in the selection of candidates for *national* office in the electoral process leading to the 2009 election. This is a key moment because MAS was in its most expansive phase, when it deployed a broad-based electoral strategy designed to capture a large constituency that would boost the "numbers" and allow the party to gain control of Congress. Thus, the lead up to that election was a highly likely period for top-down decision-making. I rely on evidence collected through interviews with over 50 MAS representatives from the departments of

TABLE 3.1 *Number of interviews with MAS deputies and senators in 2010–15 Congress, by department.*

Department	Number of interviews	Total elected under MAS	Total seats
La Paz	20	28	31
Oruro	8	11	12
Santa Cruz	8	11	28
Cochabamba	10	16	22
Other	11**		
Total	57	66	93*

* This count includes the total seats for the departments studied in this chapter, which accounts for a clear majority. The total number of seats in the Bolivian Congress is 166. Of these, the MAS has 114.

** This number includes interviews with MAS representatives from Bolivia's remaining departments (Chuquisaca, Potosí, Tarija, Beni, and Pando).

La Paz, Cochabamba, Oruro, and Santa Cruz (Table 3.1 and Map 3.1),[9] in addition to 120 interviews with key informants, to explain how candidates are selected under different party–civil society "constellations" (as defined in Figure 3.3).

Interviewees included leaders of sponsoring and allied grass-roots organizations, non-elected regional party brokers, unsuccessful aspirants, members of the executive branch, representatives of opposition parties, experts, and journalists, as well as candidates nominated for *local* office in rural and urban districts.[10] Data from interviews are supplemented by a close reading of newspapers on the process and its aftermath, and of the existing secondary literature.

The analysis developed in this chapter reveals tremendous heterogeneity across different localities. Conditions where organizations allied to MAS have a near monopoly of organization have a higher chance of being observed in the rural areas in Bolivia's western departments, including La Paz, Cochabamba, and Oruro, where single-member district candidates are more likely to emerge from social organizations and be accepted by the party leadership. This pattern of candidate selection reflects a de facto diffusion of power, in that it mirrors the balance of power between MAS and autonomous, territorially grounded grass-roots organizations – and also between these organizations themselves.

Bolivia is no exception to the rule that urban areas are generally more heterogeneous than rural areas. In some urban districts the diffusion of power

[9] While these departments do not cover the entire country, the organizational patterns observed there were also common elsewhere, as confirmed through interviews with representatives and social movement leaders from other departments in the country.

[10] Evidence from the selection of authorities for local-level office further supports the main argument of this chapter (see below).

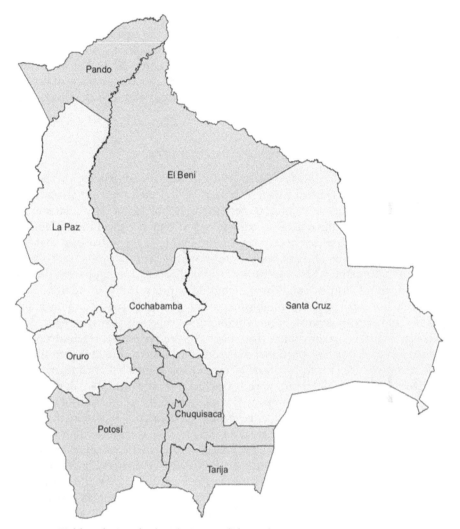

MAP 3.1 Fieldwork sites for legislative candidate selection.

among grass-roots organizations leads to a situation where agreement on candidates is difficult, while in other cases the organizational density (i.e., the presence and strength of organizations aligned with MAS) is significantly lower. In both types of situations, the candidate selection process exhibits a combination of oligarchic decision-making with grass-roots participation and consensus building. Specifically, where there are strong organizations but no consensus among them, the leadership is likely to choose a candidate acceptable to a majority of local organizations; where organizations are weak, however, the leadership is likely to select candidates that will help to build alliances to existing organizations or to attract support from particular groups that may increase electoral returns. These patterns are similar to that observed for most proportional representation candidates. Finally, in Bolivia's eastern departments, which represent relatively new arenas of competition for MAS, the social organizations linked to the party are weak. In the absence of strong organizations that can agree on candidate selection, elite decision-making is more likely to occur.

SELECTING DIFFERENT TYPES OF CANDIDATES

Bolivia's bicameral Congress consists of a Chamber of Senators with 36 seats and a Chamber of Deputies with 130 seats. All elected representatives serve five-year terms, and reelection is permitted. Members of the Chamber of Senators are elected through a closed-list proportional representation. Deputies are elected by a mixed-member proportional (MMP) electoral system that has created two different types of seats, "plurinominal" (proportional representation) and "uninominal" (single-member district, SMD), forcing parties to produce individual district candidates alongside a party list.[11] In addition, the country's 2009 constitution established a few "special" seats for indigenous peoples and Afro-Bolivians. Seventy uninominal representatives are elected by plurality vote in single-member districts, 53 plurinominal representatives are elected in a closed-list proportional representation system, and the seven special representatives are elected by plurality vote in single-member constituencies.[12]

MMPs generate different incentive structures and variable impacts on internal grass-roots participation. SMDs encourage the cultivation of a candidate's personal reputation and support within a district. To increase the probability of getting out the vote, there is an incentive to increase the participation of allied groups, which can mobilize collective support for a given candidate and thus exert significant influence on the selection process. In the case of proportional representation candidates, as the literature shows, the party leadership becomes more central to selection and list placement as district size becomes bigger. In such cases, the power of the central leadership is strengthened in relation to the grass-roots.

Uninominal Candidates

Generally, in selecting these candidates, the MAS delegates responsibilities and control to the movements and popular organizations that are present in a given electoral district. In these cases, then, candidate selection consists of procedures

---

[11] See Ardaya (2003) for a critical early assessment of this system.

[12] In the 2009 general election MAS gained 26 of 36 seats in the Chamber of Senators, 33 of the 53 plurinominal representatives, 49 of the 70 uninominal representatives, and 6 of the 7 special seats.

that provide significant opportunities for the grass-roots to influence decision-making, and candidates emerge based on the strength of the social organization they represent. Prior to an election, the National Directorate of MAS issues a call for nominations to allied grass-roots organizations throughout the country. These movements and organizations, then, are in charge of conducting screening, pre-selection, and candidate nomination processes, and they do so by electoral district and according to the norms and procedures they themselves deem adequate. In most cases, the leadership of the MAS respects the decisions by grass-roots organizations. With some exceptions, these organizations have the last word on nominations, representing a counterweight to the power of the leadership.

Formal membership in the MAS is not a condition for candidacy. Instead, "aspiring candidates need to be approved by the people in their territory" (interview with Leonida Zurita).[13] The only hard-and-fast rule that the MAS respects is that each district has to ensure rigorous gender equality: by statute, if the titular candidate for a district is a man, the substitute needs to be a woman and vice versa. Although there is no rule stipulating that uninominal candidates must have experience as a leader of a grass-roots organization, this is almost always the case. As a former deputy commented, "it is practically impossible to become a uninominal candidate for the MAS if you do not have experience as a [social organization] leader" (interview with Dionicio Núñez). Interviews with multiple uninominal representatives in La Paz, Cochabamba, Oruro, and Santa Cruz confirm this observation. Analyses based on the survey of Latin American parliamentary elites conducted by the University of Salamanca show that most of them, indeed, came from a grass-roots organization (Zegada and Komadina 2014).

The key actors are movements and grass-roots organizations with a territorial base. These gained legal status as Territorial Grass-Roots Organizations (OTBs) with the 1994 Law of Popular Participation, and they generally include neighborhood associations, traditional indigenous organizations (the *ayllus*), and modern peasant unions (the *sindicatos campesinos*). Candidate selection within the MAS ensures the representation of the OTBs that decide to join the party.[14] Below I examine subnational variation in the nomination of uninominal candidates according to the four party–civil society constellations outlined above.

---

[13] They are also required to demonstrate no history of corruption, no prior affiliation with a "neoliberal" or "traditional" party, and a demonstrated loyalty and commitment to the "process of change" led by the MAS (interview with Samuel Guarayos). These rules, however, can be overlooked under certain exceptional circumstances, predominantly due to electoral imperatives and other strategic considerations (interview with Leonida Zurita).

[14] By "joining the MAS" I mean the process by which grass-roots organizations align politically with MAS and engage in competitive nomination processes.

Strong Civil Society Aligned with the MAS

Where civil society is strongly organized, autonomous, and aligned with the MAS, as in many districts in the western departments of La Paz, Cochabamba, Oruro, and Potosí, this decentralized form of participation tends to be the norm. The process begins at the lowest organizational level of the union structure, the *sindicatos campesinos*, and then moves up to the territory's higher organizational levels, the *subcentrales* and the *centrales*. Figure 3.4 depicts a stylized version of the functional levels of the peasant union organization in Bolivia.[15] In general, the *subcentral* aligns with the territory of the electoral district, meaning that there is generally one *subcentral* per electoral district. The more specific mechanics of the process described below can only be described as a general tendency, and the following account portrays an "ideal typical" model through which the MAS selects uninominal candidates.[16]

The selectorate for such candidacies is highly inclusive, and there is a clear emphasis on extending grass-roots participation. As Vice President Álvaro García Linera commented in an interview, because "these candidates are not hand-picked, they are not the candidates of the party in a strict sense. They are selected by grass-roots organizations as a function of their territorial power, and they are the representatives of those organizations" (interview with Álvaro García Linera). In other words, in contexts where civil society is strong and aligned with the MAS, the participation and decision-making capacity of grass-roots organizations with a territorial base is high in the case of uninominal candidates.

The mechanics of selection can be summarized in three steps. First, each *sindicato* and other OTBs in a given district organize meetings to conduct a preliminary screening of potential candidates and then select their nominees. These meetings, called *ampliados* or *cabildos*, are crowded events that ensure broad grass-roots participation. The individuals who are elected at this level will then represent their organization in the competition at the next highest level of organization, the *subcentrales*. At this level, each *subcentral* holds an *ampliado* or a *cabildo* to choose among the *sindicato*-level nominees. The winner of each *subcentral* contest then goes on to compete for representation at the next highest level of organization, the *central*. The candidates for each electoral district are defined at this level, as seen below.

---

[15] The *sindicato* is the organization that brings together almost all of the families in a given community. Affiliation is voluntary and the requirements for affiliation include living and having land within that community. The *subcentral* is an intermediate structure between the *sindicatos* and the *centrales*. It is generally elected through the vote of the members of the *sindicatos*. The *central* brings together all of the *subcentrales* in a given province, and it is the highest level of authority in the local-level *sindicato* structure.

[16] Exceptions are more easily observable in urban areas, where the MAS tries to replicate the selection methods that are prevalent in rural areas. In urban settings, however, there is generally more organizational atomization. In the eastern departments, in turn, the MAS tries to replicate this "bottom-up" selection method, but this is combined with a more pragmatic approach to alliance building.

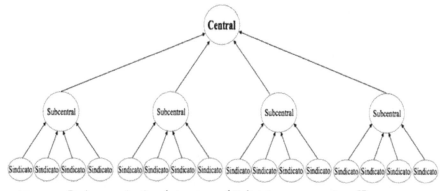

FIGURE 3.4 Basic organizational structure of Bolivia's peasant unions.[17]

Finally, the *central* organizes an *ampliado* or a *cabildo* with all of the nominees presented by the *subcentrales*. The winners at this level typically emerge as uninominal candidates if they receive the support of all the organizations involved throughout the process. This support is determined at a large congress of the authorities from all participating levels, and it is obtained by mechanisms of union democracy that have no uniform codification. The runners-up serve as substitute candidates for the district.

Strong Civil Society Aligned with Opposition
The expansion to the east, where the MAS was historically weak, pushed decision-making structures in a more oligarchic direction.[18] In parts of Santa Cruz, particularly in rural districts, the selection of uninominal candidates followed the familiar "bottom-up" pattern described above; in contrast, in the city of Santa Cruz, where there are strong organizations aligned with opposition forces, a local party structure played an influential role and nominated several candidates from its ranks.[19] However, department level selection also involved alliance and coalition building with other parties,[20] with politically

---

[17] This figure depicts a stylized version of one territorial unit with 4 *subcentrales* – which coincides with 4 electoral districts – 16 *sindicatos*, and one *central*. The *central* is generally affiliated with one of the nine departmental federations within the CSUTCB, which is the highest-level organization in the peasant union hierarchy.

[18] Jorge Silva commented that the objective for the 2009 election was "to reach an absolute majority in both chambers in the Congress at whatever cost" (interview with Jorge Silva). Thus, it is reasonable to expect a pragmatic approach to selection and alliance building.

[19] The configuration of this unusually strong party structure is a function of a deliberate decision by MAS's leadership to consolidate its presence in an area that was seen as hostile to MAS (interview with Álvaro García Linera). See more about this structure in the subsection "Additional Evidence: Local Elections."

[20] Such as the center-left Movement without Fear (MSM).

influential groups and non-traditional organizations,[21] and with a wide array of ad hoc urban organizations.[22] These alliances guaranteed representation for members of those groups and were made by the national leadership; neither the local party nor the grass-roots organizations that control the Regional Directorate created them (interviews with Isaac Ávalos, Lidia Choque, Gabriela Montaño, Reymi Ferreira, Tito Santibañez, and José Quiroz). The composition of the electoral list reflected an internal balance of power that favored those urban groups over peasant organizations, reflecting a more centralized and exclusive selection pattern, whereby the influence of a small party elite was strengthened.[23] It also revealed a strong pragmatism by the top party leadership.[24] Evidence from other eastern departments, such as Beni and Pando, where major civil society organizations are aligned with the opposition, reveals a similar pattern of candidate selection that combines participation from below with oligarchic decision-making.[25]

Strong Civil Society with Multiple Alignments

The fact that the MAS has grown fast and in a decentralized manner has given significant flexibility to newly incorporated local organizations regarding the selection of candidates.[26] In general, their decision to be a part of the MAS

---

[21] Such as the right-wing Cruceñista Youth Union (UJC).

[22] Such as the "Coordinator for Change," the "Professionals for Change," and the "Lawyers of the MAS."

[23] Lidia Choque commented that the "agreement 'from above' could have only happened because the social organizations [in Santa Cruz] are not united and each supports whoever offers the best deal."

[24] For example, Nemecia Achacollo, Bolivia's current Minister of Rural Development and a leader at the Bartolina Sisa National Confederation of Peasant Women of Bolivia, figures prominently in most of my interviews as a central actor in the design and configuration of such alliances in Santa Cruz. She is also identified as a central actor in the final configuration of the electoral lists. Juan Ramón Quintana, Bolivia's current Minister of the Presidency, figures prominently as a key operator and as a central actor in the configuration of alliances in Pando. Both ministers do not occupy a leadership position within the MAS, which shows that in configuring alliances members of the executive can wield significantly more power than the party structure.

[25] Interviews with campaign coordinators in both departments confirm this pattern, a pragmatic approach to candidate selection and alliance building that, framed as a part of a strategy to penetrate in traditionally "hostile" territories, centralizes decision-making power in the hands of a group of influential individuals, including, in some cases, President Morales himself. Indeed, alliances are not defined at the level of the grass-roots (interviews with Walter Chávez, Manuel Mercado, and Jorge Silva). Research undertaken by Do Alto and Stefanoni (2010) lends additional support to the findings reported here. See, in particular, their treatment of selection and alliance building in Pando (Do Alto and Stefanoni 2010: 348–52).

[26] As Harten (2011: 131) notes, in expanding to the cities the MAS has adopted a "laissez-faire approach" of organizational growth, through which it has sought to "benefit from specific local dynamics, as opposed to coercing these organizations into adopting a predetermined organizational style." Though this style of growth may have been prominent in urban areas, the conclusion appears to apply to non-traditional rural areas where the MAS has recently sought to insert itself.

implies mutual benefits. The MAS opens its electoral lists and gives these grass-roots organizations control over the selection process. Thus, the MAS benefits from the existing social networks and organizational infrastructure of these autonomous grass-roots organizations, which are familiar with the electoral terrain and able to organize campaigns and mobilize resources more efficiently. In turn, grass-roots organizations benefit from the association with the MAS, which generally increases their likelihood of electoral success.

This symbiotic relationship is different in rural and urban environments, however. Movements and popular organizations with a territorial base are central to selection in both settings, but in urban areas there are usually no clearly identifiable organizations that exert dominance over the territory. Rather, there is a multiplicity of neighborhood associations, professional associations, cooperatives, unions, and the like. Since they usually are in competition during the selection process, these competing organizations often have difficulty agreeing on a preferred candidate. When conflicts arise and competing organizations cannot reach agreement, a small party elite that often includes the president himself acts as an arbiter and has the last word.[27] As I describe further below, the failures of coordination among autonomous grass-roots actors create an organizational space for the leadership to centralize power, pushing internal decision-making structures in a more oligarchic direction.

Weak Civil Society

In rural areas, particularly where densely organized social actors have dominant control over the territory, the MAS has not invested much in the building of a party branch independent of these organizations.[28] In urban areas, by contrast, and particularly in places where grass-roots organizations are not strongly organized, or where they do not have dominant control over the territory, the MAS has constructed territorial party organizations of varying strength. For the most part, however, these structures lack independent decision-making power, creating an organizational opportunity for the party leadership to centralize power in contexts where civil society is weak. In such contexts, elite top-down choices are much more likely to prevail.

Summary

Systematic evidence from the departments of La Paz, Cochabamba, Oruro, and Santa Cruz, complemented by observations of other departments in Bolivia, suggests that the crucial variable determining the nature of candidate selection

---

[27] Despite this, the selection procedures for uninominal candidates in these environments follow a roughly similar path and, according to most of my interviewees representing urban districts, they try to emulate the dynamics of the rural areas. They achieve this with different degrees of success, though.

[28] Evo Morales commented some time ago that, "where the grass-roots organizations are strong, there is no need to organize MAS" (interview with Leonida Zurita).

is the strength of autonomous civil society organizations – both number of members and the ability of grass-roots organizations to reach an agreement on selection. In this scenario, the MAS diffuses power among territorially grounded grass-roots actors, which generally have the last word on selection. Once these organizations nominate a candidate, this person becomes a candidate for the MAS. However, when conflicts emerge among competing organizations, the MAS tends to concentrate decision-making power in the hands of a small party elite – and even Morales himself. These disputes are rarely resolved through formal channels, or by the local party organization. These dynamics are more commonly observed in urban areas, where the political space is more fragmented, and in the eastern departments, where MAS expanded by means of a broad-based strategy of recruitment.

Plurinominal Candidates

Districts for plurinational candidates are larger, meaning that there are different party–civil society constellations within each district. This also means that coordination among competing organizations is generally more complicated than in uninominal districts. Conflicts among such organizations create an organizational opportunity for the party leadership to centralize power.

Indeed, plurinominal candidates and candidate list placement typically emerge from agreements between the leadership of the MAS and specific social sectors, or are directly selected by Morales. These candidacies help to generate balances – territorial, corporate, urban/rural, and male/female – after the list of uninominal candidates is approved (interview with Adolfo Mendoza; also with Álvaro García Linera). In this instance the selection process is more centralized; the principal actors are national party leaders, members of the national-level government, or brokers with access to patronage resources in departmental governments, and ultimately Evo Morales himself. In comparison to the uninominal candidates, the relative power of the party central leadership is strengthened in relation to the grass-roots.

Although the selection of plurinominal candidates is more centralized and exclusive, and therefore more prone to top-down control, it serves as a part of a deliberate *strategy of addition* that allows for the incorporation of sectors and groups that do not have a territorial or an institutional corporate base. As Leonida Zurita commented, "the idea here is to include everyone – that is, professionals, non-professionals, intellectuals, non-intellectuals, indigenous and non-indigenous middle class, women, and so on. It is in that sense that our project is one of inclusion and not of exclusion." This view is akin to the view of Concepción Ortiz, the MAS's Vice President, who stated that this mechanism allows the MAS to balance its electoral lists, and is seen by the leadership as an inclusionary way to give representation to urban middle classes (interview with Concepción Ortíz).

Formal membership and a background as a movement leader are not conditions for candidacy. As a result, some plurinominal candidates, particularly those without such a background, are generally seen as unwelcome competitors by rural and peasant organizations and by candidates that emerge from these organizations. They consider themselves the authentic representatives of the MAS. Indeed, these plurinominal candidates are referred to as "invited." That characterization is used to contrast "organic" rural-based rank and file with "invited" urban and middle classes.

This form of nomination was not widespread during the early days of the MAS. Rather, as Do Alto and Stefanoni (2010: 312) suggest, the invitation of candidates only became common in preparation for the 2002 election, when MAS won significant minorities in Congress and became a national-level actor. The MAS developed an expansive strategy of electoral recruitment and coalition building in order to compete successfully for the presidency and the Congress. The idea behind this strategic maneuver was initially simple: to recruit indigenous and non-indigenous middle classes, left-leaning and nationalist intellectuals, social movement leaders, and professionals, among others, in order to expand the electoral base.

The strategy of invitation has changed over time, however, and it has served as a mechanism of accommodation that gives the MAS flexibility in changing electoral and political environments. It has also been useful since the party assumed power. According to Bolivian journalist Fernando Molina, once the MAS gained power, the growing presence of "invited" candidates has responded to two factors: "first, the need to improve the efficiency of the new regime, and second, the co-optation of the 'process of change' by bureaucratic and intellectual classes" (Molina 2010: 279). Molina's account assumes that the MAS, of necessity, has adapted to, and has been absorbed by, the state apparatus, and that "invited" candidates are just a reflection of those dynamics. However, while there are oligarchic tendencies within the legislative group, and while these have intensified since MAS assumed governing roles, Molina's conclusion can be misleading. It is possible that "invited" MAS candidates and social movement representatives do not form any sort of organic group with shared or corporate social and political interests and incentives – that is, they do not form an oligarchy. At best, they represent a temporary group of assorted representatives from diverse base organizations in a loose coalition.

Molina's functionalism also downplays the choices and power struggles within the party and the diverse selection mechanisms used by the MAS. According to Jorge Silva, the leading campaign advisor for the 2009 election, it is important to make an analytic distinction between plurinominal candidates *invited directly by Morales*, and those candidates *nominated by social organizations*. Most of the former are invited because they are considered "symbolic figures or political emblems that can give certain vitality to the government. In these cases, the selection decision does not come out from the social organizations but rather from the top down" (interview with Adolfo Mendoza). In other words, what takes place in these cases is a top-down nomination process where the source of legitimacy for these candidates comes from their accumulated symbolic capital. Examples of these candidates include

Ana María Romero de Campero in the Department of La Paz,[29] Rebeca Delgado in the Department of Cochabamba,[30] and Betty Tejada in the Department of Santa Cruz.[31] The rationale behind these nominations is to capture the median voter.[32]

The analysis provided thus far characterizes the selectorate as highly exclusive. It is therefore possible to argue that the nomination process of plurinominal candidates within the MAS resembles an "appointment system," but that would be an oversimplification.[33]

My research shows that a single leader does not invite the vast majority of the plurinominal candidates capriciously, and they are not imposed from above. Rather, many are nominated by a wide array of autonomous social movements, unions, and civic associations that, among other base organizations, compete for representation. As in the case of the uninominal candidates, prior to an election cycle MAS's National Directorate distributes an open call for nominations to sponsoring and allied organizations throughout the country. After the invitation is out, the social organizations allied to the MAS – or those that intend to join and nominate candidates – propose their preferred candidates. According to Jorge Silva, since these nominees are "neither members nor activists of the social organization nor formal members of the MAS, it is only in this sense that we can say they are invited. It is not the president who brings them or imposes them on the organizations, but it is rather the organizations that actually make the invitations" (interview with Jorge Silva).

In these cases, then, the power struggles among competing organizations to nominate their own candidates, and how conflicts emerging from these struggles are resolved, are central to selection. To increase the likelihood of nominating their preferred candidates, competing organizations need to coordinate with other groups. Coordination is not always easy, however.

An example of the selection of senatorial candidates from the Department of Cochabamba will further illustrate how the selection of plurinominal candidates works. Of the list of four senators, the first slot went to Adolfo Mendoza, who had served as a legal and political advisor to peasant organizations during the constituent assembly; the second slot went to Marcelina Chávez, who is both a miner in a cooperative and a peasant union leader; the third slot went to Julio Salazar, who was a prominent coca-growing union leader in the Six Federations of the Tropic of Cochabamba in the Chapare region; and the fourth slot went to Lidia Ordóñez, who was loosely associated to the "middle" class.

---

[29] Former ombudswoman and prominent human rights activist.

[30] Prominent lawyer and former delegate to the Constituent Assembly.

[31] Former representative for the New Republican Force (NFR) and vocal advocate for the MAS in Santa Cruz at a moment where the MAS was highly resisted in that department.

[32] Multiple interviews.

[33] On the "appointment system," see Hazan and Rahat (2010: 73–86).

Mendoza explains why he obtained the first slot:

[W]e knew that we were going to win at least two seats, but not the four seats in the Department. The Six Federations of the Tropic of Cochabamba wanted the first seat for themselves, but that would have been a risky move, electorally speaking....Since the Bartolinas and the Six Federations did not come to an agreement...they decided to invite me because they knew me by my work in the constituent assembly. I was also a visible person nation-wide, as I had led a public campaign to defend the constitution in Cochabamba before it was approved, and as a result they thought that my candidacy would secure urban middle-class votes and increase the probabilities of winning, if not four seats, at least the first three. I was someone associated with the construction of the Plurinational State, but people knew I wasn't in the MAS. In fact, I didn't become a candidate because I was a member of the MAS, or even a leader of a social organization, but thanks to my collaboration with these. And it wasn't Morales who invited me, but rather these organizations (Interview with Adolfo Mendoza).[34]

Failures of Coordination

Even in the case of uninominal candidates, competing grass-roots organizations often do not reach a consensus in the selection process, failing to nominate candidates. This leads to conflicts among organizations that constitute the party's social base. To date, there are neither clear hierarchies nor clearly established formal structures and mechanisms to resolve these conflicts within the MAS. The Regional Directorates, as intermediate-level party bodies, may play an important role in this regard. However, just like the local party apparatus, they do not have sufficient autonomy and decision-making power, and they try "not to obstruct the decisions made by the executive or by the social organizations themselves" (interview with Adolfo Mendoza). In the absence of clear mechanisms for conflict resolution, most participants end up relying on Morales to resolve them. He plays the role of an arbiter in chief, particularly in areas where the political apparatus is weaker (e.g., in Beni, Pando, and Tarija). In cases where the MAS has developed a stronger party apparatus (e.g., in Cochabamba, La Paz, and Santa Cruz), conflicts are resolved by the intervention of local powerful political actors, who exert significant influence on intraparty decisions, but also by Morales himself.

When it comes to plurinominal candidates, ad hoc committees composed by a small group of influential leaders are often formed to decide the final composition of the electoral lists. While this is an ad hoc arrangement, interviews with plurinominal candidates suggest that this group typically includes the President, the Vice President, the Presidents of Congress, top members of the

---

[34] Mendoza added that Evo Morales and the national leadership of the MAS were not pleased with his nomination, as they conceived of Mendoza as a "free thinker" or one who can "have an independent opinion and who doesn't follow 'organic' decisions by the party." Still, his candidacy was approved albeit "with a big dose of skepticism."

MAS's National Directorate, and executive authorities of the principal peasant organizations that constitute the MAS's political core. Additional leaders sometimes are included. These groups evaluate the lists proposed by social organizations in each department, and then negotiate with these organizations to determine which individuals will be selected as candidates.

These groups can also veto candidates already proposed. Their ability to do so, however, is contingent on structural elements. Two examples with differences in structural context may help illustrate this point. The first is in Santa Cruz, where civil society is strong and aligned with opposition forces. In such a context, vetoes from the top succeeded when regional organizations engaged in an alliance with the Unión Juvenil Cruceñista (UJC), a right-wing shock troop that had violent confrontations with the MAS activists during the first Morales government. This alliance would guarantee the UJC an important number of seats, which the leadership did not accept. In other cases, however, despite the veto attempts by committees, social organizations manage to nominate their preferred candidate. Generally, this occurs where strong grass-roots organizations are aligned with the MAS, as in the Department of Cochabamba.

Summary

The selection of plurinominal candidates is more centralized and exclusive than that of uninominal candidates. The process can be characterized as a combination of top-down decision-making by a small – but highly unstable and varying – group of influential leaders, and negotiation and consensus building from below. While in some cases the party leadership can exert significant influence on the order and composition of the lists, in other instances allied movements and popular organizations have more power to nominate their preferred candidate. Consistent with the main argument in this chapter, this is generally the case in areas where grass-roots organizations are stronger and aligned with the MAS. When this is not the case, the leadership has more control over candidate selection and *who* gets nominated.

SUPPLEMENTARY EVIDENCE

This subsection presents additional evidence from candidate selection for local-level office, which provides strong supplementary empirical support for the claims developed above. As sociologist Fernando García commented in an interview "understanding how the MAS selects its candidates at the local level has been inexplicably under-explored so far. It is there where the MAS expresses its full heterogeneity. And the interesting thing is that it is in those locations where the MAS decentralizes its authority and decision-making power the most" (interview with Fernando García).[35]

---

[35] García is a leading sociologist at the United Nations Development Program (UNDP) in Bolivia.

TABLE 3.2 *Subnational comparative cases.*

	Urban			Rural		
	MAS	Mixed	Opposition	MAS	Mixed	Opposition
El Alto	All levels					
La Paz	National	Local				
Achacachi				National	Local	
Villa Tunari				All levels		
Santa Cruz			All levels			

This is a slightly idealistic view about the selection of local level candidates, as the following pages demonstrate, using five municipalities that illustrate predominant trends. The criteria for selecting cases were straightforward. Taking the results of the April 2010 municipal elections, one urban and one rural district were selected with the following configurations: the MAS as electorally dominant at all levels of competition (i.e., national and municipal levels); the opposition dominant at all levels of competition; and mixed or split (neither the MAS nor the opposition clearly dominant) (see Table 3.2 and Map 3.2). Figure 3.5 summarizes the observed outcomes and leads on to a discussion of the evidence.

Strong Civil Society Aligned with the MAS

The empirical pattern that most clearly diffuses power can be observed in the municipality of Villa Tunari and, to a lesser extent, in El Alto. In both cases, where the MAS is dominant at all levels of competition, selection takes a very similar form as described above in the case of uninominal legislative candidates. In Villa Tunari, for example, the mayor and all of the representatives to the municipal council emerge from the two main coca growers' federations that are present in the district: the Special Federation of Peasant Workers of the Tropics of Cochabamba (Federación Especial de Trabajadores Campesinos del Trópico de Cochabamba, FETCT), and the Special Federation of the Yungas of the Chapare (Federación Especial Yungas del Chapare, FEYCH) (see García Linera, León, and Monje 2004: 381–457; also UMSS 2004: chapter 4).

Selection follows the *sindicato* norms, which derive from unwritten usage and customs practiced in highland communities (Van Cott 2008: 183). Once elections for municipal-level authorities approach, each local *sindicato* nominates its preferred candidate, who will then represent the *sindicato* and compete at the level of the *central*. Elections at these two stages are held either by standing in groups, or by secret ballot (interviews with Segundina Orellana and Feliciano Mamani). The winners of these contests then compete at the level of the federation, which is at the top of the local level hierarchy. The FETCT,

MAP 3.2 Fieldwork sites for local-level candidate selection.

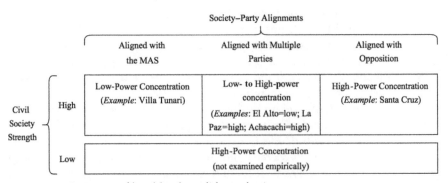

FIGURE 3.5 Summary of local-level candidate selection outcomes.

which is the largest and most powerful federation in the municipality, selects the mayor as well as eight titular candidates and eight sub-candidates for the municipal council. The FEYCH selects the deputy mayor as well as three titular candidates and three sub-candidates for the municipal council. This distribution, which is generally respected by the competing organizations, reflects the de facto balance of power in the municipality. Here the MAS as a party does not have an independent role vis-à-vis the grass-roots organizations, and indeed the two seem to be fused. As a local radio journalist summarized it, "the MAS in Villa Tunari is not a political party; it is what allows the local *sindicatos* to legally compete in elections" (interview with Walter Cassía).[36]

Strong Civil Society with Multiple Alignments

Selection in El Alto, one of Bolivia's largest cities, is similar to that in Villa Tunari.[37] The strongest popular organizations that wield power within the MAS are the Federation of Neighborhood Boards (Federación de Juntas Vecinales, FEJUVE) and the Regional Labor Federation (Central Obrera Regional, COR).[38] However, these and other smaller organizations compete with an incipient local party structure that is also involved in selection. Once elections for local office approach, both the grass-roots organizations and the local party structure nominate their preferred candidates according to their own norms and procedures. The composition of the electoral list reflects the balance of power within the "grass-roots" component, and between the "grass-roots"

---

[36] Although this "bottom up" mechanism is the general pattern, the selection process has several kinds of distortions. For example, Cordova Eguivar noted that by eliminating the need for counting, the voting system of the "lines" can be unfair and easily manipulated by powerbrokers and gatekeepers (interview with Eduardo Cordova Eguivar). In another interview, Jean-Paul Benavides commented that there are all kinds of agreements under the table that distort the "bottom up" selection process, particularly at the level of the federation. These agreements, which are typically seen as interferences by either Evo Morales directly or another member of the executive, can go against the consensus reached by the organizations (interview with Jean-Paul Benavides). Despite these distortions in the process, the presence of grass-roots organizations that can agree on candidate selection is central.

[37] For an alternative assessment of this process, see Mamani and Archondo (2010: 41–52). The main difference between their account and mine is that theirs does not address the selection of the mayor, and it focuses exclusively on what I term the "grass-roots" component. It fails to mention the existence of a territorial party structure, and it fails to explain how these two components interact during the selection process.

[38] The FEJUVE is a coordinator of residents, as well as neighborhood councils and associations, in El Alto. The COR is an umbrella organization of workers, which includes factory workers, teachers, journalists, and artisans but is dominated by street traders. Other smaller organizations that have a stake in selection include, but are not limited to, the Unique Federation of Peasant Communities in the Urban and Semi-Urban Radius of El Alto (*Federación Única de Comunidades Campesinas del Radio Urbano y Sub Urbano de El Alto*, FESUCARUSO) and the Federation of Street Traders ("the Federation").

component and the party structure.[39] It also reflects the balance of power between those two and the national MAS leadership.

For example, the COR nominated Edgar Patana, who had served as the executive secretary for the organization during the first Morales government, to run for mayor. Though the COR was not the most powerful organization in the city at the moment of selection (and it still is not), it had maintained better relations with the national MAS government by defending the government's key policies and by coordinating policies with national-level authorities (interview with Edgar Patana). This strengthened the candidacy of Patana vis-à-vis FEJUVE's preferred candidate (interviews with Edgar Patana, Néstor Guillén, and Fanny Nina). FEJUVE's authorities and the leaders of other, smaller local organizations saw Patana's nomination as an imposition from above and therefore resisted (interviews with Félix Patzi Abel Mamani and Fanny Nina).[40]

The patterns described above (in Villa Tunari and El Alto) are of special interest because they represent partial exceptions to the trend toward top-down decision-making, albeit in varying degrees. First, they demonstrate that when there is not a single grass-roots organization clearly articulating the local region and serving as a reference – or when there are no densely organized social actors – there is space for the emergence of a local party structure that will then compete for representation with the "grass-roots" component. That scenario cannot be observed in Villa Tunari, where there is virtually no room for an autonomous party structure, as the coca growers' *sindicatos* control the local political environment.

Second, the patterns show that, in a context where the territory is divided into competing grass-roots organizations, having "good relationships" with the party in government can help to shift the balance of power in one's favor during the selection process. This, in turn, can open room for top-down imposition of candidates, but such an imposition cannot be done without having the support of at least one of the strongest competing organizations. Taken together, then, the patterns described above provide additional evidence in support of the central claim in this chapter: that in districts where civil society is densely organized, autonomous, and aligned with the party, the grass-roots organizations are more likely to impose their choices of candidates and resist the top-down imposition of candidates.

---

[39] Almost all of the candidates were nominated by popular organizations, and a minority was nominated by the "party" structure.

[40] Patana almost lost the contest to a right-wing candidate of National Unity (Unidad Nacional, UN). This was surprising because El Alto had voted heavily for the MAS in the 2009 general election. Local authorities understand the "crossover voting" and the poor performance of the MAS in the 2010 local election as a result of the lack of consensus around the candidacy of Patana (interview with Jorge Silva), a conclusion shared by UN leaders (interview with Carlos Hugo Laruta).

The municipalities of La Paz and Achacachi follow a different pattern. Here the MAS has created a precarious local party structure that, together with the party's national leadership and elected representatives in Congress, selected candidates with relative autonomy from the allied grass-roots organizations. In both cases, MAS candidates emerged predominantly "from the top," but selection took slightly different forms in both municipalities.

In Achacachi, a rural district where there are strong peasant organizations with large membership and extensive territorial reach, the territorial party structure has an influential role in the selection of representatives to the municipal council and it bypasses the grass-roots organizations.[41] In 2010, for example, the mayor was "directly invited from above, by Eugenio Rojas and David Choquehuanca" (interview with Adrián Mamani Paucara).[42] That way of selection was seen by local leaders as an imposition carried out by the "MAS bureaucracy and its leadership," and as a result the candidates that emerged from local organizations ran under the ticket of a competing party (interview with Bernabé Paucara).[43] In this case, the presence of another party willing to serve as an electoral vehicle for grass-roots organizations by respecting their selection norms, gave the organizations an "exit" option.

In La Paz, where there are not similarly powerful grass-roots organizations, selection was similar, but the absence of such organizations meant that the central actors in selection were the MAS national leadership and the territorial party structure (interview with Jorge Silva). The power balance between the national leadership and the local party, however, was clearly tilted in favor of the former – that is, the local party did not have enough power to nominate its preferred candidates. Indeed, the composition of the electoral list reflects the de facto distribution of power quite clearly: most candidates nominated "from the top" were placed in the safe zone, whereas those nominated by the party were placed at the bottom (interview with Manuel Mercado).[44]

Strong Civil Society Aligned with Opposition

That last point was also true for Santa Cruz – Bolivia's largest city in the east, and one that has traditionally been considered a stronghold of the opposition. This city has a pattern that combines decentralized participation with clear

---

[41] The most powerful organization is the Federation of Peasant Workers Tupac Katari.

[42] Eugenio Rojas is a former mayor of Achacachi and a MAS senator. David Choquehuanca is Bolivia's Minister of Foreign Relations.

[43] In 2004, that party was the Pachakuti Indigenous Movement (Movimiento Indígena Pachakuti, MIP); in 2010, that party was the Movement for Sovereignty (Movimiento por la Soberanía, MPS).

[44] This was verified by interviewing all of the nominated candidates that did not fare well in the election.

top-down decision-making. The MAS has created a fairly strong territorial party structure that has an impressive mobilization capacity, and that nominates gives it a central role in candidate selection and local level governance.[45] This structure, which is led by an urban directorate,[46] draws support from two powerful urban sectors linked to the informal economy – transportation and street venders – and is territorially based in 16 political districts (interviews with Tito Santibañez and Rodolfo Zeballos). The urban structure operates "on the ground" autonomously from both the national leadership and the Santa Cruz Departmental Directorate led by peasant organizations (interview with Lidia Choque). And it wields some significant power in candidate selection, particularly in the nomination of representatives for the municipal council.

Yet, despite its organizational strength, decisions made at this level in Santa Cruz can be bypassed under certain circumstances or electoral considerations. The selection of the mayor is particularly instructive. In that case, though the territorial structure nominated Saúl Ávalos to run for mayor by an agreement with the political authorities and social bases in every district, the national leadership of the MAS considered Ávalos to be "unelectable" and vetoed his candidacy (interview with José Quiroz).[47] Through prominent elected officials from the Department of Santa Cruz – including for example the president of the senate, Gabriela Montaño – the MAS national leadership established a formal alliance with a new political party, the Popular and Solidarity Alliance (Alianza Popular Solidaria, ASIP).[48] This alliance guaranteed representation for ASIP in the municipal council, including an invitation to ASIP's president to run for mayor (interviews with Gabriela Montaño, Hugo Siles, and Freddy Soruco). Lidia Choque, a prominent peasant leader and former president of the Santa Cruz Departmental Directorate, commented that the "agreement 'from above' could have only happened because the social organizations [in Santa Cruz] are

---

[45] The configuration of this territorial structure, which is unparalleled in other cities of the country due to its density and stability, represents the peculiar historical trajectory of Santa Cruz and its organizational dynamics. It also responds to a deliberate decision by the MAS leadership to consolidate its presence in a territory that was initially seen as hostile to the MAS (interview with Álvaro García Linera).

[46] Santa Cruz is the only city in the country that has a MAS urban directorate.

[47] Electoral considerations played a central role in this decision. Indeed, opinion polls showed that Avalos's voting intention was very low in the city, and having him run as a mayor was a risky move for the MAS, particularly in its "expansive phase" to the east. In other words, the MAS could not afford to run with a candidate that, although it was nominated by the social bases, would only bring about a small voting flow.

[48] A political party founded by Roberto Fernández, the son of a former politician that formed the neo-populist party Civic Solidarity Union (Unión Cívica Solidaridad, UCS) in the 1990s. UCS made significant electoral inroads in the peripheral areas of Bolivia's largest cities, including La Paz, El Alto, and Santa Cruz. ASIP has built its precarious structure on top of the social networks developed by its antecedent.

not united and each supports whoever [whichever party] offers the best deal. Ávalos wasn't the candidate of the organizations and he had no support from them." Her statement is consistent with the central argument of this chapter: top-down decision-making is more likely to occur in contexts of strong and autonomous civil societies that (a) are not aligned with the MAS and (b) cannot agree on candidate selection.

CONCLUSIONS

This chapter examined the role of the party's grass-roots social bases in candidate selection processes within the MAS. The chapter revealed, first of all, striking levels of internal heterogeneity within the party. The MAS employs several candidate selection methods across the country. Some of those methods, or how they unfold, help to diffuse power territorially and among many grass-roots actors, acting as countervailing bottom-up correctives to hierarchy and concentrated authority. At the national level of representation, this is most often observed in the case of uninominal candidates, where densely organized and autonomous social actors wield more power and influence over the selection of candidates. Thus, electoral rules create the space for those actors to shape the process. At the local level, a similar pattern of power diffusion can be more commonly observed in municipalities where strong grass-roots organizations control the territory, something that is more commonly, though not always, observed in rural districts.

Using a wealth of original empirical evidence, the chapter identified the conditions and the political spheres under which broad and substantive grass-roots participation can be more or less effective in a movement-based party. Where civil society is strong, united, and aligned with the MAS, it can most effectively defy the tendencies toward top-down control by the leadership. Where civil society is strongly organized but lacks unity, or where it is strong but aligned with opposition parties, top-down elite choices are more likely to prevail. A similar pattern of high-power concentration occurs where civil society is weak.

Second, the qualitative evidence and findings presented in this chapter demonstrate that mitigating the trend toward top-down control can be seen both as a result of a mode of a party organizational development that privileges fluidity versus institutionalization and as a reflection of existing de facto power distributions within the MAS and autonomous social actors linked to the party – and also among these actors themselves.

This analysis is important for theoretical reasons: it has implications for understanding sources of variation in parties' organizational models and their internal power distributions. Just as parties deploy multiple strategies to attract different electoral constituencies (Luna 2014), they also look and operate remarkably differently in different settings depending on how the political space is structured. I have shown with a new source of empirical evidence that variation in the strength of autonomous civil society mobilization and patterns of party–civil society relations can shape the internal life of parties in meaningful ways. The evidence and analysis suggest that internal party processes should not be seen as a mere reflection of formal institutional rules governing a country. While these are important and are manifested, for example, in electoral rules, they do not fully explain sources of variation within parties like the MAS. To understand how these parties operate internally, then, it is crucial to examine the organizational context in which they are embedded and how this varies geographically.

Finally, I have demonstrated that, at least in the critical realm of candidate selection within the MAS, the party's grass-roots social bases wield significant power over the selection of party candidates, even though party leaders have sought to concentrate power in their own hands. The influence of densely organized grass-roots actors over candidate selection outcomes, or over *who* represents them in high electoral office, has been consequential in the Bolivian political arena: it served as a mechanism of political incorporation that led to the increased representation of previously underrepresented groups in both national and subnational political arenas.[49] In part as a result of this political incorporation, the sociodemographic composition of elected representatives has changed dramatically.

Today, representative institutions at the national and subnational levels more closely mirror Bolivia's social and cultural diversity, with the growing presence of women,[50] as well as indigenous peoples, peasants, and urban poor social groups in the formal and informal labor sectors.[51] All of these subordinate actors have gradually and pacifically displaced the hitherto dominant actors in Bolivia's political power game – a situation that resembles a circulation of political elites.[52]

---

[49] Survey data generated by the University of Salamanca's Survey on Latin American Parliamentary Elites (http://americo.usal.es/oir/elites/) provide ample evidence for this claim.

[50] Although there was a shift to greater representation of women after the 2006 Constituent Assembly, this increase can by no means be attributable only to the MAS; it is a by-product of the mobilization of Bolivia's women's movement. Bolivia introduced a gender parity law with the 2009 constitution.

[51] As an aside, the mode of nomination utilized by the MAS has ushered in a sort of Duvergerian "contagion from the left" that had an impact on how other parties select their own candidates, and *whom* they select. In 2014, even Jorge "Tuto" Quiroga – a conservative candidate – ran for the presidency with an indigenous activist as a running mate. Examples like these abound.

[52] Other analyses confirm this pattern, revealing that most legislators have a peasant background and that experience in popular organizations has replaced educational attainment as the key criterion for selection; see Zegada and Komadina (2014: 94, 61); see also Gonzalez Salas (2013) for a wonderful collection of life stories from Bolivian representatives, also confirmatory of the general pattern. Analyses at the executive level and the composition of state bureaucracies document a similar shift. See, for instance, Soruco, Franco Pinto and Durán (2014) and Espinoza Molina (2015).

Having examined candidate selection patterns within the MAS, the next chapter turns to an analysis of the degree to which greater grass-roots control over who gets into high electoral office also translates into enhanced political influence over agenda setting and greater input into national policy-making. It examines, in short, *how* societal preferences actually translate into the crafting of public policies and *who* wields power in the policy process and its institutions.

4

National Policy-Making Patterns

The previous chapter showed that the MAS's grass-roots social bases wield significant influence over the selection of party candidates for public office even though party leaders have sought to concentrate power in their own hands. This chapter examines the level of bottom-up influence in the policy-making process. It focuses on internal party politics and dynamics of autonomous social mobilization in the streets, and the extent to which both affect the crafting of public policies. In doing so, the chapter identifies the most important actors wielding power within the MAS, their sources of power, the relationships between them, and the degree to which they exert influence on the national policy-making sphere.

As I noted in the Introduction and Chapter 1, the existing literature lends overwhelming support to the argument about party oligarchization, linking the pressures of the electoral marketplace and the logics of the exercise of power with hierarchy and concentrated authority. These discussions, moreover, almost always entail a decrease over time in opportunities for participation in policy decisions by the party's social bases, with party elites becoming over time a separate caste with interests distinct from the movement base. A remedy to combat these Michelsian oligarchic tendencies, as I argue in this book, is more substantive participation in decision-making and a sense of responsiveness to societal demands. Is there anything about decision-making within Bolivia's MAS that might indicate whether such a remedy is actually at work?

To answer this question, this chapter proceeds in two ways. First, it provides a thick "anatomy" of the party's internal structures and examines whether those structures allow for grass-roots social actors to generate decisions by putting issues and priorities on the public agenda – and press for their enactment. This approach tries to capture what I call the "creative capacities" of the party's social movement bases by tracing their intervention in the legislative and executive arenas and their creative policy formulation abilities. The chapter demonstrates that while in this realm the policy process is open to some degree of bottom-up input, influence varies by policy area and remains contingent on the relative power of groups pushing for reform. Alongside the pressures in the direction of power centralization that are generally associated with the exercise of power, alternative patterns of policy-making can also be found in regard to different policy areas. In this chapter, more specifically, I show that grass-roots organizations are more likely to have creative capacities where the policies affect them directly and visibly in their productive roles.

Second, the chapter examines the extent to which internal party structures and social mobilization from below generate pressures and impose constraints on the exercise of power by the party in office. This approach tries to capture the "constraining capacities" of the party's grass-roots social bases by tracing their veto and counter-mobilization power.[1] In this chapter, I demonstrate that the constraining capacities of the party's social movement bases are largely determined by their ability to assemble large veto coalitions. It is in this area that top-down decision-making is most constrained in the case of the MAS, not only in relation to the other cases examined in this book (discussed in Chapter 5), but also in relation to earlier experiences with corporatism in Latin America (Collier and Collier 1979) and more recent experiences of state-society relations and top-down policy-making.[2]

This chapter shows that attributes of party organization defined in its early development (discussed in Chapter 2), such as its loose bureaucratic structure, provide opportunities for the party's grass-roots social bases to act autonomously, with few bureaucratic constraints, and thus shape and modify policy initiatives. In the absence of strong national and local party structures serving as "transmission belts," autonomous mobilization from below serves as the strongest mechanism counteracting hierarchy and concentrated authority.[3]

---

[1] We can think of these constraining capacities as "social vetoes" to distinguish them from the more institutional "veto points" described by Immergut (1992) or Huber, Ragin, and Stephens (1993), who focus on the degree to which constitutional structures disperse power and open channels of influence on the formulation and implementation of policy. My approach is also different from Tsebelis's (2002) notion of "veto players," which focuses on the actors whose agreement is necessary for altering the legislative status quo. I conceive of social vetoes as individual or collective actors whose behavior (in Congress or in the streets) can impose effective constraints on the authority and decision-making power of party leaders in office.

[2] A comparative example might help to illustrate the contrast. In countries like Argentina, for instance, the distribution of handouts and other clientelistic exchanges to union leaders helped to neutralize union opposition to market reforms. The inability or lack of capacity of the rank and file in labor organizations to hold their leaders accountable to their interests facilitated party control over labor movements and their demobilization (Murillo 2001), as well as the imposition of "bait-and-switch" market reforms by labor-based parties (Roberts 2015a).

[3] Important for generating and sustaining autonomous mobilization capacity is the presence of strong bottom-up channels of decision-making within those organizations that, especially at the bottom of the chain, can shape the process of mobilization. The leadership of major national organizations cannot just dictate the ways in which organizations at the base are going to

In short, the chapter stresses the theoretical relevance of the "constant cause" of strong, autonomous civil society mobilization (as defined in Chapter 1), which allows mass organized constituencies to influence, constrain, and hold the party leadership accountable in a continuous way.

MAJOR TRENDS WITHIN THE MAS

This section shows that, on balance, while the substantive influence of sponsoring and allied groups on setting the agenda and steering policy in their desired direction is limited in some areas (i.e., economy) and more open in others (i.e., mining and agrarian policy), the party's capacity to keep its leadership accountable by blocking, modifying, and constraining government policy is more prominent. The leadership, then, is sometimes held hostage by sponsoring and allied movements and is forced to discuss, negotiate, and reach compromises in ways that at least partially counteract the trend toward top-down, concentrated executive authority.

As seen in Chapter 2, becoming a governing party deeply altered the internal dynamics of the MAS. This movement-to-governing party transition involved the articulation of alliances with a wide array of peasant and urban workers' associations, which can be partially explicable in terms of the logic of supra-class electoral recruitment theorized by Przeworski and Sprague (1986). Such a coalition building strategy yielded satisfactory electoral results, but it also led to the configuration of a strikingly heterodox and loose governing coalition. After assuming office, the challenge was how to organize power – and how to actually govern with that coalition. Tensions and conflict quickly emerged between the bottom-up dynamics present in the origins and early development of the MAS and the tendencies toward top-down control associated with exercising power.

Many observers have argued that the MAS has become increasingly detached from movements and popular organizations as a governing party (Zuazo 2010; Webber 2011; Zegada et al. 2011; Madrid 2012). To support this claim, some scholars have looked at the composition and evolution of Morales's cabinet of ministers. While his first cabinet included a mix of leaders of rural and urban organizations as well as people of humble origins (Stefanoni and Do Alto 2006; Costa 2008),[4] studies have found that the presence of these in the cabinet has tended to decrease over time (Laruta 2008; Zegada, Torrez,

---

go – either *for* mobilization or quiescence. The members of these organizations at the bottom can often place strong constraints on the authority and decision-making power of their leadership – their ability to organize mobilization or dictate quiescence – and thereby help to keep the partisan allies in power responsive and accountable to their interests.

[4] This observation led Bolivia's Vice-President to characterize the Morales government as a "government of the social movements." For an argument that challenges this notion, see Zegada et al (2008).

and Camara 2008; Do Alto 2011). Indeed, the participation of representatives of social movements and popular organizations in top-level positions within the executive branch has been generally limited and isolated. With some exceptions, key positions have been occupied by a technocratic elite that is "invited" into the ranks of the party, that does not represent grass-roots organizations, and thus have few checks from below.[5]

A different story can be told about the sociodemographic composition of Congress. About 70 percent of MAS representatives in the 2009–15 Congress are men and women drawn from and nominated by a wide array of rural and urban-popular sector organizations.[6] That they overwhelmingly come from indigenous, peasant, and urban-popular groups does not mean that these organizations have a strong influence on setting the legislative agenda, however. Scholars have noted that under the Morales government, elected representatives have had a "subordinate standing" in relation to the executive (see Crabtree 2013: 287; also Fornillo 2008: 3). As Do Alto (2011: 105) points out, when the MAS became a governing party, the locus of internal decision-making switched from its elected representatives in Congress to the executive branch (see also Anria et al. 2010).

Both observations – that in Bolivia today the locus of "real" authority lies on the executive, where the presence of popular groups is generally limited and isolated – lend some support to the idea of an "oligarchization" of the MAS as a governing party. However, matters are less straightforward once we examine decision-making by looking at a broader set of internal organizational dynamics combined with the dynamics of autonomous social mobilization by popular constituencies.

When Morales assumed office in January 2006, for example, he addressed the demands set forth by the anti-neoliberal mass mobilizations of the early 2000s, which had, de facto, set the government's "post-neoliberal" agenda (Silva 2009: 143).[7] Early in his first term, Morales declared the nationalization of the hydrocarbon industry – which was actually an increase in royalty

---

[5] A key example of this is Luis Arce Catacora, who led the Ministry of Economy between 2006 and 2017.

[6] This represents an even larger percentage in comparison to the 2006–9 Congress. As noted in Chapter 3, the candidate selection methods employed by the MAS, particularly to nominate "uninominal" representatives, have led to a growing presence of popular sectors in this institution. Other analyses confirm this pattern, revealing that most legislators have a peasant background and that experience in popular organizations has replaced educational attainment as the key criterion for selection; see Zegada and Komadina (2014: 94, 61).

[7] This was also known as the "October Agenda." It was not a clear party program designed by the MAS, but more of a list of aspirations that emerged from the insurrection of El Alto in October 2003, which the MAS used for its campaign. The agenda included a wide array of popular demands to re-found Bolivia in the name of the poor and the indigenous majority. Among the key demands included in the agenda were the nationalization of hydrocarbons, an agrarian reform, and the call for a constituent assembly.

payments on multinational companies – in order to generate greater revenue (Koivumaeki 2015).[8] Morales also proclaimed an agrarian reform, promoted an anti-corruption law, and called for a constituent assembly through which popularly elected delegates would rewrite the country's constitution and establish the foundations for a "plurinational" state.[9] All of these actions can be seen as examples of Morales's positive accountability to the MAS's grass-roots social bases; that is, as attempts to follow through on the demands from the direct action protests of 2000–5, or as examples of "leading by obeying" the party's social and programmatic base. They can also be seen as attempts to foster close ties between the party in government and its organized bases of support, an effort to distance the MAS from the traditional parties in Bolivia.

Since its origins in the mid-1990s, the MAS's core constituency has been composed of the *cocaleros* in the Chapare region.[10] Together with other major peasant associations, they have maintained a strong influence over the party's platform, agenda, and policy orientation.[11] The centrality of the peasant leadership in the party is hard to overstate (Do Alto 2011).[12] Yet, as the MAS became a mass movement-based party with a national presence, it also established a broad network of alliances with other rural and urban-popular organizations (interviews with Iván Iporre, Alejandro Almaraz, and Walter Chávez). In cities that are central for winning electoral majorities, such as La Paz, El Alto, Cochabamba, and Santa Cruz, the MAS has drawn support from two powerful sectors of similar socioeconomic background: transportation and street venders. These two sectors are generally associated with Bolivia's large

---

[8] This early decision allowed the Morales government to capture windfall rents that would be used to boost public spending on health, education, and social security, without creating macroeconomic imbalances.

[9] The constitution is of particular interest because, in some ways, it exemplifies the main tendencies found in this book (Chapter 2). The 2009 Constitution reflected the MAS's attempts to follow through on the protests' repeated calls for a constituent assembly. At the same time, the outcome of the constituent assembly was a text approved by pro-government delegates only, and many people accused the MAS of forcing the constitution through in antidemocratic ways. Nevertheless, that draft was negotiated and modified in Congress, with input from opposition forces and compromises on both sides. It became law with the constitutional referendum of January 2009 (see Stoyan 2014).

[10] This point is elaborated in Chapter 2.

[11] These organizations include the Unique Confederation of Rural Laborers of Bolivia (Confederación Sindical Única de Trabajadores Campesinos de Bolivia, CSUTCB); the Syndicalist Confederation of Intercultural Communities of Bolivia (Confederación Sindical de Comunidades Interculturales de Bolivia, CSCIB); and the Bartolina Sisa National Confederation of Campesino, Indigenous, and Native Women of Bolivia (Confederación Nacional de Mujeres Campesinas Indígenas Originarias de Bolivia "Bartolina Sisa," CNMCIOB-BS).

[12] For example, Morales retains responsibility for leading both the MAS and a social movement organization, the Six Federations of the Tropics of Cochabamba, the overarching union of coca growers.

"informal" labor sector. Alliances were also made with associations representing artisans, microenterprises, pensioners, and independent mining cooperatives, among others.[13] Once in national-level power, tensions emerged between these new allies and the MAS government, particularly regarding policy choices and the distribution of political power.

These "late incorporations" complicated the decision-making processes, as growing heterogeneity in the MAS presupposed more intricate forms of consensus building among diverse constituent groups. With exceptions, such as the configuration of the Unity Pact, which brought together a wide array of organizations and provided input for the constitutional reform, the MAS did not formalize clear channels of participation and consultation in decision-making.[14] There has been a strong resistance against institutionalizing the relations between the party's grass-roots social bases and the MAS, partly because movement leaders think that formalizing these linkages might lead the MAS to operate as a conventional political party, i.e., one with "top-down" control associated with a formal hierarchical elite structure.[15]

Insofar as these mechanisms remain absent, Morales "is a referee and no one challenges his decisions" (interview with Jorge Silva). Scholars have shown that Morales has concentrated great power in the executive branch at the expense of the national legislature, as well as courts and non-partisan oversight agencies (Anria et al. 2010: 254–60; Madrid 2012: 163). And it is hard to overstate his centrality in the policy-making process (Crabtree 2013: 287–8). Yet, although he is a dominant actor in the policy process, he is not all-powerful, and he is not the sole actor. Morales cannot do as he pleases, as there are strong limits to his power that are shaped by the nature of the MAS's internal organization and the dynamics of autonomous social mobilization.[16] It is precisely the MAS's fluidity, as described in Chapter 2, or the diffuse and non-institutionalized mode of interaction between power holders, the party, and the party's grass-roots social bases that leaves wide maneuvering room for these to exert pressure on the

---

[13] The MAS has had a particularly difficult time trying to build alliances with other urban sectors, like teachers and health workers (see Do Alto 2011: 108).

[14] The Unity Pact (Pacto de Unidad) was an alliance of rural and indigenous popular organizations from the west and east of the country. Operating independently from the MAS, the Unity Pact produced a complete draft of a constitutional text and presented it to the Constituent Assembly. Above all, it provided advisory consultation. Since the new constitution was approved, however, the Unity Pact has not had active participation in decision-making processes (interview with Juan Carlos Pinto).

[15] MAS's leaders define the organization as a "political instrument" of the peasant indigenous movement, rather than a conventional party (Chapter 2). Leaders do not want such a party, and they think of it as an obsolete type of organization that can retard social and political change. In this sense, it bears noting that the parallels with the early Peronism are striking (see McGuire 1997: chapter 1).

[16] These are limitations set by Morales's own political camp. His capacity to shape policy is also limited by the opposition and domestic and international investors.

leadership (see also Anria 2013: 37). The movements and popular sector organizations that shape the party and support the government, too, have the potential to play an important policy-making role.

As is demonstrated in the pages below, these organized mass constituencies can impact decision-making in at least four ways. First, they can generate decisions by putting issues on the public agenda – be it via the party structure, their representatives in Congress, and/or their direct access to the executive branch. Second, they can deploy street power and use other pressure mechanisms to assist with the passing of legislation. Third, they can veto or block the passage of legislation via their representatives in Congress *before* the proposal becomes law. Finally, they can mobilize autonomously against the government if their interests are threatened or seen as improperly accounted for by government policy during the implementation stage (or *after* the legislation has been passed). Sometimes, they can even put enough pressure to force the leadership to reverse decisions or even take alternative courses of action, placing real constraints on the centralization of power and top-down decision-making.

CREATIVE CAPACITIES

As seen in Chapter 3, a wide array of social movements and popular sector associations in Bolivia have increasingly boosted their access to representation in Congress and other state bureaucracies via their associational linkages to the MAS.[17] The question here, in this section, is whether they have also been incorporated in the mainspring of national decision-making power (whether their increased representation has *also* meant expanded influence on decision-making) or whether greater representation has been supplanted by top-down control or more concentrated decision-making once the MAS became a governing party.

This section highlights the tensions between these two logics. It shows that while the capacity of grass-roots actors to generate decisions from below may initially seem limited, their influence should not be overlooked because decision-making is an interactive, negotiated, and contestatory process. Not only does Morales consult about strategic decisions with the leadership of major popular movements and organizations, but he also includes their demands, claims, and priorities on the agenda.[18] While the party structure lacks real influence, an analysis of the parliamentary body reveals a more mixed picture: there are clear tendencies toward the centralization of power in the

---

[17] Critics like Luis Tapia, a prominent member of a group of intellectuals known as *Comuna*, criticizes this scheme of participation by noting that the MAS "has maintained the traits of the relation between political parties and civil society that were molded in neoliberal terms, that is, access to public office goes through the party membership or negotiation with that party" (Tapia 2011: 161).

[18] For a parallel argument, see Do Alto (2011).

hands of a small group of representatives in what can indeed be seen as an executive-dominated legislative process, but at the same time the presence of powerful sectors reduces the capacity of the executive to impose its agenda, as it faces multiple social vetoes. At the executive level, bottom-up influence varies by policy area, generally reflecting the existing balance of power among competing groups and organizations. The analysis also points to the importance of considering different "constellations" of power to better understand the different positioning of actors in decision-making in changing circumstances. If the governing party lacks a majority of seats in Congress, for example, allied groups have a clearer incentive to cooperate with it – particularly if they perceive that it advances their interests. In turn, having legislative majorities increases the likelihood of the MAS to receive increasing pressures from below by dispersing demand making. In Bolivia today, this dynamic generally occurs via autonomous social mobilization from below.[19]

The Irrelevance of the Party Structure

The MAS's bureaucracy is strikingly underdeveloped. The party has very limited professional paid staff, equipment, records of membership, and finances (see Anria 2009). Its headquarters are located in a very modest office in La Paz, where members of the National Directorate meet at least once a month to coordinate activities. However, formal leadership bodies such as the National Directorate and the Departmental Directorates do not play an important decision-making role, and they lack independent authority vis-à-vis MAS office holders, particularly the president and his ministers, and also prominent leaders of social organizations.

Party structure is designed to disperse power. However, when asked about the role of party structure in shaping policy options, party platforms, campaign strategies, and overall party strategy, most interviewees agree that formal party organs have little influence. Instead, they are generally seen as "empty shells" with no real power. And in general, this is true: party organs do not generate policies and strategies.[20] As key advisor to the National Directorate, Ximena Centellas commented in an interview:

---

[19] This argument is consistent with the findings of a team of researchers in *Fundación UNIR*, who found a drastic and sustained rise in protest activity targeting the government since 2009 (UNIR 2012).

[20] Positional authority within the party generally does not correspond to "real" authority, legitimacy, or political influence. The exception is Morales, who is both the president of the MAS National Directorate and the Executive Secretary of the Six Federations of the Tropics of Cochabamba, the overarching union of coca growers in the Chapare. The question "Who is most influential in the party?" repeatedly turned up Morales, certain ministers, and prominent leaders of social organizations. With exceptions, like MAS's Secretary of Foreign Relations, Leonida Zurita, formal authorities within the party did not turn up as influential in any systematic way. Power and influence depend more on personal skill than on positional authority.

The formal party organs at the local, departmental, and national levels are 'political' bodies, and for the most part they do not have the strength or the experience to propose anything, really. Their work focuses more on dealing with intraparty conflicts, and with the conflicts that arise within allied social organizations over power struggles (Interview with Ximena Centellas; also with Concepción Ortiz).

Instead of relying on party organs for generating decisions, MAS office holders rely more on ad hoc committees for receiving input on specific topics.[21] These committees are almost always composed of small groups of influential or trusted individuals within the executive branch, who, due to their unstable and fluctuating nature, do not form any sort of organic group with shared social and political interests and incentives. In short, they do not constitute an entrenched "oligarchy."

According to the party statute, the highest decision-making body is the Regular National Congress (CON). It invites delegates of allied grass-roots organizations to participate and elect members of the National Directorate, which must be headed by leaders of peasant-based organizations (Article 18, b). The CON also invites allied movements and popular organizations to approve, reform, or modify the party's Declaration of Principles, the Program of Government, and the Statute (Article 18, c). In addition, it reviews disciplinary sanctions imposed by the Ethics Board and resolves disputes over statutory provisions. Other party conventions include the Organic Congress, which meets to decide on party organizational issues (Article 19). Although these conventions ensure broad grass-roots participation, they do not decide on public policies or on programmatic orientation. In addition, critics like political scientist Luis Tapia have described them as "moments of legitimation" of already-made decisions (cited in Zegada et al. 2011: 255).[22] Observations in party national and departmental conventions, and interviews with their participants, lend additional support to Tapia's claim.

Scholars have noted that instead of relying on bureaucratic party structures Morales prefers to have direct unmediated consultations with the leadership of grass-roots organizations prior to making decisions (Crabtree 2013: 287). And

---

[21] For example, an ad hoc political committee was formed to design the strategy for the 2005 electoral campaign. Here the party organs, as independent agents, played virtually no role. Instead, the key actors in this process were individuals who would then become ministers under the first Morales government (interview with Iván Iporre). This tendency to bypass party organs was aggravated in the 2009 presidential campaign, after having exercised power for one term, thus revealing the increasing weakness of formal leadership bodies vis-à-vis MAS office holders. Also, the development of the 2009–15 Program of Government is particularly revealing of this centripetal trend. According to Wálter Chávez, a key advisor to the government and co-writer of the program, this document was prepared by a reduced technocratic group, which "restrained itself to writing down a concise version of a program designed by Evo Morales himself" (interview with Walter Chávez).

[22] This logic of decision-making is reminiscent of the functioning of the workers' movement in 1950s Bolivia under the leadership of Juan Lechín.

most of the leaders of (principally allied) social movements and organizations interviewed for this book confirmed this pattern. The overwhelming majority of these consultation channels, however, are non-bureaucratic and non-institutionalized.[23] This makes them more likely to depend on the good will of the leader, rather than on clearly established rules and expectations. There are also annual meetings held between Morales and allied social organizations to exchange feedback and get input on public policies. However, observers have noted that over time, the tendency has been for these channels to become less important for generating relevant decisions. Drawing on interviews with key grass-roots actors, a study by a team of researchers under María Teresa Zegada found that many leaders perceive that their voices are decreasingly heard by the MAS government and that their input on decision-making is limited (Zegada et al. 2011: 249–54).[24] My interviews lend additional support to their findings, but they also suggest that additional caveats need to be introduced, for example, by looking at the behavior of the parliamentary group.

The Parliamentary Group

The party statute says little about the relationship between the formal party organs and representatives in Congress. The expectation, however, is that representatives work closely with their constituencies, that they contribute financially to the party organization, and that they regularly attend party conventions to inform authorities and the rank and file about their work in Congress (interviews with Leonida Zurita, Concepción Ortiz, Modesto Condori, and Nélida Sifuentes).

Elected representatives are only related to the party structure indirectly, as they are agents of multiple principals. Many have been nominated by popular sector organizations with which they retain strong connections; others have been nominated "from above" due to their individual contribution to the overall party list; and finally, they all have been elected by voters, most of whom are neither party nor social movement members. The interviewed representatives often provide different answers to the question of *to whom* they are really accountable: the social organizations, the MAS, the "process of change" led by the MAS, president Morales, and the voters. The lack of a strong party structure providing policy guidance means that representatives lack a common

[23] An example of this would be the Cochabamba summit of December 2011, which was an ad hoc meeting convened by Morales and the MAS to receive input on public policies from below. By the end of the summit, which ensured the participation of a wide array of allied and non-allied groups, 70 legislative proposals were made and sent to Congress. Critics argued that the MAS use these types of meetings instrumentally to boost its image and its alleged participatory ethos when its relationships with social organizations and movements are contested in the streets.

[24] This observation leads the authors of this study to conclude that the MAS has not fulfilled the promise of the principle of "governing by obeying" promoted by Morales after he gained power.

socialization inside the party. Because they come from multiple sectors of society, they have not had a common socialization outside the party either. In principle, this might enable representatives to pick and choose to which constituency they are loyal, and this explains why my interviews reveal a wide range of answers. At the same time, however, it creates incentives for the executive branch to develop its own instances of socialization and control, which serve to centralize power and discipline the behavior of MAS representatives.[25] Their behavior in office seems to follow an executive-enforced collective discipline that is at odds with the logic of constituency representation.[26]

As Vice President García Linera commented:

The presence of [representatives from] grass-roots organizations in Congress is not only symbolic; they are also heavily involved in the design of policies. The interesting thing is that the MAS, being a flexible and heterogeneous coalition, has to negotiate constantly with competing organizations to enact legislation. Every law has to be developed *with* the social organizations, and when one of them tries to dominate the process then there is the veto of another organization (Interview with Álvaro García Linera).

Although there is *some* truth in this statement, it needs to be qualified in at least two ways.

First, it is true that social movements and popular organizations have increased their representation in Congress by unprecedented levels through their relationships with the MAS. However, as noted in Chapter 3, while some representatives are selected by the grass-roots bases through mechanisms of direct participation, others are directly "invited" by the leadership and have few checks from below. Many of the "invited" leaders have quickly become the most prominent MAS representatives due to their personal skills, their ways to relate effectively to the media, and their ability to operate effectively within representative institutions.[27] That the party's structure is not strong enough to

---

[25] My observations and interviews indicate that such efforts occur in the Vice Presidency, where representatives meet weekly to decide on legislative strategy. The presence of the President or the Vice President and of key ministers is not uncommon in these meetings, and it is contingent upon the relevance of the topic. The idea behind the meetings is to generate an internal space of debate *before* legislative proposals are sent to Congress, and to avoid open discussion on the legislative floor by projecting an image of unity. While some representatives conceive of this as a "collective" agenda-setting exercise designed to ensure a balance between territorial and sectoral demands, others see it as an imposition from the top.

[26] As Komadina (2013: 23) notes, "the behavior of representatives is closely controlled by the executive … representatives thus have a limited capacity to criticize or observe legislative proposals … and acts of rebellion are sanctioned." Many of the MAS representatives interviewed, particularly those representing "uninominal" districts, expressed discontent with this decision-making pattern, conceiving of themselves as relatively powerless to generate decisions.

[27] Differential media access creates endemic conflicts among representatives. Conflicts arise when more extroverted representatives assume a role of "spokespeople" for the MAS without any prior discussion with their colleagues.

project policies and strategies has the unwanted consequence of an increase in the power of certain individual representatives, whose power often depends less on their experience as grass-roots or party leaders than on personal skills and resources.[28] From the point of view of the party's peasant leadership, however, these are generally unreliable (interviews with Leonida Zurita, Sergio Loayza, and Concepción Ortiz). If they align uncritically with the agenda of the executive, the legislative process is generally dynamic, and these leaders are praised for their loyalty. If they do not align with the executive and publicly express dissent, they can quickly be seen as traitors.[29]

Second, despite the growing presence of representatives from popular sector movements and organizations in Congress, this trend has not automatically translated into greater independent power of legislators to set the legislative agenda. Most of the legislators interviewed commented that they have limited capacity to initiate important legislation as independent agents.[30] Most of them could not identify important or controversial legislative proposals that they had introduced to Congress. Actually, most legislative proposals are brought to the floor by the executive branch.[31] However, a pattern emerging from systematic interviews with representatives and grass-roots leaders is that the presence of

---

[28] In addition to weak party structures, the informal rule of no-reelection prevailing within the MAS encourages individualistic behavior and the emergence of this type of leader; at the same time, in the longer run, it helps to prevent the consolidation of oligarchies within the parliamentary group.

[29] One of the most prominent accusations of treason occurred in early 2013, when the then-president of the Chamber of Deputies, MAS representative for Cochabamba Rebeca Delgado, criticized publicly the Asset Recovery Bill that had been introduced to the floor via the Ministry of Government. According to Delgado: "I knew that the legislative proposal, as it was sent to us, violated the spirit and the text of the constitution. Because the executive really wanted to push through this one, however, I 'obeyed' and brought the proposal to the floor. But the proposal faced strong resistance by the MAS parliamentary group, as many sectors, like transportation and street traders, would have been affected by it. And we were on the verge of not passing a bill that had been sent by the executive, which would have been unprecedented. I noticed that the executive was not willing to accept certain modifications, so I went public and criticized the proposal and its designers" (interview with Rebeca Delgado). This sparked a series of verbal confrontations between Delgado and members of the executive branch, including the minister of government and the Vice President. The Vice President called Delgado pejoratively a "free thinker" and made the bold claim that she had not respected the principle of "democratic centralism" that, for him, structures authority within the MAS. That Delgado is now regarded as a member of the opposition is a testament to the idea that party indiscipline is not tolerated.

[30] Rebeca Delgado, a former president of the Chamber of Deputies, commented: "if an individual legislator brings in a legislative proposal for a specific project, the executive branch generally does not send any financing for it. This leads me to say that, in a context where the executive gives you the agenda, constituency representation is undervalued and not fully exercised" (interview with Rebeca Delgado).

[31] To many representatives, these proposals are developed in consultation between the executive and the grass-roots organizations. Although this is hard to observe empirically, they are also correct in pointing out that many legislative proposals are imposed by the imperatives of the country's new constitution, which establishes deadlines to regulate certain provisions.

representatives coming from grass-roots organizations serves the purpose of having access to privileged information, which allows them to obstruct or modify legislation if it threatens their group interests. From the point of view of the MAS leadership the unwanted consequence is that some of the groups that join the MAS then become pressure or veto groups from within, making it difficult to pass legislation in Congress. They are also pressure groups from without, by leading resistance to legislation in the streets.

At first glance, then, the relationships between the executive and these representatives appear instrumental. Under this interpretation, groups are seen as exchanging organizational loyalty to the MAS to the extent that it delivers specific benefits – or that at least it does not threaten their interests. Examples of this pattern can be observed in the behavior of representatives of the transportation sector and cooperative miners, which are two of the strongest and most powerful groups that have gained representation through the MAS. Upon further inspection, however, it is also possible to interpret their behavior as creating incentives for the executive to negotiate constantly with allied groups. This means that the executive cannot impose its agenda without challenges, and thus setting the agenda requires negotiation.

Reflecting on the nature of political representation, legislators from these powerful sectors and leaders in their respective organizations support the idea of a "corporativist" representation. Typical responses include: "I should represent the interests of my social organization"; "as a representative from the transportation sector, I need to keep an eye on legislation that can potentially damage my sector"; "we receive pressures from below so that we defend the interests of our sector"; "we support the government but our representatives are there to keep control on unwanted legislation that can damage our sector." They are clearly not the only representatives expressing these views,[32] but they are among the few who have the power to actually veto the passage of

---

[32] Most of my interviews reveal that representatives share a common tension: whether they should be accountable to their constituencies *or* be "loyal" to Morales and the MAS. The social constituencies, particularly in the case of "uninominal" representatives, generally do put pressures on their representatives so that they defend the interests of their organizations and their territory. And consequentially these representatives are generally more reluctant to accept an imposed party line, particularly when compared to their "plurinominal" colleagues. Yet, the informal rule of non-reelection places important limits on the incentives to be responsive to their social bases. Instead, it helps to cultivate better relationships with the executive, as post-Congress career paths depend more on these relationships than on their performance in Congress or on bureaucratic procedures within the party. This is particularly acute in a context where the expectation is that the MAS will keep winning elections. For the argument on the "careerist" orientation of legislators in contexts of term limitations, see Carey (1996). His argument, however, is that the situation of presidents controlling the political fortunes of term-limited representatives leads to a reduction of party discipline and cohesiveness. In the case of the MAS, I found the opposite. Much of it has to do with the dominant nature of the MAS within Bolivia's political system.

legislation because they are backed by well-organized and very disciplined sectors with high mobilization capacity.

So far, my sketch of the MAS points to a trend toward the centralization of power in the executive that is hard to overlook. The lack of a strong party structure providing guidance and the lack of real influence of representatives to set the legislative agenda have the consequence of an increase in the power of Morales and other entrepreneurs within the executive. Yet, despite this centripetal trend, policy-making in Bolivia is a highly negotiated process, and the capacity of allied popular groups to affect decisions should not be overlooked. When grass-roots social actors are strongly organized and can mobilize large groups of people in the streets autonomously, they can put real constraints on the government's agenda and steer policy in their desired direction. A better place to examine these dynamics is within the executive branch – to which I now turn.

The Executive Branch

The literature on developmental states is useful here because it makes the general theoretical claim that in order to achieve desired goals state agencies need to be connected to their constituencies.[33] Early theorizing stresses the importance of autonomous professional bureaucracies that are connected with their business communities to achieve economic growth (Johnson 1982: 315–17; Evans 1995).[34] Although these studies highlight the need for insulation from popular pressures to ensure economic growth, more recent theorizing has noted the importance of having more meaningful engagement of grass-roots organizations with state bureaucracies for achieving successful human development outcomes (Sandbrook et al. 2007; Evans 2010; Evans and Heller 2015).[35] Popular input is seen as important, but is likely to vary greatly across areas or state bureaucracies. In ministries whose policies affect well-organized popular constituencies in a direct or visible manner, there is generally more pressure

---

[33] Chalmers Johnson (1982) raises this point in his study of the "Japanese model." In particular, he highlights the synergy produced by having close interactions between state actors and industrial elites to achieve developmental goals. Peter Evans (1995: 12) develops the concept of "embedded autonomy" to stress the importance of having bureaucracies that can operate autonomously from popular pressures but that are also sufficiently connected to their societies and particularly their business elites. In his view, these two elements are seen as necessary for a state to qualify as "developmental."

[34] For a review of this literature, see Onis (1991).

[35] This is because the twenty-first century developmental state is conceived of as a capability-enhancing state, in contrast to its twentieth century version, which was focused more on economic growth. Because policies that promote the capability of citizens require states to have accurate information and continuous feedback, the twenty-first century developmental state needs a less technocratic and more open approach to policy-making based on close ties between state agencies and broad cross-sections of civil society (Evans and Heller 2015).

from these groups to influence decisions.[36] In ministries whose policies affect more diffuse cross-sections of society rather than clearly defined constituencies, the pressure by collective actors is generally more dispersed. These agencies tend to lack strong links with grass-roots organizations for consultation and cooperation.[37]

To assess these arguments and evaluate the degree of grass-roots substantive influence at the level of the executive branch, this subsection draws on examples of policies developed by the ministries of Rural Development, Mining, and Economy, as well as the Office of the Vice Presidency. When I was conducting fieldwork, my expectation was to find different levels of grass-roots influence across government agencies. Thinking in terms of a continuum, I expected to find, at one extreme, little grass-roots presence and influence in the Ministry of Economy and the Office of the Vice Presidency. At the other extreme, I expected to find a more prominent presence and influence of powerful grass-roots social actors in the Ministry of Rural Development and Lands and, to a lesser extent, in the Ministry of Mining.

Other scholars have already noted that the Ministry of Economy and Public Finance is, for the lack of a better term, "sealed" to the participation of popular sector groups in the steering of macroeconomic policy (Stefanoni 2010: 161). My interviews with high-level officials within the ministry, including the minister himself, lend additional support to that observation: "I believe that people *have* to participate. But unfortunately, the Ministry of Economy is a very technical one; and it has to be that way, don't you think?" (interview with Luis Arce Catacora). As Chief of Staff María Nela Prada also commented,

there is an institutional inertia that tends to exclude collective actors from the exercise of power. We receive legislative proposals from social organizations, but we don't work permanently with them. Their participation is not regular; it is not institutionalized (Interview with María Nela Prada).

Despite this trend toward the marginalization of grass-roots actors, they do have some degree of access to the ministry and, in some occasions, have worked on legislative proposals alongside. Bolivia's new pension law, for example, was

---

[36] The research on land redistribution and agrarian reform is particularly useful here. It suggests that agriculture ministries and land reform agencies, whose policies generally reach large groups of clearly defined constituencies, tend to be bureaucracies highly contested by collective actors with competing interests regarding agrarian policy (Montgomery 1972; Cleaves and Scurrah 1980; Borras Jr, Saturnino and Franco 2010). In addition, the literature suggests that in order to be successful in their goals, these ministries tend to establish close connections to their key beneficiaries – be these agricultural elites, small-scale entrepreneurs, or peasant farmers (Smith 1993). Similar arguments can be extended to other ministries dealing with production and industry generally, such as the Ministry of Mining and the Ministry of Labor.

[37] The literature on social movement outcomes makes parallel arguments and lends additional support to the expectation that movement influence varies according to policy area (Amenta and Caren 2004: 462). For a comprehensive review of this literature, see Amenta et al. (2010).

developed in close dialog between the Ministry of Economy and the Bolivian Workers Central (COB), the country's national trade union federation (interviews with Luis Arce Catacora and Pedro Montes). As a symbol of this state–society cooperation, the law was promulgated on December 10, 2010 at the COB's headquarters (Niedzwiecki and Anria n.d.). However, this is more of an exception than a rule in the routine of this ministry.

A similar pattern of limited presence and influence of grass-roots actors can be observed in the Office of the Vice Presidency, which is an important producer of legislative proposals in the country. Popular sector groups are occasionally invited to present their demands and share their opinions on given proposals. However, their participation is not institutionalized and depends more on the good will of gatekeepers and other contingent factors than on firmly established rules and expectations. The Office of the Vice Presidency coordinates the relations between the executive branch and the MAS representatives in Congress (particularly with the presidents of both legislative chambers), and occasionally between these and the collective actors that might be affected by a proposed legislation (interviews with Walter Melendres, Adolfo Mendoza, and Gabriela Montaño).

The Ministry of Rural Development and Lands reveals a starkly different pattern. Since the rise to power of the MAS, powerful grass-roots actors with a rural base, including highland *peasant* movements and lowland *indigenous* organizations, have disputed the control of this ministry. On several occasions both factions have called for the resignation of various high-ranking officials, exerting enough pressure to succeed in some cases. Land issues are at the core of the dispute between organizations with competing views on the agrarian question (Bottazzi and Rist 2012: 544).[38] At the beginning of Morales's mandate, peasant and indigenous factions converged around the issue of land reform and they configured a reform coalition that developed the Law of Communitarian Renewal of the Agrarian Reform.[39] The implementation stage, however, has been anything but smooth; tensions and power struggles emerged among these groups over the distribution, reach, and pace of the reform process. Almost five years after the reform, peasant organizations such as the CSUTCB and the CSCIB led mass mobilizations arguing that the reform was unfairly benefiting

---

[38] Peasant groups favor an individual-right property regime, and indigenous groups advocate a communal conception of land ownership. The central issue here is that communal lands cannot be bought and sold.

[39] In addition to drafting the legislative proposal in collaboration with the vice-ministry of land (interview with Alejandro Almaraz), peasant and indigenous groups of the highlands and the lowlands helped to pass the enabling legislation for the Law of Renewal by exerting direct pressure in the streets when intransigent opposition forces controlled the Congress and threatened to block the government's planned reform (Bolpress 2006). This behavior is consistent with arguments in the social movement literature, which point to the importance of common enemies or "threats" in motivating actors with competing views to form reform coalitions (Van Dyke and McCammon 2010).

indigenous organizations in the lowlands and in the highlands and that it was creating a new class of indigenous "latifundistas" (interview with Rodolfo Machaca; see also Bottazzi and Rist 2012: 543). As a notable event, protests by the peasant faction forced the removal of vice-minister of land Alejandro Almaraz.[40] The decision to remove Almaraz from office reflected the power struggles and internal balance of power within the MAS, which favored the "core" peasant, productive-oriented associations vis-à-vis the "non-core" indigenous organizations (interviews with Alejandro Almaraz, Idón Chivi, Rodolfo Machaca, and Hugo Salvatierra). As further evidence of this, the government called the CSUTCB to draft a new proposal for a land law that would put an end to "latifundio" (Los Tiempos 2011).

Over time, peasant groups have gained control over the ministry. Its social composition reveals the diversity of peasant-based groups in Bolivia, and top ministerial positions (as well as positions of medium importance) are staffed by grass-roots leaders who represent civil society groups. Nemecia Achacollo, the head of the ministry since 2010, is a peasant woman with years of experience as a peasant union leader for CSTUCB's feminist branch.[41] Interviews inside the ministry and with grass-roots leaders reveal that collective actors have fairly easy and privileged access to the institution and the policy-making process. And key legislative proposals have been developed in close dialog between these groups and state officials.

An example is Law 144, the Law of Productive Revolution, which was passed on June 26, 2011.[42] The legislative proposal, which at its core dealt with the issue of "food sovereignty," has had a long history (Kopp 2011: 156–68). Under the Morales government, the Unity Pact brought the proposal to the public agenda. It was based on a broad consensus reached by the country's main rural-based national organizations.[43] These, which included both peasant and indigenous groups, agreed that food sovereignty should be a human right codified in the country's new constitution (Kopp 2011: 178–80). Their proposal would then be introduced into the constitutional text almost

---

[40] Almaraz was in charge of implementing the reform. In an interview, he commented that the "real problem pushing for my forced resignation was the idea of a communitarian redistribution of land. Peasant organizations were losing out opportunities for the commercialization of land. Peasant leaders did not want to lose their business. And they did not want indigenous groups to have large estates that would not be used productively" (interview with Alejandro Almaraz). Salvatierra made a similar assessment (interview with Hugo Salvatierra).

[41] Achacollo served as the executive of the *Bartolinas* from 2004 until 2006. She then was elected MAS deputy, and served as such from 2006 until 2009.

[42] Another example that displays similar dynamics is the agrarian reform bill.

[43] Providing spaces for discussion and also technical assistance, both national and international NGOs such as UNITAS and *La Vía Campesina* played an important role in bringing together these organizations, which often have expressed different interests and understandings of what "food sovereignty" actually means (interviews with Xavier Albó and Walter Limache). Despite their disagreements they converged on a unified proposal to address the issue of food sovereignty.

verbatim. Frustrated because things in the countryside "remained the same for quite some time" after the approval of the new constitution, the CSUTCB took the lead and developed a legislative proposal to enable the newly gained right: "it became our time to manage what happens in the countryside" (interview with Rodolfo Machaca). The proposal called for a "Decade of Communitarian and Productive Revolution" and it linked the issue of food sovereignty to rural poverty.

According to Víctor Hugo Vázquez, Bolivia's vice-minister of Rural Development, "the CSUTCB proposal was compelling, but it was technically unviable as it was proposed to us" (interview with Victor Hugo Vázquez). He commented that it needed technical adjustments to make it feasible. To assist with that, the ministry invited all the affected sectors to a round of negotiations. The ministry provided the infrastructure and technical assistance for these dialogs. Engineer Germán Gallardo, who was closely involved in the process, commented that these meetings "combined technical work with pressure from below and popular participation" (interview with Germán Gallardo). Interviews with state officials within the ministry, with key representatives in Congress, and with the leadership of the grass-roots actors involved in these negotiations concur in noting that the most influential group was the CSUTCB. At the other end of the spectrum, CONAMAQ, an organization that represents indigenous peoples in Bolivia's highlands, distanced itself from the process by noting potential environmental concerns associated with the proposal (interview with Jesús Jilamita).[44] Their concerns were legitimate. After the legislative proposal went through the Ministry of Planning for technical adjustments and modifications, it incorporated provisions easing the usage of transgenic seeds. In the eyes of CONAMAQ and other lowland indigenous groups, these were detrimental for the environment and their more traditional ways of farming.[45] Despite the pressure these groups put in the streets, the legislative proposal was sent to Congress and was approved with minor modifications (interview with Luis Alfaro).[46] It was, in the eyes of several representatives of indigenous organizations such as CONAMAQ and CIDOB, "a clear victory for the CSUTCB" (interviews with Jesús Jilamita, Rodolfo Machaca, and Lázaro Tacóo).

The Ministry of Mining is another highly disputed office. The key grass-roots actors fighting for its control are the unionized mineworkers, who are

---

[44] Their distancing also coincided with a broader tension between the government and indigenous-based organizations over the government's plan to build a highway through an indigenous territory. See "The Impact of Different 'Constellations' of Power" on "constraining" powers for more information on this conflict.

[45] The accusations of these groups were that the government was giving in to the pressures of sectors that did not participate in the negotiation stages, including big landholders and translational companies.

[46] MAS representatives from indigenous organizations such as CIDOB and CONAMAQ did not participate in the legislative sessions for the discussion of this law.

represented nationally by the Union Federation of Bolivian Mineworkers (FSTMB), and the cooperativist mineworkers, who are represented nationally by National Federation of Mining Cooperatives (FENCOMIN). The pressure exerted by these groups is determinant for shaping mining policies.[47] And mining policies generally reflect the balance of power between these competing mining sectors, rather than party professionalism or technocratic decision-making. At the beginning of Morales's first mandate, Wálter Villarroel, a cooperativist miner and former president of FENCOMIN, became the minister of mining. This was the result of a pre-electoral alliance between the MAS and FENCOMIN, by which FENCOMIN would exchange electoral support for representation in Congress and in other state institutions (interviews with Ramiro Paredes, Freddy Ontiveros, and Adalid Rodríguez).[48] The alliance, however, broke in October 2006, when cooperativist miners and the unionized mineworkers of Huanuni clashed over the control of mining activities in the Posokoni hill, the richest tin mine site in Bolivia. The armed confrontations left 16 dead and more than 68 wounded (El Deber 2006a), forcing the resignation of Villarroel, who was accused of defending the interests of his sector and not the overall general interest (El Deber 2006b).[49] This helped to strengthen the strategic relationships between the unionized mineworkers and the government, particularly when Morales appointed a new minister with ties to Bolivia's nationalist left, and someone who more closely promoted their pro-nationalization agenda. But this agenda would encounter strong challenges from below. The MAS-FENCOMIN alliance would prove to be only *temporarily* broken.

Having become an increasingly larger group and one of Bolivia's principal sources of employment – particularly in the western departments of Oruro, Potosí, and La Paz – the cooperativist miners became a key pressure group within the MAS (Espinoza Morales 2010: 238–41).[50] During the process of constitutional reform, for example, they played an important behind-the-scenes role and negotiated directly with the executive; they thus obtained important victories for the sector, like the constitutional recognition of mining cooperatives as an economic actor in the mining industry (interviews with Ramiro Paredes, Freddy Ontiveros, and Andrés Villca).[51] In addition, through their combined legislative influence via their representatives in Congress and the pressure they exerted in the streets, they were able to push through various laws and decrees that benefit the sector, particularly in matters of royalties and

---

[47] For a parallel argument, see Fornillo (2008: 14).

[48] Their support was crucial for gaining electoral majorities.

[49] For some authors, Villarroel had an "excessive corporativist attachment" (Stefanoni 2010: 161).

[50] It is notoriously hard to find reliable data on this sector. However, access to FENCOMIN's internal databases, which was facilitated by FENCOMIN's Secretary of Commerce and Exports Adalid Rodriguez, revealed that there are over 100,000 active cooperatives in the country.

[51] See article 369 in Bolivia's new constitution.

taxation.[52] Many in the government describe cooperativist miners as "strategic but uncomfortable allies." This is because they are central to gain electoral majorities, but have also become dominant in the shaping of the mining policy agenda. Their pressure has made it virtually impossible to develop a more comprehensive mining law.[53]

As a general rule, then, pressures from below are central to defining policies in the area of mining where Morales cannot impose his agenda freely. Instead, he has to negotiate constantly with competing sectors. When these sectors do not agree, there is more room for elite decision-making by pushing Morales to occupy an arbitration role. At the same time, this logic can also lead to a quasi-Social Darwinian "rule of the strongest": decisions generally reflect the existing balance of power between competing groups.

So far, my sketch of decision-making at the executive level reveals a more nuanced picture of the relationship between grass-roots movements, the MAS, and power holders than the one presented when I examined Congress. Although some ministries are "sealed" and offer little room for grass-roots social actors to exert meaningful influence, others are more penetrated by groups that engage directly in the generation of decisions and the policy process more generally. This is evident in the case of ministries whose policies affect clearly defined constituencies, particularly popular associations rooted in production or economic activity (like CSUTCB and FENCOMIN) as opposed to more identity-oriented indigenous movements (like CONAMAQ and CIDOB). The former groups have had meaningful influence on and direct participation in decision-making in key matters of agrarian policy and mining policy, reflecting once again the internal balance of power within the MAS. If these groups are strongly organized and have autonomous capacity to mobilize large numbers of people, they are more likely to keep the party open and force it to negotiate policy initiatives successfully.

The Impact of Different "Constellations" of Power

Finally, we also need to examine the role of social movements and other grass-roots organizations under different "constellations" of power, a dimension that cuts across all of the above. Here it is useful to make an analytical distinction between two time periods. The first period is between 2006 and 2009 and it coincides with Morales's first term in office, when the MAS did not control

---

[52] Cooperative miners have been central actors in the negotiations of law 175, which authorizes the Bolivian Central Bank (BCB) to purchase gold from cooperative mines, and law 186, which eliminates the added-value tax to the internal commercialization of minerals and metals sold by cooperative mines.

[53] The need for a new mining law was established in the country's new constitution, which has been in effect since 2009.

Congress and had a strong and highly mobilized opposition entrenched in Bolivia's most prosperous eastern departments – the so-called half-moon (Media Luna) region.[54] During this initial period, this opposition from traditional political elites, backed by agribusiness elites, demanded regional autonomy and threatened to secede as a reaction against indigenous mobilization (Eaton 2007: 73). The second period starts in 2009, or when Morales was reelected president and the MAS won control over Congress.[55] This meant that the MAS would confront an atomized and much weaker opposition – both in Congress and in the streets. Since that time, when Bolivian politics "normalized," a state of truce has characterized the relations between the government and economic elites.

During the first period, which was marked by high levels of polarization and stalemate, organizations allied with the MAS played a crucial role in decision-making by putting issues on the public agenda. The most notable of their contributions was the proposal for constitutional reform, which was developed by the peasant and indigenous organizations that configured the Unity Pact (interviews with Xavier Albó, Fernando Garcés, Walter Limache, Raúl Prada, and Adolfo Mendoza). Lacking an independent proposal generated by the party structure, MAS representatives adopted this draft as their own during the reform process, which pushed them to discuss "new" issues, such as the idea of a "plurinational" state with territorial and indigenous autonomies; natural resources; indigenous representation; and collective rights (Garcés 2010: 67–81). After this experience, the government also promoted other institutional innovations to facilitate a bottom-up influence beyond the constituent assembly process. The most important was the National Coordinator for Change (CONALCAM), which brought together the rural organizations that configured the Unity Pact, other urban-popular organizations such as the Bolivian Workers' Central (COB), and government officials (Mayorga 2011: 97). However, beyond becoming a space for debating and generating policy inputs, as its creators had intended initially (interviews with César Navarro and Hugo Moldiz), "it proved a useful instrument for mobilizing the government's supporters against its adversaries, particularly in 2008, when political elites in the eastern departments threatened secession" (Crabtree 2013: 287). Once the pressures from the opposition eased, the articulatory power of CONALCAM

---

[54] In the national election of December 2005, Evo Morales obtained 53.7 percent of the vote. Although these results guaranteed the MAS a majority in the Chamber of Deputies, where it won 72 out of 130 seats, they were not enough to guarantee a majority in the Senate, where the MAS obtained 12 out of 27 seats. Parties of the right won the additional seats, turning them into a majority in this legislative body. Obtaining 28.6 percent of the vote, Social and Democratic Power (PODEMOS) gained 13 seats; gaining 7.8 percent of the vote, the National Unity Front gained 1 seat; and obtaining 6.5 percent of the vote, the Revolutionary Nationalist Movement (MNR) gained 1 seat.

[55] The MAS won the 2009 election with 64.22 percent of the vote. The results allowed the MAS to have 88 deputies and 26 senators.

declined. And soon after it became defunct, with parts of indigenous organizations such as CIDOB and CONAMAQ splintering into "loyalist" and "dissident" factions and with the latter moving into opposition against the government (especially in the aftermath of the TIPNIS conflict, as seen below).

In addition to putting issues on the agenda and setting priorities, allied movements played a central role in the passage of highly contested policies during this period. Two key examples are the 2006 Law of Communitarian Renewal of the Agrarian Reform, which established that land must fulfill certain socioeconomic functions (Bottazzi and Rist 2012: 540–1), and the 2007 *Renta Dignidad*, which added a non-contributory tier to Bolivia's pension scheme (Anria and Niedzwiecki 2016: 314). While the former served as a mechanism for expropriating land from large landholders, the latter involved a redirection of revenues coming from the hydrocarbon sector, meaning that less of this money would be transferred to the regional governments. In short, both policies affected the interests of the agribusiness economic elites in the eastern departments, and this made them highly contentious. In both cases, legislative blockades by the political opposition representing those elite interests in Congress, and mobilizations by their allied groups in the streets, prevented the government from achieving the passage of its planned reforms. With the convergence of rural and urban organizations of the lowlands and the highlands around a common enemy, however, MAS supporters led a series of mass protests and counter-mobilizations. After days of sustained mobilizations in front of the Congress, both laws were enacted. In both cases, moreover, the mobilization of allied groups played a central role in the passage of legislation by counterbalancing the pressure from a united and highly mobilized opposition.[56]

Morales's reelection in 2009 marked the beginning of a different "constellation" of power. The electoral results allowed the MAS to accumulate immense amounts of institutional power, particularly as it simultaneously won control over Congress (on this point, see Mayorga 2011: 56–61; also Crabtree 2011). While this broke with the institutional stalemate, the consequences of such an overwhelming electoral victory were twofold. First, it led to the strengthening of the party leadership in relation to its social base; and second, it weakened the existing channels of bottom-up dialog and articulation, like the Unity Pact and CONALCAM (Farthing and Kohl 2014: 51). The absence of a strong institutionalized opposition, and the weakening of mobilized sectors representing their interests, also meant that movements and popular organizations aligned with the MAS would play a different role under a different "constellation" of power.

---

[56] Instances where social organizations allied to the MAS made *cercos*, or human fences, around the congress were somewhat common during this period. A noteworthy *cerco* took place in February 2008, when allied organizations surrounded Congress preventing the entrance of members of the opposition and thus facilitated the passing of the law calling for the public referendum that would decide on whether the new constitution should be approved or not.

Specifically, by dispersing demand making, tensions were accentuated between the bottom-up and the top-down logics that characterize the internal operations of the MAS (see Chapter 2; see also Levitsky and Roberts 2011; Anria 2013; Crabtree 2013; Silva 2017). The following pages examine these dynamics in greater detail.

CONSTRAINING CAPACITIES

As political scientist Moira Zuazo commented, "Morales is sometimes a hostage of the grass-roots social movements that sustain him in power" (interview with Moira Zuazo). This has become apparent after Morales's reelection in 2009, when the MAS also won a clear majority of seats in both legislative chambers, and after the MAS won the 2009 referendum on the new constitution. Winning control of the Congress meant that for some time the MAS did not have to negotiate with intransigent opposition parties in order to pass legislation. The challenge, then, switched from negotiating and seeking consensus in Congress to managing an increasingly heterogeneous governing coalition. Harmonizing the interests, demands, and priorities of core and non-core constituencies proved to be a difficult task. And as a result, the MAS has confronted increasing levels of discontent from within its own camp. There have been many instances where the party's grass-roots social base clashed with the MAS government over policy initiatives. In some cases, moreover, the MAS was unable to control autonomous social mobilization, having to reverse or modify key policies due to mass protests against their implementation. As explained in Chapter 1, I call this the "constraining capacities" of the sponsoring and allied movements that constitute the party's grass-roots social base.[57]

This subsection asks the following question: why do *some* mobilizations succeed in reversing or modifying government policy while others fail? The argument advanced here is that success in blocking or modifying government policy depends mostly on the strength of the veto coalition that popular movements manage to build. If a mobilized grass-roots actor builds a broad veto coalition with multiple segments of society, it is more likely to succeed in blocking or modifying legislative proposals. If a mobilized grass-roots actor acts alone or cannot build a strong veto coalition, then the government can more easily defeat it.

The policies under consideration below share important overarching similarities. From the government's perspective, they are all intended to address pressing issues of general interest. Important economic and political reasons underpin them and are used by the government to justify the need for such

---

[57] In a parallel argument, Silva (2017: 96) conceptualizes this pattern as a "contestatory" form of "interest intermediation" – a pattern that "involves routinized interactions where the government proposes a policy, affected popular sector organizations protest vigorously, negotiation ensues, and government abides by agreements. The pattern repeats regularly."

policies. However, their implementation directly affects the interests of movements and organizations aligned with the MAS. From their perspective, these policies are thus seen as "anti-popular."

Figure 4.1 summarizes the likely scenarios from the government's point of view. In general, the party's organizational core exercises a great deal of influence at the initiation stage, when the policy is discussed internally. Failure to secure support from the core usually means that the policy will not thrive, that it will be blocked or modified. Later, at a second stage, or when the proposal is unveiled publicly, the support of the party's core is necessary for pushing through anti-popular government proposals, as these groups can exercise significant counter-mobilization power and "defend" the government against political opposition. This, however, generally works if the veto coalition is weakly organized (Figure 4.1, Case 2). When the party's core is aligned with the government (but cannot ensure compliance from the rank and file) and a powerful veto coalition is built, the government generally finds itself having to bow to popular pressures (Figure 4.1, Case 3).

Sometimes, however, a strong veto coalition is able to block or modify government policies even if the party's core fully supports these policies. In other words, having the support of the core is not sufficient for the government to pass proposals that affect strongly organized popular constituencies; but it is necessary if the policy affects strongly organized constituencies. The case of the health workers conflict illustrates this pattern (Figure 4.1, Case 1). In a summit convened by the MAS in December 2011, popular movements allied to the government proposed an increase in working hours of doctors and health care workers, from six hours a day to eight hours a day (Ministerio de la Presidencia and Ministerio de Comunicación 2011: 21). When the government sought to impose this measure via a presidential decree (the Decree 1126), doctors and health workers organized a series of widespread marches, strikes, and street blockades in Bolivia's major cities, along with other urban sectors, like university students, transportation workers, police officers, and the Bolivian Workers Central (COB). Even though *cocaleros* and other peasant organizations aligned with the MAS – the party's core – supported and defended the policy on the streets, doctors and health care workers managed to protect the status quo (interview with Paulino Guarachi). The government was forced to reverse its policy choice after more than 40 days of sustained strikes and autonomous social mobilizations. It did so by, first, suspending the initial decree and, second, by issuing another presidential decree, the Decree 1232, and by promising to convene a summit to discuss the broader issue of health care reform (Cambio 2012).[58]

---

[58] This decree was the product of an agreement between the mobilized health care workers, university students, the COB, and the MAS government.

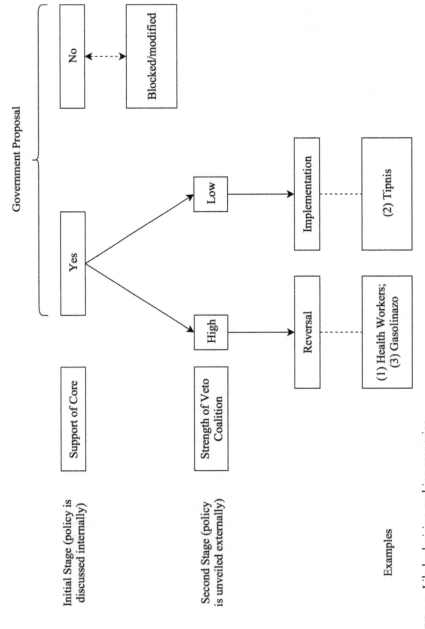

FIGURE 4.1 Likely decision-making scenarios.

The "gas riot" or *gasolinazo* crisis (Figure 4.1, Case 3) began on December 26, 2010, when the government canceled fuel subsidies by decree, in a country where gasoline had been heavily subsidized for several years. Coming as a surprise to most Bolivians, the decision quickly led to a massive increase in gasoline prices, estimated at 83 percent, as well as a general uncertainty among the population about prices and availability of basic goods, transportation prices, the stability of the government, and the next adjustment policies. The price increase was followed by popular revolts against the policy, including civic strikes, road blockades, and marches. It is interesting that the conservative right did not lead these mobilizations. Instead, social mobilizations were led by sectors that had been traditional bastions of MAS support – such as neighborhood groups and informal sector workers, miners, and even coca farmers – in key urban areas, and they demanded that Morales either annul the decree or resign. The mobilizations paralyzed virtually every major city in the country and eventually succeeded in forcing a change in policy (Crabtree 2013: 286). Strong mobilization forced the government to rescind its own decree.[59]

The idea of cutting the fuel subsidy had originally come from the executive branch, after a series of debates on the economic burden that energy subsidies actually represent (interviews with Álvaro García Linera, Noel Aguirre, Luis Arce Catacora, and Walter Delgadillo). The Ministry of Planning designed the regulatory decree, the Decree 748, which received no input from organized popular constituencies (interviews with Walter Delgadillo, Noel Aguirre, and María Nela Prada Tejada). As the Minister of Economy, Luis Arce Catacora, commented in an interview: "removing the subsidy was a completely anti-popular measure, and we knew it, but it was absolutely necessary for the health of our economy. One merit of the government was to put the issue on the political agenda" (interview with Luis Arce Catacora). Many leaders of sponsoring and allied organizations commented that there was in fact some degree of consultation before the policy was announced (interviews with Isaac Avalos, Franklin Durán, Pedro Montes, Andrés Villca, Segundina Orellana, and Leonida Zurita), but that it took the form of "seeking legitimation" of an already-made decision (interview with Rodolfo Machaca). Interviewees also concurred in noting that in those meetings, they were instructed to communicate the decision to the social bases as a way to guarantee its implementation. But things did not work out as planned. To most Bolivians, the policy came as a shock, and it hurt their household economy.

When groups began to mobilize autonomously against the policy and a broad veto coalition was formed in key urban areas, members of the executive

---

[59] In a public speech, Morales said: "I have understood the recommendations of various sectors – the workers, the unions, the provinces – and that's why, in a meeting with the Vice President, the Minister of Foreign Relations, and the rest of the ministers, we have decided, following the principle of ruling by obeying the people, to annul the Decree 748 and the rest of the decrees that accompany that policy."

branch (including Evo Morales himself) convened emergency meetings with the coca growers to explain the rationale behind the policy and to ask for their support (interview with Walter Delgadillo). The assumption was that this sector, together with the other peasant organizations that constitute the party's core, would align unconditionally with the government and that this would be sufficient to stop the mobilizations and ensure the viability of the policy. While the government and the leadership of coca growers in the Chapare region reached an agreement, it was not clear whether the rank and file, the members and affiliates, would comply uncritically (interview with Segundina Orellana). Peasant organizations like the CSUTCB defended the policy externally, but leaders commented in a series of interviews that "internally, we told the president to stop it; the policy was not really sustainable, because it was done with no real consultation, and was thus weakly designed from the beginning" (interview with Rodolfo Machaca). The policy affected the members and affiliates of these popular organizations, too, particularly as prices of food and transportation increased drastically overnight.[60] This revealed a central tension between the leadership of the movements and organizations that comprise the party's core and the rank and file. While the former supported the policy, the latter did not and it displayed a remarkable capacity for autonomous social mobilization. Having the leadership of major social organizations aligned with the government does not automatically restrain sociopolitical pressures and conflicts from below in contemporary Bolivia. Neither Morales nor the MAS can fully control popular mobilization from the top down.

While it would be inaccurate to say that *cocaleros* in the Chapare and other peasant organizations that comprise the party's core stopped the policy by themselves, their inability to align with the government unambiguously (due to the bottom-up pressures from the rank and file) was necessary for the veto coalition to succeed. When these groups told the president to reverse the policy, it was clear that not even the closest allies would be able to defend it, and that not reversing it could lead to a severe governability crisis. As Vice President Garcia Linera commented in an interview: "we reversed it when we saw that it was in the general interest to do so" (interview with Álvaro García Linera).

The case of the Isiboro Sécure National Park and Indigenous Territory (TIPNIS) (Figure 4.1, Case 2) is more complex than the other two, but the logic of policy initiative, the dynamics of autonomous social mobilization, and the actions of the party responding to (and trying to reconcile) mobilized pressure from below are similar.[61] In this case, the government made the decision to build a highway through the middle of a national park – a park

---

[60] Other interviewees, who prefer to remain anonymous, commented that because the policy led to a rise in the price of gasoline, a key input for the production of cocaine, coca growers had a clear incentive to reject it.

[61] The reconstruction of this ongoing conflict draws on newspaper coverage as well as on social conflict data generously provided by the *Fundación UNIR*.

that is also recognized as an indigenous territory.[62] The government argued that the highway was crucial for economic, social, and political reasons. Economically, the government argued, it would help to improve access to markets for the goods produced by agricultural producers in the region. Socially, it would help to improve the access to electricity and other public services in formerly neglected areas of the country. And politically, it was seen as important to advance the territorial integration of the country, as well as to break with the power of landholders and economic elites entrenched in the eastern departments, particularly in Beni and Pando (interview with Álvaro García Linera; see also García Linera 2012).[63]

However, some lowland indigenous groups living in the TIPNIS saw the highway as a threat. Those groups mobilized autonomously against the government's plan and argued that they were not consulted prior to beginning the construction of the road.[64] They claimed that, among other things, the Bolivian government was violating international agreements ratified by the country and also the country's new constitution that enshrines community rights of prior consultation (Falleti and Riofrancos 2018: 103). They also claimed that the road would lead to environmental damage and threaten their way of life.

The movements and organizations that form the party's – more "developmentalist" – core constituency strongly backed the highway from the beginning (interviews with Segundina Orellana, Omar Claros, Miguelina Villarroel, Rodolfo Machaca, and Concepción Ortiz).[65] But other key social allies not part of the core developmentalist constituency – including major indigenous movements in the eastern lowlands, like the Confederation of Bolivian Indigenous Peoples (CIDOB), and in the Andean highlands, such as the National Council of Ayllus and Marcas of Qullasuyu (CONAMAQ) – organized widespread marches and protests to defend their collective rights and stop the construction of the highway, or to at least alter its route. The marches involved violent confrontations between indigenous communities represented by these organizations, on the one hand, and coca growers (and other peasant groups) on the other hand. Unlike the *gasolinazo* crisis of December 2010, this time the government handled the conflict with violent

---

[62] The planned highway would link the departments of Cochabamba and Pando.

[63] As García Linera commented: "as long as we do not have a highway connecting La Paz and Pando, large landholders will continue to hold political power in that region" (interview with Álvaro García Linera).

[64] Former Minister of Public Works Wálter Delgadillo commented: "of course we had done informal consultation work with the local leaders and organizations inside the TIPNIS – some of this work was even quite clientelistic and manipulative – and they had agreed on the construction of the highway. But then we started with the construction, and they rejected and politicized it openly" (interview with Walter Delgadillo).

[65] Particularly the coca growers in the Chapare region represented by the Six Federations of the Tropics of Cochabamba, and also the Confederation of Intercultural Communities of Bolivia (CSCIB).

repression in a rather confusing series of events, even though, in the end, it did temporarily suspend the project by reaching an agreement with the mobilized sectors opposing the highway. It did so by issuing a law, Law 180, which declared the TIPNIS an intangible territory and prohibited the construction of the highway through it. The autonomous capacity of lowland groups to mobilize, even though they were not part of the core developmentalist coalition, was crucial for this outcome.

But the organizations that constitute the party's core rejected this law on the grounds that it violated their rights of economic development. They organized road blockades and a counter march to La Paz, arguing that, "whoever opposes the highway also opposes the economic progress of the region" and demanding to meet with the president to find a solution.[66] These groups demanded the abrogation of the Law 180, which prohibited the construction of the highway, and they also threatened to physically confront those groups who opposed the highway in a parallel march. The conflict ended when the organizations of the party's core, arriving in La Paz, met with the presidents of both legislative chambers and members of the executive branch, and reached an agreement on a legislative proposal that would allow them to implement a consultation procedure on whether to build the highway or not. The legislative proposal was then approved very quickly in Congress, becoming the Law 222, and ensuring that there would be a formal consultation.[67] The government proved to be responsive to the pressures from below from more production-oriented interests of the organizations that constitute the party's core.

Although critics may point out that this description overlooks some details, it captures the general dynamics of the TIPNIS conflict and shows the party responding to (and trying to reconcile) mobilized pressures from below. These pressures are relevant because they reveal the intense conflict and power struggles among the different sectors that attempt to shape policy-making and the internal balance of power among core and non-core constituencies.[68] Despite the autonomous capacity of the lowland groups to mobilize, and despite the temporary suspension of the construction of the highway through the national park, the government did not *fully* reverse its initial decision and instead accommodated to the policy preferences of its core constituency.[69]

---

[66] According to many actors in the political opposition, the government instigated this march and used the core organizations instrumentally. Although this is plausible, it is hard to demonstrate it empirically.

[67] The process of consultation was a long and controversial one. For a summary of the results, see Estado Plurinacional de Bolivia (2012). (Estado Plurinacional de Bolivia 2012).

[68] Though not central to the analysis in this chapter, the TIPNIS conflict also exposed the government's developmentalist policy agenda, which often comes at the expense of indigenous and environmental concerns.

[69] This firm commitment to the highway, and the way in which the government managed the conflict by repressing anti-highway protesters, led to a deterioration of the relationship between the MAS and important indigenous movements that represent large numbers of highland and

Opposition groups have not built a coalition strong enough to pressure the government to abandon the idea of the highway through the national park, and their capacity to sustain mobilization declined over time. Vice President García Linera commented: "if you look carefully, we have not reversed our policy. We have suspended the project temporarily, but will build the highway anyway because the decision is rooted on the idea of maintaining state sovereignty over the territory" (interview with Álvaro García Linera). That this position aligns with the policy preferences of coca growers (and other core peasant groups) is not accidental, however; it reveals that these are the key organized mass constituencies shaping policy and that they are also among the most powerful social actors within the government.[70] Their unambiguous support of the highway, coupled with a relatively weaker veto coalition that opposed it, meant that the government has had more maneuvering room, and the necessary support, to pursue and implement its desired policies. "If it doesn't happen now," García Linera said, "it will happen later."[71]

To summarize, the three examples examined above show that although decision-making is undoubtedly centralized in the person of the president, Morales is not an all-powerful president and his government has to discuss, negotiate, and reach compromises (or at least try to reconcile interests) regularly with the party's grass-roots social bases. Organized popular sectors may not hold the reins of power directly, but they are not left at the margins of the decision-making process either. Specifically, they can place real constraints on Morales's authority by exerting mobilized pressure from below, which in certain cases can keep the MAS open and responsive to particular societal demands. Not every popular group has the same capacity to pressure the government from below, get their favored policies, and block or modify policy proposals, however; their success is contingent on the strength of the veto coalition they manage to configure, and it varies by policy issue.

---

lowland indigenous peoples, like CIDOB and CONAMAQ. For critics like Raúl Prada Alcoreza, who is a prominent intellectual and a former MAS representative to the Constituent Assembly, "the TIPNIS conflict has revealed that the MAS government is indeed anti-indigenous" (interview with Raúl Prada Alcoreza).

[70] In the interview with García Linera, he went as far as to comment that: "the idea with the highway is to boost the economic and political power of the peasant groups and other popular and indigenous groups, in relation to the landholders" (interview with Álvaro García Linera).

[71] Several high-level government officials commented that, keeping the consequences of the *gasolinazo* in mind, the government could not afford to reverse this policy, even if it meant alienating the indigenous constituencies that oppose the highway. Otherwise, the government would be perceived as weak and permeable to all kinds of social pressures. Still, the government was able to firmly maintain its position because it counted with the unambiguous support of its core constituencies.

CONCLUSIONS

A surface-level analysis of the MAS in the realm of national policy-making may initially lend unquestionable support to the argument of top-down control by Morales. However, such a conclusion would be at best a simplification and at worst a deep mischaracterization of the actual relationships that exist between the party and its grass-roots social bases. Such a conclusion would, in fact, fail to capture a richer and more nuanced understanding of the complex, dynamic, and conflictual relationships between various social movements, the party, and power holders that I have developed in this chapter.

Using a wealth of qualitative evidence, I have shown that, on the one hand, policy-making in Bolivia's MAS is centralized in the hands of the president and a small – but varying – group of influential leaders. There is no question that Morales and trusted individuals occupy a central role in the policy process. On the other hand, however, there are elements in the structure and operations of the MAS that work against those oligarchic temptations. Most prominently, the party's loose bureaucratic structure provides opportunities for the social bases to act autonomously, with very few bureaucratic constraints. Their capacity to sustain autonomous mobilization has often put strong limits on the centralization of power and promoted leadership accountability to organized mass constituencies and responsiveness in a continuous way, contributing at least partially to counteract Michelsian oligarchic tendencies.

The main story that emerged from this chapter, then, is that of a movement-based party that allows for significant influence from below in the crafting of public policies – a story in which movements have continued to influence, constrain, and hold the leadership accountable. While oligarchic temptations are readily available within the MAS, the party's grass-roots social bases are far from being irrelevant political actors in the policy-making sphere. Their ongoing activism, and especially the strength of autonomous social mobilization, has contributed to shape the party's most important policy decisions.

This chapter further demonstrated that countervailing, bottom-up correctives to hierarchy and concentrated authority occur at two different yet related levels. If we firstly look at what I called the "creative capacities" of the allied movements and organizations (i.e., their ability to steer policy in their desired direction, to generate independent decisions by putting issues and priorities on the agenda and proposing solutions to them), the prospects for attenuating the trend toward top-down control may initially look slim. However, as the chapter demonstrated, policy-making under the MAS is a highly interactive, contestatory, and negotiated process open to societal input. Also, as the chapter showed, the capacity of the party's grass-roots social bases to generate decisions and formulate policy proposals varies from one ministry and policy sphere to another.

This argument is consistent with the expectations derived from the (old and new) developmental state literature and sociological approaches to social movement outcomes, which show that in policy areas where large numbers of well-organized people are directly and visibly affected in their productive roles there is generally more popular pressure for influencing these decisions. The MAS, as discussed in this chapter, is permeable to these pressures from organized popular constituencies. To prove this point, I examined the influence of grass-roots organizations in the development of agrarian and mining policies and demonstrated that some of the strongest and better organized groups (mostly those with production-oriented interests, like CSUTCB, COB, and FENCOMIN, among others) have been influential in shaping the public agenda and in advancing their preferred policies through their direct participation in and close interaction with the executive branch. Grass-roots organizations are more likely to have creative capacities where the policies affect them in their productive roles.

In turn, if we examine closely the "constraining capacities" of sponsoring and allied movements (i.e., their capacity to block or modify government policies), the prospects of mitigating the trend toward internal power concentration appears to be even greater in the case of the MAS. The constraining capacities, however, are determined by the ability of those groups to assemble large veto coalitions. Grass-roots groups that can mobilize broad-based coalitions involving multiple sectors of society are more likely to block or modify policy proposals. It is here – where the top-down logic of exercising power meets the bottom-up logic of autonomous social mobilization – that the Michelsian argument about top-down control finds the biggest challenge to its applicability.

Finally, the chapter highlighted the remarkable ability of the rank and file in major popular movements to sustain that autonomous mobilization capacity and thus hold their leaders accountable to their interests. This is what, in turn, helps to keep the MAS responsive to its grass-roots social bases. In this sense, the experience of the MAS in the "constraining" realm of policy-making serves as a good counter example of the trends that Murillo (2001) found in her study of the implementation of structural adjustment policies by labor-based parties in Latin America – where the inability of the rank and file to hold the union leadership accountable facilitated movement co-optation, top-down policy-making, and the imposition of policies that ran directly against the interests of those parties' social bases. The reverse appears to be at work in Bolivia under the MAS. Sustaining and reproducing that autonomous capacity to mobilize, as this book argues, is key for counteracting the trend toward top-down control.

5

The MAS in Comparative Perspective

As the preceding chapters have shown, the Bolivian MAS is an example of a movement-based party that gradually shed some of its initial characteristics between its founding in the mid-1990s and its achievement of power in 2006. Yet, even after several years in power, it remains different from other parties formed by social movements and has followed a peculiar organizational evolution. Most movement-based parties that have made the transition to national power lend overwhelming support to the Michelsian trend toward top-down control, almost always developing elite-dominated hierarchical structures that concentrate power in the leadership and de-emphasize bottom-up participation.

The literature on comparative party analysis has observed that when parties win elections, institutionalize their structures, and increasingly occupy public office, their linkages with allied social movements tend to become weaker and more intermittent. Strong grass-roots participation in the making of collective decisions seems particularly hard to sustain as the social bases of parties grow and become more diverse, and as a result of new pressures that come from sectors well beyond the party's original social base. It is also challenging to sustain given other constraints such as domestic and external economic pressures that tend to push governing parties toward further centralization.[1] In turn, all this gives rise to a top-down logic of decision-making and to a gradual suppression of the bottom-up politics that might characterize a movement-based party early in its organizational development, or when it is in the opposition.

The MAS does not fully conform to this pattern. As the present book has demonstrated, the Bolivian case offers insight into how, to what extent, and

---

[1] One might expect the trend toward top-down, centralized control under more stringent domestic and external economic constraints. This is because, at times, for instance, satisfying investors may require pushing aside the social bases.

under which conditions the trend toward party oligarchization can be mitigated in the context of exercising power. It has shown that movement-based parties may hold an advantage over other types of parties to resist power concentration and the tendencies toward top-down political control. Specifically, I have argued that the hybrid features of these parties may encourage democratic control from below by allowing for the existence of opposition among allied groups that can check power from within and keep channels open for agenda setting and influence from below. The MAS experience demonstrated that oligarchization, as defined in Chapter 1, is not inevitable or preordained: the extent to which movement-based parties can attenuate these pressures depends on organizational attributes defined early on and how they interact with both the strength of civil society and its *autonomous* mobilization capacity.

This chapter compares the origins, evolution, and power structures of movement-based parties in Brazil and Uruguay with those of the Bolivian MAS in order to further probe my key theoretical claims and shed light on the factors that make the MAS both similar to and different from other movement-based parties. The MAS in Bolivia, the Workers' Party (Partido dos Trabalhadores, PT) in Brazil, and the Broad Front (Frente Amplio, FA) in Uruguay share a common origin as opposition parties and mass movements. Yet, despite their common origins in vibrant social movements, they have organized differently and maintained varying degrees of bottom-up input on internal decision-making and different kinds of social linkages with their bases. While the PT appears to have undergone a clear Michelsian shift in its character, in the sense that it has become increasingly centralized and less participatory since its origins, the MAS and the FA have counteracted the trends toward top-down control more strongly – that is, they have remained relatively more open to input from their social bases, as well as more internally responsive. In sum, there are substantial differences across these cases in terms of how vibrant the linkages to their social bases are and how responsive these parties are to the pressures from their bases.

Table 5.1 presents some basic comparative data on these three movement-based parties, in particular on the two dimensions I have used to analyze the degree of top-down control in the MAS (Chapters 3 and 4). On the one hand, it shows that in the realm of candidate selection (the first dimension; see Chapter 3) the MAS exhibits the highest degrees of power dispersion, while the PT exhibits the lowest. On the other hand, it shows that when it comes to other areas of party decision-making, such as defining party electoral strategy, the FA stands as the most power dispersing of the three cases. In both instances, the PT appears to be the party whose internal structures concentrate power the most. Two caveats are in order. First, these data should be treated with caution, for they are based on the judgments of a relatively small group of experts and only capture little variation on processes and patterns of organization at one point in time. However, although the variation in the quantitative data is small, it points

TABLE 5.1 *Power distributions within the MAS, the FA, and the PT*

	Candidate selection	Party strategy
MAS	2.53	1.19
FA	2.46	1.30
PT	2.31	1.13

Note: Numbers are mean scores of expert response options. Responses are organized on a 1–4 scale, with 1 indicating top-down decision-making with little participation from below, and higher numbers indicating greater degrees of power dispersion. Calculated using the Kitschelt (2013) Dataset of the Democratic Accountability and Linkages Project (DALP).[2]

in the right direction: it is consistent with both monographic studies of each party (Hunter 2010; Pérez, Piñeiro, and Rosenblatt 2018) and with comparative analyses of their power structures (Schipani 2016). Second, in the absence of better comparable – and reliable – data across the cases, decisions over party strategy are used here as a proxy measure for policy-making (the second dimension; see Chapter 4). This is just for illustrative purposes. In the qualitative, comparative historical analysis below, I examine trends in the policy-making sphere more broadly.

Differences across the cases are generated by a combination of historical and constant causes. On the one hand, historical causes refer to dynamics that occur in the early stages of an institution, or in its genesis, and produce lasting legacies down the road (Stinchcombe 1968: 103). In my explanatory framework, they include: (a) organizational attributes embedded in the parties' origins and early development; (b) their experience before gaining national power; and (c) conditions surrounding their access to power. In Figure 5.1 (a) is a historical cause that creates a "weak" version of path dependency subject to positive feedback

---

[2] Data on candidate selection (the variable a_5 in the DALP dataset) are expert responses to the question: "Which of the following four options best describes the following parties' balance of power in selecting candidates for national legislative elections?" Each party level average is based on the following scaling: (1) national party leaders control the process of candidate selection; (2) regional/state-level party organizations control the process of candidate selection; (3) local/municipal actors control the process of candidate selection; (4) selection is the outcome of bargaining between different levels. Data on party strategy (the variable a_6 in the DALP dataset) are expert responses to the question: "Which of the following options best characterizes the process by which the following parties decide on electoral strategy, for example, campaign platforms and slogans, coalition strategies, and campaign resource allocations?" Each party level average is based on the following scale: (1) electoral strategy is chosen by national party leaders with little participation from local or state level organizations; (2) electoral strategy is chosen by regional or state-level organizations; (3) electoral strategy is chosen by local or municipal level actors; (4) the choice of electoral strategy is the outcome of bargaining between the different levels of party organization.

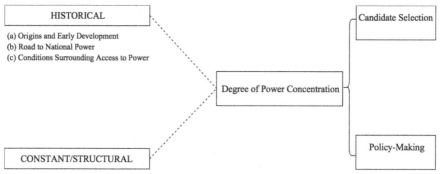

FIGURE 5.1 Power distributions within movement-based parties: a summary of the book's argument.

and self-reproducing mechanisms that are present in (b) and (c) (Mahoney 2000; Pierson 2000). Initial institutional structures, and the ensuing power distributions they produce, are path dependent (Pierson 2015: 133); though not impossible, it is difficult to deviate from them over time.

On the other hand, constant causes refer to dynamics that operate more or less continually and help to reproduce a given outcome; they may change slightly in the short-run, but most often they stay fairly stable. In my explanatory framework, conditions of societal structure linked to the parties' power base (the strength or "density" of civil society) constitute a constant cause that interacts closely with more cyclical attributes of civil society (the process of autonomous social mobilization) to shape internal power distributions. As I argue in this book (Introduction and Chapter 1), this combination of causes sets movement-based parties on distinct paths and shapes their degree of power concentration or dispersion and resulting organizational models. Figure 5.1 provides an illustration of the main components of the argument.

THE MAS IN BRIEF

Before turning to the cross-case comparisons, a summary of the experience of the MAS is in order. The MAS was formed by a rural social movement composed of coca producers and grew from a rich tradition of participatory politics found in local communities and base organizations in Bolivia's Chapare region. It then expanded to Bolivia's largest cities and became the country's largest party in less than a decade (Chapter 2). Although the transition from being a rural movement to gaining national power was accompanied by efforts to control grass-roots social movements from the top down, movements in Bolivia have retained continued levels of strength and notable degrees of autonomy from the MAS, and Chapter 3 has demonstrated how social movements and popular sector organizations in Bolivia maintained remarkable influence in the selection of candidates for elective office within the MAS at both national and subnational levels. For social groups and individuals that had been historically marginalized and underrepresented in the political arena, this channel of participation represents an important advance toward inclusion and full citizenship.

In the realm of national policy-making, there is no question that Morales and a small – but varying and unstable – group of trusted individuals occupy a central role. However, Chapter 4 has demonstrated that there are meaningful spaces for input from the social bases on political and economic decision-making. The chapter further demonstrated that bottom-up influence of collective actors on policy-making varies by policy area and remains contingent on a given group's capacity to fill the streets and that neither Morales nor the MAS can fully control popular mobilization.

In short, there are some elements in the structure of the MAS and in the dynamics of autonomous collective action in the streets that contribute to mitigate the trend toward top-down control. The bottom-up power of autonomous social movements embedded in the party's origins and early development and the legacies of popular mobilization associated with its ascent to power mean that social movements in Bolivia have remained vibrant. At times, the MAS has tried to co-opt civil society by using intimidation, threats, repression, personal disqualification, and other tactics to divide social movements, in the process threatening their autonomy. And in fact, in recent years, some of the strongest movements that initially supported the MAS have split into "loyalist" and "dissident" factions. Despite these trends, the MAS has not been able to suppress autonomous collective action from its organized social bases. Consistent with the arguments developed in this book, as Roberts (2015b: 690) notes, this ongoing capacity for collective action has contributed to "hold[ing] the government accountable to its social bases and at least partially counteract the tendencies toward top-down control associated with party bureaucratization and concentrated, charismatic executive authority."

BASIS FOR COMPARISON AND KEY ARGUMENTS

A "contextualized comparison" (Locke and Thelen 1995; Mahoney and Rueschemeyer 2003) of the MAS, the PT, and the FA is well suited for uncovering the roots of variation in internal power distributions within movement-based parties. This is for several reasons. First, they are the clearest examples available of movement-based parties that made it to national-level power in Latin America during the "third wave" of democratization. The three countries share recent histories of transitions from authoritarian rule to democracy and of transitions from highly regulated to more market-oriented economies. In such context, all three parties were spawned directly by social movements and embraced a radical left agenda in their origins. In fact, all three started out as socialist parties and yet they all adapted programmatically in part as a response to electoral imperatives; they all moved toward the center in terms of their macroeconomic policy orientation and their core programmatic agenda as they got closer to state power. Comparing their trajectories is therefore warranted as an empirical exercise.

Second, if successful new parties of any type have been rare in Latin America in the last 20 years (Levitsky et al. 2016), electorally competitive movement-based parties are even more uncommon (Kitschelt 2006). Their ability to transition from a movement to a party to government – and to even win several re-elections – is especially remarkable in the contemporary political landscape (Goldstone 2003), which makes these parties puzzling (Roberts 2015a: 275). Given these comparative challenges – and given that their internal politics remain poorly understood and under-theorized – there are great analytical payoffs in comparing Latin America's most successful movement-based parties.

Third, despite their shared sponsorship by social movements and common origins as electoral vehicles for social movement entrepreneurs, these parties vary widely in the degree to which their internal structures disperse power (Levitsky and Roberts 2011: 12). Parties can be said to disperse power when their internal structures both put limits on the exercise of power by the party leadership and encourage bottom-up input on decision-making. Notwithstanding some important differences, the MAS in Bolivia and the FA in Uruguay are examples of movement-based parties whose internal structures disperse power among their organized bases. They are also examples of organizations in which the party's top leadership more often than not finds itself needing to consult and negotiate with their social bases. They are, in short, organizations whose leadership cannot act autonomously, and they share some of the attributes that make bottom-up influence possible.

By contrast, the internal structures of the PT in Brazil facilitated greater concentration of power among a small group of political elites and gave rise to an increasingly autonomous, powerful, and unaccountable party leadership. The PT is also an example of a movement-based party that gradually suppressed social mobilization from below, a classic case of a movement-based party that confirms the tendency toward top-down control associated with party bureaucratization and concentrated executive authority. By adopting a most-similar research design in which the three cases vary on the outcome of interest – the degree of power concentration – I isolate the causal mechanisms that explain variation in their internal power distributions and the processes responsible for their reproduction. This variation, as I argue in this book, can be explained by a combination of historical and constant causes.

In the pages that follow, I demonstrate this argument by providing a detailed analysis of the origins and evolution of the PT and the FA. The analysis is organized by case, and it follows the sequence origins-roads to power-access to power, as outlined in Chapter 1. Specifically, each case narrative begins by tracing the institutional attributes defined in each party's genesis, which set parties on distinctive paths (the historical causes). It then explains how

distinctive paths are reproduced over time in different periods in the development of each party (the mechanisms of reproduction). The narrative of the cases
is then followed by a discussion of how these cases and the MAS compare with
each other.

THE WORKERS' PARTY

The Brazilian Workers' Party (PT) was founded in 1980 "by labor leaders,
intellectuals, and social movement activists" (Keck 1986: 68). The militant
unionism that spawned the party grew in strength from the mid-1970s in the
metallurgical industries of Sao Paulo to fight against the ruling military dictatorship and to search for improved conditions for workers. Also known as the New
Unionism, it was really a vibrant social movement independent of the traditional, state-controlled labor unions that dominated the scene until the late
1970s (French 2009). After being in opposition for over two decades while
growing steadily at the subnational level, the PT won the presidency in 2002 and
placed an unusual presidential candidate – Luiz Inácio (Lula) da Silva, a fourth-
grade educated union leader – in national office. The PT was then reelected three
times, in 2006, 2010, and 2014. After three complete terms, as Amaral and
Meneguello (2017: 31) note, "the party faced its biggest political and institutional crisis" and was ousted from power in 2016 via the impeachment of
president Dilma Rousseff – who presided over Brazil's deepest economic crisis
since the depression. Even before Rousseff's impeachment, the party's image and
its partisan base had become deeply damaged after top party leaders were linked
to large-scale corruption scandals (Amaral and Meneguello 2017).

Over the period from its origins to the present, a period that included 14
consecutive years in power, the PT transformed from a "democratic socialist mass
party" (Keck 1992: 247) into a party that resembles an "electoral-professional"
organization (Hunter 2007, 2010; Ribeiro 2014; Schipani 2016). Its development
lends support to the Michelsian trend toward top-down control – a trend that is
evident in decisions over candidate selection and in the policy-making sphere more
broadly (Ribeiro 2008: 226; Bolognesi 2013: 60–3).

That trend, as evidenced through signs of atrophy between the party and its
social bases, became evident soon after the PT took power (Hochstetler 2008).
Atrophy between the party and its social bases became even clearer since 2013,
when social protests initially led by popular grass-roots sectors, the party's
"natural" bases, erupted against Dilma Rousseff. Though those protests turned
into a more elite-and-middle-class conservative movement against the PT, they
demonstrated the challenges that the PT confronted, after several years in the
presidency, in terms of its openness and responsiveness to the concerns of its
own social bases (Hagopian 2016: 127). The little counter-mobilization that
the social bases of the PT posed to the questionable impeachment of Rousseff, a
president from their own ranks, is further evidence supporting the claim of the
atrophied links between the PT and its social bases.

Origins and Early Development

The PT is a quintessential example of a movement-based party – it was founded directly by highly mobilized, autonomous social movements (Keck 1992; Amaral and Power 2015: 149). The party emerged from the bottom up under military rule as a political expression of the radical New Unionism and other groups in civil society. As French (2009) notes, under the leadership of Lula, a skilled worker and union organizer (Bourne 2008), trade unions in the industrial ABC Region of Sao Paulo would try to "extend [their] fight for recognition and power into the realm of mass electoral politics" (French 2009: 165).

Since its origins, the PT sought to maintain strong linkages with a wide array of social movements, particularly with organized labor. In its formative phase, however, the PT was "not just another labor party" (Guidry 2003) because its initial social base went far beyond industrial labor to include "the organized left, Catholic activists, progressive politicians, intellectuals, and representatives of other social movements" (Keck 1992: 7). It also incorporated "segments of civil society that did not identify themselves with a class perspective, such as feminist groups, gay movements, Afro-Brazilians, human rights advocates or environmentalists" (Gómez Bruera 2013: 29), becoming a "place of convergence" for various forces from the left, including also politicians linked to the Brazilian Democratic Movement (MDB) (French and Fortes 2005: 17; Secco 2011: 27; Amaral and Power 2015: 149). The PT was also different from classic examples of labor-based parties because it was not conceived of as the political arm of a specific sector of the labor movement, and it did not establish formal institutional ties with unions. Although labor unions in the highly urban state of Sao Paulo played a central role in the formation of the party, it "was not created by the unions qua organizations" (Keck 1992: 7).

The early formal separation between the unions and the party was an attempt to protect the autonomy of each union (Keck 1986: 76; 1992: 180). Accordingly, since its inception, it did not incorporate mechanisms of collective affiliation, and those who decided to join the PT did so on an individual "party member" basis. The PT has thus followed what Roberts (1998: 75) calls the "organic" model of party development. These are parties with bottom-up extra-parliamentary origins, whose "organic relationship with mass organizations and social movements" provides "a common political space that links popular and political struggles while respecting their relative autonomy" (Roberts 1998: 277).

Much of the literature on the PT as a national-level organization has attempted to explain the extent to which the party represents something different – an exception in Brazilian and Latin American politics (Keck 1992; Samuels 2004; Hunter 2007, 2010; Meneguello and Amaral 2008; Amaral 2010). The goal here is not to assess this debate but to trace elements in the party's genesis and early organizational development that have set the party on its distinctive path down the road.

The early works of Meneguello (1989) and Keck (1992) are the essential references to trace the roots of the PT's distinctiveness in the Brazilian political system (Amaral and Power 2015: 149). Taken together, they stress three areas – links to external groups, programmatic orientation, and internal organization – that can be traced back to the formative phase of the party. Keck (1992), for instance, argues that during its first decade the PT represented an organizational "anomaly" in Brazilian politics due to its strong connections to organized society, its political proposals, and its focus on aggregating the interests of diverse grass-roots groups rather than on performing just electoral functions. Keck argues that,

...the Workers' party was a novel development among Brazilian political institutions for several reasons: first, because it is set out to be a party that expressed the interests of workers and the poor at a political level; second, because it sought to be an internally democratic party; and finally, because it wanted to represent and be accountable to its members. All these conceptions have evolved a great deal since the party was founded, but all of them remain central elements in the party's identity and are what make it an innovation (Keck 1992: 239).

Using Duverger's (1954) classic typology, others have characterized the PT as Brazil's first "mass bureaucratic" party (Meneguello 1989: 33–4) on the basis of the pattern of internal organization it adopted in its formative phase, including an articulated hierarchical structure, mass membership, strict requirements for membership, close links to organized groups in civil society, and a nationally centralized decision-making structure (see also Samuels 2004; Amaral 2010). The military regime's bureaucratic regulations forced new parties to perform onerous registration tasks within a short period of time, and that heavily influenced the adoption of such organizational pattern. Heavy regulations pushed party builders into a process of what might be called "early bureaucratization" (my term; Nogueira-Budny 2013: 115, 117). Establishing a bureaucratic, centrally organized party at the very onset of its existence was indeed necessary to permit the party's initial survival. It also contributed to the party's exponential electoral growth and future programmatic and organizational adaptations (Hunter 2010: 22; Nogueira-Budny 2013: 122). In other words, a strong tendency toward bureaucratization became a distinctive characteristic of the party's early development.

This organizational model was far from what PT founders had envisioned in the late 1970s prior to the PT's founding (de Souza 1988). Their vision was a decentralized organization characterized by bottom-up leadership and decision-making structures – called "basismo" for the emphasis on base participation (Guidry 2003: 91) – that would be a break from the pattern of elitism that had long characterized Brazilian parties. The hallmarks of this model were the party "base nuclei" ("*núcleos de base*"), which became an essential component of the PT's identity and also reflected the founders' intent to build an internally democratic party on the basis of a participating mass membership, despite the restrictions imposed by the military regime (Keck 1992: 103; Amaral 2010: 108). Base nuclei were small local groups of at least 21 party affiliates "organized by neighborhood, job category, workplace, or social movement" (Keck 1992: 104). They were to forge strong links with preexisting social movements and to promote an active and diffuse participation of party affiliates in internal party affairs.

Petistas had envisioned the base nuclei as spaces for the aggregation of interests rather than as organs focused on electoral competition. They were designed to serve "as the conduit between party and society to divulge and promote the party policies at the local level" (Nogueira-Budny 2013: 118). Although nuclei provided spaces for bottom-up participation, their activities in their initial years were "closely linked to the efforts to legalize the party" (Amaral 2010: 110; see also Keck 1992: 106), and even though they provided spaces for collective deliberation, they lacked real influence on intraparty issues (Amaral 2010: 114). Over time, particularly as the PT began to participate in (and to win) elections, these nuclei declined in importance in relation to the more hierarchical party congresses (*"congressos"*).

A centralized leadership structure would be useful to Campo Majoritário (Majority Group), the moderate faction that gained control over the party leadership in 1995. It would steer the party toward important internal transformations in a further centralizing direction (Ribeiro 2008: 160). The most relevant manifestation reflecting these changes was the 2001 reform of the party statute. Until then, the party's most important bodies for deliberation and consultation were the annual meetings (*"encontros"*) at each level of its structure, be it municipal, state, regional, or national (Partido dos Trabalhadores 1980). Their key function was (and still is) to discuss program, political strategy, tactics, alliance policy, and party-building strategies (Partido dos Trabalhadores 2001). In addition, until 2001, the annual meetings selected members of the directorates (*"diretórios"*) as well as delegates to be sent to higher-level meetings (Ribeiro 2008: 240–1). The latter would in turn select the party president. The annual meetings used to be truly representative and inclusive forums (Ribeiro 2008: 240; also 2014: 111; and Amaral 2010: 83).

But that changed. Approved "after years of conflict between the Campo Majoritário and the radical factions (with the dominant group imposing its ideas on all relevant issues)" (Ribeiro 2014: 101), the 2001 PT statute reduced the power of the base nuclei and reformed the intraparty electoral system in ways that affected the internal dynamics of party meetings.[3]

Most visibly, it introduced the PED (*Processo de Eleições Diretas*, or Direct Election Process) for the selection of party authorities and candidates at all levels, so that party authorities and candidates should "be elected by the direct

---

[3] Congresses (*"congressos"*) "started to resolve those issues whose responsibility initially resided within nuclei" (Nogueira-Budny 2013: 121).

vote of members" (Ribeiro 2014: 111), and it imposed a simple plurality internal voting system.[4] Annual meetings remained the highest-level decision-making bodies, but they now take place after the authorities are elected, which reduces their role as a body for intense internal negotiation.

While sponsors of this reform sold it as a way to deepen internal democracy and develop more inclusive decision-making processes, the adoption of the PED ended up increasing the decision-making autonomy of the party leadership by undermining the power of collective actors and appealing directly to individual party members (Hunter 2010: 39–40; Ribeiro 2014: 112). The reform made the party more inclusive, but it also promoted a participation of "low intensity" (Ribeiro 2008: 178). In addition, the PT structure became more open to new party members[5] but less permeable to pressures from the organized constituencies, allowing the leadership to operate "less constrained by the more radical holdout . . .that sought ideological purity and rejected any form of institutional change" (Nogueira-Budny 2013: 125). In short, this new system gave increased power and autonomy to the party's leadership, especially at the national level, in the selection of leaders and candidates – even if many candidates for elective office continued to be drawn from and had strong linkages to social movements, especially labor unions (see Leal 2005; also Schipani 2016: 52). By weakening the collective power of organized actors in areas like candidate selection, the advent of the PED contributed to pulling away the party's top leadership from the social bases *before* gaining national power.[6] This tendency to become less permeable to pressures from below would consolidate even further when the PT assumed governmental responsibilities, and specifically when recruiting candidates from the public administration rather than from the

---

[4] Prior to this, party authorities were selected by delegates from annual national meetings (*"encontros"*). According to Ribeiro (2014: 111), "this process differed from Brazilian party law and the practice of other parties in the greater representativeness and inclusiveness of the meetings." This is because "the criteria for participation gave greater weight to the ordinary members" in relation to the leadership. As a result, before 2001, "the PT structure was more permeable to pressure from the bottom up, from the rank and file on the leadership." For a parallel argument, see Nogueira-Budny (2013: 121).

[5] Initially, the PT had strict requirements for affiliation and demanded a high level of commitment from members (Meneguello 1989: 33). Over time, after 2001, and especially after assuming national office in 2003, the PT gradually reduced the barriers of entry to join the PT – for example, by introducing collective affiliations during electoral campaigns – and eased member obligations. In part as a result of changes in norms and rules of membership, the party dramatically increased the number of affiliates (Amaral 2010: 66). For a detailed assessment of additional explanations driving the expansion of the PT's affiliate base, see Amaral (2010: chapter 2).

[6] According to Ribeiro (2008: 265, 267), the introduction of PED can be seen as an "illusionary" democratization – that is, a "false" democratization that only boosted the autonomy of the party's top leadership, and one that transformed the PT from being a party of activists and militants into a party of voters. For the argument that the PED deepened internal democracy, see Meneguello and Amaral (2008) and Amaral (2010).

grass-roots – a tendency toward party professionalization – became increasingly common (Ribeiro 2008: 172; Perissinotto and Miríade 2009: 320; see also Perissinotto and Bolognesi 2010; and Bolognesi 2013).[7]

Beyond its increasingly centralized decision-making structures, since its foundation and early development, the PT has worked closely with a wide range of social movements, and it has also embraced a commitment to popular empowerment and participatory democracy. In 1984 the PT took a direct role organizing a broad-based coalition that brought millions of people into the streets to demand direct elections in order to accelerate the end of the military regime (*"Diretas já!"*). In terms of relationships with social movements, in the mid-1980s the PT helped to found the MST (Movimento Sem Terra, or Landless Movement) and an independent labor federation, the CUT (Central Única dos Trabalhadores, Unified Workers' Central), although both organizations remained formally autonomous (Guidry 2003: 90). The linkages between these popular movements and the party were strengthened in the 1990s, when PT representatives actively pursued their demands in Congress (Baiocchi and Checa 2007: 420). Unions, in particular, remained strong during the 1990s; they grew in membership and in terms of their mobilization capacity even during the implementation of neoliberal reforms (Schipani 2016: 51, 61–2). However, the partisan logic driven by participation in electoral arenas led to the subordination of the unions' goals to those of the party and, consequently, to a gradual loss of their capacity for autonomous collective action.

Finally, in line with the PT's emphasis on "basismo," the party generated institutional innovations at the local level where, for instance, they won political office and introduced a wide array of participatory programs (Baiocchi 2003; also Wampler 2007). A commitment to honest government and grass-roots participation would become the trademarks of the "PT way of governing" (*"modo petista de governor"*), defining the party's distinctive goal of popular empowerment and inclusion as it struggled to gain national power. These efforts to engaging organized civil society allowed the PT to maintain a distinctive profile in Brazil's politics, particularly in comparison to its competitors and even as the party structures became more centralized (Samuels and Zucco 2016).[8]

---

[7] It should be noted that despite this trend, when compared with other Brazilian parties, the PT stands out for its relatively greater inclusiveness in candidate selection procedures (Bolognesi 2013: 64) and partisan affairs more generally (Samuels and Zucco 2016).

[8] Other distinctive channels to connect the party with civil society are the "sectoral" groups (*"setorais"*), which were introduced since the founding of the party. While today these may "play an important role in cultivating affective attachments between individuals and the party" (Samuels and Zucco 2016: 353), their role in shaping party decision-making has been significantly reduced since the party's statute reform in 2001.

Road to Power: Legislative Opposition and Local Government

The PT's path to national power was indeed a long and rocky one. It followed a pattern of progressive growth from the local level to the national level in both legislative and executive elections. Along the way, it went from being predominantly urban to reaching out to rural areas (Ribeiro 2014: 88), and in 2002 Lula was elected president on his fourth try. By that time, the PT was a bureaucratic and centralized organization, and its rise to national-level power did not occur through the use of mobilization campaign tactics.

The PT first ran for office in the 1982 mayoral elections, receiving only 3 percent of the national vote (Keck 1992: 143). In light of these below-expectation results, party builders decided to "return to the base," or to strengthen the movement in relation to the party, since movement activity was seen as more conducive to social change than participation in institutions (Keck 1992: 153, 164). Although the PT performed better in the 1985 mayoral elections, particularly in state capitals, the electoral breakthrough only occurred in 1988 (French and Fortes 2005: 19), when the party gained control of 31 municipalities, including state capitals and rural districts where the MST had been active (Keck 1992: 157). Increasing governing experience in states and cities across Brazil led to a focus on institutional strategies as opposed to a strengthening of the social struggles (Lacerda 2002: 63). It also led the PT "to moderate its discourse, platform and political practices, in terms of public administration and/or its attitude toward other actors, such as in the political alliances it formed" (Ribeiro 2014: 89; see also Couto 1995). Local experiences contributed to the growth of the party and expanded its social base. PT mayors combined pragmatism and broad alliance making with institutional innovations to promote broad-based citizen involvement, such as participatory budgeting, which became the trademark of many PT administrations (Abers 2000; Baiocchi 2003; Nylen 2003). While the slogan "PT way of governing" was obviously a discursive tool to consolidate the PT as a party fundamentally different from its competitors, "it was rooted in something real: practical policies that expanded access to education, health, and housing and that improved the quality of services and goods provided" (French and Fortes 2005: 26).

The PT's "basista" ethos shaped these local governments not only due to the participatory institutional innovations implemented by its mayors but also in the sense that PT leaders did not fully abandon social mobilization strategies. Such strategies only worked under very specific circumstances that were not present in every municipality, however (Gómez Bruera 2013: 81). Above all, as a general pattern, the party's increasing experience holding local-level executive office provided a sort of "institutional school" for PT leaders that contributed to their pragmatism in office (Novaes 1993; Couto 1995; Samuels 2004). Being elected to local executive office but usually having a minority status or no stable coalitions in municipal legislatures, forced PT officials to rethink the party's approach to electoral and legislative alliance making, which initially was restricted to like-minded parties on the left (Hunter and Power 2005: 129). The commitment to working with other political forces not only signaled moderation to voters, but it also helped to strengthen the dominant coalition of party moderates – a group called the Majority Group – who would then further centralize authority and steer the PT toward the ideological center (Samuels 2004: 1008). Finally, the growing experience holding subnational level office "generated incentives for the party to place greater emphasis on electoral and institutional activity and less emphasis on mobilizational and extra institutional struggles" (Samuels 2004: 1016). The relationships between the party and its movement base would not necessarily be "weakened" or cooled down, but they would be altered in nature in response to electoral imperatives and as the PT increasingly held public office.

At the national legislative branch, where the PT increased the presence of "working class men and women, both rural and urban...including an unprecedented number of Afro-Brazilians, women, and labor and community leaders" (French and Fortes 2005: 19), the PT developed a "strategy aimed at furthering the party's distinctive profile and long-term growth" (Hunter 2010: 45). The most visible manifestation of this strategy was the anti-neoliberal policy orientation of PT representatives, who gradually moderated their views from advocating socialism and radical change to a pragmatic but progressive position aimed at reforming capitalism to protect the interests of the underprivileged.[9] Another visible manifestation of the PT's legislative strategy was the party's "distinctive organizational characteristics of cohesion, loyalty, and discipline" (Hunter 2010: 55; see also Roma 2005). The PT exerted tight control over its representatives and their legislative activity.[10] The experience in the legislative opposition progressively strengthened the party's position in representative institutions, and allowed the party to project itself onto the national political scene as a reasonable alternative to the status quo (Secco 2011). The opposition role it played also "allowed the PT to consolidate grassroots support and build a strong organization over time" (Hunter 2010: 77). All these elements would become crucial for its electoral success in the 2002 presidential victory.

Local experiences of municipal administration and long years of opposition in the legislative branch led to greater interaction between the party's union and social movement base and state institutions and bureaucracies (Avritzer 2009: 9). Some of these movements, particularly in the urban areas, "increasingly engaged in processes of negotiations with the state and deployed strategies that were less confrontational and disruptive" (Gómez Bruera 2013: 42). At the

---

[9] Amaral (2010) also notes a simultaneous process of ideological moderation among the PT rank and file. A parallel argument is found in Samuels (2004).

[10] In 2003, four representatives were expelled from Congress after opposing the PT's economic policy and its proposal for social security reform.

same time, however, "the original base of the PT, in terms of its social move-ment roots, was facing a deep crisis" (French and Fortes 2005: 26). This was particularly the case in regard to urban labor unions, as "the combined effects of economic stagnation, high unemployment rates, and productive restructur-ing drove unions into retreat" (French and Fortes 2005: 27). In light of these broader societal changes, the moderate party faction that now controlled the PT prioritized an institutional rather than a mobilizational strategy. Although social mobilization did not disappear from the stage, protest action decreased notably during the 1990s (Gómez Bruera 2013: 45).

Thus, the 2002 presidential campaign took place in a context of low-intensity popular mobilization, and it was designed when the PT enjoyed a situation of relative strength within representative institutions at the national and subnational levels. The political learning made it clear that in order to ensure governability, the party would need to shift to the center and create a broader set of alliances than only with like-minded parties on the left. In 2002, the PT allied with the small right-wing Partido Liberal (Liberal Party, PL), which provided José Alencar, a man with close ties to Brazil's business community, as the vice presidential candidate (Hunter 2007: 463).[11] In add-ition, the moderate sector led by Lula's faction (Campo Majoritário), a faction that by the early 2000s had become a cohesive, dominant coalition within the party, was able to adopt a professionalized approach for the presidential campaign. The most visible manifestation of this was the hiring of Brazil's leading PR expert, Duda Mendonça, to run the presidential campaign (Hunter 2007: 464; Ribeiro 2014: 110). This led to a move from activist-intensive campaigns, which were more characteristic during the PT's early experiences, toward a marketing-oriented campaign based on the per-sonal appeal of Lula. This was also evidence that by the early 2000s the party leadership enjoyed significant levels of autonomy in relation to the rank and file: external experts directed the winning 2002 campaign and were not subject to any internal accountability mechanisms (Ribeiro 2014: 111). The internal centralization of power and professionalization of the party had already occurred.

The election of Lula was not the product of social mobilization. By 2002, the grass-roots actors had been demobilized:

Lula's electoral victory occurred when social mobilization was not on the ascent (as would have been true if Lula had won in 1989 or 1994). Lula's election followed a decade in which mass activism had fallen off (with the notable exception of the Landless Workers' Movement, or MST), and the mass organizations built during the 1970s and 1980s were devastated by an economic liberalization that eliminated, for example, half of the industrial working class in Brazil...There is, however, one limited sense in which

---

[11] This also reflects the balance of forces in Congress and the powerful influence of Brazilian domestic capital.

Lula's election can be seen as a victory for social movements. It is very much the triumph of a remarkable generation of leaders that grew out of the dynamic protest movements that brought an end to the military regime, even if the organizations they led no longer have the same dynamism as in the past (French and Fortes 2005: 24).

The image of demobilization is perhaps more accurate in the case of urban movements; the situation was different in the countryside, "where landless workers (MST and other new groups) expanded their efforts and remained active, although profound political disagreements would cool the relationship between the PT and the MST." Despite this nuance, what matters analytically is that when Lula's 2002 campaign was designed the PT was "stronger in the institutional field but weaker in its organic base" (French and Fortes 2005: 27). This allowed party moderates to gain distance from the party's social movement base, to de-emphasize the party's socialist programmatic platform and other more radical stances, and to embrace moderation. The party also adopted modern marketing technology, such as frequent polling, as an effort to develop more targeted appeals (Hunter 2010: 139). Attempts to instill fear among potential Lula voters led Lula to release the "Letter to the Brazilian People" (da Silva 2002), which signaled to the public (and to domestic and international market operators) the PT's commitment to work within the constraints of the prevailing economic model (Samuels 2004: 1004).[12] This could be seen as a part of an electoral strategy, as Hunter (2010) argues, and also as a platform to ensure governability when the PT assumed the presidency (Gómez Bruera 2013: 90). Either way, running on a platform that avoided socialist and confrontational rhetoric, Lula won 46.4 percent of the first-round vote, reaching 61.3 percent of the valid votes in the runoff election against PSDB candidate José Serra.

Conditions Surrounding Access to Power

Once elected, Lula (2003–11) could not escape the general constraints of Brazilian politics: specifically, the highly fragmented nature of its political system – often referred to as coalitional presidentialism – that in part results from its open-list proportional representation electoral rules for legislatures (Power 2010; Amaral and Meneguello 2017). As it had happened when the PT started to accumulate local experiences of municipal administration, the PT came to national-level executive power with a weak position in both legislative chambers – as a leader of a heterogeneous and fractious governing coalition (Hunter 2010: 147; Gómez Bruera 2013: 85, 91; Schipani 2016: 64). As French

---

[12] According to Gómez Bruera (2013: 90), the letter was "drafted by a small group of leaders within Lula's entourage" and lacked intraparty consensus before it was presented to the public. As such, many within the party saw it as an imposition from the top (Gómez Bruera 2013: fn. 24, p. 188).

and Fortes (2005: 28) note, "although the PT won the largest share of seats in the Chamber of Deputies, the Left was still outnumbered by Center-Right parties in the National Congress." And it "never held more than 18% of all seats in the lower house" (Hunter 2011: 310).[13] In such a weak parliamentary position, the PT could have opted to mobilize its movement base – that is, to mobilize organized popular constituencies to promote at least certain progressive reforms by putting pressure on the legislative branch.[14]

But the PT did not do so (Gómez Bruera 2013: 91–2). The main roadblock was the PT moderates of Majority Group, who rejected mobilization because of "a fear of political and social instability" (Gómez Bruera 2013: 93). It is also plausible that large-scale mobilization was not instigated because by 2003 the PT's union and social movement base was not seen as having enough strength and mobilization capacity to support such a strategy (Gómez Bruera 2013: 94). Driven by a moderate policy agenda, the first Lula administration (2003–6) opted to engage in broad alliances across the political spectrum in order to ensure survival in office, pass initiatives in Congress, and "get things done."[15]

After Lula assumed the presidency in January 2003, the PT had a difficult time satisfying its movement base, expressing their aspirations, and translating them into policies (Hunter and Power 2007; Hochstetler 2008; Schipani 2016). The orthodox macroeconomic policies of Lula (a continuation of policies implemented by the Cardoso government), the lack of major reform in health and education, and the timid approach to land reform (Hunter 2010: 148–9, 152–3), brought about since early on "increasing conflict with, and isolation from, its base of support among social movements" (Baiocchi and Checa 2007: 411). According to Hunter (2011: 318–20), moreover, the PT governments had great difficulties upholding its signature principle of popular participation – which contributed to pulling the party away from its social bases. As a key example of these dynamics, *Bolsa Família*, the PT's signature social policy, had no role for the movement bases or for popular participation, creating angst for the traditional movement sectors of the party.

All this is not to say that the PT did not succeed in *creating* and *institutionalizing* participatory practices at the federal (and especially the subnational) levels, however (Mayka n.d.). And it is not to deny that there have been significant advances in terms of the orientation of public policies to the benefit of the PT's historical constituencies and in particular the country's poor

---

[13] According to Schipani's (2016: 64) estimations, "Center and Center-Right parties obtained, on average, 62.12% of total votes for the lower chamber throughout the PT's administrations."

[14] Mobilization was the strategy promoted by the most radical leftist factions within the PT – factions that had been marginalized from the party leadership since the mid-1990s. The opponents were the members of Campo Majoritário representing party moderates.

[15] As Amaral and Meneguello (2017) note, the distribution of ministries to allied parties was yet another way of gaining support.

majorities. Among others, these advances include greater social protection for the poor, rising minimum wages, and increased investments in health and education (Hunter 2011; French and Fortes 2012; Huber and Stephens 2012; Pogrebinschi 2012; Schipani 2016).

Nevertheless, recent political developments in Brazil, especially during the Rousseff's administrations (2011–16), indicate that the PT in the federal government created limited options for "real" input of organized civil society in shaping policy initiatives or at best that the party had great challenges "federalizing" participatory practices.[16] For some authors, that situation led to an early (and since then unstoppable) distancing between the PT and popular grassroots sectors and to a growing disappointment by the latter (Hochstetler 2008; Anderson 2011).[17] The rise of mass protests in June 2013 – as well as the weak counter-mobilization capacity of the PT social bases in light of Rousseff's impeachment – can be seen as indicative of that distancing. After 14 years in the presidency, the PT's social bases had atrophied to such an extent that the party left office with little resistance from below.

If the participation of organized civil society in the "creative" formulation of public policies was not encouraged or fully supported by PT governments (Schipani 2016: 65, 67), the ability of civil society to block or modify top-down government policy was even less evident. The process of the passage of a highly contentious Social Security Reform (*Reforma da Previdência*) illustrates this point. Put on the agenda as a way to reduce the structural deficit in Brazil's pension system, the PT proposal directly clashed with the interests of public service trade unions, a well-organized group within the Unified Workers' Central (CUT) and within the PT's base of support (Hunter and Power 2005: 131; Hunter 2010: 151). Although CUT leaders initially took a conciliatory approach and tried to negotiate with the government some of the sensitive issues of its proposal, "public sector unions...took a hard line, formally requesting that the bill be withdrawn from Congress and eventually voting for a general strike" (Gómez Bruera 2013: 141). This forced the CUT leadership to support the strike, even though the CUT as an organization would not

---

[16] See also Hunter (2011: 318) and Gómez Bruera (2013: 120). As Schipani (2016) notes, moreover, at key moments the PT governments did not fully support policies brought to the public agenda by the labor movement. An example is the proposed reform to the labor code (*Reforma Sindical*). A bill introduced by the labor movement to Congress in 2004, one aimed at strengthening unions in collective bargaining, was easily defeated because the government did not support it (Schipani 2016: 65).

[17] An alternative interpretation is presented in Pogrebinschi and Santos's (2011) analysis of the National Conferences of Public Policy, as well as in Avritzer (2010) and Samuels (2013). These studies argue that the PT managed to increase the participation of organized civil society in policy-making. As Amaral and Power (2015: 158) note, however, while this research documents the institutionalization of new participatory practices, "the casual impact of those new practices on legislative production and the elaboration of specific programs by the executive" is not immediately evident.

encourage demonstrations and "remained tacitly in favor" of the reform (Schipani 2016: 66). Despite protests organized by public servants in Brasilia, "the government prevailed over the vociferous objections of important historical constituencies within the PT" (Hunter 2010: 151). The reform was passed in Congress with little modification in response to the pressures from below, even though it included "numerous concessions" made to other parties in Congress that were central "to obtain legislative backing" (Hunter and Power 2005: 131). The passage of a top-down reform that directly collided with the interests of a well-organized historical constituency was facilitated by the party's tendencies toward top-down control associated with its bureaucratic and strongly centralized institutional structures – two characteristics traceable to its early organizational development.[18]

The Social Security Reform would not be the only instance where pressures from below did not force the party's top leadership to change its proposed policies. A number of additional times social movements and minority groups that joined the PT during its formative phase "actively opposed the construction of large infrastructure projects" (Gómez Bruera 2013: 134) that directly affected their living conditions. For the most part, these challenges were placed on the grounds of environmental concerns. The PT-led governments have to a large extent succeeded in defending large infrastructure projects, despite this opposition. In general, the PT administrations have been impervious to challenges from below. Certainly, social movements allied with the PT have obtained some benefits from their association with the PT. While the MST achieved little progress in terms of land reform (Ondetti 2008; Hunter 2011: 313), other movements have achieved substantial increases in the minimum wage and some advances in trade union legislation (Gómez Bruera 2013: 154, 162; Schipani 2016: 67–8). In both of these instances, however, allied popular movements did not mobilize autonomously; rather, they were called on by the PT leadership to show strength to opposition groups in Congress and skeptics within the party. Overall, as Gómez Bruera argues, "whenever significant changes took place the initiative of the party in government was by far the main driving force. Under the PT administration it was the party in public office, and Lula in particular, that established the main tactics and strategies" (Gómez Bruera 2013: 163).

Case Summary

The PT has movement origins. In the 1980s and 1990s, the party was a clear example of a grass-roots, internally democratic movement-based party.

---

[18] A mechanism used by the PT was the punishment of dissidence. Those who refused to agree to the proposal were expelled from the party. According to Nogueira-Budny (2013: 126–7), the mechanism of tight control over the party membership began shortly after the PT's foundation.

But the party quickly switched course. For all of its early emphasis on promoting bottom-up input, its original institutional structures (a historical cause) facilitated, even if unintentionally, power concentration and the dominance of the national party structures by a single faction – a tendency toward top-down, "hierarchical" control. Once those structures were set in and actors became used to working in those structures, deviating from them became less promising over time. Electoral imperatives, the long experience at the local level (with coalition building), and conditions surrounding the PT's access to national power (with a very weak position in Congress and the need to form broad political alliances), are responsible for the reproduction of an organizational pattern that was, since early on, pointed in the direction of power concentration. As these processes unfolded, they contributed to de-emphasizing proactive popular mobilization and to consolidating a centralized party structure – one that granted its leadership increasing levels of autonomy from the party's social base, and one that became impervious to societal pressure from below (Hunter 2007; Ribeiro 2008; also Ribeiro 2014) even if the PT still remains more participatory than its competitors (Amaral 2010; Samuels and Zucco 2016; Amaral and Meneguello 2017).

THE BROAD FRONT

The development of the Broad Front (FA) is similar to that of the PT in several ways. Its roots can be traced to the 1960s, when diverse actors on the left – including labor leaders, established left parties, popular movements, splinters of traditional parties, urban guerrilla organizations, and progressive intellectuals – converged on the idea of creating a popular front. Unity was achieved by 1971, two years before a military coup ushered in 12 years of military-authoritarian rule. Similar to the PT, the FA spent most of its formative period in opposition to an authoritarian regime (1973–84), becoming an opposition party during the post-authoritarian period (1985–2004) and then gaining national-level power in the 2004 presidential election and reelections in 2009 and 2014. Over the period since its creation, the FA has progressively been transformed from a "labor-based" "mass party" into a type of party with a broader social base that approximates the "electoral-professional" model (Luna 2014: 175). Unlike the PT, however, it has developed since its genesis institutional structures (a historical cause) that created stronger incentives for power dispersion. Compared to the PT, those structures encourage more bottom-up input and mobilized participation as well as greater limits on the power of the party's leadership. Notably, the FA has maintained such an organizational model for over 30 years – even after the party assumed and exercised power (Pribble 2008, 2013; Pérez, Piñeiro, and Rosenblatt 2018).

Origins and Early Development

Founded in 1971 "as a coalition of five fractions that included Communists, Socialists, Christian-democrats, sectors splitting from both traditional parties, and leftist independents" (Luna 2006: 416) and reflecting its diverse origins, the party initially developed a fractionalized structure and became a place of convergence for many groups on the left with different organizational identities (Aguirre Bayley 2000; Giorgi 2011). Although the number of fractions has fluctuated over time (Caetano et al. 2003: 15), the four major ones include the Communist Party (PC), the Socialist Party (PS), the Popular Participation Movement (MPP), and the Uruguay Assembly (AU). All four have leaders with varied origins, organizational structures, and grass-roots following (Luna 2014: 179–80, 192–6). The early adoption of a fractionalized structure, which is a central feature of the party's foundation that was kept alive during the military-authoritarian period, has created incentives against the centralization of power in several ways – and since early on. Specifically, it has forced competing fractions to engage in internal negotiations before reaching decisions, and it has created incentives for competition for party leadership. According to Pribble (2008: 95), "This internal competition, in turn, presents political elites with incentives to build organic ties with base organizations so as to institutionalize each fraction's power." Pribble argues that this situation "leads to the strengthening of [intraparty] mechanisms for consultation and participation."

The FA was not formed *directly* by social movements, but it has maintained close links with organized labor and the student movement, and it has drawn extensive support from them since its early years.[19] These early connections were crucial for the party to develop an organizational and an activist base during the military-authoritarian period, when some groups within the party led clandestine opposition to the military regime. Although early party builders respected the relative autonomy of mass organizations and social movements, it was clear at the time of the creation of the FA that the Communist Party had significant influence in the labor movement, and that the Socialist Party had more influence among the student movement and the urban-intellectual strata (Luna 2006: 416). According to Luna (2006), moreover, the FA developed early on a "historical brotherhood" with organized labor, which is visibly "manifested in the party's adoption of the union peak organization's platform as the keystone of its historical programmatic bases," in "the continuous interaction between union and party leaders," and in "the

---

[19] As Pérez, Piñeiro, and Rosenblatt (2018: 4) note, "the founding fathers – some of whom remain active as party elders – conceived of the FA both as a coalition and as a movement. Indeed, the party's founding proclamation expresses this notion. This implied, from the very beginning, the presence of strong bottom-up participation."

use of the union movement as a transmission belt for the party" (Luna 2006: 417). In addition, the relationship between organized labor and the party can be observed in the social composition and evolution of the FA's parliamentary group, which has a significant presence of union leaders in key positions (Luna 2014: 181). Over time, however, the labor movement has progressively gained autonomy from the FA, particularly from the PC and the PS, and became more radicalized in relation to the party leadership (Luna 2014: 182). This last factor would then become a source of conflict between the party and its social movement base when the FA made the transition to administering local governments.

As mentioned, the FA has developed a fractionalized structure since its origins, with each fraction preserving its own identity, history, and following. Such an organizational model created strong power-dispersing incentives from the outset. Further reinforcing this trend, from early on the FA sought to be an open and internally responsive party – one with "strong bottom-up participation and clear organizational structures by which grass-roots activists could influence party decisions" (Pérez, Piñeiro, and Rosenblatt 2018: 4). Accordingly, it developed a dense organization with multiple rules and mechanisms of consultation between base organizations and party elites (Pribble 2008: 93). These would provide a degree of institutionalization of grass-roots input over party platforms, candidate selection, electoral strategies, government plans, and policy orientations (Pribble 2008: 94; Pérez, Piñeiro, and Rosenblatt 2018: 3–4). Such structures would also provide the party leadership with incentives to seek broad-based consensus when making strategic decisions (Caetano et al. 2003: 9). This last point is especially important, as the FA (unlike the PT) introduced from early on an internal electoral system requiring absolute majorities. This institutional attribute complicated decision-making in the early stages; it also discouraged the dominance of the party by a single leader or fraction and, more generally, reduced the autonomy of the leadership (Caetano et al. 2003: 15, 16).

Although the degree of consultation and deliberation has tended to decrease over time, "the party continues to hold-on to some characteristics from its origins" (Pribble 2008: 92) and has not succumbed to party oligarchization (Pérez, Piñeiro, and Rosenblatt 2018). The party structures – which empowered the social bases in relation to the leadership – and mechanisms defined at early stages of development, have allowed the FA to maintain close linkages with its original leftist base of support and to promote mobilized participation of allied groups in decision-making. The parallel construction of a national network of territorial base committees (*Comités de Base*) as spaces for deliberation and collective decision-making is also an important birthmark of the party. It allowed the party to generate a large and committed activist base, helping to define the party's project of popular empowerment as it struggled to gain national power (Pérez, Piñeiro, and Rosenblatt 2018).

Road to Power: Legislative Opposition and Local Government

The FA first ran for office in the 1971 presidential election and received close to 20 percent of the vote (Lanzaro 2011). The party then spent 11 of its formative years under military-authoritarian rule, "with zero access to public office, very little access to media, and the pervasive threat of arrest and exile" (Van Dyck 2013: 373). In clandestine opposition, the FA developed a strong organizational foundation that allowed the party to survive and then to become an important actor in the pacted transition. The FA's organizational strength was clearly visible in 1983, when Uruguay democratized. The FA received 21.3 percent of the vote in the ensuing 1984 election.[20] As was the case with the PT, the FA did not come to national-level power rapidly after its foundation. The electoral expansion of the party was slow, gradual, and built on solid organizational foundations. Its vote share grew steadily at the local and the national levels. Its presidential candidate since 1994, Tabaré Vázquez, only won the 2004 presidential elections after several attempts. Along the way, the FA went from being predominantly urban-based to reaching out to rural areas and increasingly catchall in orientation. By the time it captured the presidency, the FA was a highly institutionalized and professionalized leftist party (Levitsky and Roberts 2011).

As in the case of the PT, the experience in the legislative opposition, and the governing experience at the subnational level contributed to the FA's electoral growth. The long-standing role as an opposition party in Congress allowed the party to develop a strategy aimed at differentiating itself from Uruguay's dominant parties, the Blancos and the Colorados, which had dominated Uruguayan politics for almost two centuries. This occurred in a context where the Import Substitution Industrialization (ISI) model was in crisis, and parties in power were seeking to engage in neoliberal reforms. In that context, the most visible manifestation of the FA's differentiation was the anti-neoliberal orientation of its representatives, who at times managed to function as a veto coalition largely due to the party's organizational structure and mobilizing capacity. It defended the interests of the ISI beneficiaries. This last element allowed representatives in Congress "to mount aggressive resistance to proposed [market-oriented] legislation" proposed by the dominant parties while preserving party discipline in Congress (Pribble 2008: 96).

Also similar to the PT, the experience in legislative opposition gradually strengthened the party's position in representative institutions, served as a sort of "institutional school" for its representatives, and strengthened its participation in institutional struggles. It also allowed the party to present itself in the national arena as a credible political alternative to the traditional parties. As

---

[20] The Colorado Party, which won the election, received 41.2 percent of the vote and the National Party received 35 percent.

social discontent with the dominant parties and their policies grew over time, all of these elements would be crucial for the FA's electoral success in the presidential election of 2004 (Moreira 2004).

That the FA was successful in opposing several reformist attempts not only had much to do with the cohesiveness of its congressional delegation, but also with institutional factors that facilitated the mobilization of its grass-roots base. The use of mechanisms of direct democracy made it possible for the FA to build coalitions of grass-roots actors and challenge reformist attempts in areas such as the privatization of public companies, the reform of the social security system, the budget for public education, and even the time limits for labor claims (Altman 2002: 619). Among some social groups, the FA's opposition to reform strengthened the party's position as a credible alternative to the status quo. In addition, the frequent mobilization of activists in attempts to block neoliberal reforms through direct democracy devices at the national level allowed the FA to maintain a vibrant activist base between elections, and to strengthen the ties between party leaders and their social bases. Success through mobilization in opposing neoliberal reforms would make both party leaders and movement leaders more likely to continue using mobilization tactics (and movement leaders, especially union leaders, would later on use these tactics even against the party leadership, as seen below).

At the time that the FA consolidated its position as an alternative to Uruguay's dominant parties and became a powerful actor resisting reform attempts, the FA embraced ideological moderation, even if it did not abandon its commitment to a statist model (Yaffé 2005: 95). According to Luna (2014: 252), the party gradually "changed from a Marxist mass party to an electoral-professional one...while still providing consistent opposition to neoliberal reforms." There are several explanations for this. According to Cason (2000), Uruguay's 1996 constitutional reform, which instituted presidential runoffs, forced the party leadership to engage in pragmatic alliance making to broaden the party's constituency. According to Luna (2014), the FA's ideological moderation began earlier in the 1990s in response to both electoral constraints and the constraints of the party's internal structures. The electoral constraints are associated with the idea that neoliberal reforms had imposed limits on radical leftist platforms. Internally, the shift toward the ideological center was a consequence of both the internal balance of power within the FA, which after the fall of the Berlin Wall favored the moderate party fractions (led by Tabaré Vázquez) in relation to the more radical fractions (broadly led by José Mujica), and contributed to the election of moderate *frenteamplistas* in city government (Luna 2007: 4). If the party's central challenge was to perform well electorally at the national level while maintaining strong links to its core social base of unions and other popular movements, elected officials at the local level needed to signal voters they could govern effectively while defending its historical commitments.

As with the PT, local experiences of public administration also led to a focus on electoral and institutional activity as opposed to the strengthening of mobilizational and extra-institutional strategies. The increasing experience of FA mayors (Tabaré Vázquez and Mariano Arana) governing Montevideo contributed to their pragmatism in office and to the strengthening of their position in intraparty affairs, which allowed them to circumvent organizational constraints and steer the FA toward the center. All this did not necessarily sever the relationships between the party and its union and social movement base, however. Indeed, as Luna (2014: 246) notes, this governmental experience also contributed to the *strengthening* of the linkages between the party and popular movements by developing a "close to the people administration") in Uruguay's capital. To achieve this, it implemented an administrative decentralization process that enabled activists in local committees to engage meaningfully in public deliberations and in social policy provision, bringing them increasingly closer to the state.[21] According to Luna's (2014) interview evidence, this helped the urban poor to mobilize between elections, to promote grass-roots input in regards to resource allocation, and to expand the territorial reach of the organization. The influence of the party's early organizational development, which placed heavy emphasis on consultation and consensus building with the social bases, shaped not only these experiences of local participation but also the governing dynamics. On several occasions, the *frenteamplista* governments of Montevideo clashed with unions over aspects of policy when their interests were not taken into account (Luna 2006: 417).

A tension became apparent: while the growing power of moderates within the FA and the ensuing move toward the ideological center would appear to point in the direction of centralization of party structures, the FA's promotion of grass-roots input and the labor movement–party dynamics in power would point in the direction of power dispersion. The tensions between these two logics increased as the FA pursued national-level power. Unlike the PT, however, the FA did not develop a cohesive dominant coalition that could easily control the organization from the top down. Its internal voting system prevented the emergence of such a configuration, as noted above. This contrast is worthy of further elaboration. Given the FA's diverse origins, from the beginning its leaders sought to develop an internal system of checks and balances to promote consensus building and prevent power concentration and elite entrenchment (Pérez, Piñeiro, and Rosenblatt 2018). In this spirit, it established early on the criterion of absolute majorities for deciding on certain issues such as the inclusion of new groups into the party or changes in party statutes (Caetano et al. 2003: 16). This form of decision-making, which is generally considered slower and less efficient than simple

---

[21] That Montevideo is the country's largest district and home to about half the electorate meant that even though participatory experiences were less ambitious in Uruguay than in Brazil some of these experiments engaged a proportionally larger population, and were thus more salient.

plurality systems, became even slower as the FA added more layers by incorporating new groups into its structures.[22]

The FA's most important bodies for deliberation and consultation are the National Council (Plenario Nacional, NC) and the Political Committee (Mesa Política, PC). While the former performs more of a deliberative role and one of its key functions is to develop the FA's governing plan, the latter is the political arm of the party and performs more of a monitoring and oversight function. The party is also made up of small-scale territorial units, known as base committees (*Comités de Base*), which have proliferated since the mid-1980s and forge close links with the party's rank and file. The leadership of the NC is elected every five years (two years before the presidential elections) through a system of open primaries, and it assumes the representation of both party fractions and base committees. Its hierarchical structure is comprised of "the president and vice president of the party, 72 representatives of the distinct fractions and groups that make up the party, 36 representatives from the Montevideo local committees, 36 representatives from the departmental committees, and six citizen-militants" (Pribble 2008: 93). This mixed system of representation has ensured internal balance and prevented control by a single leader or one dominant group. Over time, however, it has tended to over-represent the fractions that invest more heavily in territorial strategies (Caetano et al. 2003: 17).[23]

Despite this tendency, party structures have remained important in internal negotiations. The characteristics of the party's procedures and voting system meant that internal changes – like the move toward the ideological center and the scope of electoral alliance making – were slow processes; they were also intensely debated and challenged by the more radical fractions. While amidst these transformations labor unions remained confrontational and occasionally disruptive, the moderate FA leadership (like that of the PT) sought to strengthen electoral alliances instead of mobilizing the party's organic base to grow electorally.[24]

---

[22] The PT adopted a strict majoritarian structure in its formative phase (Nogueira-Budny 2013: 125), but unlike the FA it deepened its commitment to majoritarianism in internal reforms down the road. For instance, in 2001 the party introduced a simple plurality internal voting system (Amaral 2010: 145–56). As a consequence of this internal change, "a simple majority in a direct vote for the leadership is sufficient to impose the line of the dominant group (with a minimum of subsequent amendments) on the entire party" (Ribeiro 2014: 111).

[23] Historically, there has been routinized alternation of power within the party. However, since the MPP gained control of the leadership in 2002, there has been less alternation, which points in the direction of centralization.

[24] The alliance-making strategy had started earlier, when Vázquez formed the Progressive Encounter (EP) in 1994 as an effort to build "a macro-center-left coalition" for the 1994 election (Luna 2014: 244–5). EP was formed by splinter groups of the two traditional parties, as well as by fractions within the FA itself that had separated from it. Between 1994 and 2005, FA-EP contested elections alongside as allies.

The FA's commitment to institution building became apparent in 2002, when the party supported the incumbent "at a time when it could have forced his removal by promoting street riots like those seen in Argentina" (Luna 2014: 244). Confronting an adverse domestic situation, the FA built electoral alliances with like-minded parties of the left and with other center-left forces that contributed to the FA's gradual electoral success. The most visible of these alliances was in 2002, when New Majority (NM), which included splinter groups from the traditional parties and of the FA itself, merged with the FA and contested elections together (Yaffé 2005: 105).

Conditions Surrounding Access to Power

As with the PT, by the time the FA came to power it had already become a more professional organization and had abandoned its more radical Marxist and anti-capitalist rhetoric. Unlike the PT however, in 2005 it enjoyed a much stronger position in Congress (Lanzaro 2011: 355). This meant that the FA could pursue its historical commitments without facing an intransigent legislative opposition. It also meant that to get things done the FA did not have to engage in deal-making with conservative parties, and that it did not have to mobilize its social base to put pressure on Congress. Thus, the key for understanding the Frente's policy-making dynamics appears to lie more in the internal power struggles and negotiations among the actors that constitute the FA than in the halls of Congress. Although the FA has a dense set of formal rules and structures that regulate internal affairs (Caetano et al. 2003: 15–20), popular leaders like Tabaré Vázquez and José "Pepe" Mujica have often managed to circumvent these when they deemed it necessary for the office-seeking success of the party (Luna 2014: 248–51).

As with the PT, while internal party organs are well institutionalized for the most part, they do not generate policies or relevant decisions beyond defining the contours of the government program. It is therefore more useful to look at the relations between the FA and its constitutive units for insight into how decision-making processes actually work. According to Huber and Stephens (2012: 203), the close relations between the FA and organized social constituencies meant that policy initiatives under the FA have "tended to be more sweeping in some areas" such as in health-sector reform and in labor relations, but also were "heavily constrained in others (education reform) where their allied unions were stakeholders." In other words, under the FA governments, policy-making appears to be highly negotiated inside the governing coalition and not an imposition from the top. Policy-making under the FA requires consultation and consensus building among a wide array of organizations, a pattern that can be traced to its origins and early organizational development. The balance of power among competing actors within the FA – actors that function as veto players – can reduce the options for government proposals and can put limits on centralized decision-making.

In addition, the extent to which grass-roots groups can influence policy varies significantly across policy areas.

Bogliaccini (2012) provides further insight on these last points through his analysis of tax reform and labor reform under the FA governments. These reforms showcase the strength of the FA's historical alliance with organized labor, and how this gave leverage to labor in shaping decisions that directly affected their interests. The tax reform was one of the most important policy reforms of the FA, which can be seen as an attempt to fulfill a central aspect of the Frente's campaign promises since the 1990s (Bogliaccini 2012: 156). Submitted to Congress by President Vázquez and Economy Minister Astori, the government initiative triggered harsh internal divisions among the fractions that comprise the FA, which have different redistributive preferences and grass-roots following. This led to six months of intense negotiations inside the governing coalition and often involved strikes and demonstrations in the streets. It was opposition from within, particularly organized labor in alliance with the MPP fraction led by Pepe Mujica, that slowed down and constrained the reform process, as neither opposition parties nor organized business represented a significant obstacle to the FA (Bogliaccini 2012: 158). The result was a reform that included the input and incorporated the preferences of organized labor, even if it also introduced elements pushed from the top by Vázquez (Bogliaccini 2012: 161).

The dynamics of labor reform were different, but they also help to show the extent to which internal structures can prevent power concentration and how decisions are actually made. In that instance, labor was instrumental in bringing the reinstitution of wage councils into the legislative agenda (Bogliaccini 2012: 148). These had been suspended during the right-wing administration of Lacalle (1990–5), and were not modified during the administrations of Sanguinetti (1995–2000) and of Battle (2000–5). Coming from labor, the proposal to reinstate wage councils did not generate strong divisions inside the FA and was instead passed quickly after it was sent to Congress, since it reflected the consensus among groups within the FA. The reinstatement of wage councils, which was an instance where the grass-roots shaped the agenda, can be seen as a double-edged sword. On the one hand, it "achieved not only a more coordinated process of wage setting and an improvement of wages, but also an increase in unionization" (Huber and Stephens 2012: 186; also, Schipani 2016: 32). It has also increased the ability of labor to shape political decisions collectively, and to institutionalize grass-roots input on decision-making. On the other hand, critics can see such a pattern of institutionalized participation as promoting the demobilization of allied groups.[25]

---

[25] This critique comes mostly from the Communist Party, whose representatives seem to be "unwilling to abandon the capitalist critique" (Bogliaccini 2012: 164), and see such policies as "reformist."

The image of demobilization was only partially accurate, however. According to Pribble (2008: 94), "during the party's first experience ruling the country at the national level, there have been several instances in which FA base organizations have opposed government policy and called for a different course of action." An example of this includes the mobilizations against the free trade agreement with the United States, which forced Vázquez to abandon the negotiations. According to Pribble's interviews there is also an important degree of consultation in the area of social policy, and a principled resistance to top-down, technocratic decision-making. While the passage of time and experience in government may have led to a decrease of "organic" consultation with base organizations, this aspect "continues to be a defining characteristic and has important effects for policy outputs since the government cannot rely on autonomy from the party when formulating proposals" (Pribble 2008: 94). It is central to explaining the FA's continual ability to maintain high levels of mobilization and a remarkable organizational vitality (Pérez, Piñeiro, and Rosenblatt 2018).

Case Summary

The FA emerged from plural origins and adopted early on a fractionalized structure with a proportional electoral system. Initial institutional structures (a historical cause) ensured that no single leader or group of leaders would become dominant actors; they created incentives for power dispersion that have influenced the party's organization and behavior over time. The party's experience at the subnational level had the short-term effect of strengthening moderates, who would use their new power to circumvent party structures and steer the FA's platform toward the center as a part of an office-seeking strategy. This allowed the party to grow electorally in a gradual and sustained manner while in opposition. The experience of local administration also contributed to the increasing pragmatism of FA leaders, who once in local level office projected an image of responsible government and willingness to compromise with other forces.

At the same time, FA leaders in power did not abandon their historical commitments to their base of support in labor and other popular movements. The leaders instead mobilized them between elections through direct democracy devices. That the FA maintained a "brotherhood" with unions and social movements became clear when it came to power at the national level in 2005. While the party enjoyed a strong position in Congress, the biggest challenge to policy-making came from within its own camp. Since its origins, the party established close links with labor unions and popular movements, and it created channels and incentives for the leadership to seek broad-based consensus before reaching decisions. While the passage of time and experience in government may have encouraged the emergence of a party elite with increasing levels of autonomy that can at times circumvent party structures and pressures from below, the FA still encourages high levels of bottom-up input and privileges consensus building. Decision-making requires significant internal negotiation.

This section summarizes the evidence from the cases and discusses its importance to my key theoretical claims. As discussed in Chapter 1 (also Figure 5.1), differences in organization and bottom-up influence across the cases are generated by a combination of historical and constant causes. Historical explanations are based on a set of factors traceable to a party's genesis and early development, the experience parties gain prior to taking office, and conditions surrounding their access to power. While initial institutional structures create a "weak" form of path dependency – an inclination to develop a greater (or lesser) top-down pattern of organization – the roads traveled to come to power and the political resources parties have once in power are responsible for the reproduction of early organizational patterns. These later processes as they unfold, in short, can help to continuously reproduce particular patterns and make them resistant to change. Using the evidence from my comparison, the pages that follow discuss the factors that generate power concentration or dispersion in the first place – the initial factors that trigger one particular path versus another – and explain the mechanisms and processes that undergird path dependency.

Origins and Early Development

All three parties emerged as socialist, movement-based parties in different historical periods: the FA in the early 1970s; the PT in the early 1980s; and the MAS in the mid-1990s. They were also formed under different types of regimes: the FA at the beginning of an authoritarian regime; the PT in the latter years of a military dictatorship; and the MAS during a formally democratic regime with no legal restrictions on civil liberties but weak safeguards. Yet, despite the different historical contexts and regime types in which they were founded, all three have quite similar roots in autonomous social movements and as "outsider," opposition parties: all three were formed as labor- or movement-based parties seeking to represent the interests of previously marginalized groups in society. Since their genesis, they sought to build internally democratic organizations to permit broad-based channels of consultation and coordination between the party leadership and the social bases. All three parties approximated Roberts' (1998: 75) "organic" model of party development in their origins: they emphasized grass-roots organization; they forged intensive linkages with mass popular organizations, social movements, and community-based organizations while respecting their relative autonomy; and they all participated in elections while at the same time engaged in contentious politics in the pursuit of programmatic goals.

Two attributes that are embedded in their early organizational development require more elaboration because they trigger particular patterns of organizational evolution. The first feature relates to the bureaucratic development of each party (i.e., whether they adopted a bureaucratic or a looser organizational structure). The second relates to the initial level of organizational centralization (i.e., the extent to which internal structures initially generated incentives for consultation with organized social bases, and the effects of internal voting rules on intraparty affairs). Despite its origins in vibrant, autonomous social movements, the PT developed early on a bureaucratic pattern of organization with a clearly defined code of rights and duties for members, effective bureaucratic mechanisms of enforcement, and centralized leadership. This allowed the party to survive in an adverse context that characterized Brazilian politics during its last dictatorship (1964–85). While the PT's unionist militant founders envisioned a decentralized organization characterized by bottom-up leadership and decision-making structures (Keck 1992), legal hurdles and bureaucratic obstacles imposed by the military during the party's early development pushed the party in a centralizing and hierarchical direction. Particularly important, it developed early on majoritarian decision-making mechanisms (Nogueira-Budny 2013).[26] Subsequent rule changes such as the use of direct elections for the selection of party authorities (to be elected by the direct vote of party members, as opposed to organized groups) and the use of a simple plurality voting system for intraparty affairs since 2001, have further aggravated pre-existing hierarchies and consolidated the top-down control of a dominant faction over the life of the party. Internal decision-making, as Nogueira-Budny (2013: 123) argues, "rests squarely at the top of the party."

Also diverse in its movement origins, the FA developed from early on a bureaucratic pattern of organization with clearly defined membership rights and obligations, but one with dense rules and mechanisms that promoted internal competition among fractions and more institutionalized grass-roots participation in decision-making (Pribble 2013; Pérez, Piñeiro, and Rosenblatt 2018). Over time, party rules and procedures remained important for consultation and for internal negotiation between fractions in search of majorities to gain leverage within the party. Unlike the PT, the FA developed from the start a fractionalized structure, which created strong incentives for power dispersion. In a way, the FA functioned from early on like a "party of parties" (or a party of fractions) and each fraction preserved its own identity, history, and following. The FA's internal voting system, moreover, privileged from early

---

[26] For example, the partisan legislation imposed by the military forced the party to complete numerous bureaucratic requirements in order to obtain legal registration. Most of these requirements were time-sensitive and required quick decision-making, which discouraged bottom-up input and consultation.

on consensus building and internal balance among fractions, preventing the possibilities for control by a single leader or a dominant group within the party (even if the routinized alternation of the leadership in national party bodies has tended to decrease in recent years).

Finally, the MAS emerged organically out of the autonomous mobilization of rural social movements and grew embedded within a rich tradition of participatory politics found in local communities and base organizations, mostly in the rural areas. Since its founding and early days, it resisted developing clearly defined membership rights and obligations, as well as effective bureaucracies to ensure that these are met. Partially as a result of this, the party has become increasingly dependent on the leadership of a dominant figure, who concentrated great deals of power in his own hands (Madrid 2011, 2012; Crabtree 2013; Anria 2016). At the same time, the lack of a bureaucratic structure provided opportunities for social bases to act autonomously, with few bureaucratic constraints. And indeed, the party maintained important spaces for the input of its social bases (Chapters 3 and 4) by engaging in regular consultations (which often involve open contestation) between the party's top leadership and its social base in what is still today a loose and porous structure.

Origins matter. They leave enduring marks on parties. Although the "genesis" of a party can have lasting institutional legacies, it does not have deterministic properties.[27] The PT provides a good example. For all of the early emphasis placed by its militant union activists on extending grass-roots participation (Ferreira and Portes 2008), it went too quickly – and for most observers, unexpectedly – into an increasingly top-down direction. The party developed early on an independent leadership with few constraints on its strategic operation. Analyses of internal power distributions, therefore, need to go way past the types of sponsoring actors and commitment of founders – the actors and processes responsible for the genesis of a party – to the type of institutional structures adopted in the parties' early organizational development – the processes responsible for the reproduction of a given pattern.

In explaining the PT's counterintuitive trajectory, and thus the broader question of variation in degrees of power concentration across the cases, initial institutional structures stand out for their explanatory power.[28] They create a weak form of path dependency with self-reproducing dynamics. As actors within the party get used to working in those structures, the structures become more effective and they create vested interests – a set of "winners" and "losers"

---

[27] Using Panebianco's (1988) biological language, these elements – the organizational sponsors and their commitments – can be thought of as elements that leave "birth marks" on a party rather than immutable "genetic" features.

[28] The weakening of civil society – a contending explanation – fails to adequately explain variation across cases. For example, labor declined significantly in strength between the founding of the FA in the 1970s and its rise to power in 2004, and yet the party, relative to the PT, maintained more open structures.

(Pierson 2015: 133). In the case of the PT, its initial institutional structures allowed one faction to gain substantial advantages and consolidate power within the party. Control over those structures guaranteed control over the organization and few limits on the strategic decisions of the leadership. By contrast, the structures of the MAS and the FA created more opportunities for contestation, consensus building, and negotiation, as well as more dispersed sets of winners and actors with decision-making and veto power. Once these early organizational patterns were set up, it became increasingly difficult to switch course. As shown in the following pages, early patterns were reinforced in response to electoral imperatives and by conditions surrounding the parties' access to power.

Roads to National Power

While institutional structures set up in early stages of a party's organizational development create a greater or lesser top-down impetus, the parties' distinctive roads to power can help reinforce such trends. Electoral dynamics can serve, in short, as self-reinforcement processes of particular trends (Pierson 2015: 133). Figure 5.2 shows that in response to electoral imperatives all three parties underwent some sort of ideological moderation, from an advocacy of socialism to a more pragmatic position of reforming capitalism to protect the interests of the underprivileged. This move toward the center, which varied in intensity among the three cases, was a reflection of office-seeking strategies and a result of their experience in subnational governments. In the process, as Figure 5.2 also shows, they all increased their pragmatism and expanded the scope of their alliances, a dynamic that often pulled the party leadership away from the social bases and reinforced the trends toward power concentration.

These similarities, however, mask important cross-case variation. Relative to the MAS, the PT and the FA experienced a much slower electoral progress. Both parties gained national-level power after extensive experience at subnational and legislative levels, while the MAS had far less experience in those arenas.[29] Slow electoral progress and long experience at the local level in the first two cases helped reinforce previously adopted organizational structures; they strengthened the leverage of party moderates, who would use their increased power to become more strategic, centralize authority, and intensify internal control. The extent to which they could do so varied significantly, however. Often leading minority governments, PT mayors could circumvent internal opposition and engage in broad alliances across the ideological spectrum in order to "get things done" – a move spearheaded by an increasingly

---

[29] Levitsky and Roberts (2011: 407–10) argue that the MAS followed a "crisis-outsider" path to power, but the argument is insufficiently nuanced and it overlooks the shorter, but still relevant, experience of the MAS in representative institutions and municipal governments prior to its ascent to national power.

	Early Development	Road to Power	Conditions Surrounding Access to Power	Degree of Power Concentration
MAS *Sponsors:* coca producers and indigenous-peasant movements (Van Cott 2005; Madrid 2012)	Non-bureaucratic, loosely organized	Fast (10 years); crisis-outsider path; weak ideological moderation; little local-level experience; broad alliance making (with social movements and community organizations)	High social mobilization; mandate to "re-found" the social and political order; weak in congress	Low before assuming national power; higher after assuming national power (but remained open and responsive to social mobilization)
FA *Sponsors:* organized labor and student movement (Luna 2007; Pérez, Piñeiro, and Rosenblatt 2018)	Bureaucratic, fractionalized, emphasis on internal party consultation and negotiation	Slow (20+ years); institutional path; strong ideological moderation; long local-level experience; alliance making (with like-minded left forces)	Low social mobilization; routine turnover; strong in congress	Low before assuming national power; higher after assuming power (but maintained open spaces for input from social bases, especially urban labor)
PT *Sponsors:* labor, Catholic activists, intellectuals (Keck 1992; Meneguello 1989)	Bureaucratic, centrally organized	Slow (20+ years); institutional path; strong ideological moderation; long local-level experience; broad alliance making (including cons. and centrist forces)	Low social mobilization; routine turnover; weak in congress	High before assuming national power; higher after assuming national power (consolidation of centralized authority; reduced space for bottom-up influence from social bases)

FIGURE 5.2 Dimensions for comparison across cases.

more independent, powerful party leadership with few constraints on their strategic decisions. Constrained by its own structures and its social pillars, the FA moderated but generally allied with like-minded forces on the left. Although the experience in local government led to a focus on more institutional strategies as opposed to a strengthening of mobilizational strategies, a situation that also pointed their structures toward greater power concentration, both parties promoted broad-based citizen involvement in the political process. This helped to counterbalance the centralizing trends. Participatory programs at the municipal level were less ambitious in Uruguay than in Brazil. Nevertheless, their application took place in Uruguay's capital, which contributed to engaging a proportionally larger percentage of the national population.

Key to explaining the slow electoral progress of the PT and the FA is the relative strength of the state, or its capacity to stabilize economic or social crises. Both the PT and the FA encountered great difficulties gaining electoral support. The overall performance of the Brazilian and Uruguayan states, their capacity to contain crises, was much stronger than in Bolivia, which helped the political establishment in the first two countries resist electoral challenges by regime contenders. By contrast, in Bolivia, the weakness of the state, or its inability to contain economic and social crises, made it comparatively easier for a new movement-based party like the MAS to win elections, accelerate its rise to power, and then overwhelm a widely discredited political class. This had consequences for the internal power distributions of the three parties. The Brazilian case provides sharp contrast with the Bolivian case, and taken together they help illustrate the point. Slow electoral progress and delays in the ascension to power of the PT created strong incentives for the party leadership to make strategic adjustments, moderate, strengthen its internal hierarchical control, and even make alliances with forces seen initially as "distasteful," including conservatives and centrists – all of which was eased by the PT's increasingly centralized structures. By comparison, the leadership of the MAS encountered weaker incentives to moderate, form undesired alliances, and centralize authority during its shorter road to power.

Conditions Surrounding Access to Power

The availability of political resources once in office can also help to reinforce existing organizational trends and internal power distributions. The PT and the FA came to power when mobilization was not in ascent, unlike the case when the MAS gained power in Bolivia. In fact, the first two followed a similar "institutional path" to power (Levitsky and Roberts 2011: 405–7). Both parties "participated regularly in elections, gaining representation in legislatures and municipal governments" and contended power "within relatively institutionalized party systems that contained strong centrist and conservative parties" (Levitsky and Roberts 2011: 405–6). By the time they took office, both parties had professionalized and well-institutionalized party structures developed over long years in opposition (Hunter 2010; Ribeiro 2014; Amaral and Power 2015). But they varied in the extent to which their internal structures concentrated or dispersed power. By the time the PT won the presidency it had far more centralized, hierarchical structures (under the control of the moderate Campo Majoritário faction led by Lula) than when the FA assumed power. The FA's internal rules, defined earlier on, discouraged control by a dominant group.

The rise to power of the PT and the FA was not the result of sustained mobilization. Rather, as Levitsky and Roberts (2011: 406) note, it took place "via routine turnover, in a context where democratic institutions were not in crisis," which meant that their access to power was not premised on doing away with the existing social and political order, unlike Bolivia. While this is broadly accurate, it fails to capture notable differences in terms of the institutional position and political resources they had once they captured national office. This is important because those elements reinforced organizational structures defined in earlier phases.

That the FA won a legislative majority in both chambers meant that it did not face incentives to find "distasteful" allies to pass legislation, and that it could maintain strong ties to labor unions and other popular sector movements. Two mechanisms helped to sustain spaces for the input from its social bases and maintain more open channels of contestation and bottom-up influence. First, the legacies of labor mobilization – the early success in opposing neoliberal reforms via mobilizations – made party leaders and movement leaders more likely to continue using mobilization tactics. Once in power, union leaders would use the same tactics even against the party leadership when they disagreed over major policy initiatives. Second, internal structures defined early on, and consolidated while in opposition, encouraged the FA leadership to reach out to mobilized bases to negotiate potentially controversial reforms and policy initiatives.

By contrast, the PT came to power with a much weaker position in Congress, as leader of a larger and heterogeneous coalition, and it never won a majority (nor full control of core state institutions). This meant that a central political challenge was to generate a legislative majority to pass laws and support its policies. The PT responded to divided government by engaging in broad alliance making with parties of the center (PMDB) and even the right (PL) – a pattern it had found useful in its experiences of local administration, and one that could only be pursued once the more radical factions committed to bottom-up politics had declined in influence within the party. Ultimately, this need to establish and maintain coalitional deals pushed its internal structures toward more top-down control and eroded linkages with the social bases. Having a weak position in Congress can therefore be seen as a mechanism of organizational self-reproduction. It is part of the dynamics that kept pulling the PT leadership in a more moderate direction – and in a direction that further reinforced the detachment from the bases.

The MAS captured national office when popular mobilization was in ascent (as would have been the case had the PT won the 1989 or the 1994 election), and in a context of a profound economic and social crisis (Silva 2009: 142–3). This situation gave Morales and the MAS not only an incentive for policy reform, but also "a mandate for radical change" (Levitsky and Roberts 2011: 408) that would shape their ways of relating to its social bases.

Indeed, the MAS won national-level power by promising to convene a constituent assembly that would rewrite the country's constitution and "refound" the political order, a task for which social mobilization tactics would be essential to overcome the resistance from the guardians of the old order (interview with García Linera). This was far from the agenda in Brazil and Uruguay. Although the MAS gained office by a landslide, it did not gain full control of Congress and faced a strong and highly mobilized opposition backed by powerful economic interests.[30] Once in power, the MAS responded to legislative gridlock by encouraging mobilization from its own base. Pledging that the MAS would "govern by obeying" (Anria 2010: 109), it relied on the mobilizational capacity of affiliated movements to exert pressure on the legislative branch and counterbalance the power of political and economic elites (Crabtree 2005; Eaton 2007; Fairfield 2015; Anria and Niedzwiecki 2016).

The use of mobilization tactics created a strong incentive for power dispersion within the party. It allowed the MAS to remain open, internally responsive, and movement-influenced. The legacies of popular mobilization associated with its rise to power and first years in office meant that social movements remained vibrant. While at times the MAS attempted to co-opt movement leaders into government positions, popular sector movements did not abandon their capacity for autonomous collective action. Early success through mobilization – in overthrowing past presidents and defeating elite-based political opposition – made movements more likely to continue using such tactics, even against major policy initiatives of the MAS government. This continued capacity for autonomous collective action has helped to counterbalance the tendencies toward top-down control. As the MAS leadership and affiliated movements became used to interacting with each other in this way – not through formal party channels but by negotiating policies and party action in response to actual or threatened mobilizations – deviating from the pattern became increasingly difficult. It became hard to reverse.

Some critics may argue that domestic and external economic pressures would inevitably push parties toward top-down control – specifically, that the trend toward power concentration might be aggravated under more stringent domestic and external economic pressures. However, economic crises and severe constraints do not have uniform effects on internal power distributions.

---

[30] In its first term in office, the MAS won a slight majority in the lower chamber, but was particularly weak in the Senate (See Chapter 2).

If we take a look at ideological or policy issues, these three statements hold true: (1) the crisis context allowed the MAS to carry out a more "radical" project of state transformation; (2) the absence of a crisis – but threat of potential crisis – contributed to the ideological moderation of the PT; and (3) the aftermath of a severe crisis largely set the policy agenda and priorities for the FA in Uruguay. But policy or ideological issues do not dictate internal party governance. At one extreme, in Brazil, internal party structures moved in the direction of central-ization and top-down control *before* the PT even made it to national-level power. At the other extreme, in the case of the MAS in Bolivia, the crisis context encouraged reliance on social mobilization strategies. In short, this suggests that economic crises and severe exogenous constraints might have different effects, and that these are in turn contingent on previously adopted organizational strategies that condition parties' responses to such constraints.

Constant Explanations

The degree of internal power concentration is also shaped by constant factors linked to the "configuration" of civil society – its strength or density – and its capacity for *autonomous* mobilization – which is more cyclical than constant. Constant causes are stable conditions that contribute to reproducing an out-come and to explaining its continual reoccurrence. Organizational density – a condition of societal structure with deep historical roots – is one of such causes. Although, in effect, it might weaken or strengthen in response to state action (Rueschemeyer, Huber, and Stephens 1992: 67), drastic change requires significant time, particularly in democratic contexts. In such contexts – and especially in the short and in the medium run – levels of organizational density are therefore fairly stable.

As noted in Chapter 1, *high* organizational density in society can serve as a potential power base for movement-based parties. Existing social networks and high levels of social mobilization can facilitate the formation of new movement-based parties, provide them with invaluable organizational resources, and contribute to their long-term empowerment. In addition, when civil society is not only strong but also highly mobilized and autonomous from the state, it can generate multiple pressures from below and help to counteract the tendencies toward top-down control of an allied movement-based party in power. Weaker civil societies – those with low organizational density – or those too dependent on the state are generally more easily controlled from the top. Consequently, they tend to enable the trend toward power concentration. In short, levels of social organization can help to explain the genesis of a party – the conditions that may facilitate or inhibit party formation – and together with the degree of autonomous mobilization can help to explain the reproduction of early patterns of party development. I am concerned with the latter.

In the absence of comparable and reliable data on levels of organizational density for Bolivia, Brazil, and Uruguay, one plausible way to evaluate the strength of each movement-based party's power base is to look at the relation-ship between partisan engagement and participation in associational life – an approach similar to that of Handlin and Collier (2011). Such an approach can tell us a great deal about these parties' potential for mobilization, and about the kinds of pressures from below they might confront. Using cross-national survey data from the 2006 and 2008 waves of the Latin American Public Opinion Project (LAPOP), I examine this issue by looking at civic engagement and party–society linkages among left movement-based parties in Latin America.

The proportion of PT partisans who participate in diverse forms of social and political organization in Brazil is presented in Tables 5.2 through 5.4. Consistent with the results reported in Handlin and Collier (2011: 148, 150), I found that in Brazil, the linkages between the governing PT and urban labor unions (Table 5.2), other economic-based civic associations (Table 5.3), and

TABLE 5.2 *Importance of labor unions among left partisans (percent of left partisans participating in meetings of unions)*

	Brazil	Uruguay	Bolivia
At least once a month	2	10	20
At least once a year	8	15	31

Note: Data are responses to the question: "Do you attend meetings of a union at least once a week, once or twice a month, once or twice a year, or never?" Percentages reported for Uruguay and Bolivia are from the LAPOP 2008 survey. Percentages reported for Brazil are from the LAPOP 2006 survey. The 2008 survey was not weighted and oversampled PT supporters, which could bias the results.
Source: The AmericasBarometer by the Latin American Public Opinion Project (LAPOP), www.LapopSurveys.org.

TABLE 5.3 *Importance of labor unions or other economic-based associations among left partisans (percent of left partisans participating in meetings of unions or other economic-based associations).*

	Brazil	Uruguay	Bolivia
At least once a month	5	14	26
At least once a year	12	21	45

Note: Data reflect responses to the questions: "Do you attend meetings of a union at least once a week, once or twice a month, once or twice a year, or never?" or "Do you attend meetings of an association of professionals, merchants, manufacturers or farmers at least once a week, once or twice a month, once or twice a year, or never?" Responses were considered positive if the respondent answered affirmatively to either one of the questions or both. In the latter case the respondent was counted as a participant once. Percentages reported for Uruguay and Bolivia are from the LAPOP 2008 survey. Percentages reported for Brazil are from the LAPOP 2006 survey. The 2008 survey was not weighted and oversampled PT supporters, which could bias the results.
Source: The AmericasBarometer by the Latin American Public Opinion Project (LAPOP), www.LapopSurveys.org.

TABLE 5.4 *Importance of community-based organizations among left partisans (percent of left partisans participating)*

	Brazil	Uruguay	Bolivia
At least once a month	8	11	31
At least once a year	15	17	60

Note: Data reflect responses to the question: "Do you attend meetings of a community or group for community improvement at least once a week, once or twice a month, once or twice a year, or never?" Percentages reported for Uruguay and Bolivia are from the LAPOP 2008 survey. Percentages reported for Brazil are from the LAPOP 2006 survey. The 2008 survey was not weighted and oversampled PT supporters, which could bias the results.
Source: The AmericasBarometer by the Latin American Public Opinion Project (LAPOP), www.LapopSurveys.org.

community-based organizations (Table 5.4) are remarkably low. This finding is surprising – and perhaps counterintuitive – given the origins and history of the PT, but unsurprising if we consider Brazil's large size and the PT's organizational evolution outlined above. As Handlin and Collier (2011: 151) correctly note, "it is possible that the notion of a highly active and PT-linked civil society accurately describes some regions of the country on which monographic studies have focused but that characterization does not hold on a national level." In such a context, where associational activity on a per capita basis appears to be low, it seems more likely that stronger tendencies toward top-down control will prevail within the party.

Uruguay reveals a different pattern. Tables 5.2–5.4 portray a relatively more densely organized and vibrant civil society in Uruguay. This, however, should be interpreted with some caution. The proportion of FA partisans who participate in union meetings, meetings in other economic-based associations, and in community-based organizations is higher than in Brazil, but these numbers still make up a small number of those who voted for the FA. A salient difference between these two cases is that the FA appears to have a clearly stronger relationship with unions and other economic-based associations (Handlin and Collier 2011: 150; also Schipani 2016). This, and especially the strong union party connection, is highly consistent with the qualitative evidence and arguments developed in the pages that follow, which show that FA governments often encountered intense pressures and real challenges from its core support base in urban labor unions. Indeed, both the Tabaré Vázquez (2015–10) and the José "Pepe" Mujica (2010–15) governments found themselves having to negotiate agenda items, policies, and signature reforms with strong labor unions, in ways that at least partially put restrictions on top-down decision-making and pushed the FA leadership to expand consultation, participation, and reach compromises.

A striking difference is revealed when examining Bolivia. Participation in unions, other economic-based associations, and community-based organizations is consistently higher among left partisans, which indicates a densely organized society and high degrees of mobilization and participation. This high rate of citizen participation in civil society organizations in Bolivia has deep historical roots, as scholars in different disciplines have observed (Healy 2001; Civicus 2006; Gray Molina 2008; Lazar 2008; Vergara 2011; Crabtree 2013; Boulding 2014). As has been shown in Chapter 2, the existence of such strong civil society allowed the MAS to build a strong party from existing movements and community networks and to gain national reach by tapping into their structures. A robust civil society has also facilitated the inclusion of representatives from grass-roots popular organizations in legislatures and state institutions at the national and subnational levels through their organizational ties to the MAS (Chapter 3). At the same time, such a well-developed civil society has generated multiple pressures from below and kept open channels for agenda setting from below, which in turn contributed to disperse internal power (Chapter 4).

Constant causes – structural characteristics linked to the strength or "density" of Bolivian civil society – matter greatly. However, what has been truly decisive in the case of the MAS is the ongoing capacity for *autonomous* social mobilization that is not easily controlled from the top down, by the party or by Evo Morales. It is precisely the autonomy of social mobilization that makes it harder for a movement-based party like the MAS to exert control over social actors and succumb to party oligarchization. In short, a highly organized and autonomous civil society makes the possibility of power dispersion within movement-based parties more likely.

Other sources of data, including quantitative and qualitative assessments of the development of civil society in the three countries, are consistently supportive of the argument developed above. Figure 5.3, built on data from the Varieties of Democracy (V-Dem) Project, shows that the strength of civil society in Bolivia, measured by the involvement of people in civil society organizations, is stronger than in the other two cases. Of the three cases, moreover, Brazil appears to have the weakest civil society and Uruguay's is somewhere in the middle. The Civicus Civil Society Index, which measures civil society along four dimensions, is also consistently supportive of the argument, with Bolivia receiving the highest scores on the robustness of civil society and its powerful mobilization capacities (Civicus 2006).[31]

---

[31] The Civicus Civil Society Index consists of four dimensions, including "the organizational structure of civil society, civic engagement, perception of impact, and practice of values and the enabling environment (Civicus 2012). In the 2006 round, which were strictly designed for comparative analysis, Bolivia scored higher than Uruguay in the first two dimensions. A qualitative report highlighted the high levels of citizen participation in civil society and civil society's high capacity to mobilize autonomously (Civicus 2006: 8–10). Brazil was not covered in the analysis.

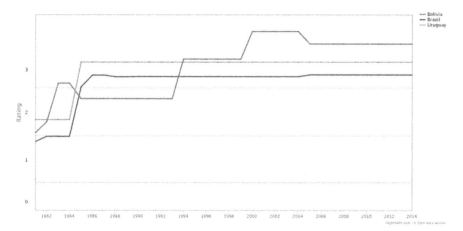

FIGURE 5.3 Citizen involvement in civil society organizations. *Note:* Data in the figure are scores of expert responses to the question: "Which of these best describes the involvement of people in civil society organizations (CSOs)?" Responses are organized on a relative scale with the following response options. o: most associations are state-sponsored, and although a large number of people may be active in them, their participation is not purely voluntary; 1: voluntary CSOs exist but few people are active in them; 2: there are many diverse CSOs, but popular involvement is minimal; 3: there are many diverse CSOs and it is considered normal for people to be at least occasionally active in at least one of them.
Source: Coppedge et al. (2017).

The processes by which constant causes contribute to continuously reproduce patterns of internal power distribution can be summarized in three propositions:

1. *Civil society shapes internal party structures.* While strong civil societies can help to generate power dispersion within parties in early stages of party organizational development, they can also help to reproduce early patterns when the party is in power. Strong civil societies can, through their "mobilization" and policy capacities, contribute to keeping parties open, internally responsive, and accountable to the social bases (Heller 2005; Lee 2016). For this to occur, retaining *autonomous* mobilization capacity is key.

2. *Party structures shape policy-making.* The internal structure of parties in power shapes the direction, texture, and scope of social policies (Pribble and Huber 2011; Pribble 2013). Parties with strong linkages to organized social actors, and those whose internal structures disperse power, tend to push social policy in a bolder, more redistributive, and more universalistic direction (Korpi 1978).

3. *Policy outcomes shape civil society and help to reproduce internal power distributions.* The higher the degree of power concentration

within parties in power, the more likely it will be that they will fail to invest resources in strengthening social organization, especially via social policies (Schipani 2016). For example, conditioned by the very centralized structures of the PT, Brazil under Lula (2003–11) and Rousseff (2011–16) followed a "poverty alleviation" strategy of redistribution that did little to strengthen social organization – an approach that is, in fact, linked to a decline in popular sectors' organizational power. The FA, by contrast, followed a more expansive "class redistributive" strategy aimed at redistributing income *and* empowering existing social organizations, an approach that has been linked to the increased empowerment of labor unions, in particular.[32] While the MAS is outside the scope of Schipani's (2016) work, related research has shown that its strong social linkages and more fluid structures have resulted in bold social policies – in pensions, tax reform, and minimum-wage legislation, to name some – that are linked to continued or even strengthened levels of social organization (Anria and Niedzwiecki 2016; Silva 2017).

CONCLUSIONS

The comparative historical analysis of the cases presented in this chapter provides robust evidence about how parties with similar origins in social movements organize their structures, the ensuing internal power distributions, and how they deal with the tension of governing while maintaining strong linkages with their social bases. While the PT became increasingly top-down, less participatory, and less responsive to bottom-up input and social mobilization over time, the FA and the MAS preserved more open channels for their social bases to influence decision-making in both candidate selection and the policy-making sphere.

Historical causes traceable to the parties' genesis and constant causes associated with the strength (and autonomy) of their social bases were identified as crucial to explaining cross-case. On the one hand, the type of institutional structures implemented during the parties' early development is a key historical explanation. It creates a "weak" form of path dependency – an inclination to develop a greater or lesser top-down pattern of organization – which is reproduced when parties contest elections and, especially, when they assume power. These later processes, as they unfold, help to reproduce patterns defined early on and make them resistant to change. While the "genesis" of a party leaves lasting institutional legacies, it is more useful to theorize about it as leaving "birth marks" rather than as constitutive of a "genetic model" that cannot be

---

[32] For example, wage councils strengthen labor unions vis-à-vis business in collective bargaining, and they have been linked to an increase in unionization (Huber and Stephens 2012: 186).

altered. The PT provides a clear example; for all of its early emphasis on extending bottom-up input, it switched course.

On the other hand, the level of organizational density – a condition of societal structure with deep historical roots – is a constant cause. It contributes to explaining the reoccurrence of particular patterns defined early on. Where civil society is not only strongly developed but also maintains an ongoing capacity for *autonomous* social mobilization, it can counterbalance the trend toward top-down control. None of these factors explain diverging outcomes in isolation. When combined, however, they create distinctive configurations of incentives and constraints for organization building, as well as shape patterns of internal power distribution in meaningful and lasting ways.

In developing this argument, I analyzed alternative arguments about external economic pressures as explanations for diverging internal power distributions, but noted that economic crises and stringent constraints do not have uniform effects. Power distributions are path dependent and heavily contingent on previously adopted organizational patterns that condition parties' responses to such constraints. For example, at one extreme the PT became more top-down in the absence of a widespread crisis, and at the other extreme a severe context of crisis encouraged the MAS to pursue mobilizational tactics and maintain open channels to involve social movement allies in decision-making.

In short, structures developed during the parties' early development, the evolution of those structures, and the conditions surrounding the parties' access to power mediate the effects of exogenous shocks and constraints, including crises. The analysis also showed that, like crises, the passing of time does not have uniform effects on internal power distributions. The case of the FA, which has been around for decades and still preserves an open space for the input of social bases, helped to discount that argument and enhance the generalizability of the findings: while time of course matters, time alone does not invariably lead to top-down patterns of organization. Historical and constant causes matter greatly.

In sum, the extent to which movement-based parties can prevent or attenuate the trends toward top-down control is best explained by how organizational characteristics are defined early on, how these are shaped by electoral imperatives, and by factors linked to the configuration of civil society – its strength and autonomous mobilization capacity. These factors shape the parties' evolution, their relationships with the social bases, and specifically the intensity of grassroots linkages they can maintain over time – and when in power. The implications of these findings are noteworthy: when looking at organizational attributes and the nature of party–society linkages, the Uruguayan FA has less in common with the Brazilian PT, with which it is often compared as belonging to the same strand of "moderate" Latin American left (Weyland, Madrid, and Hunter 2010), than with Bolivia's MAS.

As Bruhn (2015: 249) notes, this point is rarely made in the literature, and its omission has consequences. As I discuss further in the following chapter, differences *within* the moderate left are more remarkable than what the existing literature has established, and there are strong similarities between left parties classified in different typological boxes. Understanding those similarities better – by looking closely at organizational attributes and the nature of party–society linkages – can offer theoretical purchase in explaining broader macro-level processes that are still insufficiently theorized.

Conclusions

There have been several important cases of movement-based parties that rapidly rose in popularity in new democracies, with some attaining national power via competitive elections. This development calls for a new theoretical understanding of these parties' internal politics, one that helps us move beyond the stereotype of an inevitable "iron law" of oligarchy toward a more nuanced interpretation of new and – arguably – more fluid and participatory forms of organization and mobilization. As is well established in the political science literature, the pressures of the electoral marketplace and the exercise of state power create strong pressures for power concentration, pulling party elites away from their organized social bases. Whether, to what extent, and through which mechanisms movement-based parties can defy or mitigate this tendency have important political consequences, particularly once these parties are in power. When movement-based parties challenge this tendency more forcefully, they can enhance the voice and political influence of traditionally excluded groups and citizens, boosting their ability to influence the public agenda and decision-making more broadly. Resisting the trend toward top-down control associated with party bureaucratization and concentrated executive authority is important not only for the internal politics of these parties themselves, but also for shaping the options available to excluded groups to muscle their way into organized politics, and for shaping the nature and scope of redistributive policies.

This book has examined movement-based parties' options to challenge the Michelsian trend toward top-down control, or the tendency of parties to become less open and accountable to their social bases as small groups of party elites gain control over internal decision-making. Comparative politics scholars have long questioned the sources of variation in power distribution both within and across parties. Yet, despite its enduring importance, this topic remains insufficiently understood and poorly theorized. The question remains central in the study of Latin America, where dominant political figures do not have a good track record when it comes to building strong organizations that can limit their power and autonomy (Huber and Stephens 2012: 266).

The left-wing parties that won national elections in Latin America between 1998 and 2007 exhibited remarkable diversity with regard to their organizational bases of support (Cameron and Hershberg 2010; Bruhn 2015). Some of these parties, such as the MAS in Bolivia, the PT in Brazil, and the FA in Uruguay, are clear examples of movement-based parties. This development prompted scholars to investigate patterns of power concentration or dispersion within parties in an attempt to classify the existing varieties of left governments (Levitsky and Roberts 2011) and to study the effect of party organizational factors and party–society linkages on important policy outcomes, such as social welfare policies linked to reductions in equality (Pribble and Huber 2011; Pribble 2013; Anria and Niedzwiecki 2016).

The theoretical framework I develop in this book sheds light on the question of why some movement-based parties in Latin America develop more top-down structures designed to preserve and enhance the power of party elites while others develop bottom-up organizations that admit more influence from their organized social bases. My framework focuses on the impact of two causal factors that, combined, have not received enough attention in the study of comparative parties: first, historical causes traceable to a party's origins and early development and, second, constant factors associated with the "configuration" of civil society. Specifically, the analysis of the MAS indicates evidence that organizational structures and practices adopted early on can leave an indelible mark on the party and create what institutionalists call a "weak" form of path dependency that is difficult to reverse. As actors become accustomed to working within these structures, the latter become more effective and deviating from them becomes less likely over time. Though change is not impossible, the longer both the party's leadership and its social bases operate under the given rules of the game, the more accepted these become and the more difficult it becomes to deviate from those structures and from their ensuing power distributions.

Rather than allowing the party to succumb to oligarchization, the constant cause of strong, autonomous civil society mobilization reproduces over time the party's founding organizational characteristics and internal power distributions set early on. Through a comparative within-case examination of the MAS, I identified the conditions, processes, and mechanisms that provide countervailing bottom-up correctives to hierarchy and concentrated authority, as well as the overall "configurations" of civil society that make these countervailing pressures more or less effective. I have argued that the MAS is an important case for examining this question because in many ways it is an organizational anomaly. It deviates from the assumption in the political science literature that, regardless of their origins, all parties will evolve in the same direction – until they are dominated by a specialized, professionalized caste of political elites that are highly detached from and unaccountable to their social bases. Thus, by identifying the conditions most likely to lead to greater bottom-up control over party decision-making, this book contributes to theory building and lays out a series of testable hypotheses that illuminate an age-old debate in the literature on comparative political parties.

Parties make multiple decisions. Among the most important ones reflecting internal power distributions are choices about the candidates who will carry their label in elections and the policies they will pursue when in power. The comparative within-case analysis of the Bolivian MAS integrated both dimensions and provided strong evidence of the conditions most likely to lead to greater grass-roots control over these two areas of party decision-making. First, the subnational analysis of candidate selection in different districts of Bolivia and at different electoral levels (Chapter 3) showed that in contexts where autonomous civil society groups are strong, united, and politically aligned with the MAS, they can effectively impose their choices for candidates, boosting their influence over *who* represents them in national and subnational representative institutions. By contrast, where civil society is weakly organized – or where it is strongly organized, but not aligned with the party – top-down elite choices are more likely to prevail.

Second, greater control of candidate selection procedures by the MAS's organized bases of support has translated into greater substantive input into policy by shaping *what issues* come to the agenda and *how* they are decided. My analysis of the degree of bottom-up impact on national policy-making (Chapter 4) revealed that the capacity of MAS-allied groups to set agenda items, priorities, and party action varies widely by policy area and is contingent on these groups' autonomous mobilizational capacity. In policy areas that directly and visibly affect large numbers of people who are organized based on their productive roles, there is generally more effective popular pressure for influencing these decisions. Thus, some of the strongest, better organized, and most influential groups that wielded power in candidate selection were peasant movements, unions, and cooperative miners, and these groups also managed to shape the agenda and actions adopted by the party in power in policy areas such as agrarian and mining policies.

The study also examined the capacity of allied groups to challenge, block, or modify party decisions, and showed that where groups mobilize autonomously and are able to build a broad-based veto coalition with multiple sectors of society, the veto coalition is more likely to force a policy change. In other words, the political leverage of allied grass-roots groups, movements, and organizations is contingent on their ability to mobilize autonomously, across constituencies, and to link their claims to broader constituencies.

The main story that emerged, then, is one of a movement-based party that allows for significant influence from below by respecting the autonomy of allied groups and negotiating with them while pursuing compromises. Although there are strong pressures pushing toward internal power concentration – including Evo Morales's increasingly dominant and personalistic leadership and the by-products of prolonged exercise of state power – allied groups, movements, and organizations are far from being irrelevant actors to the party's most important decisions and policy processes more broadly. Policy-making under Bolivia's MAS is not insulated from bottom-up pressures from the party's organized social bases. Rather, it is best characterized as a highly interactive and negotiated process open to societal input. The past dozen years of Bolivian politics has witnessed a contentious bargaining game between the MAS and its grass-roots social bases, where in the absence of strong national and local party structures serving as "transmission belts," such groups force the party in power to respond to (or at least try to reconcile) mobilized pressure from below.[1]

GENERALIZABILITY OF THE FINDINGS

To what extent can these findings be generalized? Does my theoretical frame-work apply to other cases? I offer two key insights. First, the comparative within-case analysis of candidate selection indicates that the most robust instances of bottom-up control over party decision-making emerge in contexts with a high density of social organization and numerous grass-roots groups united in support of the governing party. In Bolivia, the first constant charac-teristic – a high level of social organization – is more likely to be observed in rural districts than in urban areas. While this characteristic may be unique to certain rural indigenous communities in only some parts of Latin America, like in Ecuador, high levels of social organization may exist in different contexts. The configuration of Bolivian civil society may not be immediately present in other countries. Nevertheless, the finding that civil society strength and the nature of political alignments can shape degrees of grass-roots control over candidate selection and thus affect internal power distributions is a testable hypothesis that can be used to study other cases with similar characteristics to those of the MAS.

Second, similar reflections apply in the realm of policy-making. My analysis shows that grass-roots substantive influence is stronger where mobilized allied groups interfere with what otherwise might be a policy success for the party in power. Such instances include challenging popular policies, constraining execu-tive authority, and forcing policy changes. Success in blocking or modifying legislation is influenced first by historical causes traceable to the party's origins and road to power. The strength and autonomy of social mobilization that shaped the party in its path to power meant that allied social movements remained vibrant after the party accessed office. Even if their leaders support or are co-opted by the party in power, and despite the government's use of tactics to divide and weaken popular movements, the remarkable ability of the

---

[1] A parallel argument can be found in Silva (2017).

rank and file in major popular movements to sustain that autonomous mobilization capacity and thus hold their leaders accountable to their interests means that movement leaders cannot always guarantee the compliance of their social bases with the government's policies. This situation has forced the MAS to step back and negotiate important policies with some of the stronger and more influential movements and popular organizations *in its own camp*, which has constrained attempts to concentrate power. Success in challenging government policies, in short, is influenced by characteristics associated with the configuration of civil society, particularly the strength of rural organizations. The presence of bottom-up channels of decision-making and the capacity of grass-roots organizations to generate and sustain autonomous mobilization constrains the autonomy of the leadership.

Bolivia is an unusual case given the central role of strong rural movements based on production. Nevertheless, the argument about the centrality of civil society configurations is not restricted to movement-based parties with strong ties to rural movements. If the case of the MAS demonstrates the role of coordination among rural and urban actors to link their demands and ensure greater responsiveness and accountability, the case of Uruguay demonstrates the capacity of strong and autonomous urban unions for ensuring party responsiveness. Uruguay is comparatively more urban than Bolivia, but the FA and the MAS operate in a similar, bottom-up manner. The degree of organization of civil society is key.

Countries with strong civil societies and well-organized social movements may have become the exception rather than the norm. Yet, as Schipani (2016) demonstrates, left parties in power can build strong civil societies through redistributive strategies. In fact, the FA's policies went a long way toward empowering private sector unions in Uruguay. Union membership increased markedly under the FA, in part due to the reintroduction of wage councils and greater regulations of industrial relations (Huber and Stephens 2012: 186; Schipani 2016: 51). To the extent that left governments invest in empowering civil society – a condition that is absent in the Brazilian case – the bottom-up dynamics of party governance observed in the cases of the MAS and the FA are more likely to occur.

The comparative historical analysis of the MAS, the PT, and the FA corroborated the importance of historical and constant causes and brought into relief some factors that did not become immediately apparent in the examination of the MAS alone. The comparative analysis reinforced the usefulness of my theoretical framework for understanding variation in power distributions inside movement-based parties more generally. As a result, there are strong reasons to believe that it can be helpful for understanding and comparing the organizational trajectories of a broader set of parties, independent of their origins, stage of development, and mode of access to power. The cases of the PT and the FA share common attributes with the MAS. All of them are left parties formed by grass-roots social movements; they all have a mass base and close links to those groups; they came to national-level power after a series of failed attempts; and they were all reelected for several consecutive terms. Unlike the MAS, however, the FA and PT came to national power in different stages of their organizational development: they were more established parties rather than movements and they experienced different organizational trajectories once in power. Over time, Brazil's PT lost much of its initial bottom-up participatory *élan* and became more centralized and less participatory, thus experiencing a Michelsian shift in its character. In contrast, the Uruguayan FA and the Bolivian MAS have maintained more vibrant grass-roots linkages and have retained more open channels for bottom-up influence.

In reflecting on the explanatory factors accounting for their different organizational trajectories, one key historical cause pushing toward power concentration in the case of the PT is the early development of an elaborate bureaucratic structure with internal rules that encouraged control of party affairs by a dominant group. This created a strong inclination for the party to develop a top-down pattern of organization that proved to be resistant to change over time – a phenomenon that historical institutionalists refer to as a "weak" version of path dependence. Lower levels of social organization – a constant or fairly stable condition of societal structure in Brazil – also help to explain the PT's trajectory. The relative weakness of autonomous social mobilization by popular constituencies helped to continuously reproduce the party's organizational pattern adopted early on.

Overall, then, the within-case and comparative cross-case evidence presented in this book point to the need to reconsider the role that both early organizational development and variation in the density of civil society organizations play in shaping the internal power distributions and long-term trajectories of movement-based parties. On the one hand, the party literature has acknowledged the importance of the first analytical dimensions, with scholars going so far as to say that parties have a "genetic model" or an organizational DNA (Panebianco 1988). The analysis of three movement-based parties demonstrated that while party origins or foundational characteristics matter greatly, the genesis of a party does not have deterministic properties. The type of institutional structures adopted during the early stages of organizational development heavily shapes whether a movement-based party becomes more or less bottom-up in the long run. These structures, and their ensuing power distributions, are fairly stable and become resistant to change the longer party leadership and rank and file operate under the given rules of the game. But organizational patterns *can* change if conditions are conducive to change. In short, although movement-based parties may have "birth marks," they do not have immutable "genetic" features.

On the other hand, more recent research on parties largely ignores or fails to measure the significance of civil society strength and its autonomous mobilization capacity. New research on party-building in Latin America has firmly established that strongly organized civil societies can serve as mobilizing structures for movement-based parties,[2] but that research uses the organizational environment to explain variation in the emergence and strength of new parties. Yet, as I have shown in this book, variation in the density and autonomy of civil society is also central for understanding variation in *power distributions* and *persistence of movement influence* within and between movement-based parties. Although the theoretical framework advanced in this book has been based on the experiences of a small subset of cases in Latin America, it offers a first step toward more nuanced understandings of the internal politics of movement-based parties more generally – an approach that is likely to travel to other cases of parties with strong connections with social movements, as well.

The comparison with other movement-based parties that reached national power in a democratic way provides a good starting point for testing the explanatory power of my theoretical framework and for identifying complementary explanations that might require more attention. There are cases, such as the ANC in South Africa, where high levels of density of civil society organizations and citizen mobilization prior to assuming power did not translate into greater bottom-up control over party decision-making once in power, but rather led to the opposite configuration. Part of this, as Evans and Heller (2015) indicate, may have to do with the logic and degrees of domestic political competition and the exercise of undisputed or hegemonic power, which can weaken civil society and encourage party–society de-alignment. This dimension – the nature of electoral competition – may be a relevant addition to the theoretical framework when it travels to other contexts, or when it is used to study longer-term organizational trajectories than the ones analyzed in this book.

BROADER SIGNIFICANCE OF THE FINDINGS

Conventional wisdom assumes that, even if some parties begin as movements, they will evolve toward oligarchies shaped by professionalization and specialization, with power highly concentrated in party elites who evolve into a separate caste with different interests from those of movement founders. A central contribution of this book is the finding that this teleological course of organizational development is not preordained or inevitable. Movement-based parties do not develop uniformly and there are mechanisms to counteract that centralizing trend. As this book has demonstrated, two key conditions – early organizational attributes and strong, autonomous social mobilization – bring these countervailing mechanisms to the fore. Analyses of how authority and power are allocated within movement-based parties, and of why some parties develop more top-down structures than others, need to consider these

---

[2] See various contributions in Levitsky et al. (2016); see also Vergara (2011).

factors, their interaction with each other, and their interplay with other variables such as the nature of party–society alignments.

Judging from their origins, movement-based parties are distinctive in that they are formed from the bottom up. They are the direct creation of social movements. Such parties follow, in essence, the reverse dynamic of party formation and organization theorized by Aldrich (1995). Yet, as this book has demonstrated, movement-based parties are internally heterogeneous organizations whose operations cannot be characterized easily as uniformly bottom-up or top-down. In effect, as this book shows, these parties look and operate differently in different structural contexts, based on the kinds of linkages they establish with the organized social constituencies from which they emerge and draw support and mobilizational power. This finding informs a long-standing theoretical debate about the conditions shaping the distribution of power inside political parties. It also adds nuance to contemporary debates regarding: (1) the nature of party linkages, particularly between parties and organized mass constituencies; and (2) the sources of variation within and between Latin American left parties, particularly those with a social movement base.

The rise of left parties, movements, and leaders in Latin America since 1998 has generated a variety of scholarly analyses of the factors that enabled the resurgence of the left.[3] Along with explaining the causes of this resurgence, much ink has been spilled in the development of classificatory schemes aiming to sort out the most relevant similarities and differences within the Latin American left and to link those characteristics to outcomes.[4] Taking into account differences in policy orientation and attitudes toward liberal democracy and market economy, some scholars have classified the left into the "good" and the "bad" types (Castañeda 2006), while others have identified a "moderate" and a "contestatory" left from a similar standpoint (Weyland, Madrid, and Hunter 2010). This literature, which advances the "two lefts" thesis, tends to group Bolivia, Venezuela, Ecuador, and Nicaragua together in the "bad" or "contestatory" strand of the left, whereas the "good" left has governed in countries like Brazil (under several PT presidencies), Uruguay (also under several FA presidencies), and Chile (under the leadership of the Concertación). Other scholars have rejected the dichotomization of the left on the grounds that it does not capture the diversity within each category (Cameron and Hershberg 2010).

Using organizational factors as classification criteria, other scholars developed more empirically accurate typologies. On the one hand, for authors like Levitsky

---

[3] See, for instance, Cleary (2006); Roberts (2007b); Weyland (2009); Luna (2010b); Murillo, Oliveros, and Vaishnav (2010); Baker and Greene (2011); Flores-Macías (2012); and Queirolo (2013).

[4] For a critique of existing typological efforts, see Bruhn (2015). Her central point is that existing typologies remain insufficiently nuanced and do not give us sufficient theoretical purchase on bigger-picture outcomes.

and Roberts (2011), the diverse lefts can be classified based on party age (or age of the political movement) and the degree to which it concentrates or disperses political authority. When combined, these two dimensions create four varieties of left parties: the populist left (Venezuela under Chávez and Ecuador under Correa), the populist-machine left (Argentina's PJ), the movement left (Bolivia's MAS), and the institutionalized left (Uruguay's FA, Brazil's PT, and Chile's PS). While the first two categories concentrate political authority in the hands of dominant leaders and have few checks from below, the latter two disperse power and are more likely to be responsive to their grass-roots base. Pribble (2013: 178) develops yet another party typology focused on two dimensions: first, whether organizational rules promote internal democracy and foster close ties with society and, second, whether parties develop programmatic or non-programmatic appeals.[5] When combined, these two dimensions yield four party types: constituency-mobilizing, electoral-professional, charismatic movement, and non-programmatic electoral. Both typologies represent welcome correctives to the previous dichotomous classifications. They also have something in common: they distinguish the lefts on the basis of the concentration of power – whether power is concentrated in the hands of party elites, or even a single leader, or whether it rests in the hands of allied groups in civil society to which the leadership remains accountable. In both of these typologies, the three movement-based parties examined in this book – the MAS, the PT, and the FA – are classified as power-dispersing organizations.

Classifying those three cases as organizations that disperse power is an important first step toward understanding emerging patterns of party–society linkage and broader macro-level outcomes. Yet, it bears noting that the classification is accurate if we look at broad national-level trends, as it only captures the *predominant* linkage strategy pursued by each party. As a result, it remains insufficiently nuanced and, in particular, may distort our understanding of what occurs at the subnational level within each party. Thus, in this book I have not attempted to come up with a new classificatory scheme of left parties, but to "bring society back in" and elucidate the crucial sources of variation in internal grass-roots participation – and the resulting power distributions within and between a subset of cases.

The empirical finding that structural variation in the relative strength of civil society and its autonomous mobilizational capacity are important determinants of within- and between-case power distributions is of great theoretical importance. It offers crucial insight into the question of why parties (*a fortiori* movement-based parties) look and operate differently in different contexts. It also points to the roots of variation in the dispersal of political authority and party–society linkages – an insight that is consistent with the idea of linkage segmentation advanced by Luna (2014).

---

[5] This typology applies to parties on *both* the left and the right.

In so doing, I have added nuance and detail to the existing classifications of left parties in contemporary Latin America. On the one hand, I have highlighted similarities between cases that are rarely compared in the literature. The analysis reveals that cases like the FA may have more in common with the MAS than with the PT, or even with Chile's PS. This point is rarely made in the literature, and its omission has important consequences. For one thing, the differences within the so-called moderate (liberal, responsible, non-populist) left are more remarkable than what the existing literature has established, and there are strong similarities among left parties commonly classified in different typological boxes.

On the other hand, this line of argument can be extended to the so-called "radical" cases with which Bolivia is often grouped together. Interestingly, however, Bolivia's MAS looks more like the FA and radically different from the governing parties in Venezuela and Ecuador. Unlike Bolivia, Venezuela and Ecuador do not have the kind of sustained, autonomous mobilization from below that contributed to the emergence of the MAS and that continued to influence, constrain, and hold its leadership accountable, as described in this book. Understanding these similarities and differences across cases, and the nature and evolution of party–society linkages, is a crucial step for delving deeper into comparative analyses of broader macro-level outcomes, such as the politics of redistribution.

The findings and evidence I present in this book also suggest that contemporary efforts to "deepen" or "democratize" democracy, a historic goal of the Latin American left (à la Roberts 1998: 3) and a central goal during the early years of the left turns in the region (Goldfrank 2011a), are heavily conditioned by historical factors and elements linked to the overall "configuration" of civil society (Rueschemeyer, Stephens, and Stephens 1992). While it has been widely recognized that achievements in democratic deepening by expanding participation and enhancing government responsiveness have been modest and varied (Levitsky and Roberts 2011: 418), the combination of historical and structural factors described in this book gives us some additional theoretical purchase to explain this variation. Specifically, it helps to explain why some left parties, like the PT in Brazil, have developed as relatively more centralized and less participatory organizations with greater power concentration and leadership autonomy, whereas others, such as the MAS and the FA, have maintained more vibrant grass-roots linkages, albeit with varying degrees of institutionalization. Out of the three cases, the MAS stands out because it remains a remarkably different case of a movement-based party, whose experience in power has led to important shifts in domestic power relations at the state and societal levels, and to the increased empowerment of subordinate groups. Whether the Bolivian experience will result in a sustained project of deepening democracy will likely depend to a large extent on the continued strength, unity, and autonomous mobilization capacity of allied groups in civil society.

The findings about the theoretical importance of civil society's strength, and especially its autonomous mobilizational capacity, merit some additional elaboration. I have shown that, enabled by "historical causes" traceable to the party's origins and strengthened by a context of heightened social mobilization, organized mass constituencies have been crucial in keeping the MAS open to societal input and responsive to popular concerns in ways that are not evident in the comparative cases. This is particularly evident in Brazil but also in cases that fall outside the scope of this book (like Venezuela under Chávez and Maduro).[6] Though that is the story of the MAS as of this writing, it is likely that the movement-based party, recently reelected for a third four-year presidential term, and with no clear successors to Morales in line, will experience a Michelsian shift in character if it becomes a hegemonic power holder. Thus, one possible scenario is that it will become increasingly centralized, with more power in the hands of Morales and his trusted circle and less political space for democratic participation of its grass-roots social bases. This is the path followed by the ANC in South Africa, which transitioned from an anti-apartheid movement-based organization into the country's electorally hegemonic governing party as the autonomy of civil society mobilization weakened (Heller 2009; Marais 2011; Evans and Heller 2015).

While this is a *possible* outcome, driven by the logics of the exercise of undisputed or hegemonic power, it does not diminish the significance of the theory and findings in this book. My analysis has specified the conditions that work both for and against power centralization and the mechanisms that can contribute to the maintenance of vibrant party–society linkages. In looking for those attributes and patterns in the comparative within-case analysis of the MAS, I identified the necessary conditions for enabling greater control of the grass-roots over party elites and party decision-making more broadly. A strong, well-organized, and *autonomous* civil society is a central necessary condition for enhancing power dispersion; the status of alignment of civil society with the party (i.e., being united in support of the party) also facilitates power dispersion, but this is contingent on the relative strength of civil society and its autonomous mobilization capacity.

The "constant cause" of strong, autonomous civil society mobilization may not always be a perfect antidote for reducing personalism, as the case of the MAS demonstrates, but to the extent that it boosts bottom-up input in the political process, it can constrain the discretion of the party leadership, enhance responsiveness, and thus make "bait-and-switch" policy-making less likely (Stokes 2001; Roberts 2015a). Given the clear connections between the latter and the process of "brand dilution" (Lupu 2016), a condition conducive to party breakdown, the findings in this book are relevant for understanding the

---

[6] It bears emphasizing that neither Venezuela nor Ecuador generated a movement-based party that carried Chávez and Correa to power. Instead, both leaders formed parties from the top down.

obverse: the conditions that might contribute to developing strong and broad-based party brands and building stable bases of support. Relatedly, the findings are relevant for understanding how parties, by responding to mobilized pressures from below, can remain vibrant in between election cycles and become effective vehicles for democratic representation. This is a core issue of concern in new scholarship on Latin American party organizations (Rosenblatt 2018).[7]

Finally, the findings presented in this book have implications for the comparative study of political parties outside Latin America. The pressures toward internal power concentration, hierarchical party-movement-relations, and greater leadership autonomy are by no means unique to parties in the region. This is particularly problematic for left movement-based parties, which, at least in principle and in their rhetoric, tend to emphasize some form of bottom-up participation as an organizational model and as a way of boosting popular sovereignty in the decision-making process. Whether they can remain open to societal input once they form governments was the subject of heated debates among students of parties, especially the European Green parties, in the 1990s and early 2000s (Müller-Rommel and Poguntke 2002).

This debate has recently received renewed attention following the rise of new left parties with a movement base in Europe (particularly in Southern Europe), such as SYRIZA in Greece, Podemos in Spain, and the Movimiento 5 Stelle (Five Star Movement) in Italy (della Porta et al. 2017). Judging by the experience of Green parties, remaining open to participation is challenging (Frankland, Lucardie, and Rihoux 2008).[8] For the most part, achieving this goal has proven to be elusive, and many Green parties have turned into elite-professional organizations with hierarchical structures and less permeability to civil society input. Others have ended up torn apart due to internal discord (Jachnow 2013; della Porta et al. 2017: 21). Some of this can be explained by the fact that the logic of territorial representation pushes party leadership to focus on multiple issues beyond the party's core concern, which in turn involves coalition building. This, in turn, tends to discourage consultation with the grass-roots social bases and increases internal conflict (Kitschelt 2006).

However, the evidence provided in this book suggests that this need not be the same fate for all parties with a social movement base, particularly for those which, by their own origins in diverse social movements, are able to incorporate a broader set of issues, actors, and demands. Resisting a Michelsian transformation might be easier for parties with a more diversified

---

[7] Rosenblatt (2018: 6) uses the term "party vibrancy" to denote "a political [party] organization that is persistently active and that engenders attachment from its members." He theorizes that four factors, when combined, contribute to developing party vibrancy: purpose, trauma, channels of ambition, and moderate exit barriers (Rosenblatt 2018: 6–11). The findings and arguments in this book add an additional *possible* causal factor in explaining sustained party vibrancy.

[8] Similar trends have been found in recent analyses of the case of SYRIZA (Hough and Olsen 2015).

grass-roots base, but the outcome is contingent on the power of organization and the continuous strength, unity, and autonomous mobilization capacity of that base. With a new wave of parties having strong connections with movements emerging, winning elections, and rising in prominence in Europe (particularly Southern Europe), the debate is open once again (della Porta et al. 2017). This book provides some tools to inform debates about European movement-based parties.

FUTURE INQUIRY

This book's findings signal several directions for future research. The pages that follow focus on three broad areas where more systematic research could significantly improve existing knowledge. First: the factors that account for variation in the strength and density of civil society as well as those that promote or hinder the density of synergetic connections between movements, parties, and states. Second: the bigger-picture trends of contemporary popular incorporation in Latin America; and, third: the interaction between incorporation and patterns of accountability.

Movements, Parties, and States

One potential avenue for further research consists of a more systematic treatment of the conditions that both facilitate and inhibit vibrant movement-party connections over time. This, as Amenta (2016: 567) rightly notes, "is something of a no-man's land in scholarship." It has the potential to analytically bridge the scholarly literatures on political parties and social movements, which often travel along parallel paths with little conversation with each other (McAdam and Tarrow 2010: 529). Although I have tried to link both literatures by showing not only how movements can form political parties, but also how they can become a critical source of variation in parties' organizational models, much more remains to be done.

Why do the connections between movements and parties (and also *states*) become strong and why do these connections grow weak in some cases and not in others? To begin dealing with this puzzle, one of the most obvious questions that can be asked starts with the Bolivian case: will the trends observed in this book be maintained in the long run? If the MAS is a positive case of a movement-based party that has retained relatively vibrant connections to its sponsoring and allied movements after assuming power, what are the implications of negative cases for developing more compelling theoretical explanations of variance. Even within Latin America, explaining variation is challenging; the data on party and civil society organizations and party-movement connections over time is scarce and not very well developed. In the absence of such data, theoretical development is best advanced through case-oriented comparative research of contemporary and historic cases. If variation within Latin America calls for more rigorous comparative research, a cross-regional perspective further reinforces this point. The ANC in South Africa could be a good point of departure, for it is a case where such connections have severely deteriorated over time. As an unambiguously negative case, its analysis would allow an exploration of the full range of variation in the outcome of interest.

Exploring this variation is not merely an academic exercise; it has deep practical implications as well. As the literature on Power Resource Theory has made abundantly clear, left parties closely linked with popular sector organizations tend to push social policy in a more progressive, universalistic, and redistributive direction, even if there is significant cross-case and historical variation (Korpi 1978; Stephens 1979; Hicks 1999; Huber and Stephens 2001, 2012). By contrast, elite parties with weaker ties to such groups tend to be less progressive and sweeping in their social policy initiatives (Pribble and Huber 2011; Pribble 2013; Garay 2017) – even though, in certain cases, those parties might in fact be very effective at delivering selective provisions of services to subordinate groups (Thachil 2014; Brooke 2017).

Evidence from policy-making within the MAS provides clear support for the Power Resource Theory, as important universalistic social policies were enacted in close collaboration between the party and its sponsoring and allied social movements (Anria and Niedzwiecki 2016). Greater degrees of bottom-up influence in the policy sphere, as described in this book, have the potential to generate more universalistic policies that in turn help to create promising policy legacies in the advancement of an agenda seeking to expand social incorporation. This, however, should not be immediately equated with good-quality democratic governance or with greater democratization.[9]

Another line of research emphasizes the importance of strong party–society linkages as providing the political foundations for building effective state policy that expands human capabilities and, ultimately, leads to more effective states (Lee 2012; Evans and Heller 2015). If social movements are seen as the starting point of strong parties and greater state effectiveness, then there is high potential payoff for research into the factors that promote or hinder the strength of civil society mobilization and synergetic movement-party–state relations. Such a research program can help unpack the factors that explain variation in development-related policy.

Although there is little systematic comparative research to explain variation in the density of civil society mobilization and movement-party–state linkages, scholars have begun to pay attention to these issues (e.g., Goldstone 2003; McAdam and Tarrow 2010). The explanation of the inner operations of the MAS presented in this book, as well as the cross-case comparative analysis, provides a preliminary map of the territory of these dynamics as a step toward theory building. It also constitutes an attempt to link scholarly literatures that

---

[9] On this point, see Niedzwiecki and Anria (n.d.).

often travel separate roads. Additional comparative research can broaden the dialog, leading to a cumulative process of theoretical development on a pressing issue with clear policy implications.

First, it would be highly valuable to examine the conditions that make the emergence of a successful movement-based party possible. Why has such a party emerged in Bolivia and not in Peru, despite the overarching similarities in the social structure of both countries, for example? Second, it would be especially valuable to examine the conditions that promote or inhibit movement-party–state connections in a more systematic fashion (for example, by examining both contemporary and historical cases and exploring variation by policy areas). This can help to identify additional explanatory factors that may contribute to strengthening or weakening links that are not easily detected with a single case study approach over a relatively short period of time. This is a worthy research program that deserves further attention and more systematic analysis.

Trends in Political Incorporation

Another area for further research relates to the question of how the findings in this book relate to new debates about Latin America's second historical process of political incorporation (Roberts 2008; Luna and Filgueira 2009; Reygadas and Filgueira 2010; Collier and Chambers-Ju 2012; Rossi 2017; Silva 2017; Wolff 2018); how this second period differs from the first labor-incorporating period described by Collier and Collier in their seminal book *Shaping the Political Arena* (Collier and Collier 1991); and the kinds of legacies it may leave in the long run.

The first period occurred during the early stages of import substitution industrialization (ISI) in the twentieth century. Class-based actors, particularly labor movements (and peasants in some countries), were crucial for the expansion of rights in the civic and social arenas. In terms of the institutional expressions of popular power, the mobilization of these groups "encouraged the formation of the first mass party organizations in the region, which often forged organic linkages to labor and/or peasant unions and drew on their human and organizational resources" (Roberts 2008: 333). In the wake of the 1980s debt crisis, the implementation of structural adjustment policies resulted in deindustrialization, the demobilization of these groups, and the emergence of new social actors that attempted to defend the interests of popular sectors (Kurtz 2004). If market policies meant the "de-incorporation" or exclusion of popular sectors, social resistance to market reforms in the "reactive phase" to neoliberalism opened up a second period of mass incorporation, a new phase of inclusion marked by a new set of social actors and more fluid institutional expressions (Roberts 2015b). Seen from this angle, the Bolivian MAS, the focus of this book, is a novel institutional expression of Latin America's second incorporation crisis – a novelty due to its origins in the autonomous mobilization of an indigenous constituency, and also due to its organizational attributes, as described in this book.

The literature on the legacies of neoliberalism shows that popular sector groups, in the Bolivian case particularly the peasant and indigenous peoples' movements, suffered from political exclusion as market reforms advanced and liberal democracies consolidated (Silva 2009: 28). The literature on democratization offers insight into how this exclusion happened. O'Donnell (1994) shows how popular groups became irrelevant in political-economic policy-making during much of the 1990s, giving rise to what he called "delegative democracies." These functioned on the basis of highly concentrated executive power. In order to advance neoliberal reforms, presidents governed with little consideration for the interests, demands, and priorities of popular sector groups "constrained only by the hard facts of existing power relations and by a constitutionally limited term in office" (O'Donnell 1999: 164). Complementing this view, the literature on social movements and parties claimed that protest and social mobilization by class-based actors during the neoliberal restructuring was difficult due to social fragmentation and rising poverty and inequality (Roberts 1998; Murillo 2001; Kurtz 2004).

In spite of the conclusions of this early literature, there were areas where popular groups found ways to make their voices heard on self-contained issues such as the environment, gender, human rights, indigenous politics, and subsistence rights, to mention a few (Oxhorn 1995; Eckstein 2001; Yashar 2005).[10] As Silva (2009: 29) notes, "as long as they kept property issues off of their agendas, these groups found the liberal democratic state to be more inclusive toward their interests."

In Bolivia, decentralization reforms in the 1990s facilitated the gradual incorporation of popular sectors in municipal governments and their penetration into representative institutions at the subnational levels. As this book has shown, the formation of the MAS and its ascendance to national-level power served as a vehicle for its realization on a larger scale.[11] Increased political incorporation also gave previously marginalized groups enhanced influence over agenda setting and policy-making and led to important shifts in domestic power relations. In today's Bolivia, well-organized grass-roots groups typically belonging to the "informal" labor sector (like coca growers, cooperative miners, and transportation unions) have expanded access to the

---

[10] Although a sharp decline in antigovernment union mobilization in the 1980s and 1990s provided support for that argument, other authors noted that market reforms in fact led to *increased* mobilization against those reforms by groups other than unions (Arce and Bellinger 2007).

[11] An early turning point was the 2002 election, when the MAS won significant minorities in both chambers, which brought several representatives from popular groups, particularly peasants, to Congress. Since then, Bolivia has experienced a circulation of political elites; actors of more diverse ethnic, class, and ideological composition have gradually, and pacifically, displaced the hitherto dominant political actors (Chapter 2).

political arena and greater influence in the policy process both from within the state (in representative institutions and state bureaucracies at all levels) and from without (through contestation, or direct pressure in the streets).[12] This is not to say they have complete control over the national agenda. Rather, it is to suggest that even if the MAS in power may have centralizing "temptations," the interests, demands, and priorities of large segments of socioeconomically disadvantaged groups have become increasingly harder to ignore.[13]

This can be seen as both a blessing and a curse. The legislative process remains under executive domination, but within that process, the growing presence of powerful organized social actors in representative institutions has given voice to sectors that before had very little "voice" and influence. However, while in some instances newly empowered groups have mobilized and served as a check on executive power via congressional oversight (Chapter 4),[14] this incorporation is based on a particularistic relationship of MAS and allied groups, and, as such, can actually be an obstacle for representative institutions to work in the interest of broader segments of society. This is especially so, given that some of these newly powerful groups have become new "veto players" alongside older ones such as the business sector.[15]

Social mobilization and organized contestation, two non-electoral forms of participation, have historically played a central role in Bolivia's political life, as many have noted (e.g., Gray Molina 2008: 124; Silva 2009; Vergara 2011). In Bolivia's first period of incorporation, which can be traced to the National Revolution of 1952, mobilization led to the development of corporatist channels of interest intermediation. They in turn provided new channels of representation and material benefits for previously excluded groups, such as peasants and workers, helping to incorporate large segments of the population into politics and society. Although those channels became easily undone when the MNR was overthrown in 1964 amidst an economic crisis, ushering in an 18-year period of military-authoritarian rule, the National Revolution consolidated the MNR as a mass-mobilizing party directly representing the interests of the marginalized (Klein 2011: 28).

[12] An interesting aspect of Bolivia is that some of the better-organized sectors are in the informal sector. For an explanation of how informal workers in the country manage to overcome collective action problems and strengthen their organizational power, see Hummel (2017).

[13] See also Rossi (2017: 260–2).

[14] As when representatives from transportation unions and street traders challenged the constitutionality of an executive-proposed asset recovery law in 2013.

[15] Interviews with representatives of the transportation sector and cooperative miners – two of the most powerful groups that have gained representation through MAS – reveal that their presence in representative institutions serves to keep an eye on legislation that can damage their sector. They are veto players; they can generate paralyzing conflicts if they do not agree with a given legislative piece.

Whether or not the emerging patterns of representation in today's Bolivia and the increased projection of popular sector groups into the state will translate into greater and sustained control of public institutions by subordinate groups is still an open question. It will require time and further investigation.

Largely thanks to commodities, the period of the MAS in government has been one of strong and sustained economic growth with significant reductions in inequality and an expansion in social welfare policies (Anria and Huber 2018). This context makes it comparatively easier to keep a movement-based party in power united than in a crisis context. Even in that favorable environment, however, social mobilization erupted several times and forced the government to alter important policies after the grass-roots social bases "spoke out," which has also contributed to maintaining cohesion on the left – a key factor in explaining the political longevity of Morales compared to other left governments in the region (Anria and Huber 2018).

In a democracy like Bolivia's, as this book has shown, a highly mobilized civil society can often be a double-edged sword. It enables subordinate groups to make their weight felt between elections and to check state power, but it can also lead to a lack of governability. In Bolivia today, the regime's inclusionary dynamics depend heavily on autonomous forms of social mobilization by popular constituencies. That mobilization has been acting more as a supplement to institutional politics rather than as its antithesis or substitute (Anria 2016; Silva 2017). Mobilization is still incorporating subordinate social groups and spurring the creation of new participatory institutions (Falleti and Riofrancos 2018: 99–105). The upshot has been a more inclusive and responsive regime, particularly when seen in the long arc of Bolivian history.[16]

But, what if a serious economic crisis hit and austerity measures were to be needed? Will the MAS implode like the MNR? While the MAS is certainly not immune to crisis, the party is built on a comparatively stronger foundation than the MNR. Part of this can be explained by its approach to coalition building. The MNR relied heavily on "extensive" linkages based on patronage and clientelism, which provided shallow coalitional foundations highly vulnerable to economic and political constraints. By contrast, the MAS pursued a more "intensive," integrative approach to crafting a coalition of support. In addition to the support of the country's largest rural movements, the MAS integrated other popular and non-popular actors – including the middle classes, urban social movements, and certain economic elites – as organizational pillars. This

---

[16] As Wolff (2018: 9) notes, this incorporation also has some inegalitarian features; explicitly *indigenous* organizations have gained access and influence over policy-making but in a subordinate position. This became especially clear in the aftermath of the TIPNIS conflict, when the relationships between the MAS and lowland indigenous movements began to deteriorate (Chapter 4).

has provided the party with a more stable basis of political support.[17] It remains to be seen whether the MAS will stay united or whether it will fracture and disperse in the face of a crisis.

Early in 2016 Morales narrowly lost a referendum that would have changed the country's constitution in order to let him run again in 2019. In the face of these results, there was a fork in the road: The MAS could have opted to find a new presidential candidate, taking steps toward de-personalization, or looked for new – legally questionable – ways to enable Morales to re-run. Blaming the media for the unfavorable results, it opted to keep Morales as its candidate, no matter what – going as far as petitioning the country's Plurinational Constitutional Tribunal to remove term limits, and obtaining a favorable result. This situation revealed a critical dilemma for the MAS, looking ahead: the challenges to sustain a political project beyond the tenure of a highly personalistic leadership. It remains to be seen what will happen in the elections scheduled for 2019, and whether in the long run the MAS will continue to perform its "incorporating" role and become a strong organizational actor independent of its current leadership, breaking a mold in Latin American politics.

Regardless of the outcome, future research on the MAS – and comparative research on movement-based parties, more generally – could focus squarely on the role of leadership within the party, its role in maintaining the party and its allied movements together, and the extent to which charismatic leaders enable or inhibit bottom-up versus top-down patterns of organization in the long run. We know precious little about this. While charismatic leaders are widely regarded as inimical to bottom-up, rank-and-file governance, the concrete effects of charismatic leadership on internal party politics are not straightforward. They should be studied more systematically rather than assumed.

Incorporation, Accountability, and Democracy

Finally, this book has generated insight into the impact of the MAS at the political regime level of analysis, and it raises additional questions. Despite significant advances in terms of inclusion and participation, as described above, observers have noted important erosions of liberal rights and freedoms, leading some to characterize the Morales-era Bolivia as non-democratic (e.g., Levitsky and Loxton 2013; Sanchez-Sibony 2013; Weyland 2013; Mayorga 2017).[18] It is frequently noted that power concentration began ramping up during Morales's first term, when his government was intent on "refounding" the state despite the challenge of a mobilized

---

[17] The distinction between "extensive" and "intensive" coalition building strategies and their effects is further developed elsewhere (Anria and Cyr 2017: 1256).

[18] Bolivian citizens also show concerns about the state of democracy. After the 2009 presidential reelection, satisfaction with democracy reached its lowest recorded point in 2012, when it stood at 49 percent; it improved slightly in 2014 (Ciudadanía and LAPOP 2014: 8).

opposition, and that this tendency was further intensified after Morales was reelected in 2009 by a 64 percent landslide and the MAS consolidated power by gaining a two-third majority of the Plurinational Legislative Assembly – a majority that it has maintained up until now.[19]

Ordinary citizens, journalists, and opposition politicians share this assessment and have many of the same complaints they had under previous governments: power is too concentrated in an executive administration that often treats opponents and the press with raw hostility. Institutions are inefficient, liberal rights are poorly safeguarded, and courts are politicized and at times used to intimidate opposition leaders (interviews with Erika Brockmann, Diego Cuadros, Carlos Hugo Laruta, and Marcela Revollo). These concerns are legitimate.[20] The fact that the government acts in ways that undermine the rights of individuals and political minorities by legal means and by controlling the media is indeed a worrisome trend. But to suggest that Morales-era Bolivia is an authoritarian regime might be going too far.

Since Morales took office in 2006, Bolivia has remained democratic. Its rankings on several quantitative measures of democracy – Freedom House, Polity IV, and V-Dem, to name a few – have remained fairly stable. According to Wolff's (2018) excellent, comprehensive review of those sources, most quantitative measures, as well as the well-known criticisms of competitive authoritarianism, do "capture the deterioration in certain dimensions of liberal democracy." But at the same time, most measures and assessments "largely miss the substantive changes in terms of participation and representation," as has been discussed in this book (Wolff 2018: 6).

With important qualifications, O'Donnell's conceptualization of "delegative" democracy is a more useful starting point to begin to understand present-day Bolivia (O'Donnell 1994; see also Luna and Vergara 2016). The concept is about how power is organized and *exercised* in a formally democratic context. Delegative democracies are a form of executive rule resting on the concentration of power resources in the hands of an elected, all-powerful president who claims to rule in the interest of the people. However, just as they lack horizontal checks on the exercise of executive power, they also admit little influence from below on the political process beyond elections. They have "deactivating" features, marked by an oddly

---

[19] As Crabtree (2013: 289) notes, this electoral tendency also appeared at the regional level. In the 2010 regional elections, the MAS won six out of nine regional governments, as well as a working majority in almost every regional legislative assembly. In the wake of slowing economic growth in 2014, however, the MAS lost a number of mayoral races, and in 2016, opposition on the left and right temporarily united and captured 51.3 percent of a referendum vote, just enough to defeat Morales' proposed constitutional change that would have allowed him to have legally seen a fourth consecutive term.

[20] There have been serious attempts to curtail freedom of expression, several politicians have fled into exile, and Bolivia has become an unfriendly environment for journalists who are not sympathetic to the MAS.

passive citizenship and a trend toward declines in social organization and the disempowerment of subordinate groups.

Those "deactivating" features are not present in Bolivia. Morales' Bolivia may exhibit some of the features of delegative democracy, but at the end of the day is fundamentally different from what O'Donnell had in mind in his thinking and theorizing of the concept. On the one hand, Bolivia showcases tendencies such as the dominance of a personalistic leadership, weak horizontal accountability, and even a strong urge to change the constitution to alter the "hard facts" of a constitutionally limited term in office. On the other hand, Morales and the MAS, in my account, are clearly accountable to organized mass constituencies in a continuous way. Thus, unlike the examples of delegative democracies, Bolivia has strong societal actors capable of exercising vertical accountability in a permanent or semi-permanent manner, or in between election cycles, through their mobilization. Autonomous grass-roots participation, inclusion, and accountability to organized mass constituencies are robust.[21]

One may question whether, despite the documented inclusionary features, violations of civil liberties, like weak protection of political minority rights and the use of courts to intimidate opposition leaders, simply render Bolivia authoritarian. However, inclusive, fair, and competitive elections continue to be held. Most crucially, defining authoritarian attributes – such as power being exercised by a clique that can supersede the will of the citizens – are not yet apparent. To the extent that violations of civil liberties weaken the liberal and republican features of the regime but do not undermine, or make ineffective, the integrity of core electoral institutions, Bolivia remains a democracy, albeit one with strong liberal deficits.[22]

While Morales has been able to concentrate power to a significant degree, the result is something still different from an authoritarian regime. Rather, going back to Dahl's (1971) two-dimensional conceptualization of polyarchy, and on the basis of the trends identified in this book, Bolivia can be classified as a democracy that has moved very aggressively in a more democratic direction in terms of participation – far more than anything Bolivia has seen in the past, with social mobilization, inclusion, and accountability to organized mass constituencies remaining robust. But at the same time, Bolivia's political regime is a democracy that has been weakened in terms of institutionalized contestation or horizontal checks and balances. The classifications

---

[21] One could argue that vertical accountability weakened in 2016 in light of the results of the February 2016 referendum. Although Morales initially admitted defeat, the MAS used legally questionable ways to remove constitutional term limits and bypass the referendum results. In addition, some groups have over time lost their capacity to mobilize autonomously and exercise vertical accountability through mobilization – this has been the case for lowland indigenous movements, for example, and especially in the aftermath of the TIPNIS conflict.

[22] This point is elaborated further in Cameron (2018: 14–5).

of Bolivia as "competitive authoritarian," by contrast, privilege this second dimension over the first one and provide a distorted and partial lens for interpreting contemporary Bolivian politics.

Which begs this question for further research and theorizing: Is there a structural trade-off between incorporation and horizontal accountability? In theory, to the extent that popular groups continue to be present in representative institutions and not only put issues on the agenda, but also perform oversight functions from within and from without, their increased representation and influence over policy-making can in the long run lead to stronger checks on the executive. Yet in practice, the logic of undisputed power might bring about greater executive dominance and decreased political input from below. It remains an empirical question as to whether the personalism of Morales' leadership, his attempts to alter the "hard facts" of a constitutionally limited term in office, and the fact that there are no clear successors being cultivated within the MAS might lead to a path of accentuated power concentration in an eventual next term in office. This remains to be seen. In any event, a civil society that can maintain its own strength and freedom of action independent of the state will prove to be one of the best safeguards that Bolivia – or any country that aspires to liberal democratic ideals – can have.

All this, in turn, suggests that in addition to theorizing about new political organizations like the MAS simply as ad hoc electoral vehicles, we should theorize about them as promising instruments for the successful inclusion into politics of groups that have traditionally been on the margins of the political power game. To understand emerging patterns of political representation, incorporation, and accountability in today's Latin American democracies, we need much more systematic comparative research on their varied institutional expressions. Such a research agenda should seriously take into account the tensions and ambiguities that characterize their internal dynamics, which often involve power concentration and pressures for power dispersion working simultaneously.

This book presents a first step in that direction. It has benefited by drawing comparisons between three movement-based parties that won state power in Latin America. However, it could be expanded to include a more systematic assessment of other institutional expressions of popular power in Latin America's second period of incorporation, like the political movements led by Chávez (and now Nicolás Maduro) in Venezuela and Correa (and now Lenín Moreno) in Ecuador. Although these leftist alternatives share with the Bolivian case a commitment to social inclusion (De la Torre 2016), they vary dramatically in terms of their organization, internal politics, and connections with social movements and popular organizations. The Bolivian MAS stands out as a new party that emerged organically from social movements themselves – a clear example of what I called a "movement-based" party – whereas the other cases do not have the same founding characteristics. Morales' leadership is deeply rooted in an autonomous logic of sociopolitical mobilization. By contrast, as

Roberts (2015b: 689) correctly notes, neither Chávez nor Correa "rose to prominence through their involvement with social movements or movement organizations." They both founded their parties from the top down, and the political processes in both countries lack the kind of sustained, autonomous social mobilization by popular constituencies present in Bolivia – and that differentiates Bolivia greatly from the leftist experiences in the other two countries.

If the first period of mass incorporation, which corresponded to the growth of ISI, led to the development of labor-based parties with a predominantly urban union base in much of the region, the second period, which is associated with post-ISI economies, has encouraged the formation of parties with more diversified social bases and radically different logics of collective action. On the basis of the analysis and evidence presented in this book, it appears that having a diversified and autonomous base (à la Bolivia's MAS) can generate diffuse pressure and greater internal power dispersion, accountability, and responsiveness. While other scholars have reached similar conclusions by looking at cases outside the region, like the Indian state of Kerala (Heller 2005), more within-region comparative research is needed to assess the institutional and organizational legacies of Latin America's contemporary period of incorporation. This research is essential to understand how the political arena has been reshaped in the region in the past few decades.

Appendix 1

List of Cited Interviews

Over 170 respondents were interviewed for this project. The following list provides the names, position (at the time of the interview), and date of interview for all interviewees cited in this book, who also agreed to disclose their names and positions. The interviewees not cited in this book, as well as those who did not explicitly consent to have their names and positions disclosed, are not included in this list.

Aguirre Ledezma, Noel. Vice Minister of Alternative and Special Education; former Minister of Planning and Development. La Paz, Bolivia, February 8, 2013.

Albarracín, Emiliana. MAS Councilwoman of the Municipality of Villa Tunari. Villa Tunari, Bolivia, March 15, 2013.

Albó, Xavier. Cofounder of the Center for Investigation and Promotion of Peasants (CIPCA). La Paz, Bolivia, December 5, 2012.

Alfaro, Luis. MAS Deputy for Tarija; MAS Delegate to the Constituent Assembly. La Paz, Bolivia, January 24, 2013.

Almaraz, Alejandro. Former Member of the MAS's National Directorate; former Vice Minister of Land. Cochabamba, Bolivia, March 11, 2013.

Ávalos, Isaac. MAS Senator for Santa Cruz; former Secretary General of CSUTCB. La Paz, Bolivia, August 30, 2012.

Benavides, Jean-Paul. Academic. Cochabamba, Bolivia, March 25, 2013.

Blanco, Bertha. Executive Member of the National Confederation of Peasant, Indigenous, and Native Women of Bolivia (CNMCIOB-BS); MAS Councilwoman of the Municipality of El Alto. La Paz, Bolivia, August 20, 2008.

Brockmann, Erika. Former MIR Senator and former MIR Deputy for Cochabamba. La Paz, Bolivia, October 5, 2012.

Burgoa, Carlos Hugo. Bolivian Consul in Tacna, Chile; former Secretary of the MAS's National Directorate. La Paz, Bolivia, April 11, 2013.

Cabrera, Justa. Indigenous Activist; President, National Confederation of Bolivia's Indigenous Women (CNMIB). Santa Cruz, Bolivia, May 8, 2013.

Cassía, Walter. Journalist; Director of Sovereignty Radio [Radio Soberanía]. Villa Tunari, Bolivia, March 18, 2013

Catacora, Luis Arce. Bolivia's Minister of Economy (2006–present). La Paz, Bolivia, May 5, 2013.

Centellas, Ximena. Advisor of the MAS's National Directorate. La Paz, Bolivia, October 31, 2012.

Chávez, Walter. Former MAS Campaign Manager; Journalist and Former Director of the fortnightly Mad Toy [Juguete Rabioso]. La Paz, Bolivia, December 9, 2012 and May 1, 2013.

Chivi, Idón. Director of Studies and Projects at the Ministry of Communication; former Advisor to CONAMAQ; member of the Presidential Representation to the Constituent Assembly (REPAC). La Paz, Bolivia, December 3, 2012.

Choque, Lidia. Former MAS-Santa Cruz President, Santa Cruz; Executive Member of the National Confederation of Peasant, Indigenous, and Native Women of Bolivia (CNMCIOB-BS). Santa Cruz, Bolivia, May 16, 2013.

Claros, Omar. Secretary General, Six Federations of the Tropic of Cochabamba. Villa Tunari, Bolivia, March 18, 2013.

Condori, Modesto. Peasant Leader; MAS Founding Member. La Paz, Bolivia, October 31, 2012.

Cordova Eguivar, Eduardo. Academic. Cochabamba, Bolivia, March 13, 2013.

Cuadros, Diego. Former Director of Territorial Organization, Ministry of Autonomy. La Paz, Bolivia, February 23, 2013.

Delgadillo, Walter. Minister of Public Works, Services, and Housing. Cochabamba, Bolivia, April 1, 2013.

Delgado, Rebeca. MAS Deputy for Cochabamba; MAS Delegate to the Constituent Assembly. La Paz, Bolivia, April 23, 2013.

Durán, Franklin. President, Confederation of Transport Drivers (Transport Union). La Paz, Bolivia, April 17, 2013.

Escóbar, Filemón. Former Leader of the FSMTB (Union Federation for Bolivian Mining Workers); former MAS Senator for Cochabamba; founding member of the MAS. Cochabamba, Bolivia, March 26, 2013.

Espinoza, Erasmo. MAS Councilman of Villa Tunari; President of the Municipal Council of Villa Tunari. Villa Tunari, Cochabamba, March 15, 2013.

Ferreira, Reymi. MAS Candidate for the Mayorship of Santa Cruz; Academic. Santa Cruz, Bolivia, May 9, 2013.

Gallardo, Germán. Planning Director, Ministry of Rural Development and Land. La Paz, Bolivia, January 10, 2013.

Garcés, Fernando. Academic; Consultant to the Unity Pact [Pacto de Unidad]. Cochabamba, Bolivia, March 8, 2013.

García, Fernando. Academic; United Nations Development Program (UNDP) in Bolivia. La Paz, Bolivia, September 3, 2012.

García Linera, Álvaro. Bolivia's Vice-President (2006–present). La Paz, Bolivia, May 4, 2013.

Guarachi, Paulino. Former Secretary General of CSUTCB. La Paz, Bolivia, September 14, 2012.

Guarayos, Samuel. President, MAS-La Paz Departmental Directorate. La Paz, Bolivia, July 28, 2008.

Guillén, Néstor. Community Leader, FEJUVE-El Alto. La Paz, Bolivia, April 9, 2013.

Guzmán, Orlando. Advisor, CONALCAM. La Paz, Bolivia, August 26, 2008.

Henríquez, Ricardo. MAS Councilman of the Municipality of Villa Tunari. Villa Tunari, Bolivia, March 15, 2013.

Huanca, Felipa. Executive Secretary of the La Paz Departmental Federation of Peasant, Indigenous, and Native Women of Bolivia (FDUMCIOPL-BS); Secretary General, National Confederation of Peasant, Indigenous, and Native Women of Bolivia (CNMCIOB-BS); MAS Candidate for Governorship of La Paz. La Paz, Bolivia, February 13, 2013.

Huanca, Luis. Former Executive, FEJUVE-El Alto. El Alto, Bolivia, August 13, 2008.

Iporre, Iván. Director, Plurinational School of Public Administration (EGPP); MAS Campaign Manager; former Personal Assistant of Evo Morales. La Paz, Bolivia, November 14, 2012.

Jilamita, Jesús. Advisor, CONAMAQ. La Paz, Bolivia, February 5, 2013.

Laruta, Carlos Hugo. Leader of National Unity [Unidad Nacional]. La Paz, Bolivia, February 6, 2013.

Limache, Walter. National Coordinator, Nina Program, Union of Institutions of Social Work and Action (UNITAS). La Paz, Bolivia, January 18, 2013.

Loayza, Román. Former MAS Deputy for Cochabamba; MAS delegate to the Constituent Assembly. Author interview. La Paz, Bolivia, July 22, 2008.

Loayza, Sergio. MAS Deputy for Beni; Former Vice President of the MAS's National Directorate. La Paz, Bolivia, November 5, 2012.

Machaca, Miguel. Former MAS Deputy for El Alto; former President of MAS-El Alto Regional Directorate. La Paz, Bolivia, August 18, 2008.

Machaca, Rodolfo. Executive Secretary, CSUTCB. La Paz, Bolivia, January 17, 2013.

Mamani, Abel. Former President, FEJUVE-El Alto; former Minister of Water. La Paz, Bolivia, February 19, 2013.

Mamani, Feliciano. Mayor of the Municipality of Villa Tunari. Villa Tunari, Bolivia, March 16, 2013.

Mamani Paucara, Adrián. Executive Secretary, Red Ponchos [Ponchos Rojos]. La Paz, Bolivia, April 19, 2013.

Melendres, Walter. Director of Legislative Administration, Office of the Vice Presidency. La Paz, Bolivia, January 24, 2013.

Mendoza, Adolfo. MAS Senator for Cochabamba. La Paz, Bolivia, November 29, 2012.

Mercado, Manuel. MAS Campaign Coordinator. La Paz, Bolivia, February 27, 2013.

Michel, Sebastián. Vice Minister of Communications. La Paz, Bolivia, April 2, 2013.

Moldiz, Hugo. Minister of Government. La Paz, Bolivia, September 26, 2012.

Montaño, Gabriela. MAS Senator for Santa Cruz; President of the Senate. La Paz, Bolivia, February 28, 2013.

Montes, Pedro. Former Executive Secretary, Bolivian Workers' Central (COB). La Paz, Bolivia, April 21, 2013.

Morales, Gerardo. Former Vice Minister of Basic Services; Councilman of El Alto. El Alto, Bolivia, August 9, 2008.

Navarro, César. Vice Minister of Coordination with Social Movements. La Paz, Bolivia, August 23, 2012 [also interviewed on August 27, 2008].

Nina, Fanny Juana. Former President, FEJUVE-El Alto. El Alto, Bolivia, April 22, 2013.

Núñez, Dionicio. MAS founding member; former MAS deputy for La Paz. La Paz, Bolivia, November 22, 2012.

Ontiveros, Freddy. Advisor, FENCOMIN. La Paz, Bolivia, October 25, 2012.

Orellana, Segundina. President, Coordinator for the Women of the Tropic (Cocamtrop); Secretary General, Six Federations of the Tropic of Cochabamba. Villa Tunari, Bolivia, March 18, 2013.

Ortega, Isabel. Vice Minister of Indigenous Justice; former MAS Deputy; MAS Founding Member. La Paz, Bolivia, November 29, 2012.

Ortíz, Concepción. Vice President, MAS National Directorate. Santa Cruz, Bolivia, November 6, 2012.

Paredes, Ramiro. Member, Plurinational Electoral Organ; Advisor, FENCOMIN. La Paz, Bolivia, October 15, 2012.

Parra, Elvira. Executive Member, National Confederation of Peasant, Indigenous, and Native Women of Bolivia (CNMCIOB-BS); MAS Delegate to the Constituent Assembly. La Paz, Bolivia, August 14, 2008.

Patana, Edgar. Mayor, El Alto; former Executive Secretary, Regional Workers' Central of El Alto (COR-El Alto). El Alto, Bolivia, April 29, 2013.

Patzi, Félix. Former MAS Candidate for the Governorship of La Paz. La Paz, Bolivia, November 28, 2012.

Paucara, Bernabé. Mayor of the Municipality of Achacachi. La Paz, Bolivia, January 14, 2013.

Peredo, Antonio. MAS Senator for La Paz. La Paz, Bolivia, August 21, 2008.

Pinto, Juan Carlos. National Director, Intercultural Service of Democratic Strengthening (SIFDE), Plurinational Electoral Organ (OEP); Member of REPAC. La Paz, Bolivia, September 7, 2012.

Poma, Martha. MAS Senator for La Paz. La Paz, Bolivia, February 14, 2013.

Prada Alcoreza, Raúl. Former MAS Delegate to the Constituent Assembly; former Vice Minister of Strategic Planning; Member of the Comuna Group [Grupo Comuna]. La Paz, Bolivia, January 29, 2013.

Prada Tejada, María Nela. Chief of Cabinet, Ministry of Economy. La Paz, Bolivia, February 1, 2013.

Quezada, Marcelo. Bolivian Ambassador to Paraguay; Campaign Advisor for the 2002 Elections. La Paz, Bolivia, July 11, 2008.

Quiroga, José Antonio. Editor, *Nueva Crónica y Buen Gobierno*; former MAS Candidate for the Office of the Vice Presidency (2002). La Paz, Bolivia, July 18, 2008.

Quiroz, José. President, MAS-Santa Cruz. Santa Cruz, Bolivia, May 21, 2013.

Revollo, Marcela. MSM Deputy. La Paz, Bolivia, February 18, 2013.

Rodriguez, Adalid. Secretary of Commerce and Exports of FENCOMIN. La Paz, Bolivia, October 25, 2012.

Rojas, Eugenio. MAS Senator for La Paz. La Paz, Bolivia, September 21, 2012.

Rojas, Roberto. MAS Deputy for La Paz/El Alto. La Paz, Bolivia, April 11, 2013.

Romero, Asterio. Secretary General, Governorship of Cochabamba; Union Leader. Cochabamba, Bolivia, March 25, 2013.

Salazar, Fernando. Academic. Cochabamba, Bolivia, March 13, 2013.

Salazar, Julio. MAS Senator for Cochabamba; *Cocalero* Union Leader. La Paz, Bolivia, December 7, 2012.

Salvatierra, Hugo. MAS Founding Member; former Minister of Rural Development, Agriculture and the Environment. Santa Cruz, Bolivia, May 15, 2013.

Sanjinez, Tito. Vice President, MAS-Santa Cruz Urban Directorate. Santa Cruz, Bolivia, May 8, 2013.

Sifuentes, Nélida. MAS Senator for Chuquisaca; Vice President of the Senate; Finance Secretary, MAS National Directorate. La Paz, Bolivia, October 18, 2012.

Siles, Hugo. MAS Councilman for Santa Cruz. Santa Cruz, Bolivia, May 14, 2013.

Silva, Jorge. MAS Councilman for La Paz; Vice President, Federation Bolivian Municipalities (FAM); MAS Campaign Coordinator; former MAS deputy for La Paz. La Paz, Bolivia, January 25, 2013.

Soruco, Freddy. MAS Councilman for Santa Cruz. Santa Cruz, Bolivia, May 8, 2013.

Tacóo, Lázaro. CIDOB Leader; Spokesperson of the Second TIPNIS Anti-Road March. Cochabamba, Bolivia, March 4, 2013.

Torres, Edgar. Union Leader, Special Federation of Peasant Workers of the Tropics of Cochabamba. Cochabamba, Bolivia, March 18, 2013.

Torrico, Gustavo. Former MAS Deputy for La Paz. La Paz, Bolivia, July 29, 2008.

Vázquez, Victor Hugo. Vice Minister of Rural Development. La Paz, Bolivia, January 9, 2013.

Villarroel, Miguelina. MAS Deputy for Cochabamba; Union Leader, Special Federation of the Yungas of the Chapare. La Paz, Bolivia, February 21, 2013.

Villca, Andrés. MAS Senator for Potosí; Former President of FENCOMIN. La Paz, Bolivia, August 30, 2012.

Villca, Juan de la Cruz. MAS Founding Member; former Executive Secretary of CSUTCB. La Paz, Bolivia, October 16, 2012.

Zeballos, Rodolfo. Advisor, MAS-Santa Cruz Urban Directorate. Santa Cruz, Bolivia, May 7, 2013.

Zuazo, Moira. Academic, Friedrich Ebert Stiftung Foundation. La Paz, Bolivia, August 29, 2012.

Zurita, Leonida. Coca Grower and Leader of the Six Federations of the Tropic of Cochabamba; Secretary of Foreign Relations, MAS National Directorate. La Paz, Bolivia, 6 November, 2012.

Appendix 2

Municipal Election Maps, MAS Vote Share

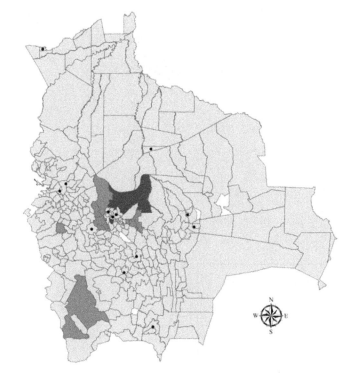

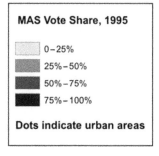

MAS Vote Share, 1995

- 0–25%
- 25%–50%
- 50%–75%
- 75%–100%

Dots indicate urban areas

MAP A2.1 1995 municipal election IU vote (rural and urban).

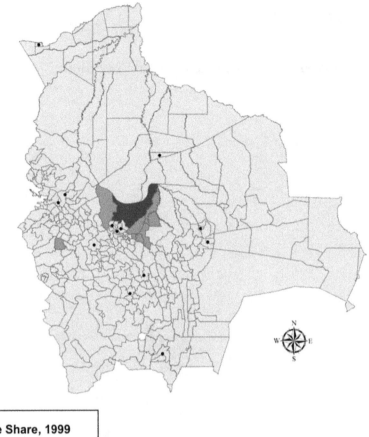

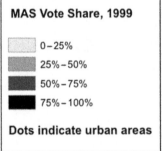

MAS Vote Share, 1999

- 0–25%
- 25%–50%
- 50%–75%
- 75%–100%

Dots indicate urban areas

MAP A2.2 1999 municipal election MAS vote (rural and urban).

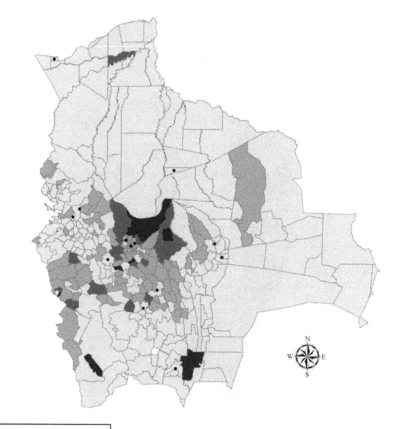

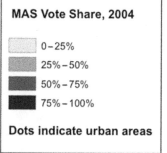

MAP A2.3 2004 municipal election MAS vote (rural and urban).

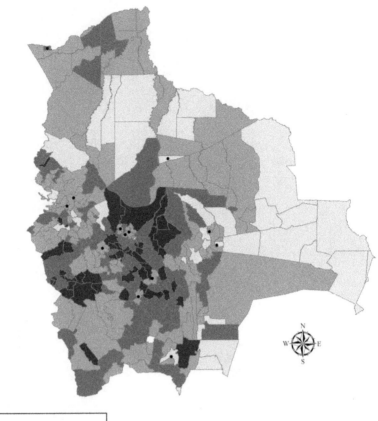

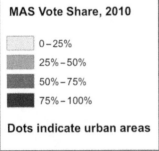

MAP A2.4   2010 municipal election MAS vote (rural and urban).

References

Abers, Rebecca. 2000. *Inventing Local Democracy: Grass-Roots Politics in Brazil.* Boulder, CO: Lynne Rienner Publishers.

Adcock, Robert, and David Collier. 2001. "Measurement Validity: A Shared Standard for Qualitative and Quantitative Research." *American Political Science Review* 95 (3): 529–46. http://doi:10.1017/S0003055401003100.

Aguirre Bayley, Miguel. 2000. *Frente Amplio: "la admirable alarma de 1971": Partido Encuentro Progresista Frente Amplio,* 2nd edn. Montevideo: La República.

Albó, Xavier. 2006. "El Alto, La Vorágine de Una Ciudad Única." *Journal of Latin American Anthropology* 11 (2): 329–50.

2008. *Movimientos Y Poder Indígena En Bolivia, Ecuador Y Perú.* La Paz, Bolivia: CIPCA.

Albro, Robert. 2005a. "Indigenous in the Plural in Bolivian Oppositional Politics." *Bulletin of Latin American Research* 24: 433–53.

2005b. "'The Water Is Ours, Carajo!': Deep Citizenship in Bolivia's Water War." In *Social Movements: An Anthropological Reader,* ed. June Nash, 249–71. Oxford and Cambridge: Basil Blackwell.

Aldrich, John H. 1995. *Why Parties? The Origin and Transformation of Political Parties in America.* Chicago: University of Chicago Press.

Alenda, Stéphanie. 2003. "Dimensiones de La Movilización En Torno a Conciencia de Patria: Hacia Un Modelo Explicativo de Un Caso de Neopopulismo Boliviano." *Revista de Ciencia Política* 23 (1): 119–35.

Altman, David. 2002. "Popular Initiatives in Uruguay: Confidence Votes on Government or Political Loyalties?" *Electoral Studies* 21 (4): 617–30.

Amaral, Oswaldo E. 2010. "As Transformacoes Na Orgaiacao Interna Do PT Entre 1995 E 2009." PhD thesis, Universidade Estadual de Campinas, Instituto de Filosofia e Ciências Humanas.

Amaral, Oswaldo E., and Rachel Meneguello. 2017. "The PT in Power, 2003–2016." In *Democratic Brazil Divided,* ed. Peter Kingstone and Timothy J. Power, 31–52. Pittsburg: Pittsburg University Press (Pitt Latin American Series).

Amaral, Oswaldo E., and Timothy J. Power. 2015. "The PT at 35: Revisiting Scholarly Interpretations of the Brazilian Workers' Party." *Journal of Latin American Studies* 48 (1): 147–71.

Amenta, Edwin. 2016. "Raising the Bar for Scholarship on Protest and Politics." *Contemporary Sociology* 45 (5): 566–70. http://doi:10.1177/0094306116664523b.

Amenta, Edwin, and Neal Caren. 2004. "The Legislative, Organizational, and Beneficiary Consequences of State-Oriented Challengers." In *The Blackwell Companion to Social Movements*, ed. David A. Snow, Sarah A. Soule, and Hanspeter Kriesi, 461–88. Oxford: Blackwell Publishing.

Amenta, Edwin, Neal Caren, Elizabeth Chiarello, and Yang Su. 2010. "The Political Consequences of Social Movements." *Annual Review of Sociology* 36: 287–307. http://doi:10.1146/annurev-soc-070308-120029.

Aminzade, Ronald. 1995. "Between Movement and Party: The Transformation of Mid-Nineteenth-Century French Republicanism." In *The Politics of Social Protest: Comparative Perspectives on States and Social Movements*, ed. J. Craig Jenkins and Bert Klandermans, 167–98. Minneapolis, MI: University of Minnesota Press.

Anderson, Perry. 2011. "Lula's Brazil." *London Review of Books*, March 31, 2011.

Anria, Santiago. 2009. "Informal Institutions and Party Organization: A Case Study of the MAS." M.A. thesis, Simon Fraser University, Vancouver.

2010. "Bolivia's MAS: Between Party and Movement." In *Latin America's Left Turns: Politics, Policies, and Trajectories of Change*, ed. Maxwell A. Cameron and Eric Hershberg, 101–26. Boulder, CO: Lynne Rienner Publishers.

2013. "Social Movements, Party Organization, and Populism: Insights from the Bolivian MAS." *Latin American Politics and Society* 55 (3): 19–46. http://doi:10.1111/j.1548-2456.2013.00201.x.

2016. "More Inclusion, Less Liberalism in Bolivia." *Journal of Democracy* 27 (3): 99–108. http://doi:10.1353/jod.2016.0037.

Anria, Santiago, and Jennifer Cyr. 2017. "Inside Revolutionary Parties: Coalition-Building and Maintenance in Reformist Bolivia." *Comparative Political Studies* 50 (9): 1255–87. https://doi.org/10.1177/0010414016666860.

Anria, Santiago, and Evelyne Huber. 2018. "The Key to Evo Morales' Political Longevity." *Foreign Affairs*, February 14, 2018. https://www.foreignaffairs.com/articles/bolivia/2018-02-14/key-evo-morales-political-longevity.

Anria, Santiago, Maxwell A. Cameron, Agustín Goenaga, Carlos Toranzo, and Moira Zuazo. 2010. "Bolivia: Democracia En Construcción." In *Democracia En La Región Andina: Diversidad Y Desafíos*, ed. Maxwell A. Cameron and Juan Pablo Luna, 243–72. Lima: Instituto de Estudios Peruanos.

Anria, Santiago, and Sara Niedzwiecki. 2016. "Social Movements and Social Policy: The Bolivian Renta Dignidad." *Studies in Comparative International Development* 51 (3): 308–27.

Arbona, Juan M., and Benjamin Kohl. 2004. "La Paz–El Alto." *Cities* 21 (3): 255–65.

Arce, Moises, and Paul T. Bellinger. 2007. "Low-Intensity Democracy Revisited: The Effects of Economic Liberalization on Political Activity in Latin America." *World Politics* 60 (1): 97–121. http://doi:10.1353/wp.0.0003.

Ardaya, Gloria. 2003. *Diputados Uninominales: Otra Forma de Representación*. La Paz, Bolivia: Plural Editores.

Avritzer, Leonardo. 2009. *Participatory Institutions in Democratic Brazil*. Washington, DC: Woodrow Wilson Center Press, Johns Hopkins University Press.

2010. "Living under a Democracy: Participation and Its Impact on the Living Conditions of the Poor." *Latin American Research Review* 45 (special issue): 166–85.

Baiocchi, Gianpaolo. 2003. *Radicals in Power: The Workers' Party (PT) and Experiments in Urban Democracy in Brazil*. London/New York: Palgrave (distributed in the USA exclusively by Palgrave).

Baiocchi, Gianpaolo, and Sofia Checa. 2007. "The Brazilian Workers' Party: From Local Practices to National Power." *Working USA* 10 (4): 411–30.

Baker, Andy, and Kenneth F. Greene. 2011. "The Latin American Left's Mandate: Free-Market Policies and Issue Voting in New Democracies." *World Politics* 63 (1): 43–77.

Ballivián, Salvador Romero. 2003. *Geografía Electoral de Bolivia: Así Votan Los Bolivianos*. La Paz, Bolivia: ILDIS.

Bartolini, Stefano. 2000. *The Political Mobilization of the European Left, 1860–1980: The Class Cleavage*. Cambridge, UK: Cambridge University Press.

Bartolini, Stefano, and Peter Mair. 1995. *Identity, Competition, and Electoral Availability: The Stabilisation of European Electorates 1885–1985*. Cambridge, UK: Cambridge University Press.

Berman, Sheri. 1997. "Civil Society and the Collapse of the Weimar Republic." *World Politics* 49 (3): 401–29. http://doi:10.1353/wp.1997.0008.

Bille, Lars. 2001. "Democratizing a Democratic Procedure: Myth or Reality? Candidate Selection in Western European Parties, 1960–1990." *Party Politics* 7 (3): 363–80. http://doi:10.1177/1354068801007003006.

Bogliaccini, Juan. 2012. "Small Latecomers into the Global Market [Electronic Resource] : Power Conflict and Institutional Change in Chile and Uruguay." Chapel Hill, NC: University of North Carolina at Chapel Hill.

Bolleyer, Nicole. 2011. "The Organizational Costs of Public Office." In *New Parties in Government: In Power for the First Time*, ed. Kris Deschouwer, 17–44. London and New York: Routledge.

2012. "New Party Organization in Western Europe: Of Party Hierarchies, Stratarchies and Federations." *Party Politics* 18 (3): 315–36. http://doi:10.1177/13540 68810382939.

Bolognesi, Bruno. 2013. "A Seleção de Candidaturas No DEM, PMDB, PSDB E PT Nas Eleições Legislativas Federais Brasileiras de 2010: Percepções Dos Candidatos Sobre a Formação Das Listas." *Revista de Sociologia e Política* 21 (46): 45–68.

Bolpress. 2006. "Tierras: El Gobierno Concerta Con Prefectos Y Los Indígenas Alistan Una Marcha." https://www.bolpress.com/?Cod=2006102513.

Borras Jr, Saturnino M., and Jennifer C. Franco. 2010. "Contemporary Discourses and Contestations around Pro-Poor Land Policies and Land Governance." *Journal of Agrarian Change* 10 (1): 1–32. http://doi:10.1111/j.1471-0366.2009.00243.x.

Bottazzi, Patrick, and Stephan Rist. 2012. "Changing Land Rights Means Changing Society: The Sociopolitical Effects of Agrarian Reforms under the Government of Evo Morales." *Journal of Agrarian Change* 12 (4): 528–51. http://doi:10.1111/j.1471-0366.2012.00367.x.

Boulding, Carew. 2014. *NGOs, Political Protest, and Civil Society*. Cambridge, UK: Cambridge University Press.

Bourne, Richard. 2008. *Lula of Brazil: The Story So Far*. Berkeley, CA: University of California Press. https://muse.jhu.edu/book/25606.

Brady, Henry E., and David Collier. 2004. *Rethinking Social Inquiry: Diverse Tools, Shared Standards*. Lanham, MD: Rowman & Littlefield.

Brooke, Steven. 2017. "From Medicine to Mobilization: Social Service Provision and the Islamist Reputational Advantage." *Perspectives on Politics* 15 (1): 42–61. http://doi:10.1017/S1537592716004126.

Bruhn, Kathleen. 1997. *Taking on Goliath : The Emergence of a New Left Party and the Struggle for Democracy in Mexico*. University Park, PA: Pennsylvania State University Press.

2015. "Defining the Left in Latin America." *Latin American Research Review* 50 (1): 242–9. http://doi:10.1353/lar.2015.0008.

Burchell, Jon. 2001. "Evolving or Conforming? Assessing Organisational Reform within European Green Parties." *West European Politics* 24 (3): 113–34.

Burgoa, Carlos, and Modesto Condori. 2011. "El Caminar Histórico Del Instrumento Político, 1995–2009." Unpublished manuscript. La Paz, Bolivia.

Caetano, Gerardo, Juan Pablo Luna, Jaime Yaffé, and Rafael Piñeiro. 2003. *La Izquierda Uruguaya Y La Hipótesis Del Gobierno. Algunos Desafíos Político-Institucionales*. Análisis y Propuestas. Montevideo: Friedrich Ebert Stiftung.

Cambio. 2012. "El Gobierno Acatará Lo Que Decida La Cumbre." *Cambio*, May 8, 2012, sec. Especial Mobilización por la Salud.

Cameron, Maxwell. 2018. "Making Sense of Competitive Authoritarianism: Lessons from the Andes." *Latin American Politics and Society* 60 (2): 1–22.

Cameron, Maxwell A, and Eric Hershberg. 2010. *Latin America's Left Turns: Politics, Policies, and Trajectories of Change*. Boulder, CO: Lynne Rienner Publishers.

Cameron, Maxwell, Eric Hershberg, and Kenneth Evan Sharpe. 2012. *New Institutions for Participatory Democracy in Latin America: Voice and Consequence*. 1st edn. New York: Palgrave Macmillan.

Carbone, Giovanni. 2008. *No-Party Democracy? Ugandan Politics in Comparative Perspective*. Boulder, CO: Lynne Rienner Publishers.

Carey, John M. 1996. *Term Limits and Legislative Representation*. Cambridge, UK: Cambridge University Press.

Carey, John M., and Matthew Soberg Shugart. 1995. "Incentives to Cultivate a Personal Vote: A Rank Ordering of Electoral Formulas." *Electoral Studies* 14 (4): 417–39.

Carty, R. Kenneth. 2004. "Parties as Franchise Systems: The Stratarchical Organizational Imperative." *Party Politics* 10 (1): 5–24. http://doi:10.1177/1354068804039118.

2013. "Are Political Parties Meant to Be Internally Democratic?" In *The Challenges of Intra-Party Democracy*, ed. William P. Cross and Richard S. Katz, 11–26. Oxford: Oxford University Press.

Cason, Jeffrey W. 2000. "Electoral Reform and Stability in Uruguay." *Journal of Democracy* 11 (2): 85–98. doi:10.1353/jod.2000.0032.

Castañeda, Jorge G. 2006. "Latin America's Left Turn." *Foreign Affairs* 85 (3): 28. http://doi:10.2307/20031965.

Centellas, Miguel. 2015. "Cycles of Reform: Placing Evo Morales's Bolivia in Context." *Latin American Research Review* 50 (1): 229–41. doi:10.1353/lar.2015.0006.

Chandra, Kanchan. 2004. *Why Ethnic Parties Succeed: Patronage and Ethnic Head Counts in India*. Cambridge, UK: Cambridge University Press.

Ciccariello-Maher, George. 2013. *We Created Chávez: A People's History of the Vene-zuelan Revolution*. Durham, NC: Duke University Press.

Ciudadanía and LAPOP. 2014. *Cultura Política de La Democracia En Bolivia, 2014: Hacia Una Democracia de Ciudadanos*. Cochabamba, Bolivia. http://ciudadaniabo livia.org/sites/default/files/archivos_articulos/Cultura%20Pol%C3%ADtica%20de %20la%20Democracia%20en%20Bolivia,%202014.pdf.

Civicus. 2006. "Civil Society Index Report: Civil Society in Bolivia – From Mobilization to Impact." www.civicus.org/media/CSI_Bolivia_Report.pdf.

———. 2012. "The Origins of the Classic CSI." https://civicus.org/index.php/media-resources/ reports-publications/151-csi-reports/719-the-origins-of-the-classic-csi.

Cleary, Matthew R. 2006. "Explaining the Left's Resurgence." *Journal of Democracy* 17 (4): 35–49. http://doi:10.1353/jod.2006.0058.

Cleaves, Peter, and Martín J. Scurrah. 1980. *Agriculture, Bureaucracy, and Military Government in Peru*. Ithaca, NY: Cornell University Press.

Collier, Ruth Berins, and David Collier. 1979. "Inducements versus Constraints: Disag-gregating 'Corporatism.'" *American Political Science Review* 73 (4): 967–86. http:// doi:10.2307/1953982.

———. 1991. *Shaping the Political Arena: Critical Junctures, the Labor Movement, and Regime Dynamics in Latin America*. Princeton, NJ: Princeton University Press.

Collier, Ruth Berins, and Christopher Chambers-Ju. 2012. "Popular Representation in Contemporary Latin American Politics: An Agenda for Research." In *Routledge Handbook of Latin American Politics*, ed. Peter Kingstone and Deborah J. Yashar, 564–78. New York: Routledge.

Collins, Jennifer. 2006. "Democratizing Formal Politics: Indigenous and Social Move-ment Political Parties in Ecuador and Bolivia, 1978–2000." PhD Dissertation, Department of Political Science, University of California, San Diego.

Coppedge, Michael. 1994. *Strong Parties and Lame Ducks : Presidential Partyarchy and Factionalism in Venezuela*. Stanford, CA: Stanford University Press.

Coppedge, Michael, John Gerring, Staffan I. Lindberg, et al. 2017. "V-Dem [Country-Year/Country-Date] Dataset v7." Varieties of Democracy (V-Dem) Project.

Costa, Jimena. 2008. "Los Poderes Fácticos de La Coyuntura." In *Los Actores Políticos En La Transición Boliviana*, ed. Horst Grebe López, 105–38. La Paz, Bolivia: Instituto Prisma.

Couto, Cláudio Gonçalves. 1995. *O desafio de ser governo: o PT na Prefeitura de São Paulo, 1989–1992*. São Paulo, SP: Paz e Terra.

Crabtree, John. 2005. *Patterns of Protest: Politics and Social Movements in Bolivia*. Latin America Bureau.

———. 2011. "Electoral Validation for Morales and the MAS." In *Evo Morales and the Movimiento Al Socialismo in Bolivia: The First Term in Context*, ed. Adrian J. Pearce, 117–42. London: Institute for the Study of the Americas.

———. 2013. "From the MNR to the MAS: Populism, Parties, the State, and Social Move-ments in Bolivia since 1952." In *Latin American Populism in the Twenty-First Century*, ed. Carlos de la Torre and Cynthia J. Arnson, 269–93. Washington, DC: The Johns Hopkins University Press.

Cross, William, and Richard S. Katz. 2013. *The Challenges of Intra-Party Democracy*. Oxford: Oxford University Press.

Cross, William P. (William Paul), and Jean-Benoît Pilet. 2013. *The Selection of Political Party Leaders in Contemporary Parliamentary Democracies: A Comparative Study.* New York: Routledge.

Cyr, Jennifer. 2012. "From Collapse to Comeback? The Fates of Political Parties in Latin America." PhD Dissertation, Northwestern University.

2017. *The Fates of Political Parties: Institutional Crisis, Continuity, and Change in Latin America.* Cambridge, UK: Cambridge University Press.

Dahl, Robert A. 1971. *Polyarchy: Participation and Opposition.* New Haven, CT: Yale University Press.

da Silva, Luiz Inácio Lula. 2002. "Carta Ao Povo Brasileiro." International Institute for Social History. www.iisg.nl/collections/carta_ao_povo_brasileiro.pdf.

De la Torre, Carlos. 2013. "In the Name of the People: Democratization, Popular Organizations, and Populism in Venezuela, Bolivia, and Ecuador." *European Review of Latin American and Caribbean Studies* 95: 27–48.

2016. "Left-Wing Populism: Inclusion and Authoritarianism in Venezuela, Bolivia, and Ecuador." *The Brown Journal of World Affairs; Providence* 23 (1): 61–76.

De la Torre, Carlos, and Cynthia Arnson. 2013. *Latin American Populism in the Twenty-First Century.* Washington, DC: The Johns Hopkins University Press.

de Leon, Cedric. 2013. *Party and Society.* 1st edn. Cambridge, UK/Malden, MA: Polity.

della Porta, Donatella, Joseba Fernández, Hara Kouki, and Lorenzo Mosca. 2017. *Movement Parties against Austerity.* 1st edn. Cambridge, UK/Malden, MA: Polity.

Desai, Manali. 2003. "From Movement to Party to Government: Why Social Policies in Kerala and West Bengal Are So Different?" In *States, Parties, and Social Movements*, ed. Jack A. Goldstone, 170–96. New York: Cambridge University Press.

Deschouwer, Kris. 2008. *New Parties in Government: In Power for the First Time.* London/New York: Routledge.

de Souza, Isabel Ribeiro de Oliveira Gómez de. 1988. *Trabalho E Política: As Origens Do Partido Dos Trabalhadores.* Petrópolis: Vozes. //catalog.hathitrust.org/Record/001536459.

Do Alto, Hervé. 2006. "Un Partido Campesino-Indígena En La Ciudad: Liderazgos Barriales Y Facciones En El Movimiento Al Socialismo (MAS) En La Paz, 2005–2006." *Bolivian Studies Journal* 13: 63–86.

2007. "El MAS-IPSP Boliviano." In *Reinventando La Nación En Bolivia: Movimientos Sociales, Estado Y Poscolonialidad*, ed. Karin Monasterios, Pablo Stefanoni, and Hervé Do Alto, 71–110. La Paz, Bolivia: Plural Editores.

2011. "Un Partido Campesino En El Poder: Una Mirada Sociológica Del MAS Boliviano." *Nueva Sociedad* 234 (julio–agosto): 95–111.

Do Alto, Hervé, and Pablo Stefanoni. 2010. "El MAS: Las Ambivalencias de La Democracia Corporativa." In *Mutaciones En El Campo Político Boliviano*, ed. García Orellana, Luis Alberto, and Luis Fernando García Yapur, 305–63. La Paz, Bolivia: UNDP.

Downs, Anthony. 1957. *An Economic Theory of Democracy.* 1st edn. New York: Harper and Row.

Dunkerley, James. 2007. "Evo Morales, the 'Two Bolivias' and the Third Bolivian Revolution." *Journal of Latin American Studies* 39 (1): 133–66. http://doi:10.1017/S0022216X06002069.

2013. "The Bolivian Revolution at 60: Politics and Historiography." *Journal of Latin American Studies* 45 (2): 325–50. http://doi:10.1017/S0022216X13000382.

Duverger, Maurice. 1954. *Political Parties, Their Organization and Activity in the Modern State.* London, Methuen/New York, Wiley: Methuen.

Eaton, Kent. 2007. "Backlash in Bolivia: Regional Autonomy as a Reaction against Indigenous Mobilization." *Politics & Society* 35 (1): 71–102. http://doi:10.1177/0032329206297145.

Eckstein, Susan. 2001. *Power and Popular Protest: Latin American Social Movements.* Berkeley, CA: University of California Press. http://search.lib.unc.edu?R=UNC b3932886.

El Deber (Santa Cruz). 2006a. "La Población Minera Continuó Sangrando." *El Deber,* October 7, 2006 edition.

2006b. "Cambian Al Ministro de Minería.," *El Deber,* October 7, 2006 edition.

Ellner, Steve. 2011. "Venezuela's Social-Based Democratic Model: Innovations and Limitations." *Journal of Latin American Studies* 43 (3): 421–49.

2013. "Social and Political Diversity and the Democratic Road to Change in Venezuela." *Latin American Perspectives* 40 (3): 63–82. http://doi:10.1177/0094582X13476002.

Emigh, Rebecca Jean. 1997. "The Power of Negative Thinking: The Use of Negative Case Methodology in the Development of Sociological Theory." *Theory and Society* 26 (5): 649–84.

Escóbar, Filemón. 2008. *De La Revolución Al Pachakutí: El Aprendizaje Del Respeto Recíproco Entre Blancos E Indios.* La Paz, Bolivia: Garza Azul.

Espinoza Molina, Fran. 2015. *Bolivia: La Circulación de Sus Élites (2006–2014).* Santa Cruz, Bolivia: El País.

Espinoza Morales, Jorge. 2010. *Minería Boliviana: Su Realidad.* La Paz, Bolivia: Plural Editores.

Esposito, Carla, and Walter Arteaga. 2006. "Movimientos Sociales Urbano-Populares En Bolivia: Una Lucha Contra Le Exclusion Social, Politica, y Economica." UNITAS – Programa Desarrollo del Poder Local. www.fundacioncarolina.es/wp-content/uploads/2014/07/Avance_Investigacion_4.pdf.

Estado Plurinacional de Bolivia. 2012. *Informe Final Del Proceso de Consulta Previa, Libre E Informada a Los Pueblos Moxeno-Trinitario, Yuracaré Y Chimane Del Territorio Y Parque Nacional Isiboro Sécure (TIPNIS).* La Paz, Bolivia: Iskra Editores.

Evans, Peter B. 1995. *Embedded Autonomy: States and Industrial Transformation.* Princeton, NJ: Princeton University Press.

2010. *The Challenge of 21st Century Development: Building Capability – Enhancing States.* New York: United Nations Development Programme.

Evans, Peter B., and Patrick Heller. 2015. "Human Development, State Transformation and the Politics of the Developmental State." In *The Oxford Handbook of the Transformations of the State,* 673–713. Oxford: Oxford University Press.

Exeni Rodriguez, Jose Luis. 2012. "Elusive Demodiversity in Bolivia: Between Representation, Participation, and Self-Government." In *New Institutions for Participatory Democracy in Latin America: Voice and Consequence,* ed. Maxwell A. Cameron, Eric Hershberg, and Kenneth E. Sharpe, 207–30. New York: Palgrave Macmillan.

Fairfield, Tasha. 2015. *Private Wealth and Public Revenue in Latin America: Business Power and Tax Politics.* Cambridge, UK: Cambridge University Press.

Falleti, Tulia G., and Thea N. Riofrancos. 2018. "Endogenous Participation: Strengthening Prior Consultation in Extractive Economies." *World Politics* 70 (1): 86–121. https://doi.org/10.1017/S004388711700020X.

Farthing, Linda, and Benjamin Kohl. 2010. "Social Control: Bolivia's New Approach to Coca Reduction." *Latin American Perspectives* 37 (4): 197–213.

2014. *Evo's Bolivia: Continuity and Change.* 1st edn. Austin, TX: University of Texas Press.

Ferreira, Marieta de Moraes, and Alexandre Fortes, eds. 2008. *Muitos Caminhos, Uma Estrela: Memórias de Militantes do PT,* Vol. 1. São Paulo: Editora Fundação Perseu Abramo.

Field, Bonnie N., and Peter M. Siavelis. 2008. "Candidate Selection Procedures in Transitional Politics: A Research Note." *Party Politics* 14 (5): 620–39.

Flores-Macías, Gustavo A. 2012. *After Neoliberalism? The Left and Economic Reforms in Latin America.* Oxford/New York: Oxford University Press.

Fornillo, Bruno. 2008. "Encrucijadas Del Cogobierno En La Bolivia Actual. Un Análisis Sociopolítico de La Experiencia Del Movimiento Al Socialismo En El Poder (2006–07)." Informe final del concurso: Gobiernos progresistas en la era neoliberal: estructuras de poder y concepciones sobre el desarrollo en América Latina y el Caribe. Programa Regional de Becas CLACSO. https://www.scribd.com/document/166479429/Bolivia-EL-MAS-en-El-Poder.

Foweraker, Joe. 1995. *Theorizing Social Movements.* 1st edn. London: Pluto Press.

Foweraker, Joe, and Todd Landman. 2000. *Citizenship Rights and Social Movements: A Comparative and Statistical Analysis.* Oxford: Oxford University Press.

Frankland, E., Paul Lucardie, and Benoît Rihoux. 2008. *Green Parties in Transition : The End of Grass-Roots Democracy?* Farnham, England: Ashgate.

French, John D. 2009. "Lula, the 'New Unionism,' and the PT: How Factory Workers Came to Change the World, or At Least Brazil." *Latin American Politics and Society* 51 (4): 157–69. https://doi.org/10.1111/j.1548-2456.2009.00067.x.

French, John D., and Alexandre Fortes. 2005. "Another World Is Possible: The Rise of the Brazilian Workers' Party and the Prospects for Lula's Government." *Labor* 2 (3): 13–31. http://doi:10.1215/15476715-2-3-13.

2012. "Nurturing Hope, Deepening Democracy, and Combating Inequalities in Brazil: Lula, the Workers' Party, and Dilma Rousseff's 2010 Election as President." *Labor* 9 (1): 7–28. http://doi:10.1215/15476715-1461059.

Fundemos. 1998. *Opinión Y Análisis. Tomo II, Datos Estadísticos Municipales 1987–1995.* La Paz, Bolivia: Fundemos.

Fung, Archon, and Erik Olin Wright. 2003. "Countervailing Power in Empowered Participatory Governance." In *Deepening Democract: Institutional Innovations in Empowered Participatory Governance,* ed. Archon Fung and Erik Olin Wright, 259–89. London: Verso.

Gallagher, Michael, and Michael Marsh. 1988. *Candidate Selection in Comparative Perspective: The Secret Garden of Politics.* London/Newbury Park, CA: Sage Publications.

Garay, Candelaria. 2017. *Social Policy Expansion in Latin America.* New York: Cambridge University Press.

Garcés, Fernando. 2010. *El Pacto de Unidad Y El Proceso de Construcción de Una Propuesta de Constitución Política Del Estado: Sistematización de La Experiencia.* La Paz, Bolivia: Preview Gráfica.

2011. "The Domestication of Indigenous Autonomies in Bolivia: From the Pact of Unity to the New Constitution." In *Remapping Bolivia: Resources, Territory, and Indigeneity in a Plurinational State*, ed. Nicole Fabricant and Bret Gustafson, 46–67. Santa Fe, NM: School for Advanced Research Press.

García Linera, Álvaro. 2006. "El Evismo: Lo Nacional-Popular En Acción." *Revista OSAL: Observatorio Social de América Latina* 19: 25–31.

2009. *Biografía Política e Intelectual: Conversaciones Con Pablo Stefanoni, Franklin Ramírez y Maristella Svampa.* La Paz, Bolivia: Le Monde Diplomatique.

2012. Geopolítica de La Amazonía: Poder Hacendal-Patrimonial y Acumulación Capitalista. La Paz, Bolivia: Vicepresidencia del Estado.

García Linera, Álvaro, Marxa Chávez León, and Patricia Costa Monje. 2004. *Sociología de Los Movimientos Sociales En Bolivia.* La Paz, Bolivia: Plural Editores.

Gargarella, Roberto. 2013. *Latin American Constitutionalism, 1810–2010: The Engine Room of the Constitution.* 1st edn. New York: Oxford University Press.

Garton Ash, Timothy. 2002. *The Polish Revolution: Solidarity.* 3rd edn. New Haven, CT: Yale University Press.

Gerring, John. 2007. *Case Study Research: Principles and Practices.* Cambridge and New York: Cambridge University Press.

Gibson, Edward L. 1992. "Conservative Electoral Movements and Democratic Politics: Core Constituencies, Coalition Building, and the Latin American Electoral Right." In *The Right and Democracy in Latin America*, ed. Douglas A. Chalmers, María Carmo Campbello de Souza, and Atilio A. Borón, 13–42. New York: Praeger.

1996. *Class and Conservative Parties: Argentina in Comparative Perspective.* Baltimore: Johns Hopkins University Press.

1997. "The Populist Road to Market Reform: Policy and Electoral Coalitions in Argentina and Mexico." *World Politics* 49 (3): 339–70.

Gill, Lesley. 2000. *Teetering on the Rim: Global Restructuring, Daily Life, and the Armed Retreat of the Bolivian State.* New York: Columbia University Press.

Giorgi, Ana Laura de. 2011. *Las Tribus de la Izquierda En Los 60: Bolches, Latas Y Tupas: Comunistas, Socialistas Y Tupamaros Desde La Cultura Política.* [Montevideo, Uruguay]: Editorial Fin de Siglo.

Glenn, John K. 2003. "Parties out of Movements: Party Emergence in Postcommunist Eastern Europe." In *States, Parties, and Social Movements*, ed. Jack A. Goldstone, 147–69. New York: Cambridge University Press.

Goldfrank, Benjamin. 2011a. "The Left and Participatory Democracy: Brazil, Uruguay, and Venezuela." In *The Resurgence of the Latin American Left*, ed. Steven Levitsky and Kenneth M. Roberts, 162–83. Baltimore, MD: Johns Hopkins University Press.

2011b. *Deepening Local Democracy in Latin America: Participation, Decentralization, and the Left.* University Park, PA: Penn State Press.

Goldstone, Jack A. 1998. "Initial Conditions, General Laws, Path Dependence, and Explanation in Historical Sociology." *American Journal of Sociology* 104 (3): 829–45. http://doi:10.1086/210088.

2003. *States, Parties, and Social Movements.* Cambridge, UK: Cambridge University Press.

Gómez Bruera, Hernán. 2013. *Lula, the Workers' Party and the Governability Dilemma in Brazil*. New York: Routledge.

Gonzales Salas, Inés. 2013. *Biografías: Historias de Vida En La Asamblea Legislativa Plurinacional*. La Paz, Bolivia: Fundación Friedrich Ebert.

Gray Molina, George. 2008. "State-Society Relations in Bolivia: The Strength of Weakness." In *Unresolved Tensions: Bolivia, Past and Present*, ed. John Crabtree and Laurence Whitehead, 109–24. Pittsburgh: University of Pittsburgh Press.

2013. "Bolivia: Keeping the Coalition Together." In *Constructing Democratic Governance in Latin America*, 4th edn, ed. Jorge I. Domínguez and Michael Shifter, 158–76. Baltimore, MD: Johns Hopkins University Press.

Grindle, Merilee Serrill, and Pilar Domingo. 2003. *Proclaiming Revolution: Bolivia in Comparative Perspective*. London/Cambridge, MA: Institute of Latin American Studies; David Rockefeller Center for Latin American Studies, Harvard University.

Grisaffi, Thomas. 2013. "'All of Us Are Presidents': Radical Democracy and Citizenship in the Chapare Province, Bolivia1." *Critique of Anthropology* 33 (1): 47–65.

Guidry, John A. 2003. "Not Just Another Labor Party: The Workers' Party and Democracy in Brazil." *Labor Studies Journal* 28 (1): 83–108. http://doi:10.1177/0160449X0302800105.

Guillermoprieto, Alma. 2006. "A New Bolivia?" *The New York Review of Books*, August 10, 2006. https://www.nybooks.com/articles/2006/08/10/a-new-bolivia/.

Hagopian, Frances. 2016. "Brazil's Accountability Paradox." *Journal of Democracy* 27 (3): 119–28. http://doi:10.1353/jod.2016.0043.

Handlin, Samuel, and Ruth Berins Collier. 2011. "The Diversity of Left Party Linkages and Competitive Advantages." In *The Resurgence of the Latin American Left*, ed. Steven Levitsky and Kenneth M. Roberts, 139–61. Baltimore, MD: Johns Hopkins University Press.

Harmel, Robert, and Kenneth Janda. 1982. *Parties and Their Environments: Limits to Reform?* New York: Longman.

Harten, Sven. 2011. *The Rise of Evo Morales and the MAS*. London: Zed Books.

Hawkins, Kirk Andrew, and David R. Hansen. 2006. "Dependent Civil Society: The Circulos Bolivarianos in Venezuela." *Latin American Research Review* 41 (1): 102–32.

Hazan, Reuven Y., and Gideon Rahat. 2010. *Democracy within Parties: Candidate Selection Methods and Their Political Consequences*. Oxford: Oxford University Press.

Healy, Kevin. 2001. *Llamas, Weavings, and Organic Chocolate: Multicultural Grassroots Development in the Andes and Amazon of Bolivia*. 1st edn. Notre Dame, IN: University of Notre Dame Press.

Heaney, Michael T., and Fabio Rojas. 2015. *Party in the Street: The Antiwar Movement and the Democratic Party after 9/11*. Cambridge and New York: Cambridge University Press.

Heller, Patrick. 2005. "Reinventing Public Power in the Age of Globalization: The Transformation of Movement Politics in Kerala." In *Social Movements in India: Poverty, Power and Politics*, ed. Raka Ray and Mary Katzenstein, 79–106. New York: Rowman & Littlefield.

2009. "Democratic Deepening in India and South Africa." *Journal of Asian and African Studies* 44 (1): 123–49. http://doi:10.1177/0021909608098679.

Hicks, Alexander M. 1999. *Social Democracy and Welfare Capitalism: A Century of Income Security Politics.* Ithaca, NY: Cornell University Press.

Hipsher, Patricia L. 1996. "Democratization and the Decline of Urban Social Movements in Chile and Spain." *Comparative Politics* 28 (3): 273–97. https://doi.org/10.2307/422208.

Hirschman, Albert O. 1970. *Exit, Voice, and Loyalty: Responses to Decline in Firms, Organizations, and States.* Cambridge, MA: Harvard University Press.

Hochstetler, Kathryn. 2008. "Organized Civil Society in Lula's Brazil." In *Democratic Brazil Revisited*, ed. Peter Kingstone and Timothy Power, 33–53. Pittsburgh, PA: University of Pittsburgh Press.

2013. "Social Movements in Latin America." In *Routledge Handbook of Latin American Politics*, ed. Peter Kingstone and Deborah Yashar, 237–48. New York: Routledge.

Hough, Dan, and Jonathan Olsen. 2015. "What Happens to the Left When It Gains Power? Look at Greece's Syriza Party." *The Washington Post*, September 2, 2015. www.washingtonpost.com/blogs/monkey-cage/wp/2015/09/02/what-happens-to-the-left-when-it-gains-power-look-at-greeces-syriza-party

Huber, Evelyne. 1980. *The Politics of Worker's Participation: The Peruvian Approach in Comparative Perspective.* New York: Academic Press.

Huber, Evelyne, Charles Ragin, and John D. Stephens. 1993. "Social Democracy, Christian Democracy, Constitutional Structure and the Welfare State." *American Journal of Sociology* 99 (3): 711–49.

Huber, Evelyne, Dietrich Rueschemeyer, and John D. Stephens. 1997. "The Paradoxes of Contemporary Democracy: Formal, Participatory, and Social Dimensions." *Comparative Politics* 29 (3): 323–42.

Huber, Evelyne, and John D. Stephens. 2001. *Development and Crisis of the Welfare State: Parties and Policies in Global Markets.* Chicago: University of Chicago Press.

2012. *Democracy and the Left: Social Policy and Inequality in Latin America.* Chicago: University of Chicago Press.

Hummel, Calla. 2017. "Disobedient Markets." *Comparative Political Studies* 50 (11): 1524–55.

Hunter, Wendy. 2007. "The Normalization of an Anomaly: The Workers' Party in Brazil." *World Politics* 59 (3): 440–75.

2010. *The Transformation of the Workers' Party in Brazil, 1989–2009.* Cambridge, UK: Cambridge University Press.

2011. "Brazil: The PT in Power." In *The Resurgence of the Latin American Left*, ed. Steven Levitsky, and Kenneth M. Roberts, 206–324. Baltimore, MD: Johns Hopkins University Press.

Hunter, Wendy, and Timothy J. Power. 2005. "Lula's Brazil at Midterm." *Journal of Democracy* 16 (3): 127–39. http://doi:10.1353/jod.2005.0046.

2007. "Rewarding Lula: Executive Power, Social Policy, and the Brazilian Elections of 2006." *Latin American Politics & Society* 49 (1): 1–30.

Huntington, Samuel P. 1968. *Political Order in Changing Societies.* New Haven, CT: Yale University Press.

Hylton, Forrest, and Sinclair Thomson. 2007. *Revolutionary Horizons: Past and Present in Bolivian Politics.* London/New York: Verso.

Immergut, Ellen M. 1992. *Health Politics: Interests and Institutions in Western Europe*. Cambridge, Cambridge University Press.

Instituto Nacional de Estadísticas (INE). 2001. *Bolivia: Características de La Población*. La Paz, Bolivia: INE.

Jachnow, Joachim. 2013. "What's Become of the German Greens?" *New Left Review* 81 (May–June): 95–117.

Johnson, Chalmers A. 1982. *MITI and the Japanese Miracle: The Growth of Industrial Policy, 1925–1975*. Stanford, CA: Stanford University Press.

Jones, Mark P. 2008. "The Recruitment and Selection of Legislative Candidates in Argentina." In *Pathways to Power: Political Recruitment and Candidate Selection in Latin America*, ed. Peter M. Siavelis and Scott Morgenstern, 41–75. University Park, PA: Pennsylvania State University Press.

Kalyvas, Stathis N. 1996. *The Rise of Christian Democracy in Europe*. Ithaca, NY: Cornell University Press.

Katz, Richard S. 2001. "The Problem of Candidate Selection and Models of Party Democracy." *Party Politics* 7 (3): 277–96. http://doi:10.1177/1354068801007003002.

Katz, Richard S., and Peter Mair. 1995. "Changing Models of Party Organization and Party Democracy: The Emergence of the Cartel Party." *Party Politics* 1 (1): 5–28. http://doi:10.1177/1354068895001001001.

2009. "The Cartel Party Thesis: A Restatement." *Perspectives on Politics* 7 (4): 753–66. http://doi:10.1017/S1537592709991782.

Keck, Margaret E. 1986. "Democratization and Dissension: The Formation of the Workers' Party." *Politics & Society* 15 (1): 67–95. http://doi:10.1177/003232928601500104.

1992. *The Workers' Party and Democratization in Brazil*. New Haven: Yale University Press.

King, Gary, Robert O. Keohane, and Sidney Verba. 1994. *Designing Social Inquiry : Scientific Inference in Qualitative Research*. Princeton, NJ: Princeton University Press.

Kirchheimer, Otto. 1966. "The Transformation of the Western European Party Systems." In *Political Parties and Political Development*, ed. Joseph LaPalombara and Myron Weiner, 177–200. Princeton, NJ: Princeton University Press.

Kitschelt, Herbert. 1989a. *The Logics of Party Formation: Ecological Politics in Belgium and West Germany*. Ithaca, NY: Cornell University Press.

1989b. "The Internal Politics of Parties: The Law of Curvilinear Disparity Revisited." *Political Studies* 37 (3): 400–21. http://doi:10.1111/j.1467-9248.1989.tb00279.x.

2000. "Citizens, Politicians, and Party Cartellization: Political Representation and State Failure in Post-industrial Democracies." *European Journal of Political Research* 37 (2): 149–79. http://doi:10.1111/1475-6765.00508.

2006. "Movement Parties." In *Handbook of Party Politics*, ed. Richard S. Katz and William Crotty, 278–90. London: Sage Publishers.

2013. "Dataset of the Democratic Accountability and Linkages Project (DALP)." http://sites.duke.edu/democracylinkage/.

Kitschelt, Herbert, Kirk A. Hawkins, Juan Pablo Luna, Guillermo Rosas, and Elizabeth J. Zechmeister. 2010. *Latin American Party Systems*. Cambridge and New York: Cambridge University Press.

Klein, Herbert. 2011. "The Historical Background to the Rise of the MAS, 1952–2005." In *Evo Morales and the Movimiento Al Socialismo in Bolivia: The First Term in Context*, ed. Adrian J. Pearce, 27–62. London: Institute for the Study of the Americas, University of London, School of Advanced Study.

Kohl, Benjamin H. 2003. "Democratizing Decentralization in Bolivia: The Law of Popular Participation." *Journal of Planning Education and Research* 23 (2): 153–64. http://doi:10.1177/0739456X03258639.

Kohl, Benjamin H., and Linda C. Farthing. 2006. *Impasse in Bolivia: Neoliberal Hegemony and Popular Resistance*. London/New York: Zed Books.

Koivumaeki, Riitta-Ilona. 2015. "Evading the Constraints of Globalization: Oil and Gas Nationalization in Venezuela and Bolivia." *Comparative Politics* 48 (1): 107–25.

Komadina, Jorge. 2013. "Culturas Políticas, Democracia Interna Y Conflicto En El Movimiento Al Socialismo." In *Partidos Políticos Del Estado Plurinacional: Estructuras Y Democracia Interna, Andamios*, 7–44. La Paz, Bolivia: PNUD-Bolivia.

Komadina, Jorge, and Celine Geffroy. 2007. *El Poder Del Movimiento Político. Estrategia, Tramas Organizativas E Identidad Del MAS En Cochabamba (1999–2005)*. La Paz, Bolivia: CESU; DICYT-UMSS; Fundacion PIEB.

Koole, Ruud. 1996. "Cadre, Catch-All or Cartel? A Comment on the Notion of the Cartel Party." *Party Politics* 2 (4): 507–23. http://doi:10.1177/1354068896002004004.

Kopp, Adalberto J. 2011. *Organizaciones Indígenas Campesinas y Soberanía Alimentaria: Contexto Boliviano e Internacional*. La Paz, Bolivia: CESA.

Korpi, Walter. 1978. *The Working Class in Welfare Capitalism: Work, Unions, and Politics in Sweden*. London/Boston: Routledge & Kegan Paul.

Kurtz, Marcus J. 2004. *Free Market Democracy and the Chilean and Mexican Countryside*. Cambridge, UK: Cambridge University Press.

Lacerda, Alan D. 2002. "O PT E a Unidade Partidária Como Problema." *Dados* 45 (1): 39–76.

Langston, Joy. 2008. "Legislative Recruitment in Mexico." In *Pathways to Power: Political Recruitment and Candidate Selection in Latin America*, ed. Peter M. Siavelis and Scott Morgenstern, 143–63. University Park, PA: Pennsylvania State University Press.

Lanzaro, Jorge Luis. 2011. "Uruguay: A Social Democratic Government in Latin America." In *The Resurgence of the Latin American Left*, ed. Steven Levitsky and Kenneth M. Roberts, 348–74. Baltimore, MD: Johns Hopkins University Press.

LAPOP. 2012. *The Americas Barometer*. Latin American Public Opinion Project. Nashville, TN: Vanderbuilt University.

Laruta, Carlos Hugo. 2008. "Organizaciones Y Movimientos Sociales En El Proceso Político Actual Diciembre 2005 a Junio 2008." In *Los Actores Políticos En La Transición Boliviana*, ed. Horst Grebe López, 67–104. La Paz, Bolivia: Instituto Prisma.

Lazar, Sian. 2006. "El Alto, Ciudad Rebelde: Organisational Bases for Revolt." *Bulletin of Latin American Research* 25 (2): 183–99.

2008. *El Alto, Rebel City*. Durham, NC: Duke University Press.

Leal, Paulo Roberto Figueira. 2005. *O PT E O Dilema da Representação Política: Os Deputados Federais São Representantes de Quem?* 1st edn. Rio de Janeiro: FGV Editora.

LeBas, Adrienne. 2011. *From Protest to Parties: Party-Building and Democratization in Africa*. Oxford: Oxford University Press.

Lee, Cheol-Sung. 2012. "Associational Networks and Welfare States in Argentina, Brazil, South Korea, and Taiwan." *World Politics* 64 (3): 507–54. http://doi:10.1017/S0043887112000111.

2016. *When Solidarity Works: Labor-Civic Networks and Welfare States in the Market Reform Era*. New York: Cambridge University Press.

Lehoucq, Fabrice. 2008. "Bolivia's Constitutional Breakdown." *Journal of Democracy* 19 (4): 110–24. http://doi:10.1353/jod.0.0023.

Levitsky, Steven. 2001. "Inside the Black Box: Recent Studies of Latin American Party Organizations." *Studies in Comparative International Development* 36 (2): 92–110. http://doi:10.1007/BF02686211.

2003. *Transforming Labor-Based Parties in Latin America: Argentine Peronism in Comparative Perspective*. Cambridge and New York: Cambridge University Press.

Levitsky, Steven, and James Loxton. 2013. "Populism and Competitive Authoritarianism in the Andes." *Democratization* 20 (1): 107–36.

Levitsky, Steven, James Loxton, Brandon Van Dyck, and Jorge I. Domínguez, eds. 2016. *Challenges of Party-Building in Latin America*. New York: Cambridge University Press.

Levitsky, Steven, and Kenneth M. Roberts. 2011. *The Resurgence of the Latin American Left*. 1st edn. Baltimore, MD: The Johns Hopkins University Press.

Levitsky, Steven, and Lucan A. Way. 1998. "Between a Shock and a Hard Place: The Dynamics of Labor-Backed Adjustment in Poland and Argentina." *Comparative Politics* 30 (2): 171–92. http://doi:10.2307/422286.

Levitsky, Steven, and Maxwell A. Cameron. 2003. "Democracy without Parties? Political Parties and Regime Change in Fujimori's Peru." *Latin American Politics and Society* 45 (3): 1–33.

Lijphart, Arend. 1971. "Comparative Politics and the Comparative Method." *The American Political Science Review* 65 (3): 682–93. http://doi:10.2307/1955513.

Linz, Juan. 2006. "Robert Michels and His Contribution to Political Sociology in Historical and Comparative Perspective." In *Robert Michels, Political Sociology, and the Future of Democracy*, ed. Juan J. Linz, with a bibliography by H. E. Chehabi, 1–80. New Brunswick, NJ: Transaction Publishers.

Lipset, Seymour, James S. Coleman, and Martin A. Trow. 1977. *Union Democracy : The Internal Politics of the International Typographical Union*. New York: Free Press [1956].

Lipset, Seymour M., and Stein Rokkan. 1967. "Cleavage Structure, Party Systems, and Voter Alignments: An Introduction." In *Party Systems and Voter Alignments*, ed. Seymour Martin Lipset and Stein Rokkan, 1–67. New York: The Free Press.

Locke, Richard M., and Kathleen Thelen. 1995. "Apples and Oranges Revisited: Contextualized Comparisons and the Study of Comparative Labor Politics." *Politics & Society* 23 (3): 337–67. http://doi:10.1177/0032329295023003004.

Los Tiempos. 2011. "Evo Morales Anuncia Nueva Ley de Tierras Para Eliminar El Latifundio En Bolivia." *Los Tiempos*, August 2, 2011.

Loxbo, Karl. 2013. "The Fate of Intra-Party Democracy Leadership Autonomy and Activist Influence in the Mass Party and the Cartel Party." *Party Politics* 19 (4): 537–54.

Lucero, Jose. 2008. *Struggles of Voice: The Politics of Indigenous Representation in the Andes*. Pittsburgh, PA: University of Pittsburgh Press.

Luna, Juan Pablo. 2006. "Programmatic and Non-Programmatic Party-Voter Linkages in Two Institutionalized Party Systems: Chile and Uruguay in Comparative Perspective." PhD Dissertation, Department of Political Science, University of North Carolina at Chapel Hill.

2007. "Frente Amplio and the Crafting of a Social Democratic Alternative in Uruguay." *Latin American Politics and Society* 49 (4): 1–30.

2010a. "Segmented Party–Voter Linkages in Latin America: The Case of the UDI." *Journal of Latin American Studies* 42 (2): 325–56. http://doi:10.1017/S0022216 X10000465.

2010b. "The Left Turns: Why They Happened and How They Compare." In *Latin America's Left Turns: Politics, Policies, and Trajectories of Change*, ed. by Maxwell A. Cameron and Eric Hershberg, 23–40. Boulder, CO: Lynne Rienner Publishers.

2014. *Segmented Representation: Political Party Strategies in Unequal Democracies*. Oxford: Oxford University Press.

2016. "Chile's Crisis of Representation." *Journal of Democracy* 27 (3): 129–38. http://doi:10.1353/jod.2016.0046.

Luna, Juan Pablo, and Alberto Vergara. 2016. "Latin America's Problems of Success." *Journal of Democracy* 27 (3): 158–65. http://doi:10.1353/jod.2016.0036.

Luna, Juan Pablo, and Fernando Filgueira. 2009. "The Left Turns as Multiple Paradigmatic Crises." *Third World Quarterly* 30 (2): 371–95.

Lupu, Noam. 2016. *Party Brands in Crisis: Partisanship, Brand Dilution, and the Breakdown of Political Parties in Latin America*. New York: Cambridge University Press.

Madrid, Raúl L. 2008. "The Rise of Ethnopopulism in Latin America." *World Politics* 60 (3): 475–508. http://doi:10.1017/S0043887100009060.

2010. "The Origins of the Two Lefts in Latin America." *Political Science Quarterly (Academy of Political Science)* 125 (4): 587–609.

2011. "Bolivia: Origins and Policies of the Movimiento Al Socialismo." In *The Resurgence of the Latin American Left*, ed. Steven Levitsky and Kenneth M. Roberts, 239–59. Baltimore, MD: The Johns Hopkins University Press.

2012. *The Rise of Ethnic Politics in Latin America*. 1st edn. Cambridge, UK: Cambridge University Press.

Magaloni, Beatriz. 2006. *Voting for Autocracy: Hegemonic Party Survival and Its Demise in Mexico*. Cambridge:Cambridge University Press.

Mahoney, James. 2000. "Path Dependence in Historical Sociology." *Theory and Society* 29 (4): 507–48.

2010. "After KKV: The New Methodology of Qualitative Research." *World Politics* 62 (1): 120–47.

Mahoney, James, and Dietrich Rueschemeyer. 2003. *Comparative Historical Analysis in the Social Sciences*. Cambridge: Cambridge University Press.

Mahoney, James, and Kathleen Thelen. 2015. *Advances in Comparative-Historical Analysis*. Cambridge: Cambridge University Press.

Mainwaring, Scott, and Edurne Zoco. 2007. "Political Sequences and the Stabilization of Interparty Competition Electoral Volatility in Old and New Democracies." *Party Politics* 13 (2): 155–78. http://doi:10.1177/1354068807073852.

Mair, Peter. 2013. *Ruling the Void: The Hollowing of Western Democracy*. London/New York: Verso.

Mamani, Julio, and Rafael Archondo. 2010. *La Acción Colectiva En El Alto: Hacia Una Etnografía de Las Organizaciones Sociales*. El Alto, Bolivia: Gregoria Apaza.

Marais, Hein. 2011. *South Africa Pushed to the Limit: The Political Economy of Change*. London and New York: Zed Books.

Mayka, Lindsay. n.d. "The Origins of Strong Institutional Design: Policy Reform and Participatory Institutions in Brazil's Health Sector." *Comparative Politics*.

Mayorga, Fernando. 2011. *Dilemas*. La Paz, Bolivia: CESU/Plural Editores.

Mayorga, René Antonio. 2006. "Outsiders and Neopopulism: The Road to Plebiscitary Democracy." In *The Crisis of Democratic Representation in the Andes*, ed. Scott Mainwaring, Ana M. Bejarano, and Eduardo Pizarro Leongómez, 132–67. Sanford, CA: Stanford University Press.

2017. "Populismo Autoritario Y Transición Regresiva: La Dictadura Plebiscitaria En La Región Andina." *Revista Latinoamericana de Política Comparada* 12: 39–69.

Mazzuca, Sebastián L. 2013. "The Rise of Rentier Populism." *Journal of Democracy* 24 (2): 108–22. https://doi.org/10.1353/jod.2013.0034.

McAdam, Doug, and Sidney Tarrow. 2010. "Ballots and Barricades: On the Reciprocal Relationship between Elections and Social Movements." *Perspectives on Politics* 8 (2): 529–42. http://doi:10.1017/S1537592710001234.

McCarthy, Michael M. 2012. "The Possibilities and Limits of Politicized Participation: Community Councils, Coproduction, and Poder Popular in Chávez's Venezuela." In *New Institutions for Participatory Democracy in Latin America*, ed. Maxwell A. Cameron, Eric Hershberg, and Kenneth E. Sharpe, 123–47. New York: Palgrave Macmillan US.

McClintock, Cynthia. 1998. *Revolutionary Movements in Latin America: El Salvador's FMLN & Peru's Shining Path*. Washington, DC: US Institute of Peace Press.

McDonnell, Duncan. 2013. "Silvio Berlusconi's Personal Parties: From Forza Italia to the Popolo Della Libertà." *Political Studies* 61 (April): 217–33. http://doi:10.1111/j.1467-9248.2012.01007.x.

McGuire, James. 1997. *Peronism without Perón: Unions, Parties, and Democracy in Argentina*. Stanford, CA: Stanford University Press.

McKenzie, Robert. 1955. *British Political Parties; the Distribution of Power within the Conservative and Labour Parties*. New York: St. Martin's Press.

Meneguello, Rachel. 1989. *PT: A Formação de Um Partido, 1979–1982*. São Paulo: Paz e Terra.

Meneguello, Rachel, and Oswaldo Amaral. 2008. "Ainda Novidade: Uma Revisão Das Transformações Do Partido Dos Trabalhadores No Brasil." Occasional Paper Number BSP-02–08. Brazilian Studies Programme Latin American Centre St Antony's College.

Meyer, David S., and Sidney G. Tarrow. 1998. "A Movement Society: Contentious Politics for a New Century." In *The Social Movement Society: Contentious Politics for a New Century*, ed. Dadid S., Meyer and Sidney G. Tarrow, 1–28. Lahnham: Rowman & Littlefield Publishers.

Michels, Robert. 1962. *Political Parties: A Sociological Study of the Oligarchical Tendencies of Modern Democracy*. London: The Free Press [1911].

Ministerio de la Presidencia, and Ministerio de Comunicación. 2011. "Primer Encuentro Plurinacional Para Profundizar El Cambio." La Paz, Bolivia. www.comunicacion .gob.bo/?q=20111219/primer-encuentro-plurinacional-para-profundizar-el-cambio.

Mitchell, Christopher. 1977. *Legacy of Populism in Bolivia: From the MNR to Military Rule*. New York: Praeger Publishers Inc.

Molina, Fernando. 2010. "El MAS En El Centro de La Política Boliviana." In *Mutaciones En El Campo Político Boliviano*, 241–302. La Paz, Bolivia: UNDP.

2018. "Tendencias Socioelectorales En La Bolivia Del Caudillismo." Nueva Sociedad | Democracia Y Política En América Latina. February 16, 2018. http://nuso.org/articulo/tendencias-socioelectorales-en-la-bolivia-del-caudillismo/.

Montgomery, John D. 1972. "Allocation of Authority in Land Reform Programs: A Comparative Study of Administrative Processes and Outputs." *Administrative Science Quarterly* 17 (1): 62. http://doi:10.2307/2392094.

Moreira, Constanza. 2004. *Final de Juego: Del Bipartidismo Tradicional Al Triunfo de La Izquierda En Uruguay*. Montevideo: Ediciones Trilce.

Mudge, Stephanie L., and Anthony S. Chen. 2014. "Political Parties and the Sociological Imagination: Past, Present, and Future Directions." *Annual Review of Sociology* 40 (July): 305–30.

Müller-Rommel, Ferdinand. 1989. *New Politics in Western Europe: The Rise and Success of Green Parties and Alternative Lists*. Boulder, CO: Westview.

Müller-Rommel, Ferdinand, and Thomas Poguntke. 2002. *Green Parties in National Governments*. London and Portland, OR: F. Cass.

Murillo, María Victoria. 2001. *Labor Unions, Partisan Coalitions and Market Reforms in Latin America*. Cambridge and New York: Cambridge University Press.

Murillo, María Victoria, Virginia Oliveros, and Milan Vaishnav. 2010. "Electoral Revolution or Democratic Alternation?" *Latin American Research Review* 45 (3): 87–114.

Navia, Patricio. 2008. "Political Recruitment and Candidate Selection in Chile, 1990 to 2006." In *Pathways to Power: Political Recruitment and Candidate Selection in Latin America*, ed. Peter M. Siavelis and Scott Morgenstern, 92–118. University Park, PA: Pennsylvania State University Press.

Niedzwiecki, Sara, and Santiago Anria. n.d. "Participatory Social Policies: Diverging Patterns in Brazil and Bolivia." *Latin American Politics and Society*.

Nogueira-Budny, Daniel. 2013. "From Marxist-Leninism to Market-Liberalism? The Varied Adaptation of Latin America's Leftist Parties." PhD Dissertation, The University of Texas at Austin.

Novaes, Carlos Alberto Marques. 1993. "PT: Dilemas Da Burocratização." *Novos Estudos Cebrap* 35: 217–37.

Nylen, William. 2003. *Participatory Democracy versus Elitist Democracy: Lessons from Brazil*. 1st edn. New York: Palgrave Macmillan.

O'Donnell, Guillermo. 1999. *Counterpoints: Selected Essays on Authoritarianism and Democratization*. Notre Dame, IN: University of Notre Dame Press.

1994. "Delegative Democracy." *Journal of Democracy* 5 (1): 55–69.

Ondetti, Gabriel A. 2008. *Land, Protest, and Politics: The Landless Movement and the Struggle for Agrarian Reform in Brazil*. University Park, PA: Penn State Press.

Onis, Ziya. 1991. "The Logic of the Developmental State." *Comparative Politics* 24 (1): 109–26.

Ostrogorski, Moisei. 1964. *Democracy and the Organization of Political Parties, Volume 1: England*. Garden City, NY: Anchor Books [1902].

Oxhorn, Philip. 1995. *Organizing Civil Society: The Popular Sectors and the Struggle for Democracy in Chile*. University Park, PA: Penn State Press.

   1998. "The Social Foundations of Latin America's Recurrent Populism: Problems of Popular Sector Class Formation and Collective Action." *Journal of Historical Sociology* 11 (2): 212–46. http://doi:10.1111/1467-6443.00061.

Panebianco, Angelo. 1988. *Political Parties: Organization and Power*. New York: Cambridge University Press.

Partido dos Trabalhadores. 1980. Estatuto, Aprovado Na Reunião Nacional de Fundação Do PT, Maio/Junho de 1980.

   2001. *Estatuto*. Aprovado em reunião do Diretório Nacional de 11 de março de 2001. www.justicaeleitoral.jus.br/arquivos/estatuto-do-partido-de-11-3-2001-resolucao-tse-no.2002.

Pateman, Carole. 1970. *Participation and Democratic Theory*. Cambridge, UK: Cambridge University Press.

Pearce, Adrian, ed. 2011. *Evo Morales and the Movimiento Al Socialismo in Bolivia: The First Term in Context, 2005–2009*. London: Institute for the Study of the Americas.

Perissinotto, Renato Monseff, and Bruno Bolognesi. 2010. "Electoral Success and Political Institutionalization in the Federal Deputy Elections in Brazil (1998, 2002 and 2006)." *Brazilian Political Science Review* 4 (1): 10–32.

Perissinotto, Renato Monseff, and Angel Miríade. 2009. "Paths to Congress: Candidates Running for and Elected to the Brazilian Chamber of Deputies in 2006." *Dados* 52 (2): 301–33. http://doi:10.1590/S0011-52582009000200002.

Pierson, Paul. 2000. "Increasing Returns, Path Dependence, and the Study of Politics." *American Political Science Review* 94 (2): 251–67.

   2015. "Power and Path Dependence." In *Advances in Comparative-Historical Analysis*, ed. James Mahoney and Kathleen Thelen, 123–46. Cambridge: Cambridge University Press.

Pérez, Verónica, Rafael Piñeiro, and Fernando Rosenblatt. 2018. *Party Organization and Activism: The Case of the Broad Front* (unpublished manuscript).

Piven, Frances Fox, and Richard A Cloward. 1979. *Poor People's Movements: Why They Succeed, How They Fail*. New York: Vintage Books.

Pogrebinschi, Thamy. 2012. "Participation as Representation: Democratic Policymaking in Brazil." In *New Institutions for Participatory Democracy in Latin America: Voice and Consequence*, ed. Maxwell A. Cameron, Eric Hershberg, and Kenneth E. Sharpe, 53–74. New York: Palgrave.

Pogrebinschi, Thamy, and Fabiano Santos. 2011. "Participation as Representation: The Impact of National Public Policy Conferences on the Brazilian National Congress." *Dados* 54 (3): 259–305. http://doi:10.1590/S0011-52582011000300002.

Postero, Nancy Grey. 2007. *Now We Are Citizens: Indigenous Politics in Postmulticultural Bolivia*. Stanford, CA: Stanford University Press.

   2010. "Morales's MAS Government." *Latin American Perspectives* 37 (3): 18–34.

Power, Timothy J. 2010. "Optimism, Pessimism, and Coalitional Presidentialism: Debating the Institutional Design of Brazilian Democracy." *Bulletin of Latin American Research* 29 (1): 18–33. http://doi:10.1111/j.1470-9856.2009.00304.x.

Pribble, Jennifer. 2008. "Protecting the Poor: Welfare Politics in Latin America's Free Market Era." PhD Dissertation, Department of Political Science, Chapel Hill, University of North Carolina at Chapel Hill.

2013. *Welfare and Party Politics in Latin America*. New York: Cambridge University Press.

Pribble, Jennifer, and Evelyne Huber. 2011. "Social Policy and Redistribution: Chile and Uruguay." In *The Resurgence of the Latin American Left*, ed. Steven Levitsky, and Kenneth M. Roberts, 117–38. Baltimore, MD: Johns Hopkins University Press.

Przeworski, Adam, and John D. Sprague. 1986. *Paper Stones: A History of Electoral Socialism*. Chicago: University of Chicago Press.

Putnam, Robert D., Robert Leonardi, and Raffaella Y. Nonetti. 1993. *Making Democracy Work: Civic Traditions in Modern Italy*. Princeton, NJ: Princeton University Press.

Queirolo, Rosario. 2013. *The Success of the Left in Latin America: Untainted Parties, Market Reforms, and Voting Behavior*. 1st edn. Notre Dame, IN: University of Notre Dame Press.

Revilla Herrero, Carlos J. 2006. "Visibilidad Y Obrismo: En La Estrategia de La Imagen Del Movimiento Plan Progreso En La Ciudad de El Alto." *Programa de Desarrollo Del Poder Local de UNITAS En DNI – El Alto*, 1–25.

Reygadas, Luis, and Fernando Filgueira. 2010. "Inequality and the Incorporation Crisis: The Left's Social Policy Toolkit." In *Latin America's Left Turns: Politics, Policies, and Trajectories of Change*, ed. Maxwell A. Cameron, and Eric Hershberg, 171–92. Boulder, CO: Lynne Rienner Publishers.

Ribeiro, Pedro. 2008. "Dos Sindicatos Ao Governo: A Organização Nacional Do PT de 1980." PhD Dissertation, Sao Carlos, Universidade Federal de Sao Carlos.

2014. "An Amphibian Party? Organisational Change and Adaptation in the Brazilian Workers' Party, 1980–2012." *Journal of Latin American Studies* 46 (1): 87–119.

Riley, Dylan. 2010. *The Civic Foundations of Fascism in Europe: Italy, Spain, and Romania, 1870–1945*. Baltimore: Johns Hopkins University Press.

Roberts, Kenneth M. 1998. *Deepening Democracy? The Modern Left and Social Movements in Chile and Peru*. Stanford, CA: Stanford University Press.

2007a. "Latin America's Populist Revival." *SAIS Review* 27 (1): 3–15.

2007b. "Repoliticizing Latin America: The Revival of Populist and Leftist Alternatives." *Woodrow Wilson Center for Scholars*, 1–11. www.wilsoncenter.org/publication/repoliticizing-latin-america-the-revival-populist-and-leftist-alternatives.

2008. "The Mobilization of Opposition to Economic Liberalization." *Annual Review of Political Science* 11 (1): 327–49. http://doi:10.1146/annurev.polisci.11.053006 .183457.

2012. "Michels and the Sociological Study of Party Organization: A Latin American Perspective." In *Annali Della Fondazione Luigi Einaudi XLVI*, 153–76. Florence, Italy: Leo S. Olschki Editore.

2015a. *Changing Course in Latin America: Party Systems in the Neoliberal Era*. Cambridge, UK: Cambridge University Press.

2015b. "Parties, Populism, and Social Protest in Latin America's Post-Adjustment Era." In *Oxford Handbook of Social Movements*, ed. Donatella Della Porta, and Mario Diani, 681–95. Oxford: Oxford University Press.

2017. "Populism and Political Parties." In *The Oxford Handbook of Populism*, October. https://doi.org/10.1093/oxfordhb/9780198803560.013.20.

Robertson, David. 1976. *Theory of Party Competition*. London and New York: John Wiley & Sons Ltd.

Robertson, Graeme B. 2010. *The Politics of Protest in Hybrid Regimes: Managing Dissent in Post-Communist Russia*. 1st edn. Cambridge:Cambridge University Press.

Rojas Ortuste, Gonzalo. 2000. "La Elección de Alcaldes En Los Municipios Del País En 1999–2000: Persistencia de La Coalición Nacional." *Opiniones Y Análisis* 49: 83–113.

Roma, Celso. 2005. "Atores, Preferência E Instituição Na Câmara Dos Deputados." PhD Dissertation, Sao Paulo, Universidade de Sao Paulo (USP), Department of Political Science.

Romero, Carlos, Carlos Bohrt Irahola, and Raúl Peñaranda. 2009. *Del Conflicto Al Diálogo: Memorias Del Acuerdo Constitucional*. La Paz, Bolivia: FES-ILDIS y fBDM.

Rosenblatt, Fernando. 2018. *Party Vibrancy and Democracy in Latin America*. New York: Oxford University Press.

Rossi, Federico M. 2015. "The Second Wave of Incorporation in Latin America: A Conceptualization of the Quest for Inclusion Applied to Argentina." *Latin American Politics and Society* 57 (1): 1–28. http://doi:10.1111/j.1548-2456 .2015.00256.x.

2017. *The Poor's Struggle for Political Incorporation: The Piquetero Movement in Argentina*. Cambridge and New York: Cambridge University Press.

Roy, Sara. 2013. *Hamas and Civil Society in Gaza: Engaging the Islamist Social Sector*. With a new afterword by the author edition. Princeton, NJ: Princeton University Press.

Rueschemeyer, Dietrich, Evelyne Huber Stephens, and John D. Stephens. 1992. *Capitalist Development and Democracy*. Chicago: University of Chicago Press.

Samuels, David J. 1999. "Incentives to Cultivate a Party Vote in Candidate-Centric Electoral Systems: Evidence from Brazil." *Comparative Political Studies* 32 (4): 487–518. http://doi:10.1177/0010414099032004004.

2004. "From Socialism to Social Democracy: Party Organization and the Transformation of the Workers' Party in Brazil." *Comparative Political Studies* 37 (9): 999–1024. http://doi:10.1177/0010414004268856.

2013. "Brazilian Democracy in the PT Era." In *Constructing Democratic Governance in Latin America*, 4th edn, ed. Jorge I. Dominguez and Michael Shifter, 177–203. Baltimore, MD: Johns Hopkins University Press.

Samuels, David, and Cesar Zucco. 2016. "Party-Building in Brazil: The Rise of the PT in Perspective." In *Challenges of Party-Building in Latin America*, ed. Jorge Domínguez, Steven Levitsky, James Loxton, and Brandon Van Dyck, 331–55. New York: Cambridge University Press.

Sánchez-Sibony, Omar. 2013. "Democratic Breakdowns via a Thousand Blows in Latin America." *LASA Forum* 44 (4): 7–9.

Sandbrook, Richard, Marc Edelman, Patrick Heller, and Judith Teichman. 2007. *Social Democracy in the Global Periphery: Origins, Challenges, Prospects*. Cambridge and New York: Cambridge University Press.

Santos, Boaventura. 2005. *Democratizing Democracy: Beyond the Liberal Democratic Canon*. London and New York: Verso.

Schattschneider, Elmer Eric. 1942. *Party Government*. New York: Farrar and Rinehart.

Schipani, Andrés. 2016. "Strategies of Redistribution: The Left and the Popular Sectors in Latin America." Presented at the 2016 REPAL Annual Meeting, MIT, Boston, MA, June 10–11, 2016.

Schiwy, Freya. 2008. *Todos Somos Presidentes/We Are All Presidents: Bolivia and the Question of the State*. Presented at the conference "Latin American Left Turns: Progressive Parties, Insurgent Movements, Alternative Policies in Latin America," Simon Fraser University, April 17–19, 2008.

Schmitter, Phillippe. 2001. "Parties Are Not What They Once Were." In *Political Parties and Democracy*, ed. Larry Diamond and Richard Gunther, 67–89. Baltimore, MD: Johns Hopkins University Press.

Schwartz, Mildred A. 2006. *Party Movements in the United States and Canada: Strategies of Persistence*. Lanham, MD: Rowman & Littlefield.

Secco, Lincoln. 2011. *História do PT, 1978–2010*. Cotia, SP: Ateliê.

Siavelis, Peter, and Scott Morgenstern, eds. 2008a. *Pathways to Power: Political Recruitment and Candidate Selection in Latin America*. University Park, PA: Penn State Press.

Siavelis, Peter M., and Scott Morgenstern. 2008b. "Candidate Recruitment and Selection in Latin America: A Framework for Analysis." *Latin American Politics and Society* 50 (4): 27–58. http://doi:10.1111/j.1548-2456.2008.00029.x.

Silva, Eduardo. 2009. *Challenging Neoliberalism in Latin America*. Cambridge and New York: Cambridge University Press.

  2017. "Reorganizing Popular Sector Incorporation." *Politics & Society* 45 (1): 91–122. http://doi:10.1177/0032329216683166.

Simmons, Erica. 2016. *Meaningful Resistance: Market Reforms and the Roots of Social Protest in Latin America*. Cambridge, UK: Cambridge University Press.

Sivak, Martin. 2010. *Evo Morales: The Extraordinary Rise of the First Indigenous President of Bolivia*. 1st edn. New York: Palgrave Macmillan.

Slater, Dan, and Erica Simmons. 2013. "Coping by Colluding Political Uncertainty and Promiscuous Powersharing in Indonesia and Bolivia." *Comparative Political Studies* 46 (11): 1366–93. https://doi.org/10.1177/0010414012453447.

Smilde, David, and Daniel Hellinger, eds. 2011. *Venezuela's Bolivarian Democracy: Participation, Politics, and Culture under Chávez*. Trade pbk edn. Durham, NC: Duke University Press Books.

Smith, Martin. 1993. *Pressure, Power and Policy: State Autonomy and Policy Networks in Britain and the United States*. England: Harvester Wheatsheaf.

Smith, William C., Juan Pablo Luna, M. Victoria Murillo, et al. 2014. "Special Section: Political Economy and the Future of Latin American Politics." *Latin American Politics and Society* 56 (1): 1–33. http://doi:10.1111/j.1548-2456.2014.00219.x.

Snyder, Richard. 2001. "Scaling Down: The Subnational Comparative Method." *Studies in Comparative International Development* 36 (1): 93–110. http://doi:10.1007/BF02687586.

Soruco, Ximena, Daniela Franco Pinto, and Mariela Durán Azurduy. 2014. *Composición Social Del Estado Plurinacional: Hacia La Descolonización de La Burocracia*. La Paz, Bolivia: Centro de Investigaciones Sociales.

Soule, Sarah A. 2012. "Bringing Organizational Studies Back in to Social Movement Scholarship." In *The Future of Social Movement Research*, ed. Jacquelien van Stekelenburg, Conny Roggeband, and Bert Klandermans, 107–23. Minneapolis, MI: University of Minnesota Press.

Stefanoni, Pablo. 2003. "MAS-IPSP: La Emergencia Del Nacionalismo Plebeyo." *Observatorio Social de América Latina* 4 (12): 57–68.

2010. *"Qué Hacer Con Los Indios…" Y Otros Traumas Irresueltos de La Colonialidad.* La Paz, Bolivia: Plural Editores.

Stefanoni, Pablo, and Hervé Do Alto. 2006. *Evo Morales. De La Coca Al Palacio: Una Oportunidad Para La Izquierda Indígena.* La Paz, Bolivia: Malatesta.

Stepan, Alfred. 1985. "State Power and the Strengh of Civil Society in the Southern Cone of Latin America." In *Bringing the State Back In*, ed. Peter B. Evans, Dietrich Rueschemeyer, and Theda Skocpol, 317–46. Cambridge, UK: Cambridge University Press.

Stephens, John D. 1979. *The Transition from Capitalism to Socialism.* London: Macmillan.

Stinchcombe, Arthur L. 1968. *Constructing Social Theories.* New York: Harcourt, Brace & World.

Stokes, Susan C. 2001. *Mandates and Democracy: Neoliberalism by Surprise in Latin America.* Cambridge and New York: Cambridge University Press.

Stoyan, Alissandra. 2014. "Constituent Assemblies, Presidential Majorities, and Democracy in Latin America." PhD Dissertation, Department of Political Science, University of North Carolina at Chapel Hill.

Subercaseaux, Elizabeth, and Malu Sierra. 2007. *Evo Morales: Primer Indigena Que Gobierna En America Del Sur.* Santiago de Chile, Chile: LOM Ediciones.

Tapia, Luis. 2011. *El Estado de Derecho Como Tiranía.* La Paz, Bolivia: CIDES/UMSA.

Tarrow, Sidney G. 2015. "Contentious Politics." In *Oxford Handbook on Social Movements*, ed. Donatella della Porta and Mauro Diani, 86–107. Oxford: Oxford University Press.

Tavits, Margit. 2013. *Post-Communist Democracies and Party Organization.* New York: Cambridge University Press.

Thachil, Tariq. 2014. *Elite Parties, Poor Voters: How Social Services Win Votes in India.* New York: Cambridge University Press.

Tilly, Charles. 1978. *From Mobilization to Revolution.* Reading, MA: Addison-Wesley.

Tockman, Jason, and John Cameron. 2014. "Indigenous Autonomy and the Contradictions of Plurinationalism in Bolivia." *Latin American Politics and Society* 56 (3): 46–69.

Tsebelis, George. 2002. *Veto Players: How Political Institutions Work.* New York: Russell Sage Foundation.

UMSS. 2004. *Atlas Del Trópico de Cochabamba.* Cochabamba: Universidad Mayor de San Simón.

UNIR. 2012. *Perfiles de La Conflictividad Social En Bolivia (2009–2011).* La Paz, Bolivia: Fundación UNIR.

Van Biezen, Ingrid, Peter Mair, and Thomas Poguntke. 2012. "Going, Going, … Gone? The Decline of Party Membership in Contemporary Europe." *European Journal of Political Research* 51 (1): 24–56. http://doi:10.1111/j.1475-6765.2011.01995.x.

Van Cott, Donna Lee. 2003. "Institutional Change and Ethnic Parties in South America." *Latin American Politics and Society* 45 (2): 1–39. http://doi:10.2307/3176978.

2005. *From Movements to Parties in Latin America: The Evolution of Ethnic Politics*. Cambridge and New York: Cambridge University Press.

2008. *Radical Democracy in the Andes*. Cambridge, UK: Cambridge University Press.

Van Dyck, Brandon. 2013. "The Paradox of Adversity: New Left Party Survival and Collapse in Latin America." PhD Dissertation, Harvard University.

2014. "Why Party Organization Still Matters: The Workers' Party in Northeastern Brazil." *Latin American Politics and Society* 56 (2): 1–26.

Van Dyke, Nella, and Holly J. McCammon. 2010. *Strategic Alliances: Coalition Building and Social Movements*. Minneapolis: University of Minnesota Press.

Vergara, Alberto. 2011. "United by Discord, Divided by Consensus: National and Sub-National Articulation in Bolivia and Peru, 2000–2010." *Journal of Politics in Latin America* 3 (3): 65–93.

Wampler, Brian. 2007. *Participatory Budgeting in Brazil: Contestation, Cooperation, and Accountability*. University Park, PA: Pennsylvania State University Press.

Webber, Jeffery R. 2010. "Carlos Mesa, Evo Morales, and a Divided Bolivia." *Latin American Perspectives* 37 (3): 51–70.

2011. *From Rebellion to Reform in Bolivia: Class Struggle, Indigenous Liberation, and the Politics of Evo Morales*. Chicago: Haymarket Books.

Weber, Max. 1946. "Politics as a Vocation." In *Max Weber: Essays in Sociology*, ed. Hans H. Gerth, and Charles Wright Mills, 77–128. Oxford: Oxford University Press.

1968. *Economy and Society: An Outline of Interpretive Sociology*. New York: Bedminster Press.

Weyland, Kurt. 2001. "Clarifying a Contested Concept: Populism in the Study of Latin American Politics." *Comparative Politics* 34 (1): 1–22. http://doi:10.2307/422412.

2009. "The Rise of Latin America's Two Lefts: Insights from Rentier State Theory." *Comparative Politics* 41 (2): 145–64.

2013. "The Threat from the Populist Left." *Journal of Democracy* 24 (3): 18–32. http://doi:10.1353/jod.2013.0045.

Weyland, Kurt G., Raúl L. Madrid, and Wendy Hunter. 2010. *Leftist Governments in Latin America: Successes and Shortcomings*. New York: Cambridge University Press.

Wickham, Carrie Rosefsky. 2015. *The Muslim Brotherhood: Evolution of an Islamist Movement*. Princeton, NJ: Princeton University Press.

Wolff, Jonas. 2013. "Towards Post-Liberal Democracy in Latin America? A Conceptual Framework Applied to Bolivia." *Journal of Latin American Studies* 45 (1): 31–59.

2016. "Business Power and the Politics of Postneoliberalism: Relations Between Governments and Economic Elites in Bolivia and Ecuador." *Latin American Politics and Society* 58 (2): 124–47.

2018. "Political Incorporation in Measures of Democracy: A Missing Dimension (and the Case of Bolivia)." *Democratization* 25 (4): 692–708. https://doi.org/10.1080/13510347.2017.1417392.

Wuhs, Steven. 2008. *Savage Democracy: Institutional Change and Party Development in Mexico*. University Park, PA: Pennsylvania State University Press.

Yaffé, Jaime. 2005. *Al Centro y Adentro: La Renovación de La Izquierda y El Triunfo Del Frente Amplio En Uruguay.* Montevideo: Linardi y Risso.

Yashar, Deborah J. 2005. *Contesting Citizenship in Latin America: The Rise of Indigenous Movements and the Postliberal Challenge.* Cambridge and New York: Cambridge University Press.

Zegada, María Teresa, Claudia Arce, Gabriela Canedo, and Alber Quispe Escobar. 2011. *La Democracia Desde Los Márgenes: Transformaciones En El Campo Político Boliviano.* La Paz, Bolivia: Muela del Diablo.

Zegada, Maria Teresa, and Jorge Komadina. 2014. *El Espejo de La Sociedad: Poder Y Representación En Bolivia.* La Paz, Bolivia: CERES/Plural.

Zegada, Maria Teresa, Yuri F. Torrez, and Gloria Camara. 2008. *Movimientos Sociales En Tiempos de Poder: Articulaciones Y Campos de Conflicto En El Gobierno Del MAS (2006–2007).* La Paz, Bolivia: Centro Cuarto Intermedio; Plural Editores.

Zuazo, Moira. 2008. *¿Cómo Nació El MAS? La Ruralización de La Política En Bolivia: Entrevistas a 85 Parlamentarios Del Partido.* La Paz, Bolivia: Fundacion Ebert.

2010. "¿Los Movimientos Sociales En El Poder? El Gobierno Del MAS En Bolivia." *Nueva Sociedad* 227 (May/June): 120–35.

Index

Other Books in the Series (*continued from page ii*)

CPSIA information can be obtained
at www.ICGtesting.com
Printed in the USA
LVHW111612160820
663336LV00003B/146